*The Future
of Childhood and*
Juvenile Justice

Contributors

LaMar T. Empey

Richard Farson

Jerome G. Miller

Kingsley Davis

Arlene Skolnick

James F. Short, Jr.

Monrad G. Paulsen

Daniel Glaser

Maynard L. Erickson

Franklin E. Zimring

Alexander Liazos

The Future
of Childhood and
Juvenile Justice

Edited by LaMar T. Empey

University Press of Virginia

Charlottesville

THE UNIVERSITY PRESS OF VIRGINIA
Copyright © 1979 by the Kenyon Public Affairs Forum

First published 1979

Prepared under Grant #78–JA–AX–0001 from the Office of Juvenile Justice
and Delinquency Prevention, Law Enforcement Assistance Administration,
U.S. Department of Justice. The result of a conference on "The Future of
Childhood and Juvenile Justice" held at Kenyon College, Gambier, Ohio,
under the auspices of the Kenyon Public Affairs Forum.

The authors alone are responsible for the opinions expressed and any policies
recommended in their respective essays and do not necessarily represent
the official position or policies of Kenyon College, the Kenyon Public Affairs
Forum, or the U.S. Department of Justice.

The Kenyon Public Affairs Forum is a nonpartisan educational program
and as such takes no position on questions of public policy.

Library of Congress Cataloging in Publication Data
Main entry under title:

The Future of childhood and juvenile justice.

   Papers from a conference held at Kenyon College, Gambier, Ohio, under
the auspices of the Kenyon Public Affairs Forum.
   1. Juvenile justice, Administration of—United States–Congresses.
   2. Children's rights—United States–Congresses.   I.   Empey, LaMar Taylor, 1923–   II.   Kenyon Public Affairs Forum.
HV9091.F87   364.36′0973   79–15129   ISBN 0–8139–0832–9

Printed in the United States of America

Contents

The Future
of Childhood and
Juvenile Justice

Introduction: The Social Construction of Childhood and Juvenile Justice

LaMar T. Empey

FOR the better part of two centuries, Americans have been described as being child-centered to an inordinate degree (Skolnick, 1973:314; Tocqueville, 1945:192–97). "We have set a new record," says Mary Goodman (1970:11). "No other people seem ever to have been so preoccupied with children."

There is much to support these contentions. During the first two-thirds of this century, the age-grading of society reached its apex. Not only were youth progressively segregated from adults, but age-grading among children themselves increased steadily: kindergarten children were separated from first graders, first graders from second graders, second graders from third graders, and so on and on. As Americans grew steadily more conscious of age, their social institutions, their beliefs, and even their scientific theories reflected that consciousness.

A host of developmental theories were expounded which elaborated and reified a bio-psycho-social process of growth that would have seemed totally anachronistic to people a few short centuries ago. As a result, parents were not only warned about the consequences of failing to take this developmental process into account in raising their children, but a whole constellation of professional child savers was enlisted to assist them: pediatricians, elementary and secondary teachers, school counselors, social workers, child psychiatrists, and recreational specialists. Even a separate system of justice, including specially trained police officers, judges, and correctional

workers, was invented, not merely to protect abused and neglected children but to treat rather than to punish those who
were deviant.

But just when it appeared that the quarantine of youth
from adult privilege and responsibility might be extended
even further, signs of change began to appear—signs that were
due not merely to dissatisfaction with the protected and segregated status of young people but to growing amounts of protest
and deviance on their parts. During the 1960s and early 1970s,
college campuses and urban centers were not only marked
by the protest of youth over their social and political impotence, the continuing presence of racism in American society,
and the continuation of the Vietnam war, but crimes against
persons and property by children under the age of eighteen
reached unprecedented proportions. The rate of arrest per
100,000 children for the FBI's seven index offenses—murder,
rape, robbery, assault, burglary, larceny, and auto theft—went
up 120 percent (FBI, 1969:4). Hence, Americans became aware
of an acute contradiction: acts of protest and predation by
the young did not square with the assumption that they are
innocent and frail and require special protections.

The response to this contradiction was by no means entirely
punitive. In 1968 Richard Nixon and Spiro Agnew did appeal
to an angry and frightened public by promising, if elected,
to wage a "war on crime." But, for the most part, policymakers
shied away from making an all-out attack on the nation's youth.
Instead, national commission after national commission suggested that youth unrest was due more to an overly protective,
unduly bureaucratic society than to something that was inher-
ently evil in young people themselves (President's Crime
Commission, 1967a and 1967b; National Advisory Commission
on Criminal Justice Standards and Goals, 1973; National Task
Force, 1977). Furthermore, these commissions were much persuaded by a body of social thought—called labeling theory—
which expressed grave reservations over society's traditional
standards of moral and legal conduct for children (Becker,
1963: Lemert, 1951; 1972; Schur, 1973).

In another era in American history, this body of thought

might have passed relatively unnoticed, but because it seemed to capture and to give expression to widespread feelings of disillusionment and cynicism, it became exceedingly popular. With regard to children, for example, it suggested that moral values which attempted to quarantine the young from adult activities and which utilized legal means in order to keep them subservient to authority and modest and chaste in their habits were no longer viable. "The basic life process today," Edwin Lemert (1967:97) instructed the President's Crime Commission, "is one of adaption to exigencies and pressures; individual morality has become functional rather than sacred in the older sense."

It would be difficult to acknowledge this change in morals at the legislative and policy level, Lemert (1967:97) went on, because "social action in America has always been heavily laden with moral purpose." Nonetheless, if the organization of childhood was to be made more functional, society should attempt to enforce only "the ethical minimum of youth conduct necessary to maintain social life in a high energy, pluralistic society." Otherwise, youth problems would only become worse, not better.

Besides stressing the dysfunctional character of prevailing moral standards, labeling theorists also resurrected the ideas of Frank Tannenbaum, who had suggested in 1938 that our organized methods for trying to control youth deviance were also dysfunctional. The final steps in making the young criminal, Tannenbaum had argued, occur, not when some basically innocent child violates the law, but when he or she becomes enmeshed in the stigmatizing processes that traditional methods of control invoke. The mischievous play of children— breaking windows, tipping over garbage cans, skipping school or shoplifting—is escalated into evil, first by concerned parents, teachers, and neighbors, and then by police, judges, and probation officers. "The process of making the criminal . . . is a process of tagging, identifying, segregating, describing, emphasizing, making conscious and self-conscious; it becomes a way of stimulating, suggesting, emphasizing, and evoking the very traits that are complained of. . . . The [young] person becomes the thing he is described as being." Therefore, the only sensible response is to refuse to dramatize evil in the first place. "The less said about it the better" (Tannenbaum, 1938:20). "Leave children alone wherever possible" (Schur, 1973:55).

The implications of this point of view, of course, were that children in the latter part of the twentieth century were more in need of protection from paternalistic do-gooders and youth-serving institutions than from an exploitive and sinful world. And whether this review was accurate or not, it was prophetic.

The first youth institution to feel its sting was society's long-standing superparent, the juvenile court. In the mid-1960s, the Supreme Court concluded that children had received the worst of two possible worlds at the hands of supposedly benefi-cent judges and probation officers. It ruled, as a result, that in future legal proceedings children should receive most of the constitutional protections afforded adults (*Kent,* 1966; *In re Gault,* 1967; *In re Winship,* 1970). Were that not enough, the practice of diverting children—delinquent or otherwise—from the juvenile court to other community agencies became a national fad, a new panacea (Carter and Klein, 1976; Klein et al., 1976). Then federal legislation was passed which stipu-lated that status offenders—runaways, sexually promiscuous children, truants, and incorrigibles—could no longer be con-fined in secure detention or correctional facilities as a method of trying to control or to reform them (LEAA, 1974:395). Fol-lowing that, such prestigious groups as the International Chiefs of Police, the National Council on Crime and Delinquency, and the farmers of the Model Act for Family Courts recom-mended that the jurisdiction of the juvenile court over status offenders should be eliminated entirely (National Task Force, 1977:3). Finally, the State of Washington heeded the obvious trend and became the first (but certainly not the last) state to free status offenders from any control by the juvenile court (Revised Code of Washington, 1977).

As might be anticipated, the movement to change the status of children was not confined merely to the juvenile court;

instead, it was paralleled by changes throughout all of society. In 1971 the twenty-sixth Amendment to the Constitution granted full political suffrage to young people at the age of eighteen rather than at the age of twenty-one (Coleman et al., 1974:42); a variety of higher court decisions supported the rights of students to free speech in the public schools (*Tinker* v. *Des Moines Independent School District*, 1969); child-labor legislation came under increasing attack, as did mandatory school attendance laws (White House Conference, 1971; Coleman et al., 1974:42); several states lowered the school-leaving age (Empey, 1978:566–67); legal restrictions on drinking by young people under twenty-one were relaxed; the "sexual revolution" questioned the scared value of premarital chastity; and the Supreme Court ruled that a pregnant teenager, no less than adult women, has the right to an abortion without parental consent (*Los Angeles Times*, July 5, 1976).

In short, significant alterations in the organization of childhood have been made in the past two decades. Yet, despite their significance, they may only be the beginning. The reason is that other alterations in American culture are taking place that, if anything, seem to be even more likely to change the organization of childhood than the changes that were initiated by the disillusionment and protests of the 1960s.

One of the most significant of these is the changing population pyramid. A decline in the birth rate, combined with an increase in life expectancy, is creating a set of conditions largely unknown to prior civilizations. We are witness to a changing population structure that is growing increasingly heavy at the top; we have suddenly become aware of a rapidly growing population of elderly people.

It is difficult to say what the precise consequences of this change will be. In the short run, it could delay current efforts to grant greater autonomy and status to the young. Their needs for jobs and services, to say nothing of middle-aged people who are poor and jobless, might be affected adversely. In the long run, however, the opposite could occur. Ever larger numbers of older people would have to be supported by a proportionately smaller and younger segment of the population. But, in either case, the chances seem more than slight that the protected status of the young will be altered.

No less important is the incipient dissatisfaction with monogamous marriage and the nuclear family as the nursery for the next generation. Helping to fuel this discontent, moreover, is the desire for equal status by women. Caught up in the conflict between the drive for personal autonomy and the responsibilities of raising children, women as well as men may find the latter task increasingly onerous. It is impossible for sex and age roles to undergo profound changes without the precipitation of ambivalence and tension. Indeed, it is entirely possible that our preoccupation with child raising will dissipate.

Other examples could be cited, but these are sufficient to indicate that we now seem to be on one of those watersheds in history when irrevocable changes are occurring in the status of children. At the same time, it is by no means certain what the outcome will be. On the one hand, the movement of recent years to extend the logic of the democratic ethic to children may enhance their status and improve their lives. On the other hand, that movement is not occurring in isolation. Instead, it is being initiated at a time when powerful movements in behalf of minorities, of women, and of the elderly have by no means realized their full objectives. Hence, there is every possibility that the Child Rights Movement will find itself in conflict with these other movements, to say nothing of the possible conflicts inherent in trying to discard traditional patterns governing the lives of children.

Given the complexity of these issues, we will be examining the Child Rights Movement and the Revolution in Juvenile Justice from several perspectives in this book. But it is important that they first be placed in an appropriate historical and cultural context. We cannot gain a good perspective on the future unless we know where we have been in the past. We cannot weigh the pros and cons of change without understanding the origins and nature of what is being changed.

The History of Childhood

In a number of recent and fascinating works, several historians have come to the conclusion that the concept of childhood with which many are now dissatisfied is a product largely of the past few centuries, at least in Western civilization (Aries, 1962; Bremner, 1970; Demos, 1970; Gillis, 1974; Hunt, 1970; Mause, 1974; Stone, 1974). These historians are not in total agreement on all the important facts; yet among the conclusions upon which they do agree is the idea that childhood has not always been a time in life to which much importance has been attached. Indeed, the opposite has often been true. For instance, Mause (1974:1) says that "the history of childhood is a nightmare from which we only recently began to awaken." And while Stone (1974:29) is somewhat more cautious, he still concludes that the historical treatment of children is a "catalogue of atrocities." How, then, did our modern concern with children come about? Why, today, are we playing so much attention to it?

Indifference to Children

Concern over children was a long time in developing. Evidence indicates that infanticide and the abandonment of newborn infants were regular practices in ancient civilizations and were not uncommon in Europe as late as the seventeenth and eighteenth centuries. Before the fourth century, in particular, newborn infants were thrown into rivers, flung into dung heaps, left to be eaten by animals of prey, or sacrificed to gods in religious rites (Mause, 1974:25). From the fourth to the thirteenth centuries, the simple abandonment of unwanted children was more the mode (Mause, 1974:51). Nonetheless, the result was usually the same, and the practice of getting rid of undesired infants was a long time in dying out. In seventeenth century England, for example, midwives had to take the following oath because of the apparent persistence of infanticide: "I will not destroy the child born of any woman, nor cut, nor pull off the head thereof, or otherwise dismember or hurt the same, or suffer it to be so hurt or dismembered" (Illick, 1974:306).

Cultural beliefs tended to define which children should, and which should not, survive such practices. Any child who was not perfect or seemed to cry too much was generally killed; boys were considered to be of much greater value than girls; and infanticide and abandonment, rather than contraception or abortion, were methods of controlling family size. Two sons might be raised, possibly three, but seldom more than one girl (Mause, 1974:26; Marvick, 1974:283–86).

Even for those infants allowed to live at birth, survival was tenuous. Up to about the eighteenth century, most children of well-to-do or even average parents spent their earliest years in the care of a wet nurse. The police chief of Paris estimated in 1780 that of approximately 21,000 recorded births, 17,000 were sent to the country to be wet-nursed; only 700 were nursed by their own mothers (Mause, 1974:35). The practice of wet-nursing was apparently denounced by moralists from the time of the ancient Greeks onward because of its apparent harm to infants. Many did not survive because commercial wet nurses were often cruel and malnourished themselves, and even killed their own infants in order to extend their money-making milk supply (Stone, 1974:29).

Other infant-raising practices, such as swaddling, burning babies with a hot iron to prevent "falling sickness," dipping them in ice water, or rolling them in the snow to harden or to baptize them, as well as disease and filth, took a high toll (Mause, 1974:31–37; Robertson, 1974:410–12; Tucker, 1974:242). Indeed, a high death rate among babies and young children may have been a major reason that childhood, as a place in the life cycle, received so little attention. As late as the seventeenth century, from one-half to two-thirds of all children died before the age of 20 (Bremner, 1970, 1:3–4; Gillis, 1974:10). "Before they are old enough to bother you," said one Frenchman, "you will have lost half of them, or perhaps all of them" (Aries, 1962:38).

Under such conditions, says Stone (1974:30), "no parent could retain his or her sanity if he or she became too emotionally involved with such ephemeral creatures as young children. Aloofness, or the acceptance of God's will, or sending one's children away from home were three natural solutions to this problem of how to deal with their deaths." Given the ephemeral character of childhood, Aries (1962;28–29) maintains that various languages in the Middle Ages and later did not possess words to distinguish babies from bigger children, and people had no conception of adolescence. And Skolnick (1973:333) says that people believed that infants existed "in a sort of limbo, hanging between life and death, more as a kind of animal than a human being, without mental activities or recognizable bodily shape."

Beyond the years of infancy, child-raising practices also revealed the continuance of relative indifference, at least in our terms. Upon reaching the age of seven, children of the poor and aristocracy alike became apprentices in the homes of their masters (Aries, 1962:35). This was the way they were prepared for adulthood, living with, and working for, others. Furthermore, the social life in which they participated was highly communal. Many children grew up in large households of as many as twenty-five people—parents, apprentices, relatives, servants, and visitors—while the lives of peasant children, though probably not less communal, were spent in smaller dwellings, on the streets, and in the fields.

Prevailing conditions meant that behavioral rules for children were vastly different from our own. Measured by contemporary standards, says Aries (1962:394), "it is easy to imagine the promiscuity which reigned in those rooms [of the communal household] where nobody could be alone, . . . where several couples and several groups of boys or girls slept together (not to speak of the servants of whom at least some must have slept beside their masters . . .), in which people foregathered to have their meals, to receive friends or clients."

Aries's comment points to the apparent fact that children were not spared a full and participatory role in all aspects of existence: sex, work, life, and death. He concludes, as a result, that, because children were not segregated by age as they are today, they led a happy and sociable life: they were the natural companions of adults.

Other historians are far less sanguine (Bremner, 1970; Illick, 1974; Lyman, 1974; Mause, 1974; Stone, 1974; Tucker, 1974). While children were not segregated from adults, historians contend that their status was at the bottom of the social scale. In antiquity, both boys and girls were often purchased at birth, subjected to castration and clitoridectomy, placed in brothels, and then became the sexual playthings of adults. The literature of the Renaissance is likewise full of moralist complaints about the sexual abuse of children. Children were also treated as economic assets. The apprenticeship system, which persisted well into the nineteenth century, even in this country, led to the exploitation of child labor. Finally, methods of social control were often brutal and countenanced severe beatings with whips, rods, and cudgels. In short, even if one took a temperate view, he might conclude as Stone (1974:29) did that children in Western civilization, until very recently, have not counted for much. Legal institutions designed to protect them from neglect, as we define it, or to punish them for lewd conduct, drinking, or staying out late, would have been ludicrous and anachronistic.

Discovery of Childhood

The forces that eventually led to the modern view of childhood apparently had their origins in the early Renaissance and, for a long time, existed coterminously with the conditions just described. Christian beliefs had long stressed the innocence and frailty of children, although in practice people had not paid much attention to them. Then, during the fifteenth and sixteenth centuries, signs of ambivalence and change began to appear. People were warned to do a better job of select-

ing wet nurses (Ross, 1974:185); the color white came to symbol-
ize children (Tucker, 1974:232); children became a source of
amusement for adults, like little dogs or puppies (Aries,
1962:129); and children in paintings began to look like children
rather than mature dwarfs (Aries, 1962:33).

By the late sixteenth and seventeenth centuries, criticisms
of prior child-raising practices also grew pronounced. Although the Renaissance, the Reformation, the Commercial
Revolution, and the discovery of the New World were undoubt-
edly influential, most historians suggest that the real innova-
tors, insofar as children are concerned, were a relatively small
band of moralists, churchmen, and schoolmen, both Catholic
and Protestant (Aries, 1962:330, 412; Bremner, 1970:I; Illick,
1974:316–17; Marvick, 1974:261). A moralization of society was
taking place in which the ethical aspects of religion were gradually taking precedence over the ritualistic. Efforts were being
made to reshape the world and to do so, in part, through
children.

Children were seen by the moralists as rather odd creatures,
fragile, innocent, and sacred, on the one hand, but corruptible,
trying, and arrogant on the other. What children needed,
therefore, was discipline and training. Their premature induc-
tion into the adult world not only injured them but affronted
adults. The remarks of two Puritan reformers in 1621 captured
this moralist theme very well (Illick, 1974:316–17): "the young
child which lieth in the cradle is both wayward and full of
affections; and though his body is small, yet he hath a reat
[wrong-doing] heart, and is altogether inclined to evil. . . .
If this sparkle be suffered to increase, it will rage and burn
down the whole house. For we are changed and become good
not by birth but by education. . . . Therefore, parents must
be wary and circumspect.

What was emerging, of course, was the modern concept
of childhood, namely, the idea that, until a child has been
given distinctive preparation, he is not ready for life. Until
he has been subjected to a sort of moral and educational quarantine, he cannot be allowed to join the adults (Aries, 1962:
411–12). In support of this idea, the moralists stressed the

importance of two societal institutions in addition to the church: the family and the school. During the Middle Ages, children were a common property and, except for a few years, were not raised by their own parents. The moralists, however, placed direct responsibility on parents, a responsibility that, among other things, probably contributed to the emergence of the nuclear family. With respect to that issue, Peter Laslett (1972:1–89) has shown rather conclusively that the English family became increasingly nuclear during the seventeenth century.

Not entirely trusting corrupt parents, however, the moralists also sought to use the school as a place for moral as well as intellectual training. Unlike the humanists of the Renaissance, who stressed the idea that learning should be pursued by people of all ages, the moralists were particularly concerned with schooling for the young. Hence, they were responsible for opening many of the first schools whose purpose was general education rather than technical training for the clergy (see Aries, 1962). While space precludes a detailed discussion of the evolution of these schools, a recognition of their importance as a social innovation designed to reorganize the lives of the young is what is most important. Along with the nuclear family, therefore, the school began to replace the apprenticeship system as a preferred institution for raising children.

The Ideal Child

By the late seventeenth and eighteenth centuries, a vision of the ideal child had been developed and widely projected. The vision is easily deduced by allusion to the child-raising principles set forth in a multiplicity of tracts, sermons, and pamphlets that were common both in Europe and in the American colonies (Aries, 1962:114–19; Bremner, 1970, I; Rothman, 1971:15–17). Briefly, the principles were these:

1. Never permit children to be alone, since they are not fit to govern themselves.

2. Discipline, do not pamper, children. They must learn submission and self-control.

3. Teach modesty. Children should not undress in the presence of others; should not lie in an immodest position, especially girls; should not sleep together if of the opposite sex; should not hear songs, read books, or observe performances that express dissolute passions.

4. Train children to work. Teach them diligence in some lawful trade.

5. Above all, teach respect for, and obedience to authority. Disobedience leads inevitably to dishonor, disease, and death. In short, the ideal child should be submissive to authority, hardworking, self-controlled, obedient, modest, and chaste. Parents who do not produce such children, and schools that fail to mold them, are suspect.

Despite the projection of this ideal, the task of incorporating it into the institutional structures of society was long and tortuous. For example, it was the new and emerging middle class—the merchants, entrepreneurs, and professionals—who were most attracted to the ideals of the nuclear family and formal schooling for their children. Thus, while they began to seek out the privacy of home and the benefits of school, the peasant class, either by force of circumstance or out of choice, clung for a much longer period of time to the practices of communal living, the apprenticeship system, and the indiscriminate mixing of the generations (Aries, 1962:414–15; Bremner, 1970, I:343). These contrasting practices, of course, were to have a lasting effect and remained in evidence well into the twentieth century.

Sexual stratification also continued. Nineteenth-century French peasants were known to declare: "I have no children, monsieur. I have only girls" (Robertson, 1974:409). And in Naples it was customary to hang out a black flag if a girl was born so that neighbors might be spared the embarrassment of coming to congratulate disappointed parents. Hence, a newly developing educational system in Europe remained off-limits to girls for some time (Aries, 1962:269–85). And while girls in the American colonies were taught to read and write, particularly those in the Northeast, they were soon relegated to domestic roles.

The pressing need for child labor also delayed the process of implementing the modern concept of childhood. Not only were children pressed into service by their own parents, but the American colonies employed large numbers of indentured children, many of whom were kidnapped by "spirits" and shipped to the colonies in large numbers (Bremner, 1970, I:5–9). Except for the time when they would eventually gain their freedom, the lot of these children was not entirely different from those of slave children. The only marked departure from the past, therefore, was in the treatment given children by their own parents. Although the young were expected to begin contributing to the survival of the family at about age six, they were not apprenticed to others until early adolescence.

As an indication of the difficulties involved in discarding the apprenticeship system and replacing it with an ideal wedding of family and school, consider the Puritans, a group who were zealously committed to the new concept of childhood. One major reason they had come to the New World was to help their children escape the "corruption" of the Old. The fountains of learning and religion had been destroyed, said John Winthrop, such that "most children, even the best wits and of fairest hopes, are perverted, corrupted and utterly overthrown" (Bremner, 1970, I:18–19).

In order to remedy these evils, the Massachusetts Bay Colony passed a law in 1624 that was designed to enforce the socialization functions of family and school (Bremner, 1970, I:–28–29). This new law required that each family teach its own children how to read and write. Parents who failed could be brought before the authorities, while children who disobeyed could be severely punished. But since parents were usually ill-equipped to teach their own children, to say nothing of insuring their survival, the General Court of Massachusetts took the first step, in 1647, toward a public educational system (Bremner, 1970, I:72–73). Furthermore, Connecticut and New Hampshire followed suit: towns of 50 households were supposed to provide a schoolmaster for elementary training, while towns of 100 were expected to have a grammar (secondary) school. But since attendance at the grammar school level was not required, and was dependent upon private support, it tended to favor the well-to-do.

Distinctions based on wealth were even more apparent in southern and middle Atlantic colonies. In these colonies the children of the poor, in particular, had to rely upon the occasional church-sponsored school or the apprenticeship system for whatever education they received. Meanwhile, formal education for slave and Indian children was simply unavailable. While some ministers and some slave owners sought to convert blacks to Christianity, they felt it was too dangerous, politically and socially, to provide them with secular skills (Bremner, 1970, I:317–18).

With all these limitations (Bremner 1970, I:74) colonial education was unmatched in Europe, reaching more children and providing them with a greater ability to read and write than a comparable number of children elsewhere. Nonetheless, it was not until after the Civil War, two centuries later, that the majority of American states passed mandatory school attendance laws, and even then such laws often proved ineffective (Hoffman, 1976:51). In 1900, for example, one-third of all workers in southern mills were children, more than half of them between the ages of ten and thirteen, and over half of them the children of immigrants (Bremner, 1970, II:601–4).

By the end of the nineteenth century, however, the Industrial Revolution had taken root, the rush westward had slowed, and the need for child labor was declining. As a result, the continued exploitation of children apparently pricked an increasing number of consciences, generating references to "cannibalism," "child slavery," and "slaughter of the innocents." The discontinuity between ideal and real, even for poor children, had begun to lessen. Thus, a crusade against child labor gathered steam, led by lawyers, social workers, various charitable groups, and even some industrialists (Bremner, 1970, II:601–4). By the dawn of the twentieth century, twenty-eight states had passed laws regulating child labor as well as requiring that children attend school.

The Invention of Juvenile Justice

Although child-labor and school-attendance laws reflected the growing sentiment that the prolongation and protection of childhood were essential to human progress, there was no special legal machinery by which to enforce such laws or to deal with children charged with crimes. Instead, delinquent children were commonly processed by lower municipal courts (Schultz, 1974:248), while those without proper supervision were often committed to houses of refuge, orphan asylums, and training schools for being "destitute of proper parental care, growing up in mendicancy, ignorance, idleness, or vice" (Platt, 1969:103). Still others were committed to adult jails and to prisons under the blanket charge of "disorderly conduct," which might cover anything from assault with a deadly weapon to building bonfires in the street or playing on the railroad tracks (Lathrop, 1916:2).

Apparently, the stage was reached when this state of affairs could no longer be tolerated. In 1870 Boston began holding separate court hearings for juveniles under sixteen, as did New York in 1877. Massachusetts also passed a law in 1869 requiring agents of the State Board of Charities to attend the trials of children to protect their interests and to make recommendations to the judge (Caldwell, 1961:400). Finally, in 1898 the Illinois Conference of Charities culminated over a decade of effort by proposing the most radical step of all—a special court just for children. The conference drafted a model court act, the Chicago Bar Association threw its support behind the act, and the Illinois legislature passed it in 1899 (Lathrop, 1925). Within 25 years, moreover, similar laws were passed in every state but two. Along with laws regulating child labor and mandating attendance at school, the juvenile court had become a part of the institutional fabric of American society.

It is difficult to overstate the importance of the functions that the juvenile court was expected to fulfill. It became an invention of revolutionary significance because it represented a response, not merely to remarkable changes in the status of children, but to the unprecedented upheavals of the late nineteenth century. At the very time when decreases were occurring in the need for child labor, when the nuclear family had been institutionalized, and when universal education seemed desirable, momentous demographic, economic, and cultural changes seemed to threaten the pursuit of these ideals. Hence, the new juvenile court would not only be expected to protect children from exploitation and abuse but would become society's superparent when unstable families and corrupt communities could no longer care for them.

Enforcing the Modern Concept of Childhood

The beliefs and aspirations that led to the creation of the juvenile court are best understood as an ideological outgrowth of the modern concept of childhood and of the assumptions inherent in that concept (see Skolnick, 1973:316–21):

1. Children go through several stages of development which require that their entrance into full adulthood be postponed until their twenties or even later.

2. Throughout the various stages of development, children are qualitatively different from adults: "Adults work and are responsible, children play and are irresponsible; adults are controlled and rational, children are emotional and irrational; adults think abstractly, children think concretely; adults are sexual, children are asexual; and so on" (Skolnick, 1973:316).

3. Until their full emotional, moral, physical and rational skills are cultivated, children should be quarantined from adult vices, activities, and responsibilitites. Though this quarantine may be reduced gradually as children proceed through the developmental process, it should not be lifted entirely until adulthood has been achieved.

The school-attendance and child-labor laws of the late nineteenth century, as well as the creation of the juvenile court, represented an embodiment of these assumptions in the legal as well as the cultural fabric of society. That is why, until almost the present day, children have been referred to court not only for violating the criminal law but for idle conduct, for intractibility, for knowingly associating with lewd or lascivious persons, for being truant, for being alone with someone of the opposite sex at night, or for one of a host of other possible "offenses." Legal definitions of child deviance were simply the obverse of the moral principles inherent in the modern concept of childhood, namely, that the ideal child should be obedient, submissive, self-controlled, hardworking, modest, and chaste (Aries, 1962:114–19; Gillis, 1974:21). A paternalistic court was expected to insure that children were stringently safeguarded, that they received an education, and that they did not behave as adults until they had outlived the quarantine associated with childhood.

Surrogate for Family and Community

The second function of the juvenile court was closely related. Its creator firmly hoped that it could become a benevolent surrogate for ineffective families and corrupt communities. That is why the first juvenile court act in Illinois specified that the law should be "liberally construed to the end . . . that the care, custody and discipline of a child shall approximate . . . that which should be given by its parents" (Revised Statutes of Illinois, 1899, Sec. 21). The inherent frailty and undeveloped natures of children would no longer tolerate the use of criminal courts and procedures for them.

Today, of course, it has become popular to question the practicality and wisdom of such a stipulation. Why, it is asked, did reformers attempt to use the formal procedures of a legal body to play a role that had been reserved traditionally for home and community?

As suggested earlier, the answer probably lies in the momentous changes experienced by Americans during the nineteenth and early twentieth centuries. Traditions derived from a rural past simply did not provide them with functional guides for raising neglected children in the bewildering world of a newly industrialized capitalistic society. In the eighteenth century, for example, chilhood had been governed by a tightly knit constellation of informal networks: home, church, and community (Rothman, 1971). Children were entirely dependent upon their families only until about age six. But between that age and the time they were apprenticed to others, they were not threatened by strangers, by busy city streets, or by neighborhood gangs. Instead, they were expected to contribute to the collective welfare and to gain the rudiments of an education. Then, at age fourteen, they assumed semiadult roles, working on the family farm, living as apprentices in the homes of their masters, or as students boarding away from home. They usually remained in that state until their mid- or late twenties, when they could afford to marry and start a household of their own. There was, then, a very short period of childhood followed by a long transitional period called "youth" and, finally, adulthood.

During this time in American history, few children or their families commanded the kinds of resources that would free them from dependence upon one another. Life was dominated by a subsistence economy in which cooperation was vital. Furthermore, marriages often turned neighbors into relatives, and daily contacts with a limited number of people fostered a reliance upon strong informal controls. Indeed, paramilitary police forces, jails, detention centers, and training schools did not exist and would have seemed anachronistic. Instead, the environmental conditions of the time produced a kind of community interdependence and age integration that made informal kinds of social control effective without them. While sin was equated with crime and punished harshly, the misfortunes of poverty and destitution were not viewed as signs of personal or community failure and turned over to the state for a solution. Rather, the fatherless child or the aged widow became the responsibility of one's kin or neighbors, By the end of the eighteenth century, however, the effectiveness of these informal methods had begun to wither (Rothman, 1971).

Between 1790 and 1830 the population of the United States grew markedly, as did the size and density of several cities and states. Massachusetts doubled in size, Pennsylvania tripled, and New York increased fivefold. When George Washington became president, most people lived in towns with less than 2,500 inhabitants. By the time Andrew Jackson was inaugurated in 1829, however, over a million people resided in towns larger than that (Rothman, 1971;57–59). Some notion of the trends that were underway can be gleaned from the fact that in 1750 there were only about 1.25 million people in this country. By 1850 the figure had reached over 23 million (U.S. Bureau of the Census, 1955).

Although such growth had never before been experienced by any society, at any time, it was only the beginning. As manufacturing, immigration, and urban expansion continued to increase, the simple economic and social organization of the early colonies became ever more ineffective. As a result, the reformers of the nineteenth century often seemed overwhelmed by the changes they observed. How was social order to be maintained? What were the best means for reducing the effects on children of poverty, urban growth, poor family discipline, and community instability?

In order to answer these questions, Americans did not first invent the juvenile court, nor did they ignore the importance of family and community. But rather than seek ways by which to enhance the effectiveness of these basic institutions, they attempted to build substitutes for them. During the first half of the nineteenth century, they built prisons for adults and houses of refuge and orphan asylums for children. Total institutions of this type had existed in some European countries for years, but the idea that they could be used to reform criminals or to substitute for the family and community as the best method for raising neglected children was entirely new. Nonetheless, optimistic and well-intentioned reformers reasoned that, if some families and communitites were no longer fit places for raising children, places of confinement could be made into effective surrogates (Bremner, 1970, I:22; Rothman, 1971:207–9; Sanders, 1970:366).

Alas, the idea was a failure. By 1850 criticisms of houses of refuge, asylums, and prisons had begun to mount; by 1870 there was an overwhelming demand for change—a demand that placed concerned reformers on the horns of a dilemma. On the one hand, rather than becoming model superparents, child-saving institutions had become prisonlike warehouses for ever larger numbers of children from the margins of society. Rather than turning out ideal juveniles, they were producing young things who either marched, thought, and acted like automatons or who seemed more angry and rebellious than ever (Bremner, 1970, I:696–97; Rothman, 1971:258–60).

On the other hand, the need for child saving also seemed to be greater than ever. All the things that reformers feared most were coming to pass. Besides the Civil War, the last half of the nineteenth century was marked by ever more immigrants, more urban growth, more mobility, and more social instability. As early as 1850 immigrant children constituted almost three-quarters of the New York Refuge, over half of the Cincinnati Refuge, and two-thirds of the Philadelphia Refuge (Rothman, 1971:261–62). The parents of these children were usually penniless when they arrived in the United States and often found it necessary to remain in the big cities, where they swelled the ranks of the unemployed and contributed to high crime rates. Consequently, by the end of that century child savers were prepared to invest the problems of childhood with even greater urgency. In this instance, however, they looked to the newly created juvenile court to provide the solution. Whereas orphan asylums and training schools had failed, an expanded legal and correctional system, with a wider array of services, would provide the necessary controls.

By way of illustrating this hope, the Educational Commission of Chicago complained in 1899 that the Compulsory School Attendance Act was not adequate to insure schooling for some children: "They cannot be received or continued in the regularly organized schools; . . . their parents cannot or will not control them; teachers and committees fail to correct their evil tendencies and vicious conduct. What shall be done with them?" (Harpur, 1899:161).

The answer was that they should be disciplined by the juvenile court. It would rescue them from their dissolute parents and see that they were properly educated. As the commission put it: "The welfare of the city demands that such children be put under restraint. . . . We should rightfully have the power to arrest all the little beggars, loafers, and vagabonds that infest our city, take them from the streets, and place them in schools where they are compelled to receive education and learn moral principles (Harpur, 1899:163–64). In short, the juvenile court was not conceived as a criminal court in the traditional sense. Instead, it would be far more than that, not only a helpful parent but a stern parent, not only a rescuer of children but an enforcer of ideal standards for them.

Delinquency Prevention

By moving in where parents, teachers and communities had failed, the juvenile court could not only keep children in school but could perform a much grander function: it could also prevent delinquency. As the Chicago Bar Association put it, the court should not have to wait until a child is "criminal in tastes and habits" or until he "is in jails, bridewells and reformatories" before it acts. Instead, it would "seize upon the first conditions of neglect or delinquency" and thereby prevent innocent children from treading the path that leads to criminality (see Platt, 1969:138–39). Furthermore, in fulfilling this role, the court should not be encumbered with all the inhibiting strictures of due process since its primary goal was in pursuing good for children, not in punishing them for evil.

Decriminalizing Children

Besides using the juvenile court to prevent delinquency, reformers also believed that it could be used to decriminalize the conduct of young lawbreakers. In the past, as Judge Julian W. Mack (1910:293) put it, children were generally "huddled together" with older criminals in the station houses, jails, and workhouses of America. Thus, "instead of the state training its bad boys so as to make of them decent citizens, it permitted them to become outlaws and outcasts of society; it *criminalized* them by the methods it used in dealing with them" (emphasis added). The new juvenile court, by contrast, would decriminalize such children by calling them "delinquents" rather than "criminals."

This could be accomplished, reformers reasoned, because the typical road to crime was paved, first, by poverty and ignorance, then by lack of family concern and discipline, then by rudeness, vice, and intemperance, and, finally, by lawbreaking itself. Consequently, they saw little need to draw subtle distinctions among the neglected child, the rude and intemperate child, and the child who broke the criminal law. Rather, said Judge Mack (1910:29), it is the duty of the state, not to ask whether a boy or girl has committed a specific offense, but "to find out what he is physically, mentally, and morally and then, if it learns that he is treading the path that leads to criminality, to take him in charge, not so much to punish as to reform, not to degrade but to uplift, not to crush but to develop, not to make him a criminal but a worthy citizen." Hence, in contrast to the efforts of today's reformers to draw sharp distinctions between "delinquents" and "status offenders," those of the nineteenth century sought to make status offenders out of *all* misbehaving children, whether they were criminal or merely neglected and unruly.

Rehabilitation

The idea that juvenile crimes should be decriminalized and their perpetrators reformed was symptomatic of the growing popularity of the concept of rehabilitation during the nineteenth century. Indeed, there is striking evidence that growing concerns about the welfare of children had percolated upward and were being expressed as concerns about adults. Nineteenth-century Americans, says Rothman (1971:66), "stripped away the years from adults and made everyone into a child."

Reflective of this idea, the Cincinnati Prison Congress of 1870, from which the principles of rehabilitation were so remarkably well distilled, concluded that great good could be accomplished if adult as well as juvenile criminals were made "the objects of generous parental care." Instead of being sentenced to suffering, they should be "trained to virtue" (Henderson, 1910;40). "A prison governed by force and fear is a prison mismanaged, in which hope and love, the two great spiritual, uplifting, regenerative forces to which mankind must ever look for redemption, are asleep or dead" (Wines, 1910:2).

It is scarcely surprising, then, that the concept of rehabilitation became a natural ally of the concept of childhood and was eagerly incorporated into the juvenile court philosophy. Ostensibly derived for the purposes of correcting criminals, the beliefs embodied in it were so like those embodied in the concept of childhood that they might be viewed as principles for raising children, not just for reforming criminals: rehabilitation, not punishment, is the primary goal of penology; punishment only degrades, correctional practices should uplift; treat people, not crimes; apply scientific methods to the task of diagnosing, classifying, and treating offenders; replace peremptory with indeterminate sentences—the task of socializing people is a task of time; make use of all educational, emotional, and industrial resources in accomplishing this task; and insure that offenders are assisted by a concerned parole officer when they return to the community (Henderson, 1910:39–63). The only way that society can be protected from the evils of crime is to insure that all offenders are socialized properly.

The only modern innovation which the Cincinnati Prison Congress failed to stress was probation. Instead, its members concluded that the most logical place to apply the principles of rehabilitation was in new, scientifically run reformatories (Brockway, 1910). But by the time the juvenile court was firmly established, this idea had lost some of its attractiveness: "However good an institution may be, however kindly its spirit, however genial its atmosphere, however homelike its cottages, however fatherly and motherly its officers, however admirable its training, it is now generally agreed . . . that institutional life is at the best artificial and unnatural, and that the child ought to be returned at the earliest practicable moment to the more natural environment of the family" (Hart, 1910:12). Early in the twentieth century, therefore, community treatment under the supervision of a probation officer became the philosophical ideal for the juvenile court. Probation, said Judge Richard Tuthill of Chicago, "is the cord upon which all the pearls of the juvenile court are strung" (Rothman, 1979). Indeed, a discerning and consecrated probation officer, together with the judge, would operate the juvenile court like a medical clinic:

The judge and the probation officer consider together, like a physician and his junior, whether the outbreak . . . was largely accidental, or whether it is habitual or likely to be so, whether it is due chiefly to some inherent physical or moral defect of the child, or whether some feature of his environment is an important factor; and then they address themselves to the question of how permanently to prevent a recurrence. (Baker, 1910:322)

Whatever he needed the unfortunate child would receive.

Triumphal Acceptance

Reactions to the invention of the juvenile court were overwhelmingly favorable. Though he had warned in 1913 that "the powers of the court of star chamber were a bagatelle compared with those of American juvenile courts," Roscoe Pound described those same courts, in 1950, as "the greatest step forward in Anglo-American jurisprudence since the Magna Charta!" (cf. Rothman, 1979 with National Probation and Parole Association, 1957:127). Similarly, Judge Orman Ketcham (1962:26) of the District of Columbia remarked that "the first two decades of the juvenile court movement produced a wealth of philosophical comment so sound in conception and so modern in tone that it has scarcely been modified or improved upon since that time."

Until very recently, then, most Americans have not been concerned with the possibility that the juvenile court might be overly patronizing and arbitrary but with finding ways by which its functions might be made more effective. The reason was that the court was not conceived as a legal body in the traditional sense. Rather, it was a logical outgrowth of the concept of childhood. No less than family or school, therefore, it should help to organize, to protect, and to discipline children. Created in an aura of benevolent paternalism, it would be law and social work, control and help, the good parent and the stern parent; it would be all things to all people (Rubin, 1976:66).

Summary and Conclusions

This review suggests that the history of childhood and of juvenile justice might be conveniently divided into two major epochs: *indifference* and *preoccupation.*

Indifference

Until about the thirteenth century, the deliberate killing or abandonment of children was regarded as casually as abortion is today. Although these practices gradually declined over the next few centuries, newborn babies were still farmed out to wet nurses, and young children were still sent to the homes of others to serve as apprentices and servants. Compared with today's exacting standards, the attitude of parents toward their own children was one of relative indifference and detachment. Childhood was not noteworthy in its own right; many languages lacked words to distinguish babies from those we now call adolescents or young adults; and little people were not shielded from adult strength or depravity, work, sex, or death. The emotionally interdependent and highly protective nuclear family, a complex and age-graded system of education, and a unique system of juvenile justice simply did not exist.

Preoccupation

From the sixteenth century to the nineteenth, age-old tendencies either to abandon, to ignore, or to exploit children were
gradually replaced with a heightened, even fervent concern
over their welfare. Childhood became a transitional period
during which family privacy and responsibility increased;
community sociability across generational and class lines decreased; a new morality for children developed; and new
forms of moral and intellectual training by family and school
began to replace apprenticeship training and early adulthood.

At the turn of the twentieth century, this preoccupation
with childhood was cast into legal stone. Child-labor laws were
passed, schooling became mandatory, and a new system of
juvenile justice was created whose purpose was both to protect
children from exploitation and to enforce the modern concept
of childhood. Society was committed to the notion that, in
order to insure their proper development, children must be
stringently safeguarded, must receive a carefully structured
education, and, only after long years of moral, physical, and
intellectual quarantine, could they be allowed to join adults.

Attenuation

Recent dissatisfaction over this way of organizing the lives
of children suggests that we may now be entering a new epoch
in history, an epoch marked by an *attenuation of childhood*.
The past two decades have been characterized by growing
protest over age segregation, the prolongation of childhood,
and the powerless status of youth; the moral standards governing childhood have been attacked; legal rules have been altered; and the power and the jurisdiction of the juvenile court
have been severely curtailed. It may be, therefore, that today's
incipient changes will be no less profound in the long run
than those which first protested societal indifference to chil-

dren during the Renaissance or which ultimately resulted in our more recent preoccupation with them

Given this possibility, current reforms will be detailed and examined in this volume. Respected and well-known advocates of both the Child Rights Movement and the Revolution in Juvenile Justice will present the cases for these movements in the first section. Then, in two subsequent sections, a number of eminent scholars will examine these movements from a variety of perspectives. Finally, after all points of view have been presented, findings and speculations will be summarized and their implications assessed.

References

Ariès, Philippe
1962   Centuries of Childhood (Trans. Robert Baldick). New York: Knopf.

Baker, Harvey H.
1910   "Procedure for the Boston Juvenile Court." Pp. 318–27 in Hasting H. Hart (ed.), Preventive Treatment of Neglected Children. New York: Charities Publication Committee.

Becker, Howard S.
1963   Outsiders: Studies in the Sociology of Deviance. New York: Free Press.

Bremner, Robert H. (ed.)
1970   Children and Youth in America: A Documentary History. 2 vols. Cambridge: Harvard Univ. Press.

Brockway, Z. R.
1910   "The American reformatory prison system." Pp. 88–107 in Charles R. Henderson (ed.), Prison Reform and Criminal Law. New York: Charities Publication Committee.

Caldwell, Robert G.
1961   "The juvenile court: its development and some major problems." Journal of Criminal Law, Criminology, and Police Science 51:593–607.

Carter, Robert M., and Malcolm W. Klein
1976   Back on the Street: The Diversion of Juvenile Offenders. Englewood Cliffs, N.J.: Prentice-Hall.

Coleman, James S., et al.
1974   Youth: Transition to Adulthood. Chicago: Univ. of Chicago Press.

Demos, John
1970   A Little Commonwealth. New York: Oxford Univ. Press.

Empey, LaMar T.
    1978   American Delinquency: Its Meaning and Construction. Homewood Ill.,: Dorsey.

Federal Bureau of Investigation
    1969   Crime in the United States: Uniform Crime Reports. Washington, D.C.: U.S. Government Printing Office.

Gillis, John R.
    1974   Youth and History. New York: Academic Press.

Goodman, Mary E.
    1970   The Culture of Childhood: Child's-Eye Views of Society and Culture. New York: Teachers College Press.

Harpur, W. R.
    1899   The Report of the Educational Commission of the City of Chicago. Chicago: Lakeside Press.

Hart, Hastings
    1910   Preventive Treatment of Neglected Children. New York: Charities Publication Committee.

Henderson, Charles R. (ed.)
    1910   Prison Reform and Criminal Law. New York: Charities Publication Committee.

Hoffman, Edward
    1976   "The treatment of deviance by the educational system: history." Pp. 41–56 *in* William C. Rhoads and Sabin Head (eds.), A Study of Child Variance (Vol. 3). Ann Arbor: Univ. of Michigan.

Hunt, David
    1970   Parents and Children in History: The Psychology of Family Life in Early Modern History. New York: Basic Books.

Illick, Joseph E.
    1974   "Child-rearing in seventeenth-century England and America." Pp. 303–50 *in* Lloyd de Mause (ed.), The History of Childhood. New York: Psychohistory Press.

In re Gault
    1967   387 & S. 1, 18L. Ed. 2d 527, 87S. Ct. 1428.

In re Winship
  1970   397 U.S.358, 25L. Ed. 2d 368, 90S. Ct. 1068.

Kent v. U.S.
  1966   383 U.S. 541, 16L. Ed. 2d 84, 86 S. Ct. 1045.

Ketchem, Orman W.
  1962   "The unfulfilled promise of the American juvenile
            court." Pp. 22–43 *in* Margaret K. Rosenheim (ed.), Jus-
            tice for the Child. New York: Free Press.

Klein, Malcolm W., Kathie S. Teilmann, Joseph A. Styles, Suzanne
  B. Lincoln, and Susan Labin-Rosensweig
  1976   "The explosion of police diversion programs." Pp. 101–
            20 *in* Malcolm W. Klein (ed.), The Juvenile Justice Sys-
            tem. Beverly Hills, Calif.: Sage.

Laslett, Peter
  1972   Household and Family in Past Time. Cambridge: Cam-
            bridge Univ. Press.

Lathrop, Julia
  1916   "Introduction." Pp. 1–15 *in* Sophonisba P. Breckenridge
            and Edith Abbott (eds.), The Delinquent Child and the
            Home. New York: Free Press.

  1925   "The background of the juvenile court in Illinois." Pp.
            290–97, 320–30 *in* Julia Addams (ed.), The Child, the
            Clinic and the Court. New York: New Republic.

Law Enforcement Assistance Administration
  1974   Indexed Legislative History of the Juvenile Justice and
            Delinquency Prevention Act of 1974. Washington,
            D.C.: U.S. Government Printing Office.

Lemert, Edwin M.
  1951   Social Pathology. New York: McGraw-Hill.

  1967   "The juvenile court—quest and realities." Pp. 91–106
            in The President's Commission on Law Enforcement
            and Administration of Justice. Task Force Report: Juve-
            nile Delinquency and Youth Crime. Washington, D.C.:
            U.S. Government Printing Office.

  1972   Human Deviance, Social Problems and Social Control
            (2d ed.). Englewood Cliffs, N.J.: Prentice-Hall.

Lyman, Richard B., Jr.
1974   "Barbarism and religion: late Roman and early medi-
        eval childhood." Pp. 108–59 *in* Lloyd de Mause (ed.),
        The History of Childhood. New York: Psychohistory
        Press.

Mack, Julian W.
1910   "The juvenile court as a legal institution." Pp. 293–317
        in Hastings H. Hart (ed.), Preventive Treatment of Ne-
        glected Children. New York: Charities Publication
        Committee.

Marvick, Elizabeth W.
1974   "Nature vs. nurture: patterns and trends in seventeenth
        century French child rearing." Pp. 254–302 *in* Lloyd
        de Mause (ed.), The History of Childhood. New York:
        Psychohistory Press.

Mause, Lloyd de
1974   The History of Childhood. New York: Psychohistory
        Press.

National Advisory Commission on Criminal Justice Standards and
    Goals
1973   A National Strategy to Reduce Crime. Washington,
        D.C.: U.S. Government Printing Office.

National Probation and Parole Association
1957   Guides for Juvenile Court Judges. New York: National
        Probation and Parole Assoc.

National Task Force to Develop Standards and Goals for Juvenile
    Justice and Delinquency Prevention
1977   Jurisdiction—Status Offenses. Washington, D.C.: U.S.
        Government Printing Office.

Platt, Anthony M.
1969   The Child Savers. Chicago: Univ. of Chicago Press.
        President's Commission on Law Enforcement and Ad-
        ministration of Justice

1967a   The Challenge of Crime in a Free Society. Washing-
        ton, D.C.: U.S. Government Printing Office.

1967b   Task Force Report: Juvenile Delinquency and Youth
             Crime. Washington, D.C.: U.S. Government Printing
             Office.

Revised Code of Washington
1977   Title 13: Juvenile Courts and Juvenile Delinquents. Pp.
             66–90, 726–29.

Revised Statutes of Illinois, 1899, Sec. 21.

Robertson, Priscilla
1974   "Home as a nest: middle-class childhood in nineteenth-
             century Europe." Pp. 407–31 *in* Lloyd de Mause (ed.),
             The History of Childhood. New York: Psychohistory
             Press.

Ross, James Bruce
1974   "The middle-class child in urban Italy, fourteenth to
             early sixteenth-century." Pp. 183–228 *in* Lloyd de
             Mause (ed.), The History of Childhood. New York: Psy-
             chohistory Press.

Rothman, David J.
1971   The Discovery of the Asylum. Boston: Little, Brown.

1979   "The Progressive legacy: development of American at-
             titudes toward juvenile delinquency." Pp. 34–68 *in* La-
             Mar T. Empey (ed.), Juvenile Justice: The Progressive
             Legacy and Current Reforms. Charlottesville: Univ.
             Press of Virginia.

Rubin, H. Ted
1976   The Courts: Fulcrum of the Justice System. Pacific Pali-
             sades, Calif.: Goodyear.

Sanders, Wiley B. (ed.)
1970   Juvenile Offenders for a Thousand Years. Chapel Hill:
             Univ. of North Carolina Press.

Schultz, J. Lawrence
1974   "The cycle of juvenile court history." Pp. 239–58 *in*
             Sheldon Messinger et al. (eds.), The Aldine Crime and
             Justice Annual, 1973. Chicago: Aldine.

Schur, Edwin M.
  1973   Radical Nonintervention: Rethinking the Delinquency Problem. Englewood Cliffs, N.J.: Prentice-Hall.

Skolnick, Arlene
  1973   The Intimate Environment: Exploring Marriage and the Family. Boston: Little, Brown.

Stone, Lawrence
  1974   "The massacre of the innocents." New York Review 14 (Nov.):25–31.

Tannenbaum, Frank
  1938   Crime and the Community. New York: Columbia Univ. Press.

Tinker v. *Des Moines Independent School District*
  1969   393 U.S. 503.

Tocqueville, Alexis de
  1945   Democracy in America (Trans. Henry Reeve). New York: Knopf.

Tucker, M. J.
  1974   "The child as beginning and end: fifteenth and sixteenth century childhood. Pp. 229–58 *in* Lloyd de Mause (ed.), The History of Childhood. New York: Psychohistory Press.

United States Bureau of the Census
  1955   Current Population Reports, Series R-25, No. 123. Washington, D.C.: U.S. Government Printing Office.

White House Conference on Youth
  1971   "Preamble," Recommendations and Resolutions. Washington, D.C.: U.S. Government Printing Office.

Wines, Frederick H.
  1910   "Historical Introduction." Pp. 3–38 *in* Charles R. Henderson (ed.), Prison Reform and Criminal Law. New York: Charities Publication Committee.

The Children's Rights Movement

Richard Farson

NOTHING is quite so invisible as the obvious. Children are so obvious, so taken for granted, so established in their place in our world that it is next to impossible for us to see how they actually live. Our discrimination against them is so deep and so widely accepted, even by children themselves, that we simply do not think of it as discrimination in the oppressive sense of, say, discrimination against blacks. It somehow feels so "natural" that it hardly seems worth our attention.

Our inability to see the obvious is one of the reasons why futurism is such a difficult enterprise. We cannot predict the future because we do not perceive the present. It is invisible to us. In 1967 two of our most respected futurists, Herman Kahn and Anthony Wiener (1967), published a book entitled *The Year 2000*, now a classic in futurist literature. In that book there is no mention whatever of pollution, ecology, or women's rights—subjects that were to dominate our national debate the very next year after its publication. The authors probably missed these issues because they were so obvious. Consider the absurdity that if the future will be as invisible to us then as the present is now, how will we know when we are there?

Despite our efforts to predict it, the future always seems to take us by surprise. This is particularly true when it comes to liberation movements. In this regard I have had my share of surprises. As a psychologist, therapist, and teacher I have always thought of myself as being in the business of human liberation, attempting to free people from the prisons of their neuroses, interpersonal styles, and limited or unfounded views of themselves and the world. Yet it seems that each time a group in our society calls for its own liberation I discover, much to my embarrassment and pain, that I am the enemy, acting both personally and professionally to limit and oppress the very people I thought I was helping.

Take women's and men's liberation, for example. All the while I was trying to respond with professional sensitivity to the delicate, subtle nuances of men's and women's personalities and interpersonal styles I was actually walking heavy-footed through their lives with a kind of locker room mentality about masculinity and femininity that was essentially invisible to me.

My transgressions do not stop here. I have been on the wrong side of other movements as well. I have tried to cure homosexuals, to teach employers to manage employees, to train teachers to handle students, and to help parents control children. In each case I was working for the powerful against the powerless, the oppressor against the oppressed, and doing it in the name of a professional attempt at human liberation.

Having had my political consciousness raised a bit on these issues, I can now recognize that when I sit across the desk from a woman, the overwhelming feature of her life is that she is a woman. That one fact is likely to be more important to what she is experiencing and probably to what is troubling her than her personality, her character, or her "neurosis." It may be even more important than her race because it more clearly defines her social position. Of course the same is true for men. Our lives are mainly determined by the simple fact that we are men.

It has been more difficult, but increasingly possible, for me to see that the same idea applies to children, only more so. Being a child is a more confining role by far than being male, female, black, or homosexual. It is nothing short of disabling. When people deal with children, they respond almost entirely to childness, not to personhood, much as they do to blindness or wheelchairness.

A new consciousness about children is beginning to develop among Americans, one that has been referred to in some quarters as a movement for children's rights (Firestone, 1970; Adams et al, 1971; Gottlieb, 1973; Gerzon, 1973; Farson, 1974a; Holt, 1974; Clark, 1975; Gross and Gross, 1977). This movement is slow in coming because we romanticize childhood as a time of carefree innocence, full of delight. We do not like to think of it as a prison.

Children represent a segment of society so huge, and so very much in their place, as it were, that the idea of children's liberation is unsettling indeed. For years we have considered women to be the largest group needing liberation, and, of course, when little girls are included in the statistics, they are. But actually there are more children than women. What's more, the changes being called for are probably more profound and pervasive.

Noting the size of the population segment in question can help to trace the manner in which our modern liberation consciousness moves from one group to another. Beginning with blacks, it has successively moved to larger and larger units: from blacks to women, to children, to animals, and to inanimate things like trees and rivers. Correspondingly, there are more women than blacks, more children than women, more animals than children, more things than animals.

The trouble with that analysis is that it is not inclusive enough. The parade of liberation groups has included too many others—gays, handicapped, or old people—who do not fit neatly into the size sequence. I'm afraid my theory of liberation movements on the basis of increasing group size must give way to the overriding fact that it is difficult to find any identifiable group that has *not* come to define itself in liberation terms. I suppose that what this means is that there is no group in the middle of society to which liberation groups are marginal, no one in the center who feels the system is working. Even the white male corporate leader who is healthy, handsome, and over six feet tall is able to make a strong case for his own need for liberation. Such is our current national mood of higher consciousness and greater discontent.

Another way of predicting the sequence of liberation movements, other than by their increasing size, is to note that the pattern reflects the inverted hierarchy to which we attribute primitive wisdom in our society. Take, for example, a typical family television program such as "Lassie." The time-tested formula is to show the wife as wiser than the husband, the children wiser than their mother, and the animals wiser than the children. That, again, has been the sequence of liberation movements. One can probably even carry it one step further to inanimate objects. What could be wiser than "Old Man River"? Or a mountain? Or a redwood? As it happens, there is a recent book by Christopher Stone entitled *Should Trees Have Standing?* (1974) arguing that trees should have the legal right to sue for their own protection.

The mistake many of us futurists make in trying to figure out where the next liberation movement is coming from is that we tend to look in the direction of those for whom we feel sorriest. This is of course precisely the opposite of what we should be doing. The people wanting liberation are those for whom we feel *least* sorry, people we think are carefree, unpressured, protected, loved, even adored. In spite of the brutality that black slaves experienced at the hands of their white masters, these same plantation owners believed that their slaves were comfortable, untroubled, and well cared for, in many instances enjoying the deep affection of the owner's family. To the masters, the slaves seemed happy in their place. Many of the same feelings prevail today in men's attitudes toward women, adults' attitudes toward children, and everyone's attitudes toward animals.

The case for liberation made by any particular group is resisted most, of course, by those with whom they are highly interdependent: southern whites with blacks, husband with wives, bosses with workers, parents with children. It is here that we are likely to find the greatest defensiveness, ridicule, and outrage.

We may see this resistance based upon interdependence become evident in this volume of papers. Those of us who professionally specialize in children have some stake in keeping childhood as it is, keeping it the way we learned to deal with it. It would be understandable if we as a group expressed considerable resistance to the ideas of children's rights, based simply upon our deeply entrenched professional attitudes about children. It is my observation that those who see the predicament of children most clearly and who are most likely to support children's rights are those who do not live or work with children.

Nor are we likely to see support coming from the children themselves. As with every other revolutionary movement, the leadership, paradoxically, is likely to come from the least oppressed, marginal members of the population or from people outside the group completely. That is the history of liberation; the nineteenth-century abolitionists, for example, were mainly white. Children are so powerless that they do not have any sense of their impotence. In order to *feel* powerless one must experience some power. The most oppressed people have no sense of their powerlessness. That is what holds them in oppression. Only after they have some power can they develop the strength, vision, leadership, and most especially the discontent that comes from the *feeling* of powerlessness that will be needed to energize a revolution. For this reason, obtaining basic rights of citizenship for children will be largely an adult effort for some time to come.

I suppose it is predictable, perhaps inevitable, that the consciousness of those with a longtime interest in civil rights will eventually extend their interest to children, as it has to dozens of other groups ranging from handicapped people to fat people to ex-felons. Moreover, in spite of the meager gains of civil rights efforts so far, it is difficult to believe that this new consciousness will eventually mean anything less than a major realignment of our fundamental social institutions. Obviously, that will not happen without considerable disruption and pain. We sustain ourselves with the hope that if we can survive the difficulties through this generation, and perhaps the next, then future generations will reap the harvest of full participation in society from the new-consciousness seeds we have sown.

Dilemmas of Liberation

Having committed myself on paper to a rather strong liberation posture toward these issues, I have a greater than average amount of interest in how this chapter in history unfolds. I must admit, however, that the events of the past few years have produced in me a significant measure of concern about the consequences of our efforts.

When we attempt to achieve social justice through the indiscriminate application of civil rights concepts appropriate for black liberation to all other groups, we are encouraged to make what I believe are some potentially serious errors. Fundamental differences exist between the elimination of distinctions between blacks and whites and the elimination of distinctions between men and women or between adults and children. We need to make more precise distinctions among the ways in which the various forms of discrimination function to oppress or to serve the groups in question. High in importance among the tasks before us will be to sort out the differences between equality and similarity, recognizing that the latter may not be necessary to the former. Perhaps we will be able to employ the principle of equifinality, the idea that the same ends can be reached by different means and that we will not have to minimize or ignore the important differences between men and women or between adults and children.

In any case, we will need to think through the basic criteria against which we can judge our policies and our actions so that we can determine whether they are likely to improve life for all concerned. For a social action to be life-enhancing, to my mind, it must first of all increase our survival capabilities as a species. Specifically, it should not seriously threaten the sexual interest of men for women and women for men. Further, it should provide for some relatively permanent and stable forms of family and community life. Debatable as they are, I take these as criteria for the validity of social action.

The trouble is that we don't always know what makes us more appealing sexually or what strengthens family and community life. Is is possible that not every desirable social action will meet such criteria. The achievement of gay rights, for example, could be questioned on these grounds. Population control advocates could even argue that we are jeopardizing our survival by being too sexually appealing. Besides, who knows what forms family and community should take to maximize our survival capabilities? The arguments could go on, but in some deep intuitive way I worry when a movement for social justice does not increase attraction for the opposite sex does not foster men and women uniting for the purpose of building families.

I have argued previously that the women's and children's rights movements would do these things. Fully equal women participating in "mainstream" (read: male) society would be more attractive to and interested in men, liberated men would be more desirable to women, and legally autonomous children would choose family life (Farson, 1971, 1974a). Maybe so. But the early signs of the effects of the women's movement do not comfort me. I see sexual hostility, male impotence, and reduced interest in procreation and family building. Perhaps these are temporary effects. We have all hoped so; believing that, while life may be difficult for a generation or two, we are simply in a disruptive transitional period and eventually life will smooth out for our children and grandchildren. I am less sanguine today about that idea as well.

In the past decade we have enthusiastically overturned many myths and taboos that have served society in some cases for thousands of years. While I surely believe in using our powers of reason to end the senseless victimization that comes from superstitions, dogma, and outdated taboos, I also believe that, when we discard many deeply held myths, we do so at our peril. Myths often serve important functions that we perceive only dimly, if at all, because they are meant not only to reflect reality but to create it. We need them to stabilize and to lubricate our human affairs and to give us hope and guidance in times when we cannot look elsewhere.

So the challenge is to find our way through these extraordinarily complex issues of social justice at a time when our society seems bent on demythologizing and overturning taboos in the name of whatever liberation movement is current. In our deliberations we must recognize the difference between needs and rights, between advocating constitutional protection for persecuted groups and approving their tabooed life-styles, between freedom and license, between the rights of one group and the conflicting rights of another, between stereotype and prejudice, between functional taboos and dysfunctional ones, between ideology and reality, and between social limitations that are life-denying and those that are life-sustaining.

Paul Goodman (1971) has said that when it comes to the difficult issues posed by the children's rights movement, we simply have no wise tradition to guide us. Instead we have the ideological narrowness that characterizes such movements. Ideology is the enemy of understanding. Can we explore the issues of children's rights unencumbered by ideology?

Probably not. But it is worth our trouble to try to understand the ideological dilemma posed for those of us who are interested in children's rights, actually for all advocates of liberation movements. On the one hand, to try to dominate nature, history, evolution, and tradition is clearly dangerous because our puny "reasonable" minds may never equal the wisdom of our primal blood. On the other hand, just as it is unthinkable to keep ethnic minorities in slavery, so it is intolerable to keep women and children in slavery. But the problems of liberating women and children are more complex, more relevant to our primitive wisdom, and more likely to ask us to violate relationships that are timeless and universal, such as the relationship of authority to age or dominance to sexuality. Nevertheless, however dangerous or even impossible it may be, we cannot remain silent and not try. So in full cognizance of the niceness of the dilemma we move ahead.

The niceness of the dilemma requires, however, that we not plunge ahead as some do who have discovered THE MOVEMENT for the first time and act as if it were the final battle between good and evil. It means rather that we move ahead carefully, hesitantly, and perhaps with some sadness for all that we endanger. This costs us the joys and excitement of a crusade, but it gives us the benefits of a moderation that might cause far less backlash and perhaps more real progress.

Advocacy with Moderation

With this in mind I have reviewed my writing on behalf of children's rights, and while I remain pleased with its substance, I now find myself more aware of the dangerous arrogance and hubris one risks in trying to dominate tradition. I now want to explore, if I can, the condition of childhood in America and the issues of children's rights with more caution, more humility, and more respect for the inescapable dilemma.

In describing the conditions under which American children live, the temptation is to begin with horror stories about abuse, neglect, and the incredible crimes of parents against their children (more young children die at the hands of their parents than from any single disease). But this approach is not likely to be in the service of a comprehensive discussion of the predicament of children, first, because it permits those of us who do not engage in such child torture to believe that we are not ourselves part of the oppressive discrimination against children, and, second, because it brings out strong protective instincts in us which, as we will see later, work against obtaining civil rights for children.

The simple fact is that children are discriminated against in every aspect of their lives—in homes, schools, communities, and in every agency, institution, and business establishment that deals with them or refuses to deal with them. Discrimination in itself is not the issue; people must make discriminations constantly, even among the various populations in our society. But children as a class are systematically segregated, ignored, exploited, coerced, incarcerated, demeaned, abused, and held powerless in a society that prides itself on its child-centeredness but in most ways is organized against children. When discrimination is so clearly life-denying, it is appropriate to counter with the protection of civil rights.

We cannot assess the potentialities of children because we have never organized society to elicit them. We have probably done just the opposite. Most of our social designs exist to keep children in their place. Children are almost totally segregated from adult life, unwelcome nearly everywhere. The have virtually no decision-making power over their own lives and little opportunity to realize their full potential.

In one sense no group in our society has ever been so well "understood" as children. They have been the subject of thousands of research studies. But the studies have one serious flaw: for obvious reasons it is impossible for the oppressor ever to gain a genuine understanding of the oppressed. Scientists can never "know" a group of people who are totally subjugated by the society to which the scientists belong, subjugated even by the scientists themselves. We cannot develop an accurate picture of the potentialities of a group when the studies themselves serve to keep that group in its place. Studying children today is like studying blacks on the plantations or women before 1968. We simply cannot know their potentialities because the unconscious or politically motivated attitudes of scientific investigators (let alone their age, race, and sex) are going to influence the methods and findings of their studies. If any population is totally subjugated, children surely are.

Over the past four hundred years, the idea of childhood has grown and the segregation of children has grown with it (Aries, 1962). Children are now regarded only as potential adults. Everything that happens to them must somehow be "good for them." As benign as it sounds, this particular attitude may be one of the most stifling and oppressive of all the attitudes we hold. It is oppressive because it does not recognize and value the child for what he or she is now, nor does it permit choices that might be satisfying or fulfilling at the moment. Everything we do, and everything they do, must pay off later on. While there are obvious examples where this attitude is necessary (e.g., dental care), one can argue that being regarded only as an adult-in-training has actually backfired and produced the opposite of its intent (e.g., "juvenile justice"). The idea of treating children as potential adults is now so deeply ingrained in all of us that we simply do not know that we hold such attitudes or that there might be any other.

Needs versus Rights

The danger in deliberations of this kind is that we can so easily fall into a discussion of children's *needs*, rather than their *rights*. Understanding children's needs is important, of course, but because our research methods for assessing their needs are questionable in the ways I have already discussed, prior consideration must be given to the protection of their rights. Indeed, it is with respect to the difference between needs and rights that child advocates fall into two categories.

The first group, by far the larger of the two, is made up of those who have traditionally been concerned with *needs*, those who believe that children need protection from the harsh realities of the adult world and that their job is to buffer children from that harshness. They try to intervene in children's behalf to end the most serious abuses against them. They tend to believe in the fundamental helplessness of children and in their right to have adult agencies monitor the ways in which children are neglected, abused, and exploited. Hence, they are likely to advocate "rights" for children that are actually needs: the "right" to a loving home, the "right" to good nutrition, or the "right" to be educated.

The second group of advocates, the group to which I subscribe, argues that the way to protect children best is first of all to protect their *civil rights*. It calls for giving children (now regarded by the courts as a "suspect category") the same protections of the Constitution enjoyed by adults. It questions the double standards of morality and behavior that may unnecessarily separate adults and children. It recognizes that children receive harsh treatment at the hands of adults precisely *because* of our efforts to segregate and protect them, especially in the institutions we have designed to serve them (schools, juvenile courts, or reformatories). The more we emphasize children's weakness and helplessness and the differences between them and us, the greater will be their ghettoization and victimization.

We would not, for example, be busing children, black or

white, into dangerous school situations if their civil rights gave them the opportunity for self-determination in these matters. You can be sure that if it were we adults who had to board the frightening buses and attend the unfamiliar and hostile schools, we would not have forced busing for long.

It is simply a myth that children do not experience harshness equivalent to that of the adult world. In many respects it is worse. It is children, after all, who are beaten by teachers, treated cruelly in juvenile penal institutions, and abused by their parents in as many as 4.2 million incidents a year (Gil, 1970). Among other distinguishing characteristics, then, children's rights advocates recognize the paradoxes of protectivism—that a protectivist posture toward children makes their lives less safe, less comfortable, less enjoyable, and far less fulfilling.

The philosophy of protectivism has always served the protector more than the protected. Plantation owners no doubt felt they were protecting their slaves when they instituted many harsh measures to control them. Women have discovered through the years that protectivism when applied to them has in fact protected them into poverty. The protective legislation for women (developed by men) which makes it impossible to ask women to work without a coffee break or to lift heavy packages or to work overtime or which requires them to have cots in their restrooms has also perpetuated an image of women that prevents them from moving into leadership and managerial positions. After all, how can we give a leadership role to someone who has to have a cot in her restroom?

Whether we are talking about such ancient practices as swaddling, torture for the exorcism of demons, the deliberate killing of deformed, illegitimate, female, or otherwise unwanted children, mutilation to aid in begging, or modern-day practices of physical and psychological beatings from parents or teachers—all have been justified as being in the interests of the child. We cannot rely on our good intentions for the protection of children. Every tyrant has thought he operated for the good of his people. Hence, we must do something far more difficult for children, something that may seem absurd: we must empower our children against us. As we will see later, this does not mean the abandonment of parental authority but rather a recognition of the nature of civil rights. To be genuine and strong, these rights must apply in the most uncomfortable places.

While it is possible to discuss children's rights one by one, as if they were separate and discrete, they are, by and large, interconnected. They do not stand well independently. One cannot expect children to be able to engage in enterprise without also having the right to sign contracts and to obtain legal assistance; this children cannot do without the full protection of law, which in turn is not likely unless they have the right to vote. By the same token, they cannot begin to gain financial independence by working unless they have freedom from compulsory education and an end to child-labor laws. Nevertheless, because these rights will not be granted all at once, it is possible and perhaps desirable to discuss them individually.

A Child's Bill of Rights

In the early seventies, when I began to work seriously on the issues of children's rights, I wrote a Bill of Rights for children that eventually formed the basis of a book (Farson, 1974a). Now, some years later, it is an interesting exercise for me to go back over what I wrote to see how much of it still stands up. While I have some embarrassment about the manner of presentation, I would probably still write much the same Bill of Rights. Just for historical purposes, let me restate my Bill of Rights as it was first published and follow that with some second thoughts about what I wrote. One cannot simply enumerate a list of rights without some need for qualification and documentation. That is why I needed an entire book to develop, explain, and defend my position. But, if you will forgive me this cursory and inadequate treatment, here is the Bill of Rights as it was excerpted from the book for a centerfold in *Ms.* magazine, March 1974 (Farson, 1974b:67)

1. *The right to self-determination.* Children should have the right to decide the matters that affect them most directly. This is the basic right upon which all others depend. Children are now treated as the private property of their parents on the assumption that it is the parents' right and responsibility to control the life of the child. The achievement of children's rights, however, would reduce the need for this control and bring about an end to the double standard of morals and behavior for adults and children.

2. *The right to alternative home environments.* Self-determining children should be able to choose from among a variety of arrangements: residences operated by children, child-exchange programs, twenty-four-hour child-care centers, and various kinds of schools and employment opportunities. Parents are not always good for their children—some people estimate that as many as 4 million children are abused annually in the United States, for instance, and that a half-million children run away from home each year.

3. *The right to responsive design.* Society must accomodate itself to the size of children, and to their need for safe space. To keep them in their places, we now force children to cope with a world that is either not built to fit them or is actually designed against them. If the environment were less dangerous for children, there would be less need for constant control and supervision of children by adults.

4. *The right to information.* A child must have the right to all information ordinarily available to adults—including, and perhaps especially, information that makes adults uncomfortable.

5. *The right to educate oneself.* Children should be free to design their own educations, choosing from among many options the kinds of learning experiences they want, including the option not to attend any kind of school. Compulsory education must be abolished, because the enforced, threatening quality of education in America has taught children to hate

school, to hate the subject matter, and, tragically, to hate themselves. Children are programmed, tracked, and certified in a process of stamping out standarized educated products that are acceptable to the university, to the military, to business and industry, and to the community. Education can change only through the achievement of new rights for those exploited and oppressed by it—the children themselves.

6. *The right to freedom from physical punishment.* Children should live free of physical threat from those who are larger and more powerful than they. Corporal punishment is used impulsively and cruelly in the home, arbitrarily in the school, and sadistically in penal institutions. It does not belong in our repertoire of responses to children.

7. *The right to sexual freedom.* Children should have the right to conduct their sexual lives with no more restriction than adults. Sexual freedom for children must include the right to information about sex, the right to nonsexist education, and the right to all sexual activities that are legal among consenting adults. In fact, children will be best protected from sexual abuse when they have the right to refuse—but they are now trained *not* to refuse adults, to accept all forms of physical affection, and to mistrust their own reactions to people. They are denied any information about their own sexuality or that of others. We keep them innocent and ignorant and then worry that they will not be able to resist sexual approaches.

8. *The right to economic power.* Children should have the right to work, to acquire and manage money, to receive equal pay for equal work, to choose trade apprenticeship as an alternative to school, to gain promotion to leadership positions, to own property, to develop a credit record, to enter into binding contracts, to engage in enterprise, to obtain guaranteed support apart from the family, and to achieve financial independence.

9. *The right to political power.* Children should have the right to vote and to be included in the decision-making process. Eighty million children in the United States need the right to vote, because adults do not vote in their behalf. At

present they are no one's constituency, and legislation reflects that lack of representation. To become a constituency, they must have the right to vote.

10. The right to justice. Children must have the guarantee of a fair trial with due process of law; an advocate to protect their rights against their parents, as well as against the system; and a uniform standard detention. Every year a million children get into trouble with the law; one out of every nine will go through the juvenile court system before the age of eighteen. At any given time, about one hundred thousand children are in some kind of jail. Some are held illegally, many have not committed any kind of crime, most have done nothing that would be considered a crime if done by an adult, and none has been given a fair trial with due process of law. The juvenile justice system was designed to protect children from the harsh treatment of the adult justice system—but it is more unfair, more arbitrary, and more cruel.

A More Tentative View

In rereading this list, my first thought is not that I no longer agree with what I proposed but that the proposals are made in such declarative and argumentative language. I must admit, too, that even though each of these paragraphs is fleshed out in the book to a full chapter, the book itself has something of that same polemical quality. If I could change anything about what I wrote, it would be to make the entire formulation more balanced, cautious, and tentative. I think at that time I was more a prisoner of the liberation ideology of the sixties that I now am. While my Bill of Rights doesn't have quite the strident quality of the statements of Youth Liberation (1972), it does, nevertheless, communicate a certainty that I no longer feel.

At the same time, the responses of others to this Bill of Rights often express outrage and disbelief: "Are you crazy? Children determining their own lives? Staying up all night? Driving cars? Having sex? Voting? Child labor?" Some of the questions are more difficult than others, but let me try to respond to the issues they raise.

Self-determination

The idea of self-determination is of course fundamental to all the others and is the one that is likely to invite the most serious objections. Avoiding for our purposes here a review of the centuries-old debate over determinism versus free will, it is, nevertheless, appropriate for us to recognize that while we may need to extend to children the right to self-determination as it is experienced by adults, no one is fully self-determined. Arguments against children's rights that use absurd but logical extensions of the question of self-determination (babies leaving home or investing in real estate) must be answered by acknowledging that the guarantee of constitutional rights for children does not mean the abandonment of reason or tradition. It simply means that reason and tradition will be both honored and questioned in the context of full civil rights for everyone involved.

For example, when someone asks, "Should a child have the right to go against the wishes of a parent?" our answer must be "Yes and no." Yes; in the event that the issue should escalate to a matter of litigation, the child's right to self-determination must be considered a fundamental right of citizenship. No; because that right must be balanced against the traditional and legal parental obligation to act in the child's behalf and to maintain a situation in which such action is possible. So if the specific instance involved, say, the child's seeking medical advice against the parent's wishes, the issue might be decided in terms of the violation of the rights of the child. If, on the other hand, it involved an argument over the use of the family car, tradition, parental authority, and the rights of the parent would no doubt prevail. As a practical matter, only the more serious disputes would be likely to escalate to court decision.

Recognizing children's rights does not mean overturning all institutions. Certainly not the family. Most of life is structured so that all of us moderate our self-determination in the light of traditional expectations of the institutions to which we belong. We follow routines and schedules, use standard operating procedures, observe social roles, obey customs and traditions, and employ all manner of carefully prescribed civil amenities. Although these limitations are seldom translated into laws, we nevertheless follow them precisely. We need to observe them and to impose them on each other in order to have what we call civilization. But they do indeed make the areas of our self-determination quite small. We move from one situation, the home for example, into another, our work or our school, in which the prescriptions for our behavior are quite explicit and demanding. I don't for a minute think we can or should throw over all the finely tuned social systems that make it possible for us to live together as a society in favor of some anarchic idea of self-determination.

Civil rights are meant to protect us in situations where tradition is not wise and when powerful people can harm us. That is why the answer to the question must be yes and no. On the one hand, we must make sure that those civil right are in place so that when a situation develops to the point that the rights of the individual have been fundamentally violated, jeopardizing that individual's right to "life, liberty, and the pursuit of happiness," there is genuine recourse in our legal system. On the other hand, in order to survive as a culture we must observe certain rites and traditions, our institutions must have sanctions, constraints, and authority, and human affairs must have boundaries and customs that will in large measure limit the self-determination of any of us, perhaps children most especially.

So the legal question in such matters will boil down not to a clearcut answer but to a muddled one, as it does in most important areas, such as abortion or custodial fights over children, in which the specifics of each case are judged on their merits and where we can only use broad guidelines to balance the various competing interests. In the future, however, those deliberations should consider the child as fully protected by the Constitution.

Unless we see these complications, we will be too easily dissuaded from the pursuit of constitutional rights for children because we will be made to feel ridiculous for endorsing the logical but absurd extremes. The courts do not endorse such extremes for adults and they will not do so for children. These are always matters for deliberation and judgment. The goal, after all, is not to offer complete self-determination to children, which is impossible, but to expand the areas of self-determination so that children are not needlessly exploited by the simple fact of their being children.

Children's Rights versus Parental Responsibility

The question of children's rights versus parental responsibility is confusing because parents are often made to act as agents of society in ways that are not necessarily beneficial to the child. Much of what parents do is determined by the social requirement that they protect their children (from speeding automobiles), control them (in restaurants designed for adults), teach them (to meet school standards), and discipline them (so that they will obey adult authority whenever encountered), all in the service of institutions that do not necessarily have the best interests of children at heart. These parental responsibilities could be eased considerably by the redesign of some basic situations and by granting the rights that we have been discussing. Nevertheless, some custodial power will always be necessary for small children, and I am prepared to support the family as the main agency for it. To maintain family structure, we must be careful not to lose the cultural and legal respect for parental authority. If we do have anything like a wise tradition, that certainly would be it.

So my answer to the question, "Should parents have power over their children?" would be, "Of course." "And," I would add, "within the context of a new consciousness of children's rights." Parents (actually fathers) used to have absolute power over their children; a parent could legally kill or sell his child. That power has eroded over the centuries to a point where

we have increasingly recognized the child's right to consideration as an independent person.

Actually, we have probably overemphasized the importance
of parental authority in raising children. In the emergency
situation, for example, authority is rarely sufficient. One must
act. I would certainly pull anyone from the path of an onrush-
ing car, child and adult alike. There is no double standard
when it comes to emergencies.

In a clash of wills over, say, eating everything on one's plate,
the parent appears to resort to authority, but it is remarkable
how often, even when the parent employs all the authority
he or she can muster, the child is still able to reach a stalemate.
Authority just *seems* important at these times. Nobody wins.

When it comes to getting children to do anything really
important such as to tell the truth, to learn, or to love, authority
is almost totally useless. It can only be used, however inade-
quately, to coerce performance or to impose behavioral limits
on less important concerns like watching television, going to
bed, or wearing a sweater.

Parents feel responsible in too many areas already, and that
responsibility is actually increasing as we continually enlarge
the job of parenting. Moreover, while parental responsibilities
are increasing, parental authority is decreasing. Naturally, we
cannot expect authority and responsibility to be equal. That
is a myth everywhere. Our responsibilities, particularly for
those we love, have always exceeded our authority to discharge those responsibilities.

With or without authority, a parent can still say, "Turn down
that stereo!" and expect to have it turned down just as one
might expect it to be turned down if that were said to another
adult. Most such responses depend not so much upon authority
as upon the power of conditioned responses to reasonable
requests that are automatic to all of us. Call it tradition or
the social graces, we almost always answer questions that are
asked and perform small favors that are requested. When we
ask people, adults or children, the time of day we are very
likely to get an answer, with or without our use of authority.

I do not, however, want in any way to diminish the importance of the authority of parents or the authority of age. Just as we cannot have strong membership without strong leadership, I think we cannot have strong children without strong parents. Weakening parental authority is no way to strengthen children. But strengthening children may actually strengthen the respect that parents have for them, because we tend to respect those who have some power to resist us.

Furthermore, we still do not know the part that identification with adult authority plays in growing up. We are coming to doubt that any particular parenting style is very important. To the extent that parents are influential at all, children are influenced by what their parents *are,* and less by what they deliberately *do.* But professional opinion, strongly supported by traditional thought, holds that children do need to have strong parental models. I, for one, would be hesitant to dismiss casually the importance of this in favor of some ideological purity in the achievement of children's rights.

Self-determination and Age

The question always arises as to what age children should be given the right to self-determination. My answer probably seems absurd: at birth, perhaps even a few months earlier. A child should have full civil rights, the protection of the Constitution at every age, even when, especially when, the child has difficulty in exercising those rights. To the extent that children or others in our society are incapacitated and unable to assert their rights, society must take extra precautions to guarantee these rights through the action of counsel, advocates, and guardians. If we try to set an arbitrary age of competence, we are bound to discriminate against some younger children who show remarkable abilities that should not be stifled by law. After all, rights are not granted only to people who are competent and responsible. If they were, many of us would lose them. Instead, the rationale for granting rights is just the other way around: we are given rights in the belief that by having those rights we will become more mature, competent, and responsible. Thus, rights are based upon citizenship, not upon competence.

The trouble is that children have never been regarded as full citizens. In this regard it is interesting to speculate as to how the average American child might compare in knowledge, literacy, and overall maturity to the average prerevolutionary American colonist who was the first beneficiary of our Constitution or to the average citizens in one of the newly democratized nations in Africa, Asia, or South America to whom we recommend our constitutional democracy. There are reasons to believe that they would not inevitably be seen as the more incompetent.

Children's Rights and Safety

Concern about children driving automobiles is not a particularly difficult problem for the children's rights advocates. If a child can pass a stringent driving examination, he or she should certainly be awarded a driver's license. As it happens, safety experts at the University of Michigan have proposed that driving would be much safer if ten-year-olds were permitted to learn. The same principle would hold in the case of children operating dangerous machinery or having resonsibility for the health and safety of others. If they can qualify on the basis of performance examinations, they should be permitted to do the work. Incidentally, in the time since I wrote the book on children's rights, a good deal of research evidence has appeared to support the idea that children could assume challenges and responsibilities at a much earlier age than we have thought possible (Skolnick, 1978).

Sexual Freedom

One item of the Bill of Rights about which I feel some vulnerability is that which deals with the right to sexual freedom. While I still agree with the main idea, I did not give sufficient consideration to the importance of sexual taboos. Every society has such taboos, even though they may be expressed in many different forms. One reason for sexual taboos is that it seems sex simply doesn't belong in relationships that are important for other reasons. That is, with the possible exception of marriage, if you have sexual relations you can't have much else. I think we have abundant evidence that such is the case. Sex does not mix well in the relationships of doctor to patient, teacher to student, or parent to child. It is not that sex totally precludes such relationships but that the relationship loses its ability to deliver on other dimensions if the sexual dimension is acted out.

Nor do I mean to encourage sexual activity at all ages, at least not until we have the legal, economic, and social-support systems to accommodate the inevitable consequences of early sexuality. In some instances we cannot achieve rights in one area without the achievement of rights in other areas. To open them up first in the area of sex may only make matters worse.

The Right to Vote

For some reason the idea of children voting produces the most derision of all the proposed rights. No doubt images come to mind of a toddler trying to reach the ballot box or of children banding together to vote for a big rock-candy mountain. Actually, giving children the right to vote would produce profound changes in the long run, but in the short run the effect would probably be imperceptible.

If all children who wanted to vote were given that opportunity, it would probably take a long time for us to notice any difference in voting patterns and outcomes. No dramatic shifts would be likely to occur because it takes a long time before newly enfranchised groups vote in their own interest. For example, to the extent they have had the vote, southern blacks have tended to vote with southern whites. For more than fifty years women have voted with the men in their lives.

Only very recently has either group begun to vote as a bloc. The real challenge, therefore, would be to encourage children to vote in their own behalf rather than to simply reflect the voting patterns of their families.

Eventually, however, important changes would doubtless come, not because some children know more about the candidates and issues than many adults (as they do), but because when children are represented, when they become someone's constituency, their interests would be reflected in new legislation designed to benefit them. Ultimately, they would be voting for candidates chosen from among them. One can only guess how the impact of children's voting for themselves would change our society. My own inclination is to think it would have a surprisingly salutary effect.

Enactment of Children's Rights

Assuming the eventual success of the children's rights movement, one can't help but speculate on the order in which we might see these various rights enacted into law. No doubt we will see progress first on those that can be accomplished with least cost, least threat, and least disruption. Beyond these considerations I would expect earliest action on those rights that are the least interdependent with other rights (i.e., could be granted without the necessity of granting other rights), those that could be achieved through a single piece of legislation or a single court decision and those that already have some visibility and political support.

Given those conditions, I would predict that we would first see major changes in the juvenile justice system. That is a fairly safe prediction because, as this volume indicates, changes have already begun. Americans are beginning to recognize the unworkability of the juvenile courts; the unfairness of indeterminate sentences; the absence of due process; the penalties for status offenses, such as truancy, running away, curfew violation, or sexual promiscuity where the crime is essentially that of being a child; and the failure of the penal system to rehabilitate youths (Wakin, 1975). It seems to me that there is a genuine readiness for change in this area.

We will change, but not because we are convinced that practical answers to the problems of juvenile crime now exist. That is surely not the case. No basic agreement exists even among professionals as to the causes or consequences of crime. Many would agree, however, that crime in America is inevitable because it is rooted in (and protective of) our basic social-political-economic system. Moreover, the entire criminal justice system is so ineffective in reducing crime that one wonders whether its functions are anything other than symbolic. Indeed, there are those who argue that it should be maintained precisely because, as a symbol of order and justice, it may deter others from committing crimes.

Its symbolic functions notwithstanding, I prefer to think of the criminal justice system as a measure of our civility as a people. It is important how we treat errant members of our society for what it tells us about ourselves. Our increasing concerns over humane processes in criminal justice may not directly reduce crime, but they are an important indicator of our advancement as a civilization. Hence, they are significant not only for their effect on crime but for their effect on us. We will always be faced with the questions, In the light of our current knowledge and development, what is today a civilized response to crime? What actions will we be proud to have taken? I would like to suggest that one answer would be to extend full civil rights to the children who are caught in the web of the justice system.

Secondly, I would expect to see an end to corporal punishment. Can the practice of spanking children in school pass another Supreme Court test? In Finland corporal punishment has been outlawed, not only in schools but in the home as well. While a majority of Americans and more than 70 percent of all educators favor the use of physical violence against children as a means of bringing about acquiescence to adult authority, it is hard for me to see this practice continuing in the face of overwhelming evidence that it is both ineffective and unjust (Reitman et al., 1972).

Third, I would anticipate an end to the prohibitions on the acquisition of information. I place this third not because I believe the resistance here is greater than for ending corporal punishment but because the ways we deny information to children are so many, so varied, and so obscure to us. Even though information is power, and we give up power reluctantly, I suspect that such changes, once we discover them, would not be as severely disruptive as other changes called for by advocates of children's rights. In my opinion, the first to change in this area will be the right to information and decision in matters of health care.

Deterrents to Children's Rights

Now for the rights that will be much slower in coming. Alternative home environments and responsive design for children produce no real argument from most Americans. Once the need is pointed out and the facts are known, people tend to go along with the intent of these demands. But because the creation of alternatives for living and the redesign of our social institutions and our physical world to accommodate children would be so costly, I would predict major changes in these areas to be rather far off.

For different reasons I would expect to see strong resistance to sexual freedom, voting, education, and economic power. As we have seen over the past two decades of the so-called sexual revolution, it is possible to have major changes in sexual consciousness that are not by and large translated into changes in behavior. Sexual patterns and sexual taboos are established so deeply in our culture, and perhaps in our genes, that they are not going to change rapidly.

Children may acquire various kinds of political power (through adult advocacy or membership on decision-making committees) before they are given voting rights. When voting rights come, they will probably be granted as they have in the past, by gradually lowering the voting age through constitutional amendment. Enfranchising blacks and women, who were expressly excluded from voting by the makers of the Constitution, required the enactment of constitutional amendments. The same will probably be true for children, although the U.S. Supreme Court might strike down the test of age as being unfairly discriminating, as they have with other proposed or de facto voting tests such as literacy or property ownership.

Ending compulsory education and ending economic discrimination against children are so strongly related that we cannot expect to see one without the other. While it would be a relatively small matter for a court to declare forced attendance at school to be unconstitutional, that possibility is remote because we are aware of the economic implications of such an act. Introducing millions of potential workers into a system already burdened by excessive numbers of surplus people could bring disaster. We do not have the economic and political inventions to accommodate such developments. Our system is still trying to adjust to the impact of the labor movement, the civil rights movement, and the women's movement. We do not know to what extent it is dependent upon sources of cheap labor to continue. No doubt people will fear, and rightly so, that opening the economic system to children so that they might exploit it rather than only be exploited by it may be just too much unemployment for capitalism to handle.

Curiously, children themselves will probably oppose all of these changes. One of the paradoxes in all liberation efforts is that the victims are their own worst enemies, but this is even stronger when it comes to the achievement of children's rights. That is probably one reason why the children's rights movement has not "taken off" as other movements have. The problem is too deep. Children are simply too powerless to be able to recognize their own plight. They are not yet strong enough to mount any campaign to benefit themselves. They have few solid political allies, although old people would benefit equally from an end to ageism, and small or physically handicapped people would stand to gain considerably by new social and physical designs to accommodate children.

Perhaps the most important reason that the children's rights movement is slow in getting started is that it is not easy to see what society has to gain by supporting it. We are left with having to act on children's rights only as a matter of conscience, because not even children themselves are completely sure that we would have a safer and better society if they were admitted to full participation in it. Unfortunately, conscience has not proved to be as powerful a motivator as self-interest.

Perhaps we fear victimization by children. We simply don't want them around, don't want to have to deal with them, don't want to incorporate them in our decisions, in our discussions, or in our lives. Probably nothing is more obnoxious to adults than demanding children. It may be that simple.

But perhaps, too, we are afraid of what children might lose in the process. I suspect that we really believe children are in many ways superior to us, just as I suspect that men believe women are superior to them. Granting rights to children is threatening to us because we do not want to jeopardize that precious mystique, dispel the indispensable mystery that is a child. Sometimes we forget how we humans need mystery as well as reality; how we secretly value children's innocence, spontaneity, and clear-eyed perceptions; how we long for our lost selves that children show us.

Finally, we must not forget that the major difference between the children's rights movement and other movements of liberation is that childhood is temporary. Children grow out of it. They can see light at the end of the tunnel even in the earliest years. Remember, too, that older children get a kind of perverse enjoyment out of oppressing younger children.

To turn out backs on the problem, however, by saying that they will grow out of it imposes upon 40 percent of our population a long sentence of oppression. As our society moves toward higher morality (and we are), we will find it impossible to continue our present posture. Ultimately, there is no moral alternative but to grant children the fundamental rights to which their citizenship and their humanity entitle them.

What will eventually raise our consciousness about the predicament of children and their need for civil rights? Perhaps it will come indirectly, as we are faced with other dilemmas that are related to children's rights, animal rights, for example. What will be the effects on our ideas of children's rights when we become more aware of animals as conscious, communicating beings? Flora Davis in her book *Eloquent Animals* (1978) describes the remarkable abilities of chimps and apes to communicate complex ideas through sign language or through the medium of computers. The implications are staggering. One professor she interviewed said that he didn't know what he would do if some day one of the chimps said, "I don't want to be operated on!"

References

Adams, Paul, et al.
  1971   Children's Rights: Toward the Liberation of the Child.
          New York: Prager.

Ariès, Philippe
  1962   Centuries of Childhood (Trans. Robert Baldick). New
          York: Random House/Vintage.

Clark, Ted
  1975   The Oppression of Youth. New York: Harper & Row.

Davis, Flora
  1978   Eloquent Animals. South Rutherford, N.J.: Coward,
          McCann & Geogheghan.

Farson, Richard
  1971   "A new man is emerging." New Woman 1 (June):90.

  1974a   Birthrights. New York: Macmillan.

  1974b   "Birthrights: a children's Bill of Rights." Ms.
          (March):67.

Firestone, Shulamith.
  1970   The Dialectic of Sex. New York: William Morrow.

Gerzon, Mark
  1973   A Childhood for Every Child: The Politics of Parent-
          hood. New York: Outerbridge and Lazard.

Gil, David G.
  1970   Violence against Children: Physical Child Abuse in the
          United States. Cambridge: Harvard Univ. Press.

Goodman, Paul
  1971   "Reflections on children's rights." In Paul Adams et al.
          (eds.), Children's Rights: Toward the Liberation of the
          Child. New York: Prager.

Gottlieb, David (ed.)
  1973   Children's Liberation. Englewood Cliffs, N.J.: Prentice-
          Hall.

Gross, Beatrice, and Ronald Gross
    1977   The Children's Rights Movement: Overcoming the Op-
            pression of Young People. New York: Anchor/Double-
            day.

Holt, John
    1974   Escape from Childhood. New York: E. P. Dutton.

Kahn, Herman, and Anthony Wiener
    1967   The Year 2000. New York: Macmillan

Reitman, Alan, J. Follman, and E. T. Ladd
    1972   "Corporal punishment in the public schools: the use
            of force in controlling student behavior." ACLU Report
            (March).

Skolnick, Arlene
    1978   "The myth of the vulnerable child." Psychology Today
            2 (February):56.

Stone, Christopher D.
    1974   Should Trees Have Standing: Toward Legal Rights for
            Natural Objects. Los Altos, Calif.: William Kaufman.

Wakin, Edward
    1975   Children without Justice. New York: National Council
            of Jewish Women.

Youth Liberation of Ann Arbor
    1972   Youth Liberation. Washington, N.J.: Times Change
            Press.

The Revolution in Juvenile Justice: From Rhetoric to Rhetoric

Jerome G. Miller

OVER the last ten to fifteen years there has been a dramatic change in our understanding of juvenile delinquency and approaches to juvenile justice in the United States. Beginning with the *Kent* (*Kent,* 1966) and *Gault* (*In Re Gault,* 1967) decisions of the Supreme Court, there has been a growing awareness of the shortcomings of the juvenile court, approaches to understanding delinquency, and the means for dealing with it. Surely there can be no greater indictment of a system of care than to suggest that the best service one can do for a potential client of that system is to divert him or her from it. Yet this was precisely what President Johnson's Commission on Law Enforcement recommended (President's Commission, 1967).

Since the late 1960s this recommendation has led to an emphasis on such reforms as decriminalization, diversion, due process, deinstitutionalization, and the variations on these themes. It has been said that a new revolution for dealing with juveniles has been spawned. Yet it is striking that support for this revolution has come from both civil-liberties–oriented liberals and from conservatives concerned with issues of law and order. This seeming paradox is not only indicative of the degree to which we have become disillusioned with the juvenile justice system of the past half century, but it may indicate that we are dealing with something less than a revolution. A careful review of prior revolutions in the treatment of the young suggests that such may be the case.

Institutionalization: Revolution in the 1800s

The attention to the establishment of the juvenile court in 1899 has often obscured the fact that there was an even earlier revolution in the approach to juvenile offenders in this country. Dating from the early 1800s, a tradition developed favoring the institutionalization of juveniles in facilities ostensibly designed to be different from adult jails and prisons. This tradition had become so entrenched that, long before the turn of the twentieth century, several attempts were made to reform it. Before Dorothea Dix sought better institutional care for the mentally ill, Samuel Howe of Massachusetts was pointing out the unconscionable conditions in existing juvenile institutions in that state. Likewise, one cannot read the descriptions of the Boston House of Reformation by Alexis de Tocqueville and Gustave de Beaumont (1964) without realizing that an earlier revolution had already taken place in the treatment of certain juveniles. In their report to the French government on the penitentiary system in the United States, they described in great detail such experiments as inmate self-government, exclusion of corporal punishment, and what would generally be described—at least until recently— as an enlightened approach to the treatment of delinquents. They noted, for example, that

corporal chastisements are excluded from the [Boston] House of Refuge; the discipline of this establishment is entirely of a moral character and rests on principles which belong to the highest philosophy.

Everything there tends to elevate the soul of the young prisoners, and to render them jealous of their own esteem and that of their comrades; to arrive at this end they are treated as if they were men and members of a free society. . . .

. . . The early use of liberty contribute[s], perhaps, at a later period, to make the young delinquents more obedient to the laws. And without considering this possible political result, it is certain that such a system is powerful as a means of moral education. (Wines, 1910:379)

The founder of the Boston House of Reformation, the Rev. E. M. P. Wells, was a young Episcopal minister whose ideas about "juvenile wickedness" differed considerably from those accepted at the time. In writing about him, a later reformer, Frederick Wines (1910:376), noted:

Wells believed that bad boys were no worse by nature than others and was convinced that a boy "can always be reformed while he is under 15 years old, and very often after that age." He became superintendent in 1828 and first drew attention to himself by introducing an educational curriculum that was wholly unlike anything that the staid overseers of delinquents at that time had ever seen. Regulated play and gymnastics figured prominently in the program and Wells frankly admitted that the "mechanical" parts of education such as arithmetic, writing and spelling, held a low place in his opinion.

Contrast the above description of a training school of the early 1800s with a report on the St. Charles School for Boys by the Illinois Crime Commission in the late 1920s, almost three decades after the establishment of the juvenile court in Illinois:

All whippings were administered by a disciplinary officer who went . . . to each cottage each evening after supper and whipped any boys who had been reported earlier by the house father, or for whom the house father requested punishment at that time. Some boys were punished by being locked up in the "hole" for up to thirty-two days with no shoes and no mattress. They slept on wooden boards nailed to the concrete floor. Some were handcuffed to iron pipes and kept manacled day and night. (Platt, 1969:150)

When comparing this twentieth-century institution for delinquents with its nineteenth-century counterpart, one is less impressed with the revolution brought on by the establishment of the juvenile court. However, we seem to be becoming a nation of lawyers, and it may be that the legal confirmation of certain realities is more important than the realities themselves. Whether or not this is true, it does seem to be the case that, by the time the juvenile courts were established, the reforms intended by the establishment of juvenile institutions in the nineteenth-century had not been successful but had been effectively undone.

Juvenile Court Revolution

We are all familiar with the invention of the juvenile court and with the revolution it was said to represent. Hailed as signaling a new era in the treatment of children, it was established in all states but three by 1917. By 1932 there were over six hundred independent juvenile courts across the land. Yet the evidence is clear that it failed to disrupt the older pattern of confining juveniles in unspeakable institutions.

In 1925 Louise Bowen (Platt, 1969:151) noted that the Cook County Detention Home had "every appearance of being a jail, with its barred windows and locked doors—the children have fewer comforts than do criminals confined in the County jail. They are not kept sufficiently occupied and have very little fresh air." These comments were made seven years after a report to the Cook County Civil Service Commission on the investigation of the juvenile detention home had been submitted. The study commission called upon such persons as Mrs. Bowen, Miss Jane Addams, Amelia Sears, Dr. William Healey, Judge Franklin Chase Hoyt of the Children's Court of New York, Judge Edward F. Waite of Minneapolis, and a variety of others who would probably be characterized today as representative of the child-saver movement. This study group noted that

the [detention] home as taken over by the County was founded largely in the idea that it was wrong to detain children in jail and in police stations with criminal adults. The ideal was to maintain for them a home. The idea has been carried out partly—children are not now detained in jail with criminal adults, but dependent children, children mildly delinquent, are housed together and eat together with delinquents as deteriorating in their influence, as that of many adults in the jail. Neither is our juvenile detention home a home. For the dependents and the minor delinquents it has some of the qualities of a jail. (Cook County Commission, 1917:4)

As a result of their findings, the commission recommended that some juveniles be deinstitutionalized and that settings in which others were confined be made more homelike—recommendations that might as easily have been made in 1978 as in 1917. The commission said:

For the seriously criminal its detention qualities [the Cook County Detention Home] are inadequate. Can the County protect its children by a better separation of the dependents and the tractable from the incorrigible, the immoral, the confirmed juvenile delinquents? Can the Home give to its children or a *deserving* portion thereof a little more of a real home during their detention period? (Cook County Commission, 1917:5, emphasis added)

Consistent with its stance, the commission recommended that the delinquents housed in juvenile detention homes be separated and reclassified, that a strong effort be made to keep children in their own homes, and that children charged with lesser delinquencies might be amenable to mild forms of discipline. It argued that, for those who must be detained and are responsive to discipline, "a special portion of the Home may be reserved where they may receive less custodial care, more recreation and out-of-door play and perhaps simple vocational work. The few attendants necessary for their care should live at the Home with the children."

For all of its progressive recommendations, however, the Commission Report suggested that *"for the remaining children, the immoral girls, the incorrigible and unruly boys and girls, the present juvenile detention home and the present custodial care are none too severe. In Detroit individual separation rooms are installed for and occupied by the incorrigibles who deserve complete isolation, which we also recommend"* (Cook County Commission, 1917:6, emphasis added).

The distinction of the commission between "incorrigible" or "undeserving" delinquents and those who are relatively "innocent" or "deserving" helped to perpetuate a paradox that has characterized reform movements from Elizabethan times to the present. Instead of demanding reforms for all delinquents, the commission proposed to use humane reforms

only for the "deserving," while the "undeserving" would continue to receive the most stringent forms of traditional discipline. Hence, as in the past, reforms were not meant to deal
head-on with those labeled as "undeserving," only with those
who were "deserving."

Given this stance, the problem then became one of diagnosis
and labeling, of deciding who should become the beneficiaries
of new and humane services and who should remain isolated
from them. The answer to that problem of course, was
provided by the ideologies and belief systems of the time.
Diagnosis always represents a response to contemporary constructions of social and political reality. But, as Laing points
out, these constructions may be relatively unintelligible to
the person being labeled, even though they prescribe a particular set of social responses:

The unintelligibility of the experience and behavior of the diagnosed
person is created by the person diagnosing him, as well as by the
person diagnosed. This stratagem seems to serve specific functions
within the structure of the system in which it occurs. . . . The label
is a social fact and the social fact a political event. This political
event, occurring in the civic order of society, imposes definitions
and consequences on the labeled person. It is a social prescription
that rationalizes a set of social actions. (Laing, 1968b:18)

It seems quite clear that the definitions made within the
context of the new juvenile justice system were not the result
of the unique needs of individual children but were the result
of treatment options that antedated the creation of that system, primarily institutionalization for the "undeserving." This
tended to be the case because the political power and influence of the institutional industry was predominant when the
juvenile court entered upon the scene. Consequently, it was
that industry which had the greatest impact on the way children were diagnosed and labeled.

By the late 1800s, and certainly by the early 1900s, it was
the ruling boards of institutions who were largely responsible
for designing our systems of treatment, not only for juveniles
but for the mentally ill, the retarded, and, to a large degree,
even the poor:

These authorities were created to meet two great groups of problems: 1. The diversity of practice, inadequacy of equipment, competitive relationships and often wasteful methods characteristic of the care of wards for whom institutions, whether state or local, had been established; and the same lack of uniformity, the same inadequacy of service, the same wastefulness characteristic of the "outdoor" care of persons in distress given by local authorities. (Breckenridge, 1927:32)

Even though "outdoor" care as well as institutionalization came under the purview of these boards, Francis M. Rush, Jr. (1978:31) shows quite clearly that their major concern was with the latter. In Massachusetts, for example, the new board had general responsibility for "the local almshouses, a state hospital on Rainsford Island, three state lunatic asylums, a state prison, a state reform school, a state industrial school for girls, and a school ship *(The Massachusetts)*, and partially controlled by the state, the Massachusetts General Hospital, the Massachusetts School for the Blind, and the Massachusetts School for Idiots." Rush (1978:32) comments further that emphasis was *"on administrative rationality that would result in efficiency and economy."*

This emphasis was carried over into the Conference of Boards of Public Charities, formed in 1874 when the members of the boards of New York, Wisconsin, Connecticut, and Massachusetts met with the American Social Science Association to share views. The Conference (The National Conference of Charities in Corrections after 1879), which ultimately became the professional organization of social workers, emphasized administration and practice rather than scientific inquiry. By the 1870s, therefore, it was evident that the care of the mentally ill would be determined less by superintendents of individual institutions and more by centralized boards seeking to develop comprehensive and unified policies toward dependent groups of all kinds. (Rush, 1978:32)

One sees here the degree to which administrative and practical institutional considerations would influence later approaches, ideology, and even so-called scientific inquiry into issues of concern, such as juvenile justice. Indeed, Platt suggests that they led to the demise of theories of the born criminal: "The concept of the natural criminal was modified with the rise of a professional class of correctional administrators and social servants who promoted a medical model of deviant behavior and suggested techniques of remedying 'natural' imperfections" (Platt, 1969:35). It was within this context that the juvenile court and the so-called helping professions emerged.

In summary, it is clear that the revolution heralded by the founding of the juvenile court could have been of great importance. Roscoe Pound's famous statement (1950) that the juvenile court represented one of the most significant advances in the administration of justice since the Magna Charta reflected his awareness of the profound issues that *could* have been forced upon the scene by the establishment of the juvenile court. Likewise, George Herbert Mead (1961), in his classic article "The Psychology of Punitive Justice," noted that the juvenile court had forced a breach in the wall of the criminal justice system. Unfortunately, the ambivalence Mead saw reflected in the society around him—whether to treat or to punish—permeated the establishment of the juvenile justice system and the traditions of the juvenile court. This ambivalence was amplified by the bureaucratic structures which had been set up for treatment or punishment and which *already existed* at the time the juvenile court was created. Predictably, the clientele were soon receiving the worst of both worlds— no due process, followed by punishment labeled treatment. Seen in retrospect, therefore, such decisions as *Kent* and *Gault*, which guaranteed elements of due process and equity in sentencing, were probably inevitable.[1] The fervent hopes

---

[1] It now seems odd now that a system seen by the Supreme Court as essentially punitive—one which called punishment "treatment"—should more recently be perceived as mollycoddling young offenders. Even more interesting, much of the current revolution in juvenile justice is seen as responsive to both the above-mentioned criticisms. This is accomplished by shifting official response, depending upon the target population involved: reserving the benefits (diversion, deinstitutionalization, prevention) of the revolution for the "deserving" delinquent and the strict sentences (due process, waivers to adult court) for the "undeserving." This is, or course, repeating the pattern which turned out to be the major weakness of the child-saving movement and of the juvenile court begun in the early part of this century.

surrounding the juvenile court were undone by bureaucratic growth and practice.

Rather than terminating existing institutional child care or treatment bureaucracies, the juvenile court sustained and nourished them. Indeed, as new bureaucratic systems developed around the court, they began to escalate the labels and programs by which the net of the juvenile court could be thrown even wider. Under early banners of delinquency prevention, the juvenile justice system became involved with larger numbers of lesser, but "deserving," offenders. Meanwhile, legal statutes in most states permitted the court to bind "undeserving," and presumably more serious, delinquents over to adult courts. Indeed, in states such as New York, the age levels for the juvenile court were made so low as to insure the extrusion of most "undeserving" offenders into the adult system. Although "incorrigible" as well as "delinquent" children had always been seen as fit clientele for intervention or commitment to a reform school, such intrusions became virtually guaranteed as the system grew more formalized and bureaucratic.

Professionalism in Juvenile Justice

Along with bureaucracy, professionalism became the handmaiden of juvenile justice. There has always been a strong belief in this country that professionalization in and of itself guarantees quality services and scientifically informed problem-solving. Hence, large numbers of psychiatrists, psychologists, and particularly social workers were introduced into the juvenile justice field. Indeed, it still remains true that if an administrator of a juvenile correctional agency wishes to gain credibility or to deal with the problems of a hostile legislature or press, he can usually do so by introducing greater numbers of "qualified" personnel and "professional" consultants. Meanwhile, his approaches or ideology need not change, nor, in fact, do these consultants need to affect the institutional equilibrium of his operation. As a result, it has been a common administrative ploy in the juvenile justice field to professional-ize ineffective or, at times, brutal systems.

Given these conditions, professionalism provides a paradox in fields that have a captive clientele. Although professionals can at times advance the humaneness of a system, an indirect effect has been to give credibility to those that are ineffective and to insure their survival. In short, the professional is more likely to be used by the bureaucracy than he or she is likely to change it. The screening processes for selecting profession-als, for culling out the obstreperous ones, and for socializing the remainder to the institutional world have all served to dilute conflicts and to bless and ratify the system.

We have often maintained the naive view that professional treatment of the juvenile offender is an objective, science-based exercise. In fact, diagnosis in the juvenile justice system is in large part a political problem that culminates in a bureau-cratic process we call treatment. The terms attached to the clientele are skewed toward maintaining equilibrium within the juvenile justice bureaucracies. Indeed, some labels, such as "psychopath," fairly demand maltreatment! Thus, manage-ability is the issue, and the labels are enrolled to that end. Professionalization gives a rationality to the jargon that effec-tively masks the process.

Mead understood well the value and normative issues that would predispose the child-saver revolution in juvenile jus-tice to failure. Although he had hoped the juvenile court would provide some means of breaking out of the traditional criminal law system—something that Roscoe Pound prob-ably perceived as possible—Mead's own analysis of the role of the criminal in our society should have warned him otherwise:

Seemingly without the criminal the cohesiveness of society would disappear and the universal goods of the community would crumble into mutually repellent particles. The criminal does not seriously endanger the structure of society by his disruptive activities and on the other hand he is responsible for a sense of solidarity, aroused among those whose attention would be otherwise centered upon interests quite divergent from those of each other. Thus, courts of criminal justice may be essential to the preservation of society even when we take account of the impotence of the criminal over against society, and the clumsy failure of criminal law in the repression and suppression of crime. I am willing to admit that this statement is distorted, not, however, in its analysis of the procedure against the criminal, but in its failure to recognize the growing consciousness of the many common interests which is slowly changing our institutional conception of society, and its consequent exaggerated estimate upon the import of the criminal. (Mead, 1961:882)

Mead suggests, in short, that society could not tolerate the removal of a significant segment of the population (adolescent offenders) from the criminal labeling process. To do so would threaten the underpinnings of society itself. It would also give meaning to the trend of moving certain juvenile offenders into the adult criminal justice system while at the same time justifying the juvenile court's spreading a wider net into noncriminal behavior, dependency, and incorrigibility.

If Mead had investigated the internal dynamics of the system, it is likely that he would also have noted how they reinforce the broader macrodynamics. An instance here are the problems of the interplay of appointed or elected judges with the politically sensitive court and correctional bureaucracies that comprise the juvenile justice system. Such arrangements are skewed toward professional conservatism because of the bureaucratic risk involved in moving too far away from traditional criminal justice procedures. Consequently, there has been a built-in bias against dealing in new and innovative ways with "undeserving" offenders—those whose problems are the greatest and whose acts are the more serious. Instead, there has been much to gain by concentrating upon "deserving" children—those who resemble one's own middle-class offspring. If one is to justify treatment, one must show success, and there is no better way for doing that than to deal successfully with those who would probably be a success anyway. Meanwhile, the system can demonstrate its commitment to the protection of society by continuing to isolate and to immobilize its "undeserving" failures. As a result, those "undeserving" individuals who have always populated our detention centers and reformatories have remained largely unaffected by the professionalization of juvenile justice.

The Growth of Professionalism

As noted earlier, professional theory and practice first gained a foothold in this country through their ties to the institutional industry of the nineteenth century. After the turn of the twentieth century, however, professionalism became increasingly academic and gained a measure of independence because of its ties to hospitals and universities (Rush, 1978:42). The consequences of this development for the profession of social work are dramatically demonstrated by comparing the themes around which its national conferences in 1893 and 1928 were organized. Clearly, there was a marked shift from a concern with administering institutions to a concern with a broader set of academic and substantive issues (Rush, 1978:42):

National Conference of Charities in Corrections *1893*	*National Conference of Social Work* *1928*
1. State Boards of Charities	1. Children
2. Charity Organizations	2. Delinquents and Correction
3. Indoor and Outdoor Relief	3. Health
4. Immigration	4. The Family
5. Child-Saving	5. Industrial and Economic Problems
6. Reformatories	6. Neighborhood and Community Life
7. The Prison Question	7. Mental Hygiene
8. The Feeble-Minded	8. Organization of Social Forces
9. The Insane	9. Public Officials and Administration
	10. The Immigrant
	11. Professional Standards in Education
	12. Educational Publicity

Concomitant with this change was the development of standardized professional methodologies, such as Mary Richmond's book *What Is Social Casework?* (first published in 1922). Regarding these standards, Willard stated in 1925 that

social work no longer attends chiefly to the confinement and management of state wards, but derives its problems from community processes far beyond state institutions. . . . On account of the necessary reference to social ends involved in social work thus broadly conceived, those ends must be fixed through appreciation of the social processes themselves in any state, and their merits defined in terms of social values. (Willard, 1925:55–56)

In theory, at least, social work joined the professions of psychiatry and clinical psychology in widening its perspective and in fostering the rehabilitation ethic. Yet there are several grounds on which it might be argued that professional theory continued to differ widely from professional practice.

First, there is the fact that institutional management bureaucracies, backed by a century of experience, heavily influenced the on-the-job training of professionals. The categories, labels, processes of management, and interorganizational relations of these bureaucracies have often been far more influential in determining the actual practices of professionals than the theories they have learned in the classroom. A child-saving ideology, for example, is more likely to be swallowed up or diluted by a complex bureaucratic system than it is to change that system.

Secondly, there is the seductive tendency to justify the continued use of coercion by the manipulation of new diagnostic labels. In a 1947 essay, Lionel Trilling argues that "some paradox in our nature leads us, once we have made our fellow men the objects of our enlightened interest, to go on to make them the objects of our pity, then of our wisdom, ultimately of our coercion" (see Rothman, 1978:72). Trilling's perception is accurate so far as it goes, but it does not go far enough. Although the helping professions have used coercive methods with enthusiasm, there are other, more complex, ways for dealing with unresponsive and undeserving juveniles—ways

that avoid the risk of moral conflict between stated professional and democratic goals and the use of coercion.

A safer response by professional helpers in a bureaucracy
is to adjust diagnostic categories and thereby to remove the
need for the coercion of the clients with whom professionals
deal. This insures that failures are defined as being outside
the expertise and responsibility of the helping professional.
That is why the deep-end diagnoses and the hard-core labels
survive whatever professional or ideological era we find ourselves in. Furthermore, that is why treatment systems reserved for the "undeserving"—extrusions, exclusions, and
isolation—also persist. Labels change, but the process remains
essentially the same.

Ironically, these inhumane systems also serve to validate
the label. D. L. Howard (1960), for example, has shown how
English practices of the late nineteenth century dovetailed
nicely with Lombrosian theories regarding the identification
and labeling of the criminal. Although entering a punitive
and brutal prison machine as people, men and women later
emerged as Lombrosian animals, easily recognizable as criminal types by the Victorian middle classes. Thus, as Denis Chapman (1968:237) notes, the whole system was "logical,
watertight, and socially functional." Furthermore, while our
systems today are more complex, the same social dynamics
tend to persist.

While there are a large number of persons who would
change or abolish punitive institutions, there are others (perhaps the majority) who see the correctional system as one
of punishment and social isolation. Unfortunately, it is at this
point that the self-interests of professionals often dovetail with
those of bureaucrats. In their diagnostic labeling processes,
they dance a ritual choreographed to fulfill latent functions
of social control while touting the manifest functions of science
and care. The professions provide the new labels that change
from decade to decade, while the basic treatment of the
"undeserving" continues unchanged; for example, the treatment of the "moral imbecile" in the late nineteenth century,
the "constitutional psychopathic inferior" in the early 1900s,

the "psychopath" in the 1930s and '40s, the "sociopath" in the 1950s, the "antisocial personality" in the 1960s, the person "unresponsive to verbal conditioning" in the 1970s, and, most recently, the "criminal personality" of the middle 1970s. In this sense, Chapman (1968:237) is probably correct in referring to the helping professions as "latter-day Lombrosos whose social function is to provide the 'scientific' explanations required by the culture."

Such labels also remove the professional from responsibility for dealing with the phenomenon he names. He is thereby able to withdraw from the situation or enter into it at will, wearing success as a halo and placing failure on the head of the client. The degree to which the professions become involved with those juveniles seen by the society as violent or most dangerous becomes a function of bureaucratic and political considerations, though couched in professional jargon. One can anticipate that psychiatrists, psychologists, and social workers will become involved to the degree that clientele with lesser or virtually no problems are unavailable. It is a seller's rather than a buyer's market emerging from a system with a captive clientele to be redefined, reassigned, or extruded from the system by those who, paradoxically, claim the expertise for dealing with the problem.

It is important, therefore, to question whether the nomenclature, training, and treatment modalities of the helping professions are relevant to dealing with serious juvenile delinquents. This leads to more telling questions. For example, if professionals cannot deal with these youngsters, will they leave the field (and the budget) open for other agents of change? But, rather than engaging in the difficult self-appraisal inherent in trying to answer this question, they have characteristically switched focus, usually finding a more felicitous target group of clientele with whom to deal—middle-class, "neurotic" delinquents or status offenders. Hence, the sad truth is that, despite the rhetoric, we have had an inverse system whereby those who are most likely to present major problems to society in terms of violence or repeated crimes are systematically excluded from the system of care by professional diagnosis and are thereby relegated to the largest and most impersonal human warehouses—jails, prisons, training schools—places where they find the fewest and least qualified professional helpers. At the same time, those who are *least* likely to become involved in serious crimes are most likely to be dealt with by professional helpers. The rationale given is that of a diversionary or preventive exercise. This is why the new revolution with its emphasis on diverting status offenders or deinstitutionalizing programs for them has been so fully embraced by the professions.

Trilling's fear that we tend to move toward the coercion of those most in need of care is well-founded. One might make a case for the thesis that professional coercion in juvenile justice follows naturally from professional inadequacy. First, labels (e.g., psychopath) that cry out for coercion are coined. Then, paradoxically, the coercion that follows, having been prescribed by professionals, is usually dispensed by nonprofessionals in lower-level staff positions. One can only conclude, therefore, that this whole exercise is more a measure of the inadequacies of the professions than of the appropriateness of the coercion. Moreover, it also points to a certain fragility in the power of the juvenile justice professions. If Hannah Arendt (1970:56) is right when she says that power and violence are opposites—"where the one rules absolutely, the other is absent"—then the history of the involvement of psychiatry, psychology, and social work in juvenile justice over the past fifty years has not been felicitous either for the clientele or the professions. "Loss of power becomes a temptation to substitute violence for power—and that violence itself results in impotence" (Arendt, 1970:54).

In summary, disillusionment with the child-saving movement and cynicism with the juvenile justice system are well-founded. This disillusionment, however, is more a function in the nature of reality than of the ideals that were promulgated. The treatment actually afforded juveniles has never approached the goals envisaged. Perhaps it never could, given the characteristics of a system that is accountable only to those who run it rather than to its captive clientele. And perhaps it is of the essence of juvenile justice that captives can never have legitimate power. If that is so, reform will always be subject to the altruism of those who provide the service. Yet, as experience teaches, altruism is notoriously undependable and eventually is worn away in bureaucracies. Indeed, the product of unresponsive bureaucracies is apathy and finally violence. And that, of course, has been the history of the juvenile justice system from 1900 to the present.

Why haven't we broken out of this vicious cycle? The reasons reside in the system itself. Even its widely touted cures are not so much cures as they are means of providing reassurance to the rest of society. Too often, as Edmund Leach (1967) points out, they represent "the imposition of discipline by force—the maintenance of the existing order against threats which arise from its own internal contradictions." To the degree that this is so, the success of revolutions in juvenile justice has been, and will continue to be, limited.

The New Revolution in Juvenile Justice

In much the same way, many of the issues surrounding the current revolution in juvenile justice have to do more with rhetoric than with substance. Its principal catchwords—decriminalization, diversion, due process, and deinstitutionalization—are part of that rhetoric. There is little evidence that youth service bureaus, for instance, set up as diversionary, have lowered the numbers of juveniles going into the criminal justice system. Generally, they have dealt with other, more "deserving" youngsters. Thus, it is difficult to prove that they either prevented delinquency or diverted delinquents.

Likewise, Vinter and Sarri (1975:46), in their massive national study, have shown that deinstitutionalization has not occurred on a uniform basis. It is certainly clear that it has not happened in adult corrections, with its record numbers in prisons and jails, and, though there are states in which institutional populations in training schools have fallen dramatically, there are others which have maintained or increased the numbers of juveniles in institutions. The reasons for this failure, moreover, are usually bureaucratic in character rather than academic or ideological. Indeed, there are some who say that we traditionally institutionalize a certain percentage of the population in our society (Brizius, 1976). As we close one type of institution, we fill another. Similarly, William Nagel's study (1977) on prisons implies that we fill prisons to occupy empty cells. Those states that build more prisons have more prisoners, those that do not build more prisons have less prisoners—and both phenomena are unrelated to crime rates.

All of this is not to suggest that diversion, deinstitutionalization, and other reforms are not important. It is simply to point out that such reforms are seldom applied to the target population for which they were initially justified. For example, state correctional bureaucracies rarely dramatize their support for new reforms by transferring appropriate portions of their budgets from institutional programs to community-based alternatives. Furthermore, their reasons for failing to do this are eminently practical: the juveniles ordinarily assigned to diversionary or preventive programs are generally not those already in institutions or likely to be sent to them. Instead, new programs require *additional* budget because existing monies are needed to service the institutionalized youngsters who use up the bulk of most state juvenile correctional budgets (usually over 90%). Thus, only if state correctional agencies were disposed to *terminate* ineffective institutional programs could one anticipate the transfer of institutional budgets into alternative programs. However, this does not happen because (1) alternative programs are not really *alternatives* for institutionalized juveniles, and (2) institutions survive whether or not they are effective, since they are there to provide for other needs, such as employment in remote areas, contracts with vendors, political patronage, and a sense of safety and solidarity for the public.

Ideology and the New Revolution

Along with the now familiar statements that juveniles have received the worst of two possible worlds and that more fair and effective ways must be found for dealing with them, there are a number of less well known ideologies that should be considered in examining the so-called revolution in juvenile justice. The first is Robert Martinson's (1974) assertion that "nothing works"—an assertion that dovetails nicely with the position of the helping professions vis-à-vis corrections.[2] These professions, though perceived by the public as expert in the area of juvenile delinquency, have, as indicated earlier, tended to withdraw from dealing with more difficult delinquents. Hence, Martinson simply provided confirmation of the ineffectiveness of the professions with serious delinquents and insured that whatever involvement they might have in the future could be limited by them to the more expensive, professionally well controlled pilot and research-demonstration projects.

Another issue contributing heavily to the rethinking of the juvenile justice model has been the recent emphasis upon rising juvenile crime—particularly violent crime. Although there are a number of indications that this problem is receding and that it peaked somewhere between 1973 and 1975, the media, particularly the liberal media, have projected the problem as a continually growing, if not exploding, one. This projection has coincided with the growing interest in the conservative views of James Q. Wilson (1975), Ernest van den Haag (1975), and others who argue that a more practical (punitive) approach to crime should be taken.

Significantly, Wilson is a Harvard professor and van den Haag, who presents himself as a psychoanalyst and social critic, is one of the founders of the New York Conservative Party. Although their neoclassical views might be questioned on theoretical grounds, the most significant thing about their writings for our purposes is their ideological character. Wilson (1975:60) has criticized the field of criminology for being polemical and nonscientific, and he is correct. What masquerades as science is often, in fact, the bias of individual criminologists who are influenced by personal ideological convictions rather

---

[2] Martinson's (1974) views have become increasingly ideolological as they have received acceptance in the media—though more recently he is saying "everything works."

than by facts or objectively based theories. Wilson's work, no less than van den Haag's, is in the same genre. The only difference is that it is conservative whereas other criminologists have been liberal.

Even more striking is the extent to which formerly liberal criminologists have moved to the right in recent years as the liberal media have hyped the violence issue. Without doubt, the current revolution in juvenile justice is confronted with a conservative counterrevolutionary thrust that would warp current changes into its own reactionary mold.

Along with the movement to the right has been a rising moral indignation in society around the issues of crime. Some have pointed out that when a nation is not united in war against other outside nations, it will look inwardly for scapegoats, concentrating primarily upon the poor and the criminal. Perhaps the law-and-order sources of the current revolution in juvenile justice owe something to the cessation of the Vietnam war. For example, Svend Ranulf (1964), a Danish sociologist, argues that the expansion of criminal law is attributable to moral indignation. Such indignation, in turn, is connected with the rising power of the lower middle classes. He notes, for instance, that the reform of German criminal law, advocated by the national socialists and published by the minister of justice in 1933, proposed a widening of crimes to be punished with severity. The minister's memorandum on this issue reads like the comments of today's conservative critics of juvenile justice. "It is even doubted," he said, "that the state had a right to punish at all. It seemed that the welfare of the criminal, and not the welfare of the people, was the main purpose of the criminal law" (Ranulf, 1964:11). Even though history reads otherwise, comments of this type enjoy increasing popularity.

With reference to the joining of the right and the left around the present revolution, perhaps the most telling issue has been the decline of faith in the indeterminate sentence. We appear to have come full circle on this issue. Havelock Ellis, in his treatise on the criminal in 1903, states that the great fault of our prison system is its "arbitrary character." In recommending reforms for the treatment of the criminal, he notes that "the first reform necessary is the total abolition of the definite and predetermined sentence. The indefinite sentence is no longer new, either in principle or practice; all that is needed is its systematic extension. It has been adopted by many of the American states, including Illinois, Massachusetts, Pennsylvania, Ohio, Wisconsin, Minnesota, and Colorado. It was first introduced at the famous state reformatory of New York at Elmira by an act passed in 1877" (Ellis, 1903:321).

Although the indeterminate sentence is attacked by contemporary critics as an artifact of the helping professions—primarily psychiatry—it was in fact begun by *institutional managers.* Ellis pointed out that the establishment of the indeterminate sentence "was due to the genius and experience of Mr. Z. R. Brockway, who had had a long practical training in prison management, and who was well acquainted with the nature of criminals" (Ellis, 1903:321). In truth, the indeterminate sentence was developed out of needs for control and management in prison bureaucracies, not out of the needs of offenders. The professional helpers who embraced it needed it in their roles as managers. But, as has happened so often in the history of corrections, early discussions centered around the rhetoric—or what Robert Merton might call the "manifest values" of the case; that is, whether rehabilitation or punishment is appropriate. Unrecognized was the fact that correctional systems rested on more latent issues related to bureaucratic calm and political peace—issues which provided the glue for those systems. Rehabilitation versus punishment is not the issue, since rehabilitation has rarely been tried.

Ironically, both sides of the political spectrum have made exactly the same mistake today. Andrew Von Hirsch (1976), in his book *Doing Justice*—a report of the predominantly liberal Committee for the Study of Incarceration—draws conclusions similar to those of Ernest van den Haag (1975) in his conservative tome *Punishing Criminals.* The Committee for the Study of Incarceration concluded that rehabilitation in prisons and institutions does not seem to have worked. Hence, they recommended that it be abandoned and prison sentences shortened. Of course the opposite will in fact happen. The committee was legally correct but politically naive.

The committee would have dealt more squarely with the issues if it had refused to discuss altogether the rehabilitative model—since it is for the most part rhetoric in prison settings—and dealt rather with the management issue, which is what the indeterminate sentence is about. But, having failed to do that, its report, along with *Punishing Criminals,* was welcomed by conservatives as rejecting the "two myths that have vitiated so much of the discussion about criminal justice—the view that criminals are 'sick' individuals who are not morally responsible for their offenses, and the view that criminals are political rebels struggling against oppression. In place of these myths, both authors affirm the eminently sensible proposition that criminals are lawbreakers who deserve to be punished for their illegal actions" (Plattner, 1975:114).

These comments accept as fact the belief that prisoners generally have been treated as sick—which, of course, is not true. Though the rhetoric of certain criminologists may have stressed this sort of issue, the budgets of the correctional bureaucracies have always fostered systems of neglect or punishment—jails, training schools, and prisons. If one wishes to understand the latent realities of a system, therefore, one must not look to the manifest rhetoric but to more mundane considerations, such as how the money is spent. For the most part, in juvenile or adult corrections, it is not spent on rehabilitation or in dealing with the concerns of political rebels. Those are catchwords meant for use by politicians and academics.

The Ideological Middle Ground

A middle ground in the current revolution, which walks a tightrope between abolishment of the juvenile court and total support of the juvenile court system, seems to have been taken by the Twentieth Century Fund Task Force on Sentencing Policies Toward Young Offenders. This report states bluntly:

The theory behind the juvenile court is not merely obsolete; it is a fairy tale that never came true. The court has helped some young offenders, but it has punished others. From the beginning, juvenile court judges have considered the interests of the state as well as those of the offender. It is pointless to pretend that social policy toward youth crime is based solely on the best interests of the young offender or that the best interests of the offender and those of the state are always the same. But the juvenile court need not rely on hypocritical rhetoric to jsutify its jurisdiction over youths charged with crime. (Twentieth Century Fund, 1978:6)

The report then goes on to justify a "discrete policy" toward youth crime which includes the principles of culpability, diminished responsibility resulting from immaturity, providing room to reform, and proportionality. It recommends parameters of sentencing dictated primarily by the level of the offense and supports the idea of custodial confinement and limited waiver to adult court of selected cases. It also recommends reform of the management principles which have governed institutions and criticizes the attitudes, actions, and professional inadequacies of certain judges, police, corrections officers, and magistrates.

Despite its recommendations, the conclusions of the task force represent a compromise—the kind of compromise one expects from the membership of a task force consisting primarily of lawyers, retired judges, commissioners of youth service, and academics. Consequently, there is little that is new in the document. Rather, it simply represents a realignment of issues on a continuum between the existing juvenile court system and the existing adult correctional system. Indeed, it appears in many ways to be a retreat or rear-guard action against what is perceived as a law-and-order backlash. Certain types of crimes and certain delinquents are moved closer to the adult system, while others are seen as more appropriate to the juvenile system. Very few new or alternative approaches are suggested—the tack being one of wedding proportionality of sentence to seriousness of crime rather than wedding effective and humane methods of treatment to those who need it most.

The Techniques of the New Revolution

Along with the traditional hope that delinquency can be prevented, the current revolution has actually concentrated most
upon diversion and deinstitutionalization, with due process
being seen as integral to these. Except in rare instances, however, the decriminalization of status offenses has not been
widespread.

Prevention. In considering so-called delinquency prevention,
Lundman and Scarpitti (1978) estimate that since 1965 alone
over 6,500 different attempts at prevention have been
launched. The authors found 1,000 citations in the literature
regarding delinquency prevention programs and set about
trying to examine 127 of them in careful detail. In only 25
previous projects, and 15 continuing ones, however, did they
find useable information on the nature and results of these
projects. Based on this information, therefore, they concluded:

> . . . Most projects reported in the professional literature did not
> permit reliable assessment of results. And those projects with experi-
> mental designs and objective measurement of delinquent behavior
> had not successfully prevented delinquency. . . .
> . . . We found little reason to believe that a major breakthrough
> in delinquency prevention is forthcoming. (Lundman, 1978:207)

The authors did find other things, however, that should interest those involved in the current revolution in juvenile
justice, a revolution seen as throwing off the coercive protec-
tiveness of the earlier child-saver revolution. One example
is that of a Georgetown University psychologist, Juan B. Cortes
(1972), who proposed a delinquency-prevention project based
upon early—and largely unsupported—theories about the relationship between body-type and delinquency. In Washington's "wickedest" precinct, he maintained, a program should
be organized and aimed at identifying families who have children under the age of seven, determining those who are "potentially delinquent" families, studying those families, and

classifying them into two main groups: (1) those with parents who would not or could not cooperate, and (2) those with parents who would and could cooperate. Techniques for "tactfully and helpfully informing and training the parents of the second group in the necessary modifications of their child-rearing practices and in their relationships with each other" were suggested. Both cooperative and uncooperative families, he concluded, should be helped.

Significantly, Cortes's approach was based upon the Glueck Delinquency Prediction Scale, which Lundman and Scarpitti found had a prediction error of 84 percent. Hence, they were sufficiently impressed by its questionable merits that they felt constrained to warn against its intrusive potential: "Generally, these subjects have not been found guilty of anything beyond possession of characteristics or behaviors which someone believes are predictive of delinquency. In our zeal to help, we must not lose sight of the fact that juveniles who have not been adjudicated delinquent have the right to refuse that help" (Lundman, 1978:220).

Another approach to prevention and diversion was that advanced in 1972 by the Youth Development and Delinquency Prevention Administration of HEW (Gemignani, 1973). The YDDPA recommended a national strategy for the prevention of juvenile delinquency that had largely evolved from a meeting called by YDDPA in early 1970. It called for the nationwide establishment of youth services systems "which will divert youth, so far as possible, from the juvenile system by providing comprehensive, integrated, community-based programs designed to meet the needs of all youth, regardless of who they are or what their individual problems may be." Preventive programs would be implemented for troubled but predelinquent youth, while community-based rehabilitation programs would be used as alternatives to incarceration for those who were delinquent.

Commendably, the strategy projected a 25 percent decrease in the rate of youth in court delinquency cases with an annual saving of the same amount. If enough services were supplied, it was argued, the numbers going into the juvenile justice system would inevitably decline. It is unfortunate, however, that, in placing blind faith in the rationality of the bureaucracies that would administer the new strategy, its progenitors failed to heed Durkheim's (1964) conclusion that any society continues to criminalize a certain proportion of its membership, even though its standards of morality may move markedly upward:

Imagine a society of saints, a perfect cloister of exemplary individuals. Crimes, properly so-called, will there be unknown; but faults which appear venial to the layman will create there the same scandal that the ordinary offense does in ordinary consciousness. If, then, this society has the power to judge and punish, it will define these acts as criminal and will treat them as such. For the same reason, the perfect and upright man judges his smallest failings with a severity that the majority reserve for acts more truly in the nature of an offense. Formerly, acts of violence against persons were more frequent than they are today, because respect for individual dignity was less strong. As this has increased, these crimes have become more rare; and also many acts of violating this sentiment have been introduced into the penal law which were not included there in primitive times. (Durkheim, 1964:68–69)

Durkheim's remarks suggest why it may be that diversionary and preventive programs are usually reserved for other populations than the more serious juvenile offender. If the latter were reformed, penal populations would drop and it would be necessary to assign labels and penalties to other, less serious, groups in order to fill the jails, detention centers, and prisons reserved for the "undeserving" members of society. As a result, it is unlikely that the usual clientele of juvenile justice could be reduced.

Diversion. Diversion is generally defined as the channeling of cases to noncourt agencies or systems in instances where these cases would ordinarily have been processed by the juvenile court. Nejelski (1973) says that the most significant part of this definition is the second half, namely, that diversion should involve those who would normally have been handled by the juvenile court. What he found, however, was that the children who were actually being diverted were *not* those who fit into this category. Rather, they were persons who ordinarily would have been released. Meanwhile, the usual cases continued their parade through the court. Hence, he concluded that "these projects may be useful in themselves because they aid juveniles, but they increase state intervention without reducing the workload of the courts. They are supplemental, but they are not diversionary" (Nejelski, 1973:83).

Nejelski's findings were not unique. As with preventive programs, there is little to show that diversionary programs lower the numbers of juveniles being inserted into the deep end of the juvenile system. A truly diversionary program should be able to show one less detained or institutionalized youngster, or at least one less person on a juvenile court docket, for every person diverted. Allowing for shifts in population and unusual surges in crime rates, this would mean that if a particular community diverted a thousand youngsters in a given year, the juvenile court docket would fall by at least a thousand. Of course, such measures are seldom if ever applied. Instead, most new programs only widen the net of official bureaucracies, not decrease it.

There are also other questions that merit close scrutiny with respect to diversion: (1) Who will be diverted? and (2) How much intervention, with or without coercion, can be tolerated without due process? There is question, for instance, whether referral to a youth service bureau is actually voluntary when the alternative is to be labeled a juvenile offender and to be threatened with a training school or reformatory should the diversion fail. But, while juveniles are now provided with some of the benefits of due process in court proceedings, such is not true when they are placed in the hands of diversionary bureaucracies.

The resulting potential for destructive labeling is great. As Nejelski (1976:108), points out, "Diversion does not absolve society from making diagnoses. Diversion merely redesignates or shifts the responsibility for making these decisions. Fundamental questions remain. By whom are these individuals to be judged and upon what evidence? By focusing on diagnosis as he does, Nejelski immediately turns it into a "due process" issue. Diversion *does*, in fact, shift the responsibility; whole new systems, formal and informal, come into play. These systems, in turn, base their use of diagnostic labels upon the options they have available for treating juveniles. Hence, there is potential for either good or bad.

If those making the diagnosis have at hand a wide range of treatment alternatives, the chances are increased that the diagnosis itself will become less rigid and less restricted to either-or types of choices (e.g., either home or an institution, either probation or training school). The possibilities are enhanced for greater choice, less bureaucratic risk, and ultimately less coercion. Conversely, the possibilities for negative labeling and punitive reactions are greater where the helping bureaucrat has fewer options available. The juvenile is more at risk. Furthermore, it should not be forgotten that, even when alternatives exist, a conservative bias is usually inherent in the choices made. In short, if a long continuum of options is created by the diversionary ethic, due process is less an issue, but, if it is limited and short, it poses a series of age-old problems.

Unfortunately, those concerned with diversion often see matters in terms of a dichotomy rather than as a continuum. Nejelski (1976:114) comments that the notion of due process runs counter to the social-contract theory suggested in the *Gault* (1967) decision. "That theory," he says, "may be interpreted as aruging that the juvenile court could dispense with due process if in fact the court were treating and correcting its clients." Nejelski (1976:115) argues, however, that "a sounder basis for according due process is simply the fact that the state is coercively intervening in the life of its citizens." Wherever coercion appears, due process should be guaranteed, whether in diversionary or court programs.

A final issue with respect to diversion has to do with the target population it proposes to help. To often it has simply been a means for carrying out the traditional pattern of separating the "deserving" from the "undeserving." For example, in the case of the New Jersey Juvenile Conference Committee (a diversionary program), criticisms were levied that, while local communities had been successful in diverting middle-class youth, they had not been successful with those in the urban ghettos. The juvenile courts continue to be flooded with poor kids from minority backgrounds (Nejelski, 1973:89). Given the history of reforms in this country, one might have anticipated this result. To the degree that the pattern is solidi-fied, therefore, the current Revolution may be sowing the seeds of its own destruction.

Deinstitutionalization. Deinstitutionalization is another catch-word in vogue. It has to do with the removal of juvenile offend-ers from institutional settings (detention centers, training schools, and jails) and their placement in a variety of commu-nity alternatives. Although it would be difficult to find another issue over which so much has been said, the existing evidence relative to its implementation is difficult to find and to inter-pret.

The first problem has to do with the lack of reliable statistics. In a study conducted in the state of Pennsylvania (Office of Children and Youth, 1977), for example, it was found that the numbers of juveniles in jails were underreported by as much as ten times by the official reporting body, the state Juvenile Court Judges Commission. Only by going to the jails, reading the log books, noting the ages of inmates, and counting heads were investigators able to find out how many were actu-ally being kept in jails.

Secondly, it is by no means clear that systematic efforts are being made to deinstitutionalize existing programs. Al-though the National Assessment of Juvenile Corrections (Vin-ter, 1976) showed some drop in institutional populations in the early 1970s, there are other indications of a rising popula-tion in juvenile institutions in the late 1970s. Indeed, the whole picture is clouded by the absence of standardized and reliable information. For example, the first report by the National As-sessment Project (Vinter, 1976) indicated that Utah ranked fourth in its efforts to deinstitutionalize its programs. Yet, when this writer visited Utah in 1978, there were close to

200 juveniles in the state boys' school. At that rate of incarceration, a state the size of Massachusetts, with an average institutional population of 75 to 100 (in closed facilities), would have had between 1,600 and 2,000 in institutional settings.

Even then the Utah data were questionable for another reason. On the one hand, that state could show a dramatic decrease in the number of juveniles committed to the training school by the courts. Yet, on the other hand, that same facility became the site for a rapid increase in the number of juveniles being held either for diagnostic workups or simple detention. Thus, although the labels had changed, the numbers in the Utah institution actually rose in late 1978—though if one were to read official reports, one would find a drop in juveniles committed to the state training school.

Similar ploys have been seen in other states. For instance, the California Probation Subsidy Program showed a dramatic drop in youth committed to state Youth Authority institutions. Yet, at that very same time, California was harboring in its detention facilities—county-run and state-approved—the largest per capita population of any state in the union (California Youth Authority, 1975).

Finally, in some states there is evidence that conservative trends will contribute to a deliberate increase in the use of institutional facilities. The state of Washington, for example, projects a doubling of its institutional population over the coming years. This is a result of a new determinate sentencing law backed by civil libertarians that got out of hand in the legislature. Although the new law provides for the transfer of jurisdiction over status offenders from the juvenile court to the Department of Social and Health Services, it mandates the use of structured sentencing procedures for delinquents, based primarily on prior record and instant offense. Gone is the notion that the court should treat the offender and not the offense. Furthermore, a cynic might predict that the transfer of status offenders to the Department of Social and Health Services will simply result in many of them continuing to be institutionalized under a child welfare, rather than a juvenile court, rubric.

Such changes lead one to conclude that there has been no massive deinstitutionalization movement in the United States. The recent concentration by LEAA in the Office of Juvenile Justice and Delinquency Prevention upon the so-called status offender, though laudable, is but a variation on the theme of the "deserving" versus the "undeserving" delinquent. It is doubtful that the effort to remove status offenders from institutional settings will in fact lower the total numbers of juveniles in institutional settings. Indeed, if the usual bureaucratic processes come into play, one can anticipate one of two possible outcomes.

If, on the one hand, status offenders are removed from institutions, labels applied to other juveniles will be escalated to justify a given number of youngsters to fill a given number of slots in institutional settings. If, on the other hand, it is too risky bureaucratically to redefine the needed number of juveniles by escalating their diagnoses, the labels placed on institutions will be de-escalated to justify their continued usage. For example, when it became illegal in some states to assign nondelinquent youth (PINS) to training schools for delinquents, the schools were simply renamed as treatment centers for "persons in need of supervision."

Perhaps the most tragic example of this kind of euphemistic manipulation recently occurred in Ohio, where the legislature actually passed a law that required the Fairfield School for Boys at Lancaster to keep a minimum number of boys (300) in that school whether they were "appropriately" assigned to it or not. As a result, the chairman of the Ohio Youth Commission is on record as having said that he has had to "practically kidnap" boys in order to keep the minimum called for by the legislature and has had to keep them long past their release dates in order to obey the law.

Although the amendment mandating this procedure was introduced by a legislator from the district in which the training school is located, he has denied that it had anything to do with jobs or employment in the area. Instead, he insists that he was motivated by a need to keep "quality vocational programs" in the facility and that to do so he had to keep its population at a given level (Institutions, Etc., 1978). Whatever the rationale, one seldom sees the issue so well defined.

There have been studies that exhibit an understanding of the Parkinsonian dynamics just described. For example, consider the report produced by the National Association for the Care and Resettlement of Offenders in Great Britain, chaired by Peter Jay, formerly British ambassador to the United States (Jay, 1977). This group concluded, first of all, that it might be possible to remove as many as 95 percent of the 12,000 children in Great Britain presently in residential care (including group homes):

Those of us who favor the approach in this chapter (decarceration) believe that there is sufficient evidence to reach the practical conclusion now that, even for the 12,000 minority of young offenders now adjudged to be in need of residential treatment, any approach based on institutional care and theories of individual "treatment and cure" do not have a sufficiently good prospect of general success to warrant the huge deployment of resources, to say nothing of the dedicated application of the staff involved, which present arrangements imply and would imply under any conceivable development in reforms of the current approach. (Jay, 1977:49)

Secondly, the group concluded that any use of incarceration for juveniles should be confined to those who are "dangerous"—"not more than about 400 children throughout England and Wales on any given day." But, unlike considerations of this type in the United States, be it of the old or the new revolution, the British group went on to conclude that *"the definition of the 'dangerous' child is a politically negotiable one."* Hence, it recommended a regular and scrupulous review of the necessity for continued detention based on statutory criteria relating to "dangerousness":

We have said that on the best estimates available to us there are not more than 400 children in this category (dangerous). To an extent the decision will be arbitrary. What is crucial is that no amount of persuasion and pressure should allow the number to increase except in the light of a fundamental review of the strategy. In practice the effect of such a limit will not be very different from the position that faces magistrates and social workers under our present system.

[As it is now], a child cannot be sent to a community home unless a place is available or the management is willing to accept him. While we fully appreciate the constraints that a limitation on numbers in secure accommodation will seem to impose, we firmly believe that if a strategy of decarceration is to be adopted, this is the only way to ensure that the number of young offenders in institutions will not escalate. (Jay, 1977:52)

Of interest to those proposing reform in the American system should be the fact that the only dissenter to this conclusion among the ten-person working party was the chairman of the London Borough's Childrens Regional Planning Committee, who suggested that institutional care must be tied to consistent social work practice in the field.

All of the foregoing is by way of illustrating the difference between the manifest and latent functions of institutions for juveniles. Usually these institutions are justified on the basis of their manifest functions, couched in terms of law and order, public safety, or in terms of child welfare and proper treatment. Actually, latent functions are often of much greater importance—employment in remote areas, political patronage, contracts with vendors of services, arrangements between specific institutions and the particular courts, or the self-interests of professional and custodial groups. Much of the juvenile justice system remains geared to these considerations, not to its manifest functions.

In order to attack this problem, programs such as diversion and prevention should be tied to deinstitutionalization in practice, not just in rhetoric. As it is now, however, they seldom deal with the youngsters who actually populate our institutions. If they did, deinstitutionalization for most juveniles would occur as a natural by-product of proposed reforms, and only the most serious offenders would be confined. Were that done, we would be free to discuss alternative types of residential care for those who need such control, those juveniles on the deep end of the delinquency continuum who are the most dangerous and violent offenders. We could develop caring, decent, small residential settings which, on the one hand, would guarantee the control society demands but which, on the other, would mitigate the violence that currently flows from the monolithic, single-sex settings in which offenders are now confined. Furthermore, the same criteria that should underlay an effective diversionary or preventive program should underlay effective deinstitutionalization: some element of choice, guarantees, and the accountability of the service-giver to the client—in this case, the offender.

The Future of Juvenile Justice

It is hazardous to try to predict the future course of events in juvenile justice. Yet, on the basis of past events, one might expect a repetition of the cycles of the past hundred or more years. Public scandals and unrest, followed by calls for reform, followed by increased funding, followed by a reformed system, followed by scandals and unrest, followed by calls for reform, and so on. Although a case could be made for the idea that, as the cycle has turned over and over, a certain progressiveness has characterized the treatment of juveniles, it is doubtful that juvenile justice has done little more than lag along behind the larger society in reflecting the current life-styles, norms, and values, keeping up only to the degree that the basic dichotomy between insiders and outsiders is maintained and the solidarity of society sustained.

Although from a contemporary vantage point one might see a great difference between the whipping of a youngster in a reform school of the late 1880s and the cutting off of a youngster's hair in a training school of the early 1970s, the subjective experience may not be all that different. Even in those cases where there is clearly some advance in humanitarian handling of juvenile offenders, it lags behind the treatment of young people who are the offspring of society's priviledged groups, the insiders. For example, it is unlikely (but not impossible) that we will return to flogging of adolescents; yet the systems which we have substituted for flogging have maintained the basic labeling process, social prescriptions, and the patterns of isolation and rejection which follow therefrom.

Robert Theobald once commented that what we need these days for understanding the future is not so much a map as a compass. The problem with this analogy, true as it is, is that in the juvenile justice system our preconceived maps actually create the terrain that we then later explore. If we could drop our maps and set out sketching what we find, rather than what we have created, the future for juvenile justice might hold more promise.

What Will Happen

Having said this, let me venture what I think will happen and then distinguish it from what could or perhaps should happen. One can anticipate the introduction of new technologies into the juvenile justice system over the next few decades. One can further predict that those technologies will gain widespread acceptance and will be justified by one or more ideologies. Nonetheless, whether the rhetoric is "rehabilitation," "just desserts," or some other, the new technologies will lend themselves to more control in management: juvenile corrections will appear more humane and professional while being less incident-prone and chaotic, and the punishment-rehabilitation argument, being a sham issue, will probably become diluted as legal and therapeutic bureaucracies become more effective and clientele are made less obstreperous.

Their innovative character notwithstanding, the new systems of control will provide the same functions detention centers and training schools have always provided—though they will be harder to recognize. In addition, one can also anticipate growing professionalism in the field that will further fix-in the system. It will include interesting approaches and models for the "deserving" offenders—the general rule of thumb being that the more the offender looks like, talks like, and acts like a judge's or legislator's son or daughter, the more likely he or she will be to receive help from the more progressive models of professional care. Meanwhile, as the determinate sentences of the "justice model" replace the indeterminate

sentence and become longer and more punitive, "just desserts" will become more and more the fate of the "undeserving" youngsters. Their isolation from the benefits of humane
and decent programs will become even greater.

What all of this suggests is that the child-saver revolution
of the early 1900s and the rethinking of these issues in the
current revolution are but two sides of the same coin. The
current revolution has picked up on those youngsters that
the child savers saw as their proper clientele. As the juvenile
court has lost credibility, another system has come into play
to deal with "deserving" delinquents, whereas the "undeserving" were always meant to be handled not as one would deal
with a threatening acquaintance but as a threatening stranger.
This pattern will likely continue. The only variation will be
associated with the greater use of due process for the "undeserving." Court adjudication will be followed either by acquit-
tal or imprisonment. But, in either event, "undeserving"
delinquents will be denied the understanding and help envisaged by the child savers and hopefully anticipated by Mead.

Meanwhile, our rhetoric will continue to bounce back and
forth between rehabilitation versus punishment and the bureaucracies and political constituencies which that dichotomy
engenders. Yet it is not likely that either the child saver or
the legal bureaucracy will ultimately win—at least not for
any sustained period of time. Indeed, the very existence of
these bureaucracies will itself restrict the parameters of the
debate and will make it difficult to break out of existing parameters. Mead (1961:882), put it another way:

But the two attitudes, that of control of crime by the hostile procedure of the law and that of control through comprehension of social
and psychological conditions, cannot be combined. To understand
is to fogive and the social procedure seems to deny the very responsibility which the law affirms, and on the other hand the pursuit by
criminal justice inevitably awakens the hostile attitude in the offender and renders the attitude of mutual comprehension practically
impossible. The social worker in the court is the sentimentalist, and
the legalist in the social settlement, in spite of his learned doctrine,
is the ignoramus.

That is the problem for the future.

Finally, the current idea that "nothing works" has in it the seeds of despair, what medieval theologians called the ultimate sin. For with the assertion that nothing works (probably a false assertion) we turn our backs on the possibility of helping another human being. The consequence is more tragedy than premise.

Giving up the rehabilitative model negates the hope (admittedly unrealized) of understanding (not excusing) deviant behavior. Perhaps because of the rigidities of professionalism, such understanding was not about to occur. Certainly recent approaches to criminal deviance based upon clinical practice would indicate that it is not presently occurring. Perhaps, therefore, we should deprofessionalize "help." Yet to do that would be to discard the hope that educated, intelligent persons can learn something from their clients, can give moral and intellectual meaning to that knowledge, and can carry it back to the larger society. But even then such hope is threatened by the popular abandonment of the rehabilitative ideal and the potential it bears for learning.

In summary, it does not seem unlikely that in 2078 a convention of correctional experts will be convened to determine why the ideals of correctional experts in 1978 were not realized. If they do, they will be repeating history. The American Correctional Association met in 1970 to determine why the enlightened principles of the Cincinnati Prison Congress of 1870 were not implemented. Indeed, had they been implemented, they would have already resulted in the dissolution of the correctional system as we know it.

What Should Be

With reference to what could or should be, let me set forth a few possibilities. The problem is not one of techniques or technology, not knowing what to do or how to do it. As the chapter by Professor Glaser in this book shows, certain approaches work with certain clientele and we know what they are. The research of Ohlin, Coates, and Miller (1978) shows clearly the directions that an effective and humane system of juvenile corrections should take. It should: (1) follow the principle of the least restrictive alternative consonant with public safety; (2) place stress upon family supports; (3) provide residential care in the most familylike setting possible; (4) see that group living situations should have strong community linkages; (5) make secure care a last resort (knowing that there is little evidence one can do more than provide a least harmful program); and (6) apply the definition of "dangerous" or "in need of care" only when all other avenues have been exhausted.

However, the problem of designing an effective and humane system for the future is more basic than the above. It is not a question of not knowing what to do or in which directions we must turn to provide humane and effective juvenile corrections. The problem is that, in taking those steps, we must impinge upon a network of political, professional, and bureaucratic relationships now so deeply imbedded as to make the very notion of basic change sound revolutionary—which, rationally, it need not be. To move toward an effective system, certain basic steps must be taken.

The most basic relates to the introduction of some elements of the democratic ideal into the juvenile correctional system. The problem is one of building some element of choice into a system designed for keepers and captives. It is a problem of accountability to clientele who have no power to demand such accountability. It is not whether one should become involved in more punishment or more treatment: shorter terms versus longer terms or discipline versus permissiveness. Variations on this theme have been with us as long as human memory. By the same token, it is not a question of specific types of helping or therapy—behavior modification versus transactional analysis, therapeutic communities versus psychoanalytic regimen, or institutional versus community-based programs. Variations on these themes have also been with us in one form or another for the last century and a half. Rather, any new possibilities in corrections will have to emerge from a close look at the bureaucracies that define and treat the outsiders. Unfortunately, present reforms do not consider this.

If one were to look for a model, it would approximate that proposed by Etzioni which, though applied in another context, has meaning in juvenile corrections. Speaking of an ideal of "authentic societal guidance," Etzioni (1968:619) says: "We refer to the combined sources of social regulation and change, the downward and the upward flows, as social *guidance,* while we reserve the term *social control* for downward flows and consensus formation for upward ones." It is precisely this reciprocity in authentic social guidance that is lacking in our juvenile correctional system. It suggests that we think the unthinkable—the possibility of de-escalating levels of social control and building in some elements of consumerism. In the introduction of authentic consumerism, there is hope for meaningful systems change.

From this it follows that there must be in the labeling and diagnostic process a potential for *authentic* listening whereby those who apply the labels develop a capacity for understanding more clearly the world the juvenile offender brings to the juvenile justice system. The categories of reference must be constantly readjusted by this experience. Whatever social prescriptions emerge from the labeling processes must themselves be subject to at least some elements of consumerism. The youngster must be able to influence the labeling categories and have some choice between and among prescribed courses of action. A wide variety of options and programs heightens the possibility of informed choice and diminishes the potential for rigidity and coercion. There must be built into this the potential for a least restrictive alternative and for movement into more restrictive alternatives only on a staged basis—with due process entering as freedom diminishes.

But even those at the deepest end—those who have committed the most heinous crimes—must be (1) understood, and (2) given some element of choice in their treatment. There is no reason, for example, if a decision is made that a person who has committed a violent crime cannot be free for a given period, that that person could not have some choice over the conditions under which his or her freedom will be denied. Further, there should be the possibility for movement between and among alternative settings (even secure settings) based upon the perceptions of the client rather than the service-giver. Those programs and facilities that can guarantee public safety and still be the choice of dangerous offenders (admittedly a choice among lesser evils) should be sustained. Those facilities and programs that cannot should be closed. It is not a question of permissiveness versus control but rather one of making our correctional bureaucracies in some way accountable. Even Phillips-Exeter Academy, given a solely captive population of students, would deteriorate over time. The best of educators, therapists, or administrators will not sustain their altruism without some means of accountability to clientele being in the structure.

In whatever correctional system might evolve in the future, there should be an understanding that certain problems must remain insoluble, for their very solution invites tragedy. The category, for example, of the "most dangerous" offender must remain a negotiable one, open to constant reconsideration. This is not to say that such offenders do not exist but to point out that they represent, as well, the quintessential outsider. They are, thereby, those individuals upon which bureaucratic and political careers can be made through mistreatment, neglect, and scapegoating. Juvenile offenders who fall into this category are the keystone of the juvenile justice system. They must be treated deftly. This sad group carries the potential of telling us more about our society and ourselves than of themselves. They also provide the only legitimate test of our labeling and treatment systems.

Finally, none of this can happen until there is a wide variety of alternative resources available. With growing awareness of how limited our resources are, we are not likely to sustain many new approaches until we can reallocate existing resources. This means taking money from where it is—primarily in institutions—and giving it to new approaches and programs. That, in turn, means the termination of certain existing bureaucracies. And this, of course, is the major barrier to any substantive change. Anyone who would attempt such changes could aptly be described as foolhardy. But there is a time for fools. Send in the clowns.

References

Arendt, Hannah
    1970   On Violence. New York: Harcourt Brace.

Beaumont, Gustave de and Tocqueville, Alexis de
    1964   On the Penitentiary System in the United States and Its Application in France. Carbondale: Southern Illinois Univ. Press (1833).

Breckenridge, Sophonisba P.
    1927   Public Welfare Administration in the United States: Select Documents. Chicago: Univ. of Chicago Press.

Brizius, Jack
    1976   "Rates of institutionalization in U.S., 1900–1970." Unpublished paper, Chief Planner, National Governors' Assn., Washington, D.C.

California Youth Authority
    1975   Hidden Closets. Sacramento: California Youth Authority.

Chapman, Denis
    1968   Sociology and the Sterotype of the Criminal. London: Tavistock.

Coates, Robert B., Alden D. Miller, and Lloyd E. Ohlin
    1978   Diversity in a Youth Correctional System: Handling Delinquents in Massachusetts. Cambridge: Ballinger.

Cook County Civil Service Commission
    1917   Report on Investigation of Juvenile Detention Home. Chicago: Clohesy & Co.

Cortes, Juan B.
    1972   Delinquency and Crime: A Biophysical Approach. New York: Seminar Press.

Durkheim, Emile
    1964   The Rules of Sociological Method. Glencoe, Ill.: Free Press.

Ellis, Havelock
      1903   The Criminal. New York: Charles Scribner.

Etzioni, Amitai
      1968   The Active Society. New York: Free Press.

Gemignani, Robert J.
      1973   "Diversion of juvenile offenders from the juvenile jus-
                tice system." In New Approaches To Diversion and
                Treatment of Juvenile Offenders. Washington, D.C.:
                U.S. Dept of Justice, LEAA (June 1973).

Howard, D. L.
      1960   The English Prisons. London: Methuen.

In Re Gault
      1967   387 U.S. 1, 18 L.Ed. 2d 527, 87 S.Ct. 1428.

Institutions, Etc.
      1978   I. E., Investigative Newsletter on Institutions 1:8. Wash-
                ington, D.C.: National Center for Action on Institutions
                and Alternatives.

Jay, Peter
      1977   Report of NACRO Working Party: Children and Young
                Persons in Custody. Peter Jay, Chairman. Chichester
                & London: Barry Rose.

Kent v. *U.S.*
      1966   383 U.S. 541, 16 L.Ed. 2d 84, 86 S.Ct. 1045.

Laing, Ronald D.
      1968a   The Politics of Experience. Middlesex, England: Pen-
                guin Press.

      1968b   "The obvious," *In* D. Cooper (ed.), To Free a Genera-
                tion. New York: Macmillan.

Leach, Edmund
      1967   A Runaway World: The BBC Reith Lectures. London:
                BBC.

Lundman, Richard J., and Frank R. Scarpitti
      1978   "Delinquency prevention: recommendations for future
                projects." Crime and Delinquency (April 1978).

Martinson, Robert
   1974   "What works? questions and answers about prison re-
            form." The Public Interest (Spring 1974).

Mead, George H.
   1961   "The psychology of punitive justice." Pp. 876–86 *in*
            Talcott Parsons (ed.), Theories of Society, Vol. II. Glen-
            coe, Ill.: Free Press.

Merton, Robert K.
   1957   Social Theory and Social Structure. Glencoe, Ill.: Free
            Press.

Miller, Alden D., Lloyd E. Ohlin, and Robert B. Coates
   1978   A Theory of Social Reform: Correctional Change Pro-
            cesses in Two States. Cambridge: Ballinger.

Nagel, William
   1977   The Case for a Moratorium on Prison Construction.
            Washington, D.C.: National Moratorium on Prison Con-
            struction.

Nejelski, Paul
   1973   "Diversion of juvenile offenders in the criminal justice
            system," *In* New Approaches to Diversion and Treat-
            ment of Juvenile Offenders. Washington, D.C.: U.S.
            Dept of Justice, LEAA (June 1973).

   1976   "Diversion: unleashing the hound of heaven?" *In* Mar-
            garet K. Rosenheim (ed.), Pursuing Justice for the Child.
            Chicago: Univ. of Chicago Press.

Office of Children and Youth
   1977   Study of Juveniles in Detention and County Jails in
            Pennsylvania. Harrisburg, Pa.: Office of Children and
            Youth.

Ohlin, Lloyd E., Robert B. Coates, and Alden D. Miller
   1978   Reforming Juvenile Corrections: The Massachusetts Ex-
            perience. Cambridge: Ballinger.

Platt, Anthony M.
   1969   The Child Savers: The Invention of Delinquency. Chi-
            cago: Univ. of Chicago Press.

Plattner, Marc F.
1975   "The rehabilitation of punishment." The Public Interest 44.

Pound, Roscoe
1950   Address to annual meeting of the National Council of Juvenile Court Judges.

President's Commission on Law Enforcement and Administration of Justice
1967   The Challenge of Crime in a Free Society. Washington, D.C.: U.S. Government Printing Office.

Ranulf, Svend
1964   Moral Indignation and Middle-class Psychology. New York: Schocken.

Rothman, David J.
1978   "The state as parent." *In* Doing Good: The Limits of Benevolence. New York: Pantheon Press.

Rush, Francis M., Jr.
1978   "Social and historical factors in the development of total institutions: their relevance for the discipline of public administration." Unpublished manuscript.

Sarri, Rosemary C., and Robert D. Vinter
1975   National Assessment of Juvenile Corrections. Ann Arbor: Univ. of Michigan.

Twentieth Century Fund
1978   Confronting Youth Crime: Report of Twentieth Century Fund Task Force on Sentencing Policy toward Young Offenders. New York: Holmes & Meier.

van den Haag, Ernest
1975   Punishing Criminals. New York: Basic Books.

Vinter, Robert D. (ed.)
1976   Time Out: A National Study of Juvenile Correctional Programs. Ann Arbor: National Assessment of Juvenile Corrections, University of Michigan.

Vinter, Robert D., George Downs, and John Hall

1975   Juvenile Corrections in the States: Residential Programs and Deinstitutionalization. Ann Arbor: National Assessment of Juvenile Corrections, Univ. of Michigan (November 1975).

Vinter, Robert D., and Rosemary C. Sarri

1975   National Assessment of Juvenile Corrections, Ann Arbor: Univ. of Michigan.

Von Hirsch, Andrew

1976   Doing Justice. New York: Hill & Wang.

Willard, D. W.

1925   "Form, function, and objectives." *In* Howard W. Odum and D. W. Willard, Systems of Public Welfare. Chapel Hill: Univ. of North Carolina Press.

Wilson, James Q.

1975   Thinking about Crime. New York: Basic Books.

Wines, Frederick H.

1910   Punishment and Reformation: A Study of the Penitentiary System. New York: Thomas Crowell.

Demographic Changes and the Future of Childhood

Kingsley Davis

THE agencies and mechanisms that govern juvenile behavior are much the same as those that govern adult behavior. The agencies are primarily the nuclear family, the relatives beyond the nuclear family, the local neighborhood, and the organs, private and public, of the local community and the state. The principal mechanisms by which these agencies exercise control are three: first, the expression of opinion (an individual wants to be approved and hates to be ostracized or downgraded); second, personal cooperation or retaliation (if I fail to meet the expectations of others, they will not meet mine either); and third, formal rewards and punishments. Necessarily, these channels of social control work best when they work together. For instance, formal rewards and penalties, which govern behavior when the ordinary channels of everyday control cannot do so, are most effective when they reinforce rather than replace or oppose the other controls.

Any special difficulty with adolescent behavior arises from the fact that adolescents are expected to shift in a short period from childhood dependency to adult independence. They thus must reduce the authority of those on whom they have depended during childhood. This is not difficult with respect to authority figures (teachers, coaches, dentists) who function only temporarily, but it is delicate with respect to parents. The parent-child relation is expected not only to endure but to move from complete dependence to complete independence. Once a face-to-face relationship of authority has lasted for a long time, however, it is difficult for the subordinate party to shake his subordination. Also, it is difficult for a person to emancipate someone voluntarily over whom he has long exercised authority.

In industrial societies, the problem of erasing parental authority is mitigated by the child's leaving home to attend college, take a job, or get married; but this usually does not occur early enough to avoid potential conflict. While the child is still at home, strife is most likely to be avoided if the other agencies of the community are all operating effectively to reinforce the norms with respect to adolescent behavior. If the relatives, friends, and neighbors all know the adolescent and his parents, encourage restraint on both sides, and help maintain surveillance outside the home, the parent-child devolution of authority may run smoothly. If, however, conditions are such that the nuclear family is isolated and unsupported, the conflict inherent in the relationship will tend to materialize.

In the present chapter I shall maintain that the demographic changes occurring in industrial societies have in some ways facilitated and in other ways complicated the social control of adolescent behavior. In general, the more purely demographic the change, the more favorable it appears to be, but this effect has tended to be canceled or distorted by developments of a sociological origin. To see this, let us begin with the most fundamental aspect of the demographic revolution— the gain in longevity.

The Gift of Life

Before the Industrial Revolution, average life expectancy was only about 30 years. A child born when his mother was 25 and his father 30 had only about 57 percent chance of enjoying the company of both of them when he reached the age of 15.[1] Today, by contrast, when average life expectancy for whites in the United States has reached 73.5 years, the chances

[1] The preindustrial probability is for Costa Rica in 1892 (see Arriaga, 1968:86–87). The 1976 U.S. probability is calculated from National Center for Health Statistics (1978a).

are 95.1 percent that an adolescent will have parents who are still alive (National Center for Health Statistics, 1978a). There is relatively little chance that he will be orphaned by either parent. Hence, to the degree that living parents are important in controlling and directing the lives of their children, the child's transition to adulthood should be enhanced and the incidence of maladaptive behavior reduced.

Family Disorganization

The potentially stabilizing influence wrought by this increase in life expectancy, however, has been nullified by social and cultural changes of a striking nature. Consider, for example, recent rises in illegitimacy and in the voluntary dissolution of marriages.

The rate of divorce and separation in the United States rose from 6.1 per thousand existing marriages in 1933 to 21.1 per thousand in 1978. As a result of this threefold increase, the chances are only between 50 and 60 percent that an adolescent will still be living with his parents at age 15.[2] In short, while U.S. divorce statistics make precise estimation difficult, they do suggest that the likelihood that an American child will remain with both parents throughout childhood has reduced to about the same level that it was in the preindustrial era.

The contemporary departure from the traditional nuclear family is also being accelerated by increases in illegitimacy and single parenthood. While this rise is poorly documented

[2] Assuming that a child of 15 was conceived after two years of marriage and that the divorce rate of 1978—approximately 26 divorces per year per 1,000 married women aged 14–44—was to continue steadily, the probability that the parents would still be married at the end of the child's fifteenth year is only 51.5 percent. This estimate, however, does not take into account any deterrent effect that children may have on divorce. Also, it assumes that the divorce rate of 1978 will neither fall nor rise. For analyses of changes in the divorce rate and in the probability of a marriage ending in divorce, see Glick and Norton, 1973; McCarthy, 1978; and Preston and McDonald, 1976.

in American statistics, available evidence suggests that it has been spectacular. In 1976 some 14.8 percent of all births in the United States were illegitimate. Among whites the figure was 7.7 percent, and among blacks 50.3 percent (National Center for Health Statistics, 1978b:17). Between 1974 and 1976 the ratio of illegitimate to legitimate births rose 314 percent for the total population, 315 percent for the white population, and 169 percent for the nonwhite population.

When these spectacular increases are combined with the rising divorce rate, we can understand the rapid rise in the number of children living with one or two stepparents or in single-parent families. Existing data do not provide a precise knowledge of stepparent cases, but surveys of marital status and living arrangements by the Census Bureau (1970, 1978) permit estimates of those with one or two parents. These estimates for adolescents aged 14–17 are shown in Table 1.

Table 1. Living arrangements of children 14–17 by race, 1969 and 1977

| | Percentage of children 14–17 | | |
Date and living arrangement	All races	White	Black
1969			
With both parents	82.1	86.1	56.3
With mother only	11.8	9.1	30.3
With father only	1.8	1.4	3.1
With neither parent	2.7	2.0	7.7
Not in families	1.6	1.4	2.6
Total	100.0	100.0	100.0
1977			
With both parents	77.3	82.2	48.3
With mother only	16.7	12.8	40.0
With father only	2.5	2.5	2.7
With neither parent	2.6	1.6	8.1
Not in families	0.9	0.8	0.9
Total	100.0	100.0	100.0

SOURCES: Bureau of the Census, "Marital Status and Family Status: March 1969," *Current Population Reports,* Series P-20, No. 198 (March 25, 1970):21; "Marital Status and Living Arrangements: March 1977," Ibid., No. 323 (April 1978):26.

In only eight years the number of teenagers living with both parents dropped from about 82 percent in 1969 to about 77 percent in 1977. The decrease for blacks, however, was greater than that for whites. Indeed, by 1977, less than half of all 14- to 17-year-old black adolescents (48.3 percent) were living with two parents. It should be noted as well that these figures may slightly overestimate the number of adolescents living with two parents, particularly with their own genitors, since the information provided by the Census Bureau for 1977 did not account for the living arrangements of institutionalized populations, itinerants, and vagrants and since it included children who were living with stepparents as well as with blood parents.

No one knows whether, or to what degree, the trend revealed in Table 1 will continue. Nonetheless, there is evidence that it will continue for some time. By way of documenting this conclusion, we can compare the living arrangements for children under the age of 5 in 1977 with those for the same age group in 1969. They are shown in Table 2.

The number of young children in the entire population

Table 2. Living arrangements of children 0–4 by race, 1969 and 1977

Date and living arrangement	Percentage of children 0–4		
	All races	White	Black
1969			
With both parents	86.6	91.6	59.3
With mother only	9.8	6.6	26.9
With father only	0.5	0.5	0.9
With no parent	3.1	1.3	12.9
Total	100.0	100.0	100.0
1977			
With both parents	80.7	87.3	43.5
With mother only	14.7	10.1	40.8
With father only	0.7	0.7	0.9
With no parent	3.9	1.9	14.8
Total	100.0	100.0	100.0

SOURCES: Same as Table 1.

not living with both parents increased from 13.4 percent in 1969 to 19.3 percent in 1977. Although this increase is noteworthy in its own right, it is dwarfed by differences between the races. Whereas the number of white children who were not living with both parents increased from 8.4 percent in 1969 to 12.7 percent in 1977, the number of black children in similar circumstances increased from 20.7 percent to 56.5 percent. In short, well over half of the latter group were not living with two parents.

Finally, the data in Tables 1 and 2 reveal some striking findings when changes in the living arrangements of young children aged 0–4 are compared with those of adolescents aged 14–17. One would anticipate that infants and young children, because of their age, would be more likely than adolescents to be living in two-parent families. Tables 1 and 2 show that, in general, such still continues to be the case; that is, when all young children, black and white, are lumped together, a greater proportion of them, in both 1969 and 1977, were living with both parents than were adolescents. However, when distinctions between the races are drawn and when the current trend toward single parenthood is taken into account, the picture changes markedly.

First, in 1977 the proportion of white children aged 0–4 separated from one or both parents (12.7 percent) was almost as large as the proportion among adolescents 14–17 in 1969 (13.7 percent). Such evidence suggests that the trend toward single parenthood has accelerated in recent years and that, by the time the 1977 cohort of children reaches adolescence, the incidence of broken families for them will be much higher. Secondly, the trends for young black children are even more striking. Not only were more of them living apart from two-parent families in 1977 (56.5 percent) than were black adolescents in 1969 (43.7 percent), but it was they, and not adolescents, who experienced the higher incidence of broken homes in 1977 (56.5 percent for children 0–4 vs. 51.7 percent for adolescents 14–17). In short, contemporary trends toward single parenthood are even more marked in the black than in the white community.

Table 3 elaborates further on this difference and again sug-

Table 3. Percentage change between 1969 and 1977 in proportion of children in different living conditions

| Living arrangements | Percent change, 1969–1977 | | | | | |
| | Children all races | | White children | | Black children | |
	0–4	14–17	0–4	14–17	0–4	14–17
With both parents	−6.8	−5.8	−4.7	−4.5	−26.7	−14.2
With mother only	+50.9	+41.2	+52.7	+41.3	+51.7	+32.1
With father only	+27.8	+42.6	+42.6	+72.7	+4.6	−11.9
With neither parent	+30.7	−4.0	+69.0	−16.2	+16.8	+5.5
Not in families	+3.4	−45.3	+4.7	−42.1	−5.3	−67.2

SOURCES: Same as Table 1.

gests that, unless some unanticipated but remarkable change occurs to alter the trend of the past few years, we can expect a substantial increase in the number of adolescents in single-parent families during the next decade.

Some notion of the magnitude of this increase can be determined by extrapolating the trends observed in Tables 2 and 3. This can be done in two different ways. We can either extrapolate the trend for 14- to 17-year-olds between 1969 and 1977 (Method 1) or we can first extrapolate the change for 0–4 year olds for the same period and then apply the average ratio between this group and the 14- to 17-year-olds to get an estimate for the adolescents of the future (Method 2). The results of this exercise are shown in Table 4.

Table 4. Current and projected percentage of children 14–17 not living with both parents

Year	Percentage of children 14–17		
	All races	White	Black
1969	17.9	13.9	43.7
1977	22.7	17.8	51.7
1985 Projected			
Method 1	27.1	21.5	58.5
Method 2	28.4	21.7	70.6

It will be observed that the two methods yield similar results except for the black population; that is, while both methods suggest that in 1985 approximately one-fifth of all white adolescents will *not* be living with two parents, Method 1 suggests that the figure for blacks will be 58.5 percent, while the second suggests that it may be as high as 7 out of 10. Although it is startling, this latter figure cannot be ignored because it stems from the rapid rise between 1969 and 1977 of young black children who were being reared in single-parent families. The proportion of black children aged 0–4 lacking at least one parent jumped from 40.7 percent in 1969 to 56.6 percent in 1977 (Table 2).

The social and political implications of this change are

considerable because almost all of the increase in the black community between 1969 and 1977 was absorbed by female-headed families, while such was not true in the white community (Table 3). Not only did white fathers assume a larger share of the increase (42.6 per cent vs. 52.7 for mothers), but the numbers of children involved were proportionately smaller. Thus, it seems quite clear that the rapid rise in the illegitimacy ratio among black births is having the effect of putting an even higher percentage of young black children than in the past into families headed by mothers. In 8 or 10 years there is likely to be a much higher percentage of black adolescents in mother-headed households.

Further confirmation for this conclusion is provided in Table 5. It shows the actual rise in the ratio of female-headed to two-parent families between 1969 and 1977 and projects figures for 1985. Again, the startling increase in female-headed households in both black and white populations is documented, but while the black population did not increase its ratio much faster than whites between 1969 and 1977, it started from such a large base that its absolute increase was much greater. Indeed, if current trends continue, the ratio of female-headed black households per 100 two-parent families may reach as high as 117.9 in 1985 vs. 19.1 for whites.

The implications of these trends for children, particularly

Table 5. Past and projected increases in the ratio of female-headed to two-parent families

| | Female-headed families per 100 two-parent families (Females 14–44 years of age) | | | Percent change in ratio |
| | Actual | | Projected | Years |
	1969	1977	1985	1969 to 1977
All races	9.7	18.1	33.8	87.0
White	6.9	11.5	19.1	66.3
Black	42.0	70.4	117.9	67.5
"Spanish"	NA	23.7	NA	NA

those who are black, are nothing short of profound. Without attempting to speculate on the eventual long-run consequences of changes in the structure of American families, one sees that in the short run the results will be often disruptive and traumatizing. History clearly teaches that, during periods of rapid change, when the socializing influences of traditional structures are diminished and when newer structures have not yet replaced them, the incidences of lawbreaking, of suicide, of escape through drugs, and of other such signs of personal disorganization can be expected to increase. Indeed, current concerns over the inabilities of schools to educate, of the justice system to control youth crime, or of neighborhoods and communities to exercise effective informal controls are thrown into new light when these figures are considered. For well over two hundred years, with the dwindling influence of extended kin and neighbors, industrial society has placed increasing reliance upon the nuclear family as the foundation for the next generation, as the device through which young people can be prepared to assume adult roles. In light of the progressive destruction of that unit in recent years, current bewilderment over the behavior of the young is scarcely surprising. Increasing numbers of them have been socialized in a context for which tradition provides little direction and control.

If these conclusions are at all valid for white children, they are doubly so for those who are black. Not only have the latter been hampered in their attempts to succeed by a family structure that relied heavily upon female-headed households, but the signs are that, instead of diminishing, that model has been expanding. Were the females who head young families today mature women, were they well-educated and economically self-sufficient, recent trends might foster less concern. But they are not. Instead, it has been the younger, least-educated, and poorest segment of the black female population that has tended increasingly to become the heads of households. If the black family was disorganized when Patrick Moynihan (1965) wrote about it a few years ago, it is even more disorganized now.

The Birthrate, Siblings, and the Age Structure

If many of the favorable effects of the mortality revolution have been canceled by sociological changes, what about the effects of that other demographic phenomenon, the decline in the birthrate? To answer that question, one must realize that the trend in the birthrate has not been steady, like that in the death rate, but has fluctuated wildly. For this reason two quite different demographic effects of birthrate changes have a bearing on juvenile behavior. One of these—the production of unprecedented alterations in the age structure—is due to temporary fluctuations in the birthrate. The other, due to the overall long-run decline in the birthrate, is the reduction in the average number of siblings each adolescent has. I shall consider both of these effects, but first let us examine the fertility trend more closely.

Fluctuations in the Birthrate

If we start just before World War I and record the peaks and troughs in fertility, we get the results shown in Table 6. It can be seen that there has been a cycle in which the fertility rate fell by half in roughly twenty years and then recovered

Table 6. Peaks and troughs in U.S. fertility, 1914–1976

	Births per 1,000 women 15–44 years of age			
Date	Total	Whites	Nonwhite	Black
1914	126.6	124.6	NA	NA
1936	75.8	73.3	95.9	NA
1957	122.7	117.6	161.7	NA
1976	65.8	62.2	87.6	87.2

SOURCE: National Center for Health Statistics, *Vital Statistics for the U.S., 1974,* Vol. 1, "Natality," pp. 1–6; and "Final Natality Statistics 1976," *Monthly Vital Statistics Report,* Vol. 26, No. 12 Supplement (March 29, 1978), p. 8.

in approximately twenty more. Such gyration in fertility is unprecedented. Before the Great Depression the history of the fertility rate was one of rather steady decline, setting in just after the middle of the nineteenth century. At the end of this decline, however, during the depression and at the present time, the reproductivity of women in industrial countries became so low that, if it had continued, it would eventually have failed to replace the population. That also is without precedent for national populations.

Low Fertility and Lack of Siblings

From a theoretical standpoint, the low fertility generally characterizing industrial nations during the present century should, other things equal, have aided parents in socializing their young and in decreasing the incidence of deviant behavior. With fewer children to train and to supervise, parents would have more time and energy to devote to the child's development. Indeed, a continued reduction in the birthrate inevitably produces an increase in the number of one-child families. As yet we do not know the consequences of such a trend, whether it gives rise to egocentrism and lack of constraint or to greater responsibility, nor do we know whether supervision by an increasing number of mother-surrogates will decrease or increase the effectiveness of the socialization process. Whatever the eventual outcome, the trends of the past decade favor a reduction in family size.

In 1965, in the United States, the mean number of children per family was 1.44; by 1978 this figure was down to 1.10 (Bureau of the Census, 1978:3–5). However, since these averages include families with no children at all, it is important to recognize that, in those families which did have children, the average number in 1978 was 1.96. Yet families with multiple children have been on the decline. There are as a result more families today with an only child than with any other number. The following figures show the shift between 1965 and 1978 (Bureau of the Census, 1966:15 and 1978:3–5).

	Percentage of all families with own children under 18	
	1965	*1978*
With one child	31.2	38.2
With two children	29.6	35.8
With three or more	39.1	26.0

A further factor with respect to these trends, as noted already, is the increasing proportion of single-parent families. Indeed, the increase in such families has contributed to the very low fertility of the present time, because it is very hard to rear even one child alone, much less two; hence, in one-parent families the proportion with only one child is particularly great. In 1978, for example, the distribution was as follows (Bureau of the Census, 1978:3–5).

	Percentage of all single-parent families with own children under 18
With one child	44.4
With two children	30.2
With three children	25.4

It was suggested earlier that, insofar as single parenthood is gaining ground, it may be lessening the improvement in child development that low fertility makes possible. The shift from a two-parent to a one-parent family means a 50 percent reduction in supervisory personnel. The decline in fertility does not compensate for that kind of reduction in parents. Apart from the structure of the family, changing fertility affects the age structure of the entire population and thus the situation of children.

Low Fertility and the Age Structure

Changes in fertility exercise more influence than changes in mortality on the age structure, because fertility feeds people into the population only at age zero, whereas mortality removes them at all ages. Accordingly, two features of the age structure in modern times can be traced to antecedent fertility changes. These are, first, the general aging of the population, which derives from the long-run secular decline in fertility, and, second, the changing ratio of one cohort to another in size, which derives from the gyrations in the birthrate since World War I. I shall now discuss each of these influences with respect to their possible effect on juvenile behavior.

How an aging population affects youth. In 1890 only 4.0 percent of the American population were over 65. Today the figure is 10.9 percent. In the most probable projection of the Census Bureau, the proportion rises in the year 2000 to 12.2 percent. Simultaneously, the proportion of young people aged 15–19 has been generally shrinking. It was 10.5 percent in 1890, is 9.8 percent today, and will be, according to the Census Bureau's Series II projection, 7.8 percent in the year 2000.

The significance of this trend for our subject lies in the fact that, in effect, the young and the old have become competitors for largesse from the rest of society. This competitiveness has grown sharper as time has gone on because both age groups have increasingly withdrawn from productive work— the elderly through more frequent and earlier retirement and adolescents through greater attendance at school and greater unemployment. The result is that both are now mainly classifiable as dependent populations, and they are both more costly than other dependent age groups, such as infants or young children.

In the struggle for largesse, the young have advantages as well as disadvantages. Generally they have parents who can fend for them, whereas the old do not; they have youth and vigor, whereas the old lack these. They have much to look forward to, and the society has an interest in them, whereas the old are on their way out. On the other hand, the old have experience and better command of means. They occupy high political offices and command public as well as private funds. Above all, they have leisure. They can, therefore, lobby for their own interests, whereas this is difficult for teenagers.

On net balance, it looks as though the battle will go to the elderly, especially since they now outnumber youth.

Exactly what this evolving and gradually more uneven contest will do to juvenile behavior is hard to say, for the condition is essentially new. For most of human history the young and the old both worked insofar as they were able; hence they did not compete in large numbers as dependents. In modern industrial nations, by contrast, their competition is increasingly severe in the sense that at both ends of the age scale the labor force is shrinking. The person engaged in productive work, therefore, has an increasing burden of dependents, and as the per capita demands of these dependents rise, the burden in the form of taxation becomes ever heavier. The productive worker finds it impossible to reduce the burden of the elderly, for they are taken care of through the impersonal agency of the state and retirement schemes. He can, however, do something to alleviate the burden of young-age dependents: he can simply reduce the number of his offspring, and that is precisely what he has done.

It would be surprising if these few offspring, when approaching adulthood, did not find the outlook discouraging. They face a crowded world in which resources are diminishing in relation to the rapidly expanding human population, in which they must bear a heavy burden of old-age dependency at home and of young-age dependency abroad, in which they believe (erroneously, to some extent) that jobs are scarce and the age-differential in pay is too large because the older workers protect themselves, and in which, finally, they feel that housing and recreational facilities are scarce because the elderly retirees as well as the older workers place heavy demands on these.

Thus it seems that in the competitive struggle the young are caught in a dilemma. On the one hand, in the backs of their minds they firmly hold to the myth that there are only so many jobs and that consequently their advantage lies in having older persons retire as early as possible. On the other hand, the more the elderly withdraw from productive activity, the greater is the tax burden placed on the young worker.

As a consequence, the young feel doubly disadvantaged, although half of their complaint rests on a fallacy.

The problem is not that the old hang onto their jobs too long, but the opposite: they withdraw too early from productive labor. Were they to stay longer, their dependence would decrease. A major deterrent, however, is the fact that many older workers are paid too well. If these workers were working and getting paid in proportion to their talents, rather than to their seniority, their rising numbers would be less of a problem. But, in truth, many employers are glad to have the elderly retire because the principle of seniority has pushed the salaries of elderly workers well above the cost of employing workers who are younger.

Whatever the motives, the decline in the employment of the elderly has been spectacular. In 1951, 44.9 percent of all males aged 65 and over were in the labor force; by 1976 the number was only 19.4 percent. As the aged have become more numerous, therefore, fewer of them have remained in the labor force (Bureau of the Census, 1975:15 and 1977a:387).

Paradoxically, this decrease has not been accompanied by a compensatory increase in the employment of the young. First, consider the status of young males age 16–19. Their participation in the labor force declined from 67.9 percent in 1951 to 60.3 percent in 1976 (Bureau of the Census, 1975; 1977a). Furthermore, it should be remembered that being "in the labor force" does not mean that the person is actually employed because the concept includes "looking for work." For the young in particular the rate of unemployment is high. In 1976, for example, 19.2 percent of all males aged 16–19 who were in the labor force were unemployed. Furthermore, because many others in this age group were not in the labor force (48.7 percent), but were still dependent upon others for support, less than half of the total age group (48.7 percent) were actually working.

The only thing that has kept the total American labor force from falling is the ever greater entry of women into paid work (Table 7). As the employment of males has decreased, the employment of females has accelerated. This trend, how-

Table 7. U.S. labor force and unemployment, 1951–1976

| Date | Percent in labor force | | | | Percent labor force unemployed | | |
| | Population aged 16+ | | Population aged 16–19 | | | Aged 16–19 | |
	Males	Females	Males	Females	Total	Males	Females
1951	87.3	34.7	67.9	42.5	8.2	NA	NA
1960	84.0	37.8	59.4	39.4	14.7	NA	NA
1970	80.6	43.4	58.4	44.0	15.2	NA	NA
1976	78.1	47.4	60.3	49.8	NA	19.2	18.7

SOURCE: Bureau of the Census, *Historical Statistics of the United States, Colonial Times to 1970* (Washington: Government Printing Office, 1975), p. 131; Statistical Abstract of the United States 1977, p. 387.

ever, is not a pure gain. In the first place, it cannot be assumed that women are now productive but were previously unproductive. They were working in the home and caring for children, and the money earned by their husbands constituted their "pay." Their transfer to workplaces outside the home, therefore, has not been a clear advantage for the productive side of the economy. Secondly, and equally significant, is the fact the growing employment of adult women has placed them in direct competition with the young for a place in the world of work, and at the very time when advocates of the Child Rights Movement are calling for the right of the young to be employed. Indeed, Carter and Glick (1976:424) point out that virtually all of the increase in female employment in recent years has occurred among married women, not among single teenagers. Hence, among young women, 16–19, as well as among young men, unemployment rates are high—18.7 percent in 1976 for those who were in the labor force (Table 7).

The potential for youth unrest produced by this state of affairs is great. Ordinarily, if young people are not at work and are not looking for work, they are in school. But if they cannot find work and are not in school, they are at loose ends. In the future, therefore, few things seem so important as the reduction of the sizable percentage who are idle. Although some of the difficulties inherent in trying to accomplish this have been highlighted, the class struggle between old and young is one in which demographic changes, institutional rigidities, and popular myths are intertwined in a complicated, poorly comprehended, and never ending tragedy. Hence, when there is frustration without comprehension, the resulting behavior is apt to seize the wrong targets and to be self-destructive. This is particularly true when the persons involved are vigorous but immature. Indeed, given the relative powerlessness of the young, we can begin to understand the raging youth revolt of the 1960s and early 1970s. But with the analysis so far made, we cannot say why it erupted at the particular time it did or why it died down. To understand this, we have to move from consideration of the long-run aging

of the population to another facet of change in the age structure—namely, the distortion in the size of cohorts due to prior
fluctuations in the birthrate.

Cohort size and juvenile conduct. Each generation, each cohort of people born at roughly the same time, bears throughout life the marks of the special conditions affecting it. Among
these conditions are the sheer size of the cohort relative to
earlier and later ones and the socioeconomic circumstances
prevailing during the cohort's formative years. For much of
recorded history, societies did not change rapidly enough to
create great differences between the circumstances of one
cohort and the next, but this is not true of industrial societies.
Ordinarily, too, the main difference between the size of one
cohort and the next is simply a reflection of the rate of population growth, but again this is not true of industrial countries.
Social and demographic changes nowadays create pronounced
differences between successive cohorts.

By way of example, consider the cohorts most relevant to
this discussion. Those Americans who were born during the
period from 1905 to 1920 were adolescents or young adults
during the Great Depression of the 1930s. They had insecurity,
hard work, and thrift stamped into them. Although they were
fairly numerous themselves (for birthrates were substantial
1905–20), they had few children, producing the lowest birthrates that had been known up until that time. As a result,
the low fertility of the depression years was to have a marked
impact on the subsequent age structure of American society.

Between 1940 and 1955 the total population of the United
States increased by 25 percent; yet, because of low birthrates
during the depression, the youth population actually *declined*
by 9.7 percent. By contrast, the population aged 35–54 gained
22.9 percent, a growth that was almost as fast as the growth
of the total population. As a consequence, there were far more
middle-aged adults to supervise the young at about mid-cen-
tury. In fact, there were 3.7 of them per youth in 1955, whereas
in 1940 there had been only 2.7 (see Table 8).

Table 8. The youthful population in relation to the adults who look after them, United States, 1940–2000

Date	Population (thousands)		Percent increase in prior period		Ratio: 35–54 ÷ 15–19
	Aged 15–19	Aged 35–54	Aged 15–19	Aged 35–54	
1940	24,032	33,946	—	—	2.74
1955	21,966	41,736	−8.6	22.9	3.73
1975	40,244	46,584	83.2	11.6	2.22
1990	34,730	61,903	−13.7	32.9	3.69
2000	36,625	77,219	5.5	24.7	3.91

SOURCE: 1940 from *Statistical Abstract of U.S. 1963*, p. 26; 1950–1955 from Bureau of the Census, *Current Population Reports*, Series P-25, No. 146 (November 12, 1956); 1970–1977 from Ibid., No. 721 (April 1978); 1990–2000 from Ibid., No. 704 (July 1977), pp. 50, 60.

After 1955 the situation reversed itself. The prolonged baby boom, lasting approximately from 1946 to 1960, gave rise to a rapid expansion of the youthful population, while the older cohorts, born during the low birthrate period of 1928–45, were either shrinking or hardly growing. Between 1955 and 1970, for example, the population aged 15–19 jumped by 72.6 percent, while the adult population aged 35–54 increased by only 11.3 percent. The ratio of middle-aged adults to each youth therefore dropped from 3.7 to 2.4.

It is hard to observe these statistics without concluding that the explosion of the teenage population had something to do with the youthful revolt of the 1960s and 1970s and the rapid rise in crime rates during the same period. Needless to say, there were other factors. One group of children during the 1960s—those in the middle and upper classes—grew up in the lap of relative luxury under a regime of permissive child raising. Yet these were the youngsters who put up barricades in city streets, bombed Bank of America branches, made non-negotiable demands, went for unisex clothing, drugs and hair styles, and threatened professors with physical injury. Ironically, this group sought to deny the competitive philosophy of their elders. Yet, because of their sheer numbers, they were in a more competitive situation than any prior cohort.

By contrast, a second group—the children of the lower class—grew up in the lap of poverty. Under a climate characterized more by complete anomie than by mere permissiveness, they were witness to burning neighborhoods, looting, and riot. Lacking the organizational skills of their more affluent peers, they engaged in unparalleled levels of street crime and interpersonal violence.

In order to understand those behaviors, it is necessary to recognize that they were due not merely to the social and political climate of the time but also to the high ratio of adolescents to older adults during the period. In terms of sheer numbers alone, the integration of the generations was at an all-time low. When such an imbalance of successive cohorts occurs, conflict and disruption can be anticipated.

Significantly, it is the generation nurtured in this tumultuous period that is now taking charge of the nation. Yet it is obvious that as they reach adulthood they have not reacted well to childbearing, given the sense of security and social trust that it requires. Instead, a generation raised in turmoil and self-doubt is a generation that cannot tolerate the frustrations associated with long-term commitments to marriage and to family. Thus, low birthrates, higher rates of illegitimacy, increasing signs of family disorganization, economic inefficiency, and the high crime rate characterizing the country today can perhaps be traced, at least in part, to the size and characteristics of this cohort and to the unique set of social and political circumstances in which it grew to maturity.

Were these conditions not of sufficient complexity, a major development that is likely to deepen the underlying disadvantage of this generation and of its offspring is not only the continued aging of the population but the impoverishment of the world in general due to the exhaustion of natural resources and energy. Today's young people, those born in the 1960s, seem more cautious and conservative than those who preceded them, but it is unlikely that they can achieve the stability of earlier generations. They and their children will confront a world which has not only undergone unprecedented changes in the recent past but which will likely see more such changes in the future.

Intrusions between Parent and Child

As a final issue with respect to the future of childhood, we can consider the question of authority. Here one should recall some previous points; namely, that the human being is helpless at first and requires guidance and training for an extraordinarily long time, that societies have usually assigned these tasks to parents, and that along with these responsibilities must go authority, albeit an ever changing authority that is complete at the beginning but is zero at the end. In contemporary societies, however, the family is a tiny unit in a huge mass society. Urban anonymity, impersonal neighborhoods, individual transportation, occupations and amusements outside the home—all make effective parental supervision difficult, if not impossible. Furthermore, contemporary societies are characterized by intense specialization. There are hundreds of agencies and institutions, many of them dealing in a specialized way with children, which have inevitably weakened the already delicate authority of parents. Indeed, they have done so not only with respect to adolescents but with respect to young children.

Compulsory school attendance not only puts the child under the authority of educators for much of each day but now, with busing, he may no longer attend a neighborhood school. Under the Serrano decision, he is not allowed to have educational advantages commensurate with the local community's enterprise and means but must be subject to those of ever-larger units. Family planners are permitted by law to offer contraceptive and abortion services to minors without parental knowledge or consent. Medical decisions frequently override parental decisions with respect to medical treatment of the young. Social welfare services easily replace the father in furnishing support for a mother and her children, thus freeing the father from his parental obligations, or else they collect funds from the father by virtue of their governmental authority even though he may be denied the right to see, let alone control, his children. Businesses, universities, and professional schools are forced by administrative rules to offer jobs to women regardless of their family status, thus tending to erase the division of labor that once characterized the family. Several states have instituted "no-fault divorce," which means divorce by will of either party and an equal division of the community property, regardless of what either partner has done. Political parties, consumer magazines, and television programs point their messages directly to the young. Though this catalog could be continued ad infinitum, all of the intrusions into the family have a persuasive rationale behind them because they are carried out by experts, whereas parents are only amateurs. The fact remains, nonetheless, that such intrusions tend to remove the child from parental control and, thereby, to reduce the satisfactions as well as the responsibilities of family life.

Little wonder, then, that the birthrate has dropped precipitously. To many people, the costs of children seem to exceed the benefits, especially after they have had one or two offspring. In 1965, for example, American wives aged 18–24 expected to have enough births during their lifetime to make an average of 3.1 per wife; by 1976, only eleven years later, the expectation had fallen to 2.1, and even this expectation was ahead of the actual performance. With the age-specific fertility rates exhibited in 1976, each woman would have only 1.8 children during her lifetime—clearly not enough to replace the population (Bureau of the Census, 1977:2).

It is true that a social system can tolerate a great amount of deviant behavior and that youthful rebellion is nothing new; but a society in which the young are given to robbery, rape, violence, and drugs and in which adults fail to replace themselves cannot last long. Either current industrial peoples will be displaced or they will somehow manage to restore effective training, guidance, supervision, and control of juveniles. If they accomplish the latter, it will require that authority over children be maintained, that it be durable and firm, and that it be backed up instead of dissipated by the various agencies of the society. At present there seems no candidate for this task other than parents, but there is little evidence that parents will be sufficiently held responsible or rewarded and backed up by the community. The problem cries out for attention.

References

Arriaga, Eduardo E.
   1968   New Life Tables for Latin American Populations in
           the Nineteenth and Twentieth Centuries. Berkeley:
           Univ. of California, pp. 86–87.

Bureau of the Census
   1966   "Household and family characteristics: March 1965."
           Current Population Reports, Series P-20, 153 (August
           5):15.

   1970   "Marital status and family status: March 1969." Current
           Population Reports, Series P-20, 198 (March 25):21.

   1975   Historical Statistics of the United States, Colonial Times
           to 1970. Washington, D.C.: U.S. Government Printing
           Office.

   1977a   "Fertility of American women: June 1976." Current
           Population Reports, Series P-20, 308 (June):2.

   1977b   Statistical Abstract of the United States. Washington,
           D.C.: U.S. Government Printing Office, p. 387.

   1978   "Households and families by type: March 1978 (advance
           report)." Current Population Reports, Series P-20, 327
           (August):3.

Carter, Hugh, and Paul C. Glick
   1976   Marriage and Divorce: A Social and Economic Study
           (rev. ed.). Cambridge: Harvard Univ. Press.

Glick, Paul, and Arthur Norton
   1973   "Perspectives on the recent upturn in divorce and re-
           marriage." Demography 10 (August):301–4.

McCarthy, James
   1978   "A comparison of the probability of the dissolution of
           first and second marriages," Demography 15
           (August):345–359.

Moynihan, Daniel Patrick
    1965   The Negro Family: The Case for National Action. Wash-
            ington, D.C.: U.S. Department of Labor.

National Center for Health Statistics
    1978a   "Final mortality statistics, 1976." Monthly Vital Statis-
            tics Report 26 (12).

    1978b   "Final natality statistics." Monthly Vital Statistics Re-
            port 26 (12) (March 29):17.

Preston, Samuel H., and J. McDonald
    1976   "The incidence of divorce within cohorts of American
            marriages contracted since the Civil War." Center for
            Studies in Demography and Ecology, Seattle. (mimeo).

Children's Rights, Children's Development

Arlene Skolnick

Do psychological studies of children's development contain messages regarding children's rights? Or, coming at the issue the other way, are there legal and social-policy questions concerning children for which psychological research can provide the answers? It seems, at first glance, that there must be some connection between legal conceptions of childhood and empirical findings concerning children's development. Yet the connection is by no means clear and direct. What follows is an attempt to show why the path from child development to children's rights is so problematic. This is not to deny that psychology has important contributions to make to social-policy debates concerning children. Rather, the point is that psychology cannot itself resolve these debates.

It is impossible to make policies dealing with children without the implicit or explicit application of some developmental theory. Policy decisions are inevitably predicated upon assumptions, however loosely organized, about the needs and capacities of children, how these change with age, what circumstances are good or bad for them, and some notion of where to draw the line between childhood and adulthood. These assumptions, however, are not usually stated explicitly; most often they are tacitly assumed. Indeed, Kalven (1973:509) has observed that legal systems sometimes are based on "premises so mundane and commonplace as not to need any systematic confirmation."

This state of affairs generally stems from one of the three stances taken by policymakers, lawyers, and judges toward psychology (and the other social sciences): (1) they ignore it, by far the most common approach; (2) they rely on it for expert advice, assuming that research findings contain clear policy mandates waiting to be put into effect; or (3) they tend to be manipulative in using it—the expert is called in to put the stamp of science on what is basically a value judgment (Mnookin, 1977). By contrast, I propose a fourth alternative, namely, that legal and policy decisions concerning children should be informed by developmental research, even though such decisions cannot be determined by psychological considerations alone.

The issues involved in children's rights are comparable to the tangled relations of law and psychiatry concerning the insanity defense. Indeed, there is some overlap between the two areas in that they both involve concepts of mental competence and criminal responsibility. The inadequacies of the traditional legal definition of insanity—the ability to distinguish right from wrong—led lawyers to turn to psychiatry in the hopes of arriving at a definition that would better fit social realities, particularly in light of the possibility that a person could have a sense of right and wrong and still be "crazy." As yet, however, an adequate definition of legal insanity remains to be written.

The moral of this tale is not that psychiatrists have unduly muddied the waters but that psychiatric knowledge has revealed the highly complex nature of the issues with which psychiatrists are expected to deal. Although such knowledge may not translate easily into legal standards, it would be foolish to ignore psychiatric expertise in the making of insanity decisions. Yet, as complicated as it is, the issue of legal insanity has at its core a fairly direct question that can be stated in gross terms—is he (or she) crazy?

By contrast, no such simple question lies at the core of children's rights. The term does not refer to any coherent doctrine, but, rather, to a complex and contradictory mixture of political, moral, social, and psychological issues. As one writer put it, children's rights is a "slogan in search of a definition" (Rodham, 1973). The term has been invoked in the name of such diverse and even contradictory "rights" as the right to freedom from poverty, to have a loving home, to vote at an early age, to have a childhood, and to have adult autonomy. Further, the legal status of children touches on difficult issues concerning family privacy, government intervention, social and economic practices and institutions, and psychological needs and capacities.

Were these complexities not sufficient, the field of developmental psychology is a huge, diverse, and ever shifting field in which methods and concepts are undergoing continuing change. To illustrate this, let me quote from a recent review article on cognitive development in the 1978 *Annual Review of Psychology.* The author, Rochel Gelman (p. 297) observes that in the past two years there has been "an explosion" of research in a variety of new areas, and to report carefully on these new trends one needs to know a fair amount of logic, linguistics, philosophy, and physiology. The need to know so much about other disciplines, she confesses, led her to consider reneging on her agreement to write the review— a temptation I faced also in regard to this assignment. Yet just as Gelman decided to write her review because she found important shifts away from the view that very young children are cognitively inept, so I decided to write this paper for similar reasons. There are important new ideas and findings emerging in development research that should be included in considering the changing of children's rights. Further, knowledge about the limits of what we know can be as useful to policymaking as any positive information that developmental psychology has to offer.

What Are Children's Rights?

As a first step, it will be useful to distinguish among the various kinds of claims being made under the heading of children's rights and to see how developmental psychology relates to these claims. Most commentators distinguish between two somewhat contradictory thrusts to the Child Rights Movement: the first seeks to secure special rights *for* children on the basis of their special needs; the second seeks to extend adult rights *to* children. For example, Mnookin (1977) has labeled the two dominant varieties of child advocates as the "child savers" and the "kiddy libbers."

Similarly, Rogers and Wrightsman (1978) have found that attitudes toward children's rights can be scaled along two independent dimensions: a "nurturance" dimension, which stresses the provision of services for children, and a "self-determination" dimension, which calls for the right of children to have control over various aspects of their lives.

In addition, Wald (1978) has isolated four claims in behalf of children that also conform to these dimensions. The first two clearly conform to the nurturance dimension: (1) such "rights against the state" as adequate housing and parental care; and (2) greater state protection from abuse by parents, by other authority figures, and even by such adults as television advertisers. The second two, by constrast, stress self-determination: (3) constitutional protections in actions involving the state, such as the right to legal counsel in juvenile court proceedings, due process in school expulsions, or First Amendment rights to wear armbands or to distribute pamphlets; and (4) the right to challenge parental authority—to act independently of parents, to seek legal redress against parental demands, or to have the freedom to obtain abortions and other medical services without the need for parental consent.

In short, it is quite clear that the current Child Rights Movement is not united by a common set of focal concerns. The rights of children mean quite different things to different people. Further, nurturance rights are not always free from controversy, while those which stress self-determination are surrounded by it. For example, Wald's first right (generalized claims against the state for nurturance) is probably as controversial as his fourth (the claim that children should be autonomous from parents).

The first is controversial because of what is being claimed, namely, the idea that the psychological and physical needs of children can be easily translated into constitutional claims against the state. Without denying that the basic needs of many children in this society are shockingly neglected—statistics on infant mortality, child health, and the number of children living below the poverty line tell part of the story— several writers point to serious flaws in the strategy of attempting to meet these basic needs by labeling them rights. As Wald observes (1978), these are not claims for adult rights that are denied children. Rather, they are moral and social goals that would benefit adults as well. They cannot be obtained by court order but must be addressed by the political system. Likewise, Stier (1978) warns that the failure to distinguish legal rights from moral obligations to care for children may dilute the concepts of legal rights, such as the claim to equal protection and due process, without improving the well-being of children.

The fourth right, meanwhile, is controversial because it pits children against parents. As Wald (1978:16) observes, "It is one thing to argue . . . that a school without compelling reasons should not be able to dictate to a child and his parents the length to cut the child's hair before sending him to school. It is quite another to argue that the child who wants long hair should be able to have a court order his parents not to cut his hair." While we are used to seeing parents act in concert with their child to promote the child's interest against the state, we are not accustomed to seeing the state join with the child to promote the child's interest against his or her parents. Hence, the social and psychological implications of this possible outcome are great. Where, then, does developmental psychology fit into the conflict over children's rights?

The Role of Developmental Psychology

First, let it be said that psychological considerations are not uniquely relevant where the issue is one of fundamental human rights; a month-old child is, or should be, as much a person in the eyes of the law as an adult. But developmental psychology does have an important role to play when questions are being raised about children's needs, their psychological capacities, or their relations with their parents. Relevant to these questions, therefore, psychology has traditionally had a great deal to say concerning the nurturance needs of children. Indeed, psychologists have been prominent in drawing up children's Bills of Rights that stress this particular point of view. Meanwhile, they have been less involved in seeking to promote the autonomy of children, preferring instead to support the traditional legal view of children as dependent and incompetent beings. Indeed, developmental psychology's view of childhood as dependent and long lasting has had two contrasting effects.

On the one hand, psychology has contributed enormously to what Fromm has called "the revolution of the child." Before the nineteenth century the infant and the very young child were thought to be incapable of genuine thought, feeling, or suffering. Childhood was viewed as "an unfurnished antechamber to adulthood" (Kessen, 1966). Heredity or fate was generally held responsible for how a person turned out. But with the advent of Sigmund Freud, such views began to change. As the most influential of a number of nineteenth-century theorists and reformers, Freud articulated a new view of the child. He argued that rather than being blank and insensitive organisms, the very young were passionate beings, with powerful feelings and emotions and with complicated thought processes. As a result, the history of developmental psychology in the twentieth century is an elaboration of this basic insight.

On the other hand, psychological research and theory have also helped to promote the view that children are incompetent and dependent, despite the contention that they are possessed of powerful emotions and thought processes. David Bakan (1971) suggests, for instance, that, while studies and theories in the psychology of adolescence have drawn attention to an important period in the lives of contemporary individuals, they have also stressed the pathology of adolescence, thus depreciating the value of adolescents as persons:

By stressing, for example, the presumptive emotional instability and unformed nature of people of that age . . . Hall and others tended to put a gloss of psychopathology on this age period. Since it has long been a principle in our society that persons regarded as psychologically pathological are to be relieved of rights, the effect of this literature has been to serve the general disability of persons under legal ages. In this way, the workers in the field of adolescence have tended to conspire, certainly unwittingly, with some of the forces depriving adolescents of their rights. (Bakan, 1971:989)

In addition to describing adolescents as emotionally unstable and beset by identity crises, psychologists have tended to describe all young people in terms of their inadequacies rather than their competencies: preschool children are said to be "egocentric," while school-age children are described as "pre-operational" or "morally unsophisticated" in their thinking.

Studies of Cognitive Development

The traditional way of doing research in developmental psychology has also contributed to this polarized adults-have-it, children-don't, view of competence. In what has been called the "modal developmental study" (Brown and Campione, 1978), children of varying ages are compared on a single task purporting to represent some basic cognitive process, such as logical inference or moral reasoning. Children who succeed at the task are assumed to have the capacity in question; those who fail at it are said to lack it.

Recent research, however, has challenged these assumptions in a number of areas—cognitive development, social role taking, moral reasoning. Tasks that were assumed to be *the* tests of the capacity in question have been revealed to have certain flaws in them. When new tests are devised or standard tests are modified, younger children no longer appear so incompetent. The preschool child no longer appears globally egocentric, and the school-aged child no longer appears morally unsophisticated. Cognitive capacities are not an all-or-nothing phenomenon.

Kohlberg's work on moral development is frequently cited by legal writers as the definitive work on children's moral reasoning. Kohlberg asks children to solve hypothetical story dilemmas about interpersonal or moral issues such as the choice between duty to family and duty to community. For example, his best-known story dilemma asks whether a man should steal an overpriced drug he cannot afford to cure his wife of cancer. Kohlberg finds no consistent moral thinking about this dilemma in children under ten, and the highest level of morality is not reached until the end of adolescence. In fact, the highest levels are reached by a surprisingly low proportion of adolescents and adults.

Recent research, however, seriously questions Kohlberg's findings. His inability to find coherent moral thinking in children under ten seems to result more from his choice of dilemmas based on adult social concerns than from cognitive capacities inherent in children. Thus, when children are presented with issues arising out of their own social realities—a fair distribution of candy or pizza, how a child should respond to parental authority when it is inconsistent and arbitrary, the ability to distinguish between social conventions, such as not addressing teachers by their first names, and immoral acts such, as stealing or killing—children are capable of remarkably sophisticated reasoning (Damon, 1977). By the end of childhood (ages 8–10), in fact, children seem able to take into account a multiplicity of claims for justice and to choose the claims that seem most suited to specific situations. In short, the adult-centered methods used in previous studies did not permit these abilities to emerge.

The presumed egocentricity of preschoolers also appears to be the result of asking them about complex and unfamiliar tasks. But by presenting problems to children in simple and familiar forms, psychologists have been able to push ever lower the ages at which cognitive capacities can be found in very young children, such as the capacity to reason in moral terms or to take another person's point of view.

Limits on Cognitive Capacities

Despite the newly revealed capacities of the preschool child, the evidence is also clear that there may be some general limits on cognitive reasoning. There are indications, for example, that a major revolution in the child's cognitive capacities occurs at around the age of seven. Children become markedly less egocentric. They are more capable of conceiving of a problem from another person's point of view and can enact a variety of social roles. They are able to understand the consequences of their behavior and its effects on other people. They are often willing to engage in altruistic behavior, even at some cost to themselves.

Given the nature of such findings, it is interesting to note that they are quite consistent with the presumptions of many traditional societies that children acquire adultlike sense at about seven years of age. Both the English common and the Catholic canon law define this age as the time when the child becomes capable of knowing right from wrong and therefore of being liable to trial or ready for communion and confession.

At the same time, such findings should not be interpreted as suggesting that there are no differences between the preschooler, the schoolchild, and the adolescent. Young children still do not do well at tasks involving sophisticated forms of abstract reasoning, and their use of their capacities is erratic and fragile. Hence, social sophistication of the preadolescent will be shaken up when adolescence presents him or her with a range of new social concerns—sex, intimacy, work, and responsibility to self and society. Yet it is clear that children are much less globally inept than they have been portrayed in the traditional developmental literature.

Questions about Adult Cognition

Paradoxically, while one body of research has suggested that the age of cognitive competence should be lowered, a second body indicates that the traditional view of adult competence may be off the mark. The final stage of cognitive development, according to Piaget (Inheder and Piaget, 1958) is the state of formal operations. It is the ability to reason logically, to solve abstract hypothetical problems. At present, however, serious questions have been raised about the universality of formal operational thinking. Although the more mature forms of thought do not emerge until adolescence or later, they are by no means the typical modes of thought for most adults most of the time. As Flavell (1977) points out, the higher the Piagetian stage, the less inevitable its attainment by normal individuals across a variety of environments. Indeed, Piaget himself recognizes that most adults may be capable of the most mature levels of thinking only in areas of their greatest experience or interest. Even well-educated adults have trouble dealing with formal-logical problems such as the distinction between, "If A then B," and "If and only if A, then B."

This research on adults illustrates the point made earlier in reference to children: tests of cognitive performance are not reliable guides to a person's cognitive capacities. For example, cross-cultural research reveals that non-Westerners may do poorly on Western cognitive tasks yet be capable of solving complex cognitive problems in life situations that are real to them. In short, in trying to understand the cognitive competence of children or adults in any culture, it is not enough to know how they perform on laboratory tasks alone; we must look at functioning in settings familiar to the person being studied.

Implications of Cognitive Research

Although much current research has sought to make laboratory tasks simpler and more closely related to children's interests and experience, developmental psychology still does not study children growing up in actual life circumstances. Bronfenbrenner (1974), for example, argues that psychology is a science that studies the influence of strange adults on children in strange situations. Laboratory research has produced enormously useful information, but its relevance to real life, hence its usefulness to the making of social-policy decisions, is questionable. Bronfenbrenner argues that developmental psychology "needs" social policy; increased attention to policy-related research would provide important answers to scientific questions about the interaction between development of children and their enduring environments.

Similar problems arise in trying to translate developmental findings into statements about children's rights. Newer research that finds a lack of egocentricity in preschoolers and the capacity in school-aged children for sophisticated reasoning about social relations would seem to support the argument of rights advocates that adult rights should be extended to children. Indeed, it is interesting to note in this regard that the American Psychological Association did enter the legal arena in support of the concept of the "mature minor." The APA participated as *amicus curiae* in a class action suit involving institutionalization of children under the age of eighteen by their parents (*Bartley* v. *Kremens,* 1975).

The brief prepared by the APA and by other mental health organizations argues that children ages twelve and older should be accorded the same due-process protections as adults. In commenting on the brief, Stier (1978) observes that the age of twelve is an increasingly preferred dividing line for according children majority status; "mature minor" rules are part of a liberalizing trend particularly evident in the area of medical treatment and health care; the choice of the age of twelve seems to reflect the work of Piaget and the notion of mature cognitive capacities emerging at adolescence.

On the other hand, the more traditional view of children and adolescents as emotionally dependent and cognitively immature is also alive and well (See, e.g., Baumrind, 1978). While the newer research reveals children to be surprisingly sophisticated in many ways, it does not say that children or adolescents are the same as adults. Conclusions are drawn from the data in the same way that one decides whether the glass is half full or half empty—according to how one prefers to view the world.

Children, Values, and Politics

One of the major difficulties confronting discussions of children's rights is the assumption that children are beyond politics. The attitude of all sides is that they are speaking in "the best interest of the child." Those who would extend children's rights claim to speak in behalf of those interests, while those who defend the status quo claim that current practices are already fulfilling that standard. As a result, strong rhetoric is exhibited on both or all sides of this issue without much attention to the value positions that are concealed in whatever stance is taken.

When we discuss children, the family, and the state, we are dealing not only with philosophical preferences, fine points of the law, and the latest research findings from developmental psychology but with gut-level, high-voltage emotional reactions. There are no value-free ways of looking at these issues. For example, many advocates of children's rights view children as oppressed minorities comparable to blacks, American Indians, and women. They argue that, just as a person's legal autonomy should not be restricted because of race or sex, it should not be restricted by age either. Critics of this position, by contrast, consider this analogy to be absurd, an insult to women and racial minorities, and a danger to family and social stability. Across such rhetorical barricades, reasoned discussion can be difficult indeed.

It is not only in making policy decisions for children in general that values must be confronted. Even the seemingly less politicized atmosphere of decisionmaking for the individual child involves value choices. What is in the best interest of the child is often indeterminate and speculative. Mnookin (1977), for example, spells out some of the problems confronted by a judge in trying to determine the best interests of a child in a custody dispute. Assuming that it is possible to make accurate predictions about alternative outcomes (which, in fact, it is not), what set of values should a judge use to make his decision about a child's best interest? Should it be the child's present happiness or happiness in adult life? Should happiness at any age be the deciding value? What about economic productivity, spiritual development, or warm relationships? As Mnookin (1977:6–7) observes, deciding such questions involves ultimate assumptions about the purpose and value of life itself.

Ambivalent Objects: The Child, the Family, and the State

The power of children to evoke strong and ambivalent emotional responses did not, of course, begin with the children's liberation movement. Throughout Western history the child has symbolized both good and evil. The child has represented naked innocence, naked impulse, and both subordination to and rebellion against authority. Indeed, attitudes toward impulse are the key to understanding attitudes toward childhood.

The ambivalence toward children which many observers have noted in contemporary American society reaches back several centuries. Calvinist theory had as a prime tenet of childrearing the doctrine of infant depravity—the infant was doomed to sin and evil unless controlled by parents. Likewise, the Counter-reformation promoted the same dark view of childhood. As a result, Kessen (1965:33) observes that, particularly in England and America, there has been a "curious conflict between childhood as innocence and the grim portrait of an evil being who must be scourged to his salvation."

Toward the close of the eighteenth century the theme of childhood innocence was forcefully reasserted by Rousseau and the Romantic school of writers, most notably Blake, Wordsworth, and, later, Dickens. Rather than being innately depraved and in need of vigilant adult guidance to develop properly, the child, argued Rousseau, would develop naturally toward virtue with a minimum of adult training.

For the Romantic writers the child served as a counter-modern symbol of protest against the emerging forces of industrialization. While "dark Satanic mills" blighted the landscape, the child stood for imagination, sensibility, and the multiple possibilities of human development. Later in the century, however, the image of the child was sentimentalized into cloyingly sweet symbols of Victorian innocence, such as Little Eva and Peter Pan.

Freudian theory, in turn, overthrew the image of childhood innocence and introduced a modern version of Original Sin. The Calvinist idea of infant depravity was reborn in the Freudian concept of the id as a seething cauldron of lustful and murderous impulses. Like the Calvinists, therefore, Freud emphasized the role of parents as tamers of the child's animal nature and as agents of civilization.

The Child

The ideological implications of the various images of childhood are more complicated than they appear at first glance. Although Calvinist views, on the one hand, could be, and often were, used to justify brutal childrearing methods, such views signified an increase in the status of children. The growth of interest in the child's soul symbolized both an increasing concern for the child as a person and a greater degree of emotional involvement between parents and children (Morgan, 1944; Stone, 1977).

On the other hand, Rousseau's celebration of childhood was not without an ironic twist. In stressing the natural childishness of the child, he helped to emphasize the distance between children and adults—the childishness of the child was the complement of the supremacy of the adult. Hence, Rousseau's work is full of pleas for parental authority over the child, not of pleas for the autonomy of children.

What all of this means is that a sensitivity to the various stages of childhood and youth is not necessarily evidence of concern with the child's welfare. Rothman (1971), for example, has pointed out that there is a "darker side" of age grading, that it may be "part of an effort to lock-step the child into rigid and predetermined modes of behavior." Thus, a sensitivity to age differences may reflect an attempt on the part of those charged with the management of children to make their tasks easier.

Similarly, a concern with childrearing by the family may not be an index of pure concern with the child's welfare. "Enlightened" childrearing may reflect not so much a decline in parental authority as a shift in tactics from coercion to manipulation. Thus Sunley (1955) has suggested that the emergence of interest in the child and in the problems of childrearing may have reflected a new emphasis on the child as the agent of parental ambitions and as a representative of the parent's status in society.

The Family

Just as there are different images of children in our culture, so are there different images of families. The dominant view of the family is a romantic, idealized one. The family is seen as the foundation of civilization and the social order; it molds the characters and destiny of its children, thereby insuring the survival of society from one generation to the next. Currently, a nostalgic rhetoric is in vogue; many people feel that the family is falling apart and abandoning its time-honored function of socializing children and providing a haven of peace and security for adults; if only we could return to the stable, harmonious family life of earlier times, many, if not all, of our modern ills would be cured.

A minority of writers have dissented from this "sentimental model" of the family, and a minority of this minority have actually gone to the extreme of attacking the family as an oppressive institution and the source, rather than the potential cure, of all our ills. Over a century ago, for example, Herbert Spencer (1946:87) pointed out the fallacy in assuming that people are transformed into infallible and virtuous rulers in relations with their children. He observed that "the citizens we do business with, the people we meet in the world, we know to be very imperfect creatures. In the daily scandals, the quarrels of friends, in bankruptcy disclosures, in lawsuits, in police reports, we have constantly thrust before us the pervading selfishness, dishonesty, brutality." But we take for granted that in the family "the virtues are with the rulers and the vices with the ruled."

Both extreme views of the family overlook the reality that there is no such thing as "the family," only families, some of which fit the idealized image, some of which are oppressive, with most falling in between, or mixing oppressiveness and nurturance together. Children grow to maturity not through some simple process of parental molding or the internalization of family norms but by raising themselves by their cognitive and emotional bootstraps from the ambivalent brew of family life.

The State

The third corner in the triangle of forces affecting our concept of childhood is the state. It, too, is the center of controversy: is it a check on individual selfishness or an agency of class oppression? Is it an instrument of the public will or a body of power-hungry bureaucrats enriching themselves at the public's expense? In these days of tax revolt, hostility toward government agencies spreads across the entire political spectrum from right to left. Thus, it is something of an understatement to say that the citizenry are ambivalent in their attitude toward the state.

This attitude notwithstanding, some advocates of children's liberation would like the state to play a greater role, not a lesser one, in the lives of children and their parents. They have suggested, for example, that the state should provide for the routine screening of parents to detect potential child abusers, for national health authorities who would inspect homes and compel preventive medicine, and even for the licensing of parents before they are permitted to have children.

Needless to say, there is opposition to such a point of view. Other child advocates are either opposed to greater intervention by the state or would like to see some of its powers decreased. They feel that past attempts to regulate family life and to save children have created greater evils than they have prevented. The state, they argue, already has too much power to intervene in family life and to remove children from the custody of their parents. In short, attitudes toward the state are little less ambivalent than those toward our current concepts of childhood and family life.

Children's Rights and Development in Social Context

Underlying the various issues mentioned above are some basic social and historical realities. Discussions of both children's rights and developmental psychology are often carried on as if development took place in a social vacuum. Yet we cannot debate about the proper allocation of responsibility for childrearing among the parents, child, and state without taking into account the way the balance among these three is affected by the social and cultural contexts of family life. Nor can we talk about psychological development or the competence of children as if these were biological invariants. The needs, roles, and capabilities of children are affected by the structure and functioning of the family, the economy, the quality of community life, the child-care system, and the age-stratification system, as well as by the prevailing political and religious ideologies.

Over the past century, for example, there has been a decline in the social bonds that tie families to communities. While there is debate about the concept of the isolated nuclear family and the persistence of such institutions as the extended family, the neighborhood, and the church, there is little doubt that such ties have lessened in recent decades and that family privacy has increased (see Laslett, 1974). Troubled families, as a consequence, are likely to find themselves with fewer informal supports than those in the past. Meanwhile, the state, other formal organizations, and professional helpers have been called upon to fill the gap. Indeed, the very ease with which writers in the area of children and the law speak of the triad of child, family, and state indicates how thoroughly the community has been obliterated as a factor in the regulation of family life.

This obliteration of traditional ties has spawned a great deal of nostalgia for some golden age of family and community life. We should not idealize excessively the small towns and neighborhoods of previous eras. Not only are they unlikely to return, but their passing is not an unmixed loss—they could be intrusive, intolerant, and hostile to individual and family autonomy. Nevertheless, families were less likely to find themselves without social support and in need of assistance from courts and state agencies.

Several other historical changes have also had a profound impact on children and families: the increasing segregation and differentiation of different segments of the life span, the transformation of children from economic assets to economic liabilities, and shifts in ideologies concerning the family and the role of children in it. All such changes, as well as the foregoing, are the familiar concomitants of modernization. And, though it is true that historians and some sociologists, as well as some developmental psychologists, professionals, and policymakers are familiar with them, a detailed knowledge of childhood in other times and places has not really affected contemporary thinking about children. Writing of developmental psychology in particular, Keniston (1971), has described the problem of "chronocentrism": the tendency to take the developmental patterns of contemporary Western children as a universal norm of human development.

Transition to Adulthood

The most fundamental shift in family life is the change in children's economic roles. In historical and cross-cultural perspective, this shift has made our own culture decidedly deviant in the way it deals with the transition from childhood to adulthood. As anthropologist William Stephens (1963) points out, there are three aspects to this transition. The first deals with work and occupational roles, the second with marriage and parenthood, and the third with the emancipation of children from parental authority. In all three ways the transition to adulthood in our culture is unusual. While our young people become adults relatively late in terms of their assumption of work and marital roles, they are emancipated from parental authority both abruptly and at an early age.

In most traditional societies, by contrast, parental authority ends only with the death of the parent. In the Irish countryside, for example, Arensberg and Kimball found many forty- and fifty-year-old "boys," unable to marry or work the land for themselves. As one informant said, "You can be a boy forever, as long as the old fellow is alive" (Arensberg, 1950:59).

In Western society, because of our tradition of neolocal residence, getting married usually means the end of parental authority. In most other societies, marriage is no such turning point. Even after the death of parents, the individual remains in a childlike position with respect to his or her elder kin or to the spouse's kin. Thus, most adults will occupy the status of "married child" for a large part of their lifetimes (Stephens, 1963:393).

Work Roles

The idea that children should fulfill productive work roles is so alien to contemporary notions of childhood that it is hard to realize how odd we are historically and cross-culturally. In nearly all societies known to ethnographers (including early eras of our own society) work begins very early. This is not to say that age differences are not recognized. Instead, it is expected that children between the ages of three and six will begin to perform some useful work. Then, after age six, their responsibilities are increased so that at some point between nine and fifteen they will become, occupationally speaking, "a fully functioning adult" (Stephens, 1963:386). Although some of the work performed by children consists of chores not directly leading to adult work—such as errand-running and trash disposal—most of their duties clearly take the form of apprenticeship for adult work roles. This is particularly true in societies that are precariously close to the subsistence level.

The contributions and responsibilities of children are vital to survival.

Our current conceptions of child labor were shaped by the terrible exploitation of children that occurred in the mines and factories during the early era of industrialization, exploitation that was gradually put to an end by child-labor and compulsory education laws. But in preindustrial settings, when work took place within the family, participation in the workaday world was not necessarily oppressive. For example, when the Whitings recently compared the lives of children in African agricultural settlements with those in new African cities, they did not find that the latter were necessarily better off. From the age of three, rural children are expected to help with gardening and herding, while little girls often have full responsibility for the care of younger siblings. They concluded:

There is no indication that this type of labor overtaxes the child. At that age between three and eight when children are so eager to play the role of adults, they are permitted to do so and are made to feel that they are important contributors. It is true that their parents exert more pressure towards obedience and are more punitive when they fail to perform their tasks responsibly, but this is not surprising when one considers that 5–7 year olds are being entrusted with human lives and valuable stock. (Whiting, 1972:4–5)

The Symbolic Role of Children

At first glance it would seem that modern parents have been the losers in the modernization game, children the winners. The traditional parent could look to a child as a current economic asset, a support in old age, and a lifelong subordinate. The modern parent, by contrast, enjoys few of these ancient rewards of parenthood.

Yet the value of children to their parents has not been lost; rather, children have been transformed from economic assets into psychological and symbolic ones. Love and mutual identification have come to be the medium of exchange in family relations, rather than goods, services, and obedience. If the home in modern times, as Christopher Lasch (1977) puts it, has been viewed as a "haven in a heartless world," it is children who have served as the heart of the home.

Before relatively recent times, love was not considered an important element in parent-child relations (Kagan, 1977). Parental attitudes were not thought to be a source of mental illness in later life. Children who had been subjected to severe discipline did not necessarily assume that their parents had been hostile or remiss in their duty. By contrast, twentieth-century society believes that a lack of parental love can have disastrous consequences later on. These beliefs can act as self-fulfilling prophecies: parents believe that if they fail to love their children enough they will harm them. Children and adolescents, in turn, learn of scientific and popular theories relating lack of parental love to unhappiness and psychological illness. Thus, as adults, they interpret their emotional problems as delayed reactions to a lack of love during childhood, rather than to fate, to witchcraft, or to evil spirits.

Children are not only love objects but sources of pride, hopes for the future, sources of meaning and connectedness in an impersonal society. They also give parents the opportunity to exercise a degree of power not possible anywhere else. Blau and Duncan (1967:428) observe that, while successful middle-class men are able to find support for their status from their occupational roles, "the unsuccessful find a substitute in the authority they exercise in their role as fathers over a number of children."

It is these emotional dynamics of modernized family life that make the idea of children's liberation within the family such a touchy issue. For a child to challenge the wisdom and good will of a parent is not only a challenge to parental authority but it strikes at the very raison d'être of the family. What parent has a child with the idea of being hauled into court some years hence in a dispute over bedtime, haircuts, curfews, or allowances? Quite apart from the practical and political problems of increasing the public surveillance of private life, the enforcement of children's rights within the family would throw the roles of parent and child even more out of balance than they already are.

Developmental Theory and Social Reality

Given the conditions just described, it seems quite clear that, despite the child-centeredness of the modern family, growing up is more of a problem in contemporary industrial societies than it was in the past. On the one hand, there is little to be gained from idealizing the past because children were less likely to be considered sensitive human beings and often were treated in less humane ways. On the other hand, the task of managing the lives of children was often less difficult than it is now. For example, when the home is no longer the center of economic life, as it is today, childcare becomes a problem. The homes of the preindustrial past were not child-centered. Yet their economic functions assured that adults would be available to look after the children, and old people could also participate. Economists have pointed out that the most "efficient" way of caring for young children is in a setting in which other activities are being carried out, since children require full-time availability but not full-time attention (Boocock, 1976:422).

Adolescence, as well as early childhood, is also a major time in life when psychological needs are often out of step with social realities. The reason was enunciated by Ruth Benedict (1938) four decades ago. She pointed out that modern industrialized cultures maintain sharp discontinuities between the behavior demanded of the child and that demanded of adults: children play while adults work; the child is supposed to be obedient, the adult dominant; the child is supposed to be sexless, while the adult is expected to be sexually active and competent. In few other cultures, Benedict points out, do people have to learn one set of behaviors as children and then unlearn and reverse these patterns as they grow up. Thus, much of the familiar turmoil of adolescence can be explained in terms of the reversal of roles demanded of young people in transition between childhood and adulthood. But this is not all; a reversal of roles is not the only problem.

There are certain cultures that, like ours, demand radical changes of behavior in moving from one age category to another. But, in contrast to ours, most of these provide highly organized social supports and rituals to help bridge the gap. Meanwhile, modern adolescents must negotiate the difficult passage from the dependence of childhood to the independence of adulthood by themselves. It should come as little surprise, therefore, that serious problems of adjustment and identity are often encountered.

In the years since Benedict and Margaret Mead first pointed out that modern adolescence is not a universal developmental stage in the lives of people, some of the most interesting studies on the topic have looked at variations among adolescents in American society. Several of them have challenged the traditional belief of developmental psychology that the teen years in America are necessarily a time of storm and stress, generations gaps, rebellion and nonconformity (Douvan and Adelson, 1966; Elkin and Westley, 1955). While some adolescents do experience difficulty, others quietly internalize their parents' own roles or their parents' aspirations for them and diligently apply themselves to the task of becoming "mature." In short, contrary to the developmental view of adolescence, there is more than one kind of adolescent experience.

Recent historical studies have also exploded the notion of a uniform kind of transition between childhood and adulthood. Instead, the belief that all children go through the same developmental stages is but another consequence of the age-stratification system in modern societies. People of the same age are generally expected to be in roughly the same stages of their careers at the same time: schooling, work, marriage, parenthood. Before the modern era, however, there was less uniformity in life-cycle transitions. Children might start school very early or else not begin their educations until adulthood. Around 1840, for example, 10 percent of the children in Massachusetts under the age of four, were enrolled as regular students (Vinovskis, quoted in Boocock, 1976). Furthermore, the time at which students left school was not a significant turning point either. Instead, it was common for young people to move back and forth between school and work, according to family needs and the availability of jobs (Hareven, 1978).

The shortage of labor that had existed throughout most of American history insured that anyone willing to work could do so. During most of the nineteenth century a large proportion of young people left school and went to work at twelve or fourteen. Many also left home at this age, either to live in other families as apprentices or simply to be on their own.

Joseph Kett (1977), in his history of adolescence in America, uses the term "semidependence" to describe the status of youth, aged ten to twenty-one, in the preindustrial nineteenth century. In contrast to today's youth, young people in the past could be much more independent of their parents and yet remain tied to them even while living away from the parental roof. Similarly, Marks (1975) points out that, for the first three-quarters of the nineteenth century, the courts recognized a doctrine of emancipation; that is, a boy as young as thirteen or fourteen could be freed of the obligation to turn over his wages to his parents and still continue to live at home. Meanwhile, his parents would be legally free from the responsibility of supporting him. (It is important to note, however, that the courts were not so willing to recognize the emancipation of girls.)

By the end of the nineteenth century, however, there was no longer a need for children and other unskilled labor. Young people who had been mature enough to be workers in earlier times now were considered immature, useless, and even dangerous. The presence of large numbers of idle young people in the streets of American cities was perceived as a threat to the social order. This "crisis" of youth led to major social movements and new social and legal policies for dealing with children. Child-labor laws, compulsory education, and the juvenile court and child-guidance clinic were products of this ferment. The laws, with their precise age requirements, set a clear boundary for the end of adolescence. Adolescence was now marked off from childhood by puberty and from adulthood by legal barriers to working, leaving school, and living apart from parents. "By the early twentieth century, the notion that a child upon reaching puberty could assume a status independent of his parents had virtually disappeared. The state compelled the extension of childhood—enjoining longer supervision, more protracted education, and the postponed assumption of adult economic roles" (Marks, 1975:88).

For middle-class youth the economic changes at the end of the nineteenth century altered the conditions for success and created new demands on families. Formal education beyond puberty was now required to place children on the track to positions in the new bureaucratic middle class. In the past, when the middle class was composed of entrepreneurs, artisans, and self-employed professionals, the road to adult success was a meandering one. Detours into the world of casual labor or an erratic and incomplete education did not preclude economic attainment later in life. Indeed, an independent and autonomous youth could be a precondition for success in the business world of the nineteenth century.

By 1900, however, a youth's desire for independence and autonomy came to be seen as "prescriptions for failure" (Kett, 1977:172). No longer a meandering road, the route to success came to be more and more a steep ladder, a series of age-graded tasks. A missed step anywhere along the line could be disastrous. There was a new emphasis on achievement, obedience, purity, and self-restraint. Parents who now had to sacrifice the earnings of their teen aged children expected this sacrifice to be repaid, not in money, but in conformity to the demands of family, school, and society.

Significantly, it was during this period that developmental psychology emerged as an academic discipline. But rather than projecting a view of human development that was relatively free from the perspective of a particular time and place in history, it not only reflected the changes just described but actually influenced the direction they took. Indeed, the view of adolescence as a period of storm and stress, first suggested by G. Stanley Hall and then elaborated by other psychologists, had a tremendous impact on the treatment of young people for much of the twentieth century.

The key factor in this "invention of the adolescent" (Kett, 1977) was the use of a biological framework to interpret the problems of youth. Young people between the ages of ten and twenty-five—particularly young men—had been a problematic age group in other eras. And puberty had been recognized as a time of life that could bring drastic changes. Nonetheless, the novelty in what Hall and the others had to say was the idea that adolescence was a universal phenomenon, determined principally by a biological, not a biosocial, process of maturation. Hence, as Benedict (1938) noted, the social and scientific consequences were great. When adolescent storm and stress is explained in physiological terms, she pointed out, we overlook the possibility of developing social institutions that might lessen the strains on adolescents and their families; instead, "we elaborate a set of dogmas which prove inapplicable under other social conditions" (p. 27).

The Future of Childhood

The road from these observations to social policy is complicated. To say that adolescence is largely the product of social, economic, and legal arrangements, rather than the expression of some universal biological necessity, is not to say that it can be readily changed. It is a fallacy to think that if something is biological, it is immutable, but if it is social, it can be easily altered. Often, the reality is the other way around.

For example, although the incompetence and dependency of children may be largely a product of cultural belief and practice, rather than an inherent condition, this is not to say they are unreal. The existing social and economic context places limits on the exercise of children's competence and responsibility. Children do have further to go to achieve adult levels of competence in advanced technological societies than they do in small, subsistence-level ones.

Similarly, although the discontinuity between children and adults in sexual matters is also culturally based, this does not mean that current family structures could accommodate unrepressed child sexuality. Nor is it likely that the majority of families would be willing, or psychologically able, to provide or tolerate a genuinely egalitarian relationship with children. So long as children are economic dependents, and so long as parents remain responsible for them—legally, morally, and, above all, emotionally—parents cannot easily tolerate the notion that children should be both equal and autonomous.

At the same time, given the profound changes that are now occurring in our beliefs and theories about children, it would seem unreasonable to assume that our present conceptions of childhood will remain in force indefinitely. If the views of childhood and of human development have changed in the past, they are capable of changing again. Thus, although it is difficult to predict the precise directions of social change, a new view of childhood may be visible on the horizon, and new stages of development may emerge from these changes.

Although the adult world is still sharply marked off from the world of the child, there is a certain blurring around the edges. The norms of conventional age grading appear to be losing their previous decisive influence. "Adolescence" is spreading at both ends—younger children are absorbing teenage culture and attitudes, and many of those in their twenties and beyond are refusing to progress to "adulthood." Dress and amusements no longer distinguish children and adults as sharply as they once did. Current clothing styles are not only unisex, they are increasingly uniage. Where fairy tales once were shared by all age groups, now television is.

The recent public and professional interest in adult "development" is another sign of lessened differentiation between adult and child roles. Ironically, while there is increasing public dissatisfaction with education for children and youth, more and more adults want and need to continue their learning over their life span. Some have suggested, as a result, that the schools should be opened to people of all ages and that children should be integrated into work activities. Should this occur, the distinction between economic and educational institutions would become blurred.

The 1970 White House Conference on Children suggested something like a revival of the apprentice system: workplaces would be modified to include the young in productive work so that they would be able to divide their time between learning and actual work. Similarly, schools might become communities in which children could carry out responsible service as well as educational activities. If these kinds of changes are forthcoming, the life cycle would no longer consist of an early period of full-time school and full-time work later, but rather a combination of the two activities over many years.

Robert Lifton (1969) argues that the conditions of life in the twentieth century have produced a new kind of individual whom he calls "protean man" after the mythological figure who could assume any shape. People today not only live in an age of identity crises that may last a lifetime, but settled identities may change to other settled identities, and more than once.

Future conceptions of the stages of life may be more like those of premodern times than those of the industrial age. After "infancy"—the years from birth to age seven—adults and children will not be seen as so sharply different from each other. Yet it seems unlikely that the child of the future will be seen simply as a smaller version of the parent, as he or she was in medieval or tribal societies, an heir to the parent's place in society who is subject to parental authority until the death of the parent.

The research of Berger and his associates (1972) into communal childrearing suggests a model of childhood, one that may point the way to future patterns of the larger society. Having rejected middle-class notions of maturity, they note, communards have had to rethink the definitions of childhood, adulthood, and the relations between them. These investigators observed a transition from infancy to "person" status after the age of four to seven years, as in Aries's (1962) description of medieval times. When children are no longer dependent on adults, they are treated and tend to behave as just other members of the extended family. Indeed, Berger believes that the single most important belief governing adult-child relations in the communes is that the behavior of the children does not reflect on the parents in any way. Adults are not characterized by what they do, or do not do, with or to their children, or how their children turn out.

Such adult-child relations may well become the future pattern in the larger society. This development, however, would not require that everyone become a member of a rural commune. Rather, such an outcome would seem to be implicit in a variety of trends now going on in a society at large. There is evidence, for example, that we are moving away from the child-centered, mother-focused, expert-guided family of past decades—the family that replaced the patriarchal, adult-centered family ideal of earlier times (Rapoport et al., 1977). In its place new balances are being sought between the needs of children and those of adults.

This new trend, which has been documented in opinion polls (Yankelovich, 1977), has alarmed many observers and seems to be further evidence of the decline of the family and evidence of "the new narcissism." Yet this state of alarm overlooks the costs of the child-centered approach to both children and parents. The danger of child neglect does not contradict the opposite danger. When parents sacrifice their own interests and satisfactions on "the altar of child centered family life," they are likely to damage the child as well (Rapoport et al., 1977). The overprotective, double-binding, guilt-inducing families who fill the pages of the psychiatric journals are none other than well-respected middle-class families who are trying to live up to the roles prescribed for them.

In short, the roles of children and adults in contemporary Western societies have been out of balance. Just as the casting of the sexes into sharply different roles—the strong breadwinning male versus the weak dependent female—imposes costs on both men and women, so a sharp split between child and adult roles also takes its toll. On the one hand, adult work roles seldom allow for the imaginative, growing, and feeling aspects of the human experience. On the other hand, dependent children lack power, social standing, and responsibility even though they are given opportunities to play, experiment, and make mistakes (Stern et al., 1975:117). As a result, the prolonged uselessness of children deprives them of opportunities to develop self-esteem through responsible and productive action.

Implications

In conclusion, I would like to discuss the implications of the themes of this paper for social policy. Mainly, I want to warn against attempting to translate findings from developmental, historical, or cross-cultural research directly into specific social policies. For example, it is one thing to say that the contemporary practice of excluding children from work is historically and culturally unusual and that children are cognitively more competent than they have been thought to be, and quite another to say that child-labor laws should be abolished, the public schools closed down, and children set "free" to enter the labor force at the age of seven.

To say that children have been capable of carrying out more adult roles in other times and places does not mean that today's children could function as adults in our own society right now. If the roles and statuses of children are determined to a greater or lesser degree by social structure, they will be difficult to change unless the social structure also changes. For example, if adolescence was "invented," at least in part, because the economy no longer needed the labor of young people, it is likely to remain a part of the life cycle until the economy changes enough to absorb adolescents into the labor force. In a society which cannot provide full employment for adults, the prospects for young people becoming workers seems quite dim.

But suppose that we could turn the clock back and return to the nineteenth century of child industrial labor. Or suppose that today's industries did suddenly need a large new influx of workers? Would we want children in mines, steel mills, asbestos and chemical plants? There is no comparison between the conditions under which children worked on farms and preindustrial workshops and those that prevail in the industrial age. The child-labor reforms at the turn of the century were a protest against the inhuman working conditions of industrial capitalism and at the same time a capitulation to those conditions. Although the children would be saved, adult workers would have to bear the brunt of an expanding industrial economy.

In short, then, the idea that children are capable of productive work does not mean that they could be easily integrated into the economy or that they should be made to do any particular kind of work. Similar arguments apply to the other inferences that might be drawn from the themes discussed in this paper. For example, if children and adolescents are not categorically different from adults in their cognitive and moral reasoning, why should they not be treated as adults in the criminal justice system?

One problem is translating cognitive-development notions into legal policy is that legal categories are crude and artificial. A person is either a minor or an adult in the eyes of the law. Thus, young people are shifted from one category to the other at age eighteen or twenty-one, regardless of their cognitive capabilities before or after. Yet the practice of defining all children as minors obscures the striking differences among children of different ages as well as the similarities between older children and adults. The six-month-old child, the one who is six years old, and the sixteen-year-old are all children in the eyes of the law. By contrast, psychological research in cognitive development, whether or not it is based on the idea of distinct stages, recognizes gradations in the degree to which children are capable of different cognitive tasks or moral reasoning.

In his essay in this volume, Zimring argues for a "learning theory permit" of adolescence and for an asymmetrical view of privilege and responsibility for youth. He suggests that there is a period of transitional learning during which young people are ready to begin a new adult activity, such as driving, but before they are ready to assume full responsibility for all their acts. During this period, therefore, they should be protected from the full consequences of their misbehavior as a social investment in their future development. The view of cognitive development outlined in this paper is compatible with this image of privilege and responsibility.

Here again, it is one thing to say that children and adolescents are capable of knowing right from wrong and of realizing the consequences of their acts, and quite another to leap to the conclusion that they should be treated by the criminal justice system as fully responsible adults. It would be ironic if, at the very time when there is great disillusionment with the adult criminal justice system and with the prison as an institution, a new population of young people were to be incarcerated. What is needed is a system of justice which recognizes varying degrees of cognitive and emotional maturity and which, therefore, is more capable of judging moral and legal responsibility.

References

Arensberg, Conrad M.
> 1950   The Irish Countryman. Gloucester, Maine: Peter Smith.

Ariès, Philippe
> 1962   Centuries of Childhood (Trans. Robert Baldick). New York: Knopf.

Bakan, David
> 1971   "Adolescence in America: from idea to social fact." Daedalus 100:979–95.

Bartley v. *Kremens*
> 1975   402 F. Supp. 1039, (E.D. Pa.). *Amici curiae* brief of American Psychological Association et al. Washington, DC: Mental Health Law Project.

Baumrind, Diana
> 1978   "Reciprocal rights and responsibilities in parent-child relations." Journal of Social Issues 34:179–96.

Benedict, Ruth
> 1938   "Continuities and discontinuities in cultural conditioning." Psychiatry 1:161–67.

Berger, Bennett M., B. M. Hackett, and R. M. Millar
> 1972   Child-rearing Practices in the Communal Family. Unpublished progress report to the National Institute of Mental Health.

Blau, Peter M., and Otis D. Duncan
> 1967   The American Occupational Structure. New York: Wiley.

Boocock, Sarane S.
> 1976   "Children and society." Paper prepared for presentation at the American Association for the Advancement of Science Annual Meeting (January 1975). Reprinted in Arlene Skolnick (ed.), Rethinking Childhood. Boston: Little, Brown.

Bronfenbrenner, Urie
  1974   "Developmental research, public policy, and the ecol-
          ogy of childhood." Child Development 45.

Brown, A. L., and J. C. Campione
  1978   "Permissible inference from the outcome of training
          studies in cognitive development research." Quarterly
          Newsletter of the Institute for Comparative Develop-
          ment 2:46–53.

Coveney, Peter
  1967   Image of Childhood: The Individual and Society, a
          Study of the Theme in English Literature. Baltimore:
          Penguin.

Damon, William
  1977   The Social World of the Child. San Francisco: Jossey,
          Bass

Douvan, E., and J. B. Adelson
  1966   The Adolescent Experience. New York: Wiley.

Elkin, F. A., and W. A. Westley
  1955   "The myth of adolescent culture." American Sociologi-
          cal Review 20:680–684.

Flavell, John H.
  1977   Cognitive Development. Englewood Cliffs, N.J.: Pren-
          tice-Hall.

Gelman, Rochel
  1978   "Cognitive development." Annual Review of Psychol-
          ogy 29:297–332.

Inhelder, Barbel, and Jean Piaget
  1958   Growth of Logical Thinking from Childhood to Adoles-
          cence. New York: Basic Books.

Hareven, Tamara
  1978   "Historical adulthood and old age." Pp. 201–16 in E.
          Erikson (ed.), Adulthood. New York: Norton.

Kagan, J.
  1977   "The child in the family." Daedalus 106:33–56.

Kalven, H., Jr.
    1973   Quoted in Margaret Rosenheim, "The child and the law." *In* B. Caldwell and H. Ricciuti (eds.), Child Development Research (Child Development and Social Policy) 3:509.

Keniston, Kenneth
    1971   "Psychosocial development and historical change." Journal of Interdisciplinary History 2:2:329–345.

Kessen, William
    1965   The Child. New York: Wiley.

Kett, Joseph F.
    1977   Rites of Passage: Adolescence in America. New York: Basic Books.

Lasch, Christopher
    1977   Haven in a Heartless World. New York: Basic Books.

Laslett, B.
    1974   "The family as a public and private institution: an historical perspective." Journal of Marriage and the Family 35 (August):480–94.

Lifton, Robert
    1969   "Protean man." Yale Alumni Review (January):17–21.

Marks, F. Raymond
    1975   "Detours on the road to maturity: a view of the legal conception of growing up and letting go." Law and Contemporary Problems 39:3:78–92.

Mnookin, Robert H.
    1977   "Children's rights: beyond child savers and kiddie libbers." Address to the American Psychological Association.

Morgan, Edmund S.
    1944   The Puritan Family. Boston: Public Library.

Offer, Daniel
    1969   Psychological World of the Teen-ager. New York: Basic Books.

Rapoport, Rhona, Robert N. Rapoport, A. Strelitz, and S. Kew.
    1977   Fathers, Mothers, and Society: Toward New Alliances. New York: Basic Books.

Rodham, Hillary
    1973   "Children under the law." Harvard Educational Review 43:487–514.

Rogers, C. M., and L. S. Wrightsman
    1978   "Attitudes towards children's rights: nurturance or self-determination." Journal of Social Issues 34:59–68.

Rothman, David J.
    1971   "Documents in search of a historian: towards a history of childhood and growth in America." Journal of Interdisciplinary History 2:2.

Spencer, Herbert
    1946   Essays on Education. New York: Dutton.

Stephens, William N.
    1963   The Family in Cross-cultural Perspective. New York: Holt, Rinehart and Winston.

Stern, D., S. Smith, and F. Doolittle
    1975   "How children used to work." Law and Contemporary Problems 3:93.

Stier, Serena
    1978   "Children's rights and society's duties." Journal of Social Issues 34:46–58.

Stone, Lawrence
    1977   The Family, Sex and Marriage in England, 1500–1800. New York: Harper and Row.

Sunley, Robert
    1955   "Early nineteenth-century American literature on child rearing." Pp. 150–67 in Margaret Mead and Martha Wolfenstein (eds.), Childhood in Contemporary Cultures. Chicago: Univ. of Chicago Press.

Wald, M.
    1978   "A framework for analyzing children's rights issues." Unpublished manuscript, Stanford Law School.

Whiting, B.
    1972   "Work and the family: cross-cultural perspectives."
            Harvard Graduate School of Education. Paper pre-
            pared for Conference on Women: Resource in a Chang-
            ing World.

Yankelovich, Daniel
    1977   Quoted in "A new kind of parent." San Francisco Chron-
            icle (April 21):1.

Social Contexts of Child Rights and Delinquency

James F. Short, Jr.

THE future of the Child Rights Movement—and more broadly of delinquency and childhood—is rooted in the past and is very much dependent on events and trends in the larger society. We are agreed on this, though we may disagree as to the precise roots of these phenomena and on the extent and degree of their dependence on external forces. Among the more important of these forces are the social contexts of child rights and delinquency—their variations and directions vis à vis a variety of social movements, institutional developments, and the general context of social change.

The history of childhood can be traced in many ways, and one of our tasks is to explore the implications for the future of varying perspectives on the past. Whatever perspective is adopted, it is clear that much has changed; this is somewhat humorously (some may say ominously) reflected in a news clipping I saved some time ago from the now defunct *National Observer*. Entitled "Freedom of Screech," the article reads, in part:

A 200-year-old Massachusetts law prohibits "throwing stink bombs, garbage, nails, or similar substances in public passageways," the state's Supreme Court recently ruled, but it doesn't mean you can't hurl a tirade of four-letter words in a department store aisle. The ruling came after a teenage boy, reportedly piqued following an argument with a saleswoman, shouted obscenities for 40 minutes in a Jordan Marsh store in Boston. The youth was charged under a state disorderly conduct law. But the Massachusetts high court ruled that the First Amendment's freedom-of-speech provision protects the use of vulgar and offensive words that do not "inflict injury" or tend to "incite injury" or tend to "incite an immediate breach of the peace." (Dwight Buell, National Observer, Fall 1975)

Age Groups as Interest Groups

That ruling surely would have shocked the justice's forebears in the Massachusetts Bay colony under whose strict Puritan code being a "stubborn or rebellious" son was a capital crime (Powers, 1970). Yet the law is essentially conservative, relying heavily on precedent, forging new proscriptions and prescriptions out of the experience and percevied interests of a variety of groups. While the young have often been the target of new laws and appellate decisions, it has not been *their* perceptions of common interests but those of their elders that have dominated lawmaking and enforcement vis à vis the young. Indeed, until very recently age groupings as such have not been active *as interest groups* in making and implementing law.

The one major exception has been the emergence of "gray power"—the banding together of older people in recent years to further their own collective self-interest. This phenomenon is instructive because of what it reveals about the Child Rights Movement. For, while it can be argued that membership in youth culture—more correctly, youth cultures—abounds, the diversity of interests among young people, often countercultural in nature, is such that it has contributed to the lawmaking and enforcement activities of other people, based on their perceptions of what is right, rather than to lawmaking that is based on what young people perceive to be in their own self-interest. When the members of youth culture have been involved in the pursuit of legal (i.e., political) objectives, therefore, it has more often been via protest rather than through traditional electoral and lobbying activities.

The civil rights movement and the Vietnam War mobilized many young people in both protest and electoral activities, but these were not in the interest of child rights or even of the young as an interest group (Skolnick, 1969). Furthermore, it is well to remember that many young people were hawkish with respect to the war and that Governor Wallace's national political ambitions received major support from among the young (Lipset, 1971). Likewise, I have noted elsewhere that, at the height of civil rights activism in the early 1960s, while white gang members in Chicago were opposing efforts to integrate public facilities and neighborhoods, members of black gangs were uninvolved in the struggle and apathetic toward it (Short, 1976.) It was not they but the children of middle-class black families who pressed outward from the restrictions of ghetto living and who bore the brunt of civil rights confrontations. Even then these middle-class youth acted more as individuals—as members of black families and occasionally as participants with pro–civil rights groups in the civil rights movement—than as members of a group that was uniquely youthful. Meanwhile, their counterparts in the slums were isolated from that struggle and preoccupied with their own largely internecine conflicts. Some ghetto youth as individuals broke out of this type of self-defeating struggle by participating in heavily underwritten higher education programs. But the results of these programs were limited at best because they were designed and financed by well-meaning, but often naive and misguided, groups who had little appreciation for the special problems of ghetto youth in middle-class (and often elite) colleges and universities.[1]

A few gangs reached for legitimate status during the salad

[1] I know of no systematic evaluations of such programs, but my impression is that the failures far outnumber the successes. The extremes of success and failure are illustrated by two young men of my acquaintance. One, a strapping young man of considerable physical prowess, was perhaps the outstanding gang leader in Chicago's west side during the early 1960s. He was placed in an elite eastern college where he hung on for two years, occasionally engaging in athletic competition. The semirural setting of the college remained foreign to him, however, and he returned to the streets at every opportunity. He finally dropped out, became addicted to heroin and deeply involved in the street-level drug traffic. The second boy, somewhat younger than the other, never joined a gang, though friends and relatives were active in the same west side gang with which the other young man was associated. This boy was picked out by a screening examination in his public high school, sent to an eastern preparatory school for his last two years, and subsequently graduated from an elite western university. He was an excellent student, and when I met him he was applying for admission to several of the top graduate business schools in the country.

days of the War on Poverty, again with the encouragement of well-meaning adult organizations (and a few individuals who for ideological or other intellectual reasons adopted their cause—see Fry, 1969, 1973; Dawley, 1973; Poston, 1971). But, again, the failures of these efforts were often spectacular, while successes were of short duration and limited to a few marginal business and cultural enterprises and to occasional individuals who sold themselves as experts in self-help who possessed special means for solving ghetto youth problems (Poston, 1971). A gullible, sometimes desperate public was willing for a time to believe and to be entertained by—and some to exploit and be exploited by—these enterprising young men. Inevitably, important opposition developed within city political organizations, which were affronted and threatened by the prospect of economically prosperous and politically powerful "young hoods." Whether or not that prospect was at all realistic, the end results of such efforts were hardly encouraging to the gangs or their supporters (Sherman, 1970; Short, 1974).

More recently the campaign against the "new prohibition" (Kaplan, 1971) of legalized marijuana growth, manufacture, and usage has attracted major support among the young through organizations such as NORML (National Organization to Reform Marijuana Legislation). Here again, however, there is also much opposition among the young, and such mobilization as has occurred is focused on specific interests rather than on the diffuse interests of an entire age group.

Impact of Change: On Youth, Crime, and Delinquency

The impact of social change falls unevenly across the age spectrum. For a variety of reasons, the impact of many social changes is greater on the young than on other age groups. Margaret Mead, among others, has remarked on the difficulties faced by the older generation in socializing the young for a future that will be so very different from the past which their elders have experienced. Contributors to this volume, I suspect, can testify to this insight, and those younger can recount some of the consequences of the problem. But the brunt of social change is borne by the young. Some of these impacts are direct—others indirect.

The Panel on Youth of the Presidents Science Advisory Committee (Coleman et al., 1974) notes that the population aged fourteen to twenty-four increased in the United States by 52 percent during the 1960–70 decade—by far the largest increase in our history. Equally dramatically, the ratio of the population aged fourteen to twenty-four to that aged twenty-five to sixty-four increased by 39 percent during the decade, compared to *decreases* experienced in every decade of our history except for the 1950–60 decade, during which no change occurred in this ratio. The impact of this change was felt throughout American society, but it was the young whose lives were most shaped by its consequences. The change meant, for example, that the most crime-prone age grouping in our society increased enormously during the 1960s, in contrast with our entire history as a nation. Following the very large increase in the population aged fourteen to twenty-four during the 1960s (52%), an increase of 11 percent is projected in 1970–80 and a decrease of 8 percent during the 1980s.

This dramatic demographic change created great pressures on childrearing institutions, especially schools, pressures that were exacerbated by a burgeoning civil rights movement that focused increasingly on schools following the 1954 decision of the U.S. Supreme Court. Riots in urban ghettos, assassinations of prominent political and civil rights leaders, and an unpopular war abroad also contributed to the turmoil of growing up during the 1960s. These and other developments occurred against a background of longer-term trends of increasing proportions of females in the work force and of nuclear family breakdown, as well as increased differentiation of childhood and state assumption of responsibility for child welfare.[2]

[2] Boli-Bennett and Meyer (1978) argue convincingly (and present data in support of their argument) that increased power and authority of the nation-state, on a worldwide scale has resulted in a world system in which "differentiated and state-managed childhood" have become ideologically dominant.

High Crime Rates

For whatever reasons—changing values and standards of conduct, socialization practices, ineffective controls—increases in
arrests for illegal behavior in recent years have been higher
for the young than for other age groups. For the more serious
(Class I) crimes, increases among the very young have been
especially dramatic for the violent crimes of homicide, robbery, and aggravated assault. Already these trends are shifting,
as the adolescents born in the late 1950s and early sixties pass
into young adulthood.

A second recent trend appears to be less affected by this
passage, however, namely, the increasing involvement of
young women, especially in serious common crime. Most of
the age-related trends referred to above can be acounted for
by the dramatic increase in the youthful population in the
United States during the decade of the 1960s (Ferdinand, 1970;
Blumstein and Nagin, 1974; Coleman et al., 1974). Increases
in criminal and delinquent behavior by females cannot. It is
hard to resist the conclusion that the success of the feminist
movement has had among its consequences a change in social-
control practices and in socialization with respect to behavior
options for females. These in turn have had the consequence
that behavior once thought inconceivable for females has become increasingly accessible to them (Harris, 1977). Once
again, the impact of such changes has been greatest on the
young. Relaxed controls on female children in families and
schools have had the effect of permitting, if not encouraging,
behavior that is defined as delinquent.

Both self-reports by young people and arrest data suggest
that increasing proportions of young females have become
involved in delinquent and criminal behavior over the past
few years. Patricia Miller's (1977) comparison of self-reports
from Illinois youth in 1972 with data collected earlier by the
same means in several Illinois communities and elsewhere
suggests that the prevalence of most types of delinquent behavior among males has changed little over the past twenty

years or more but that substantially more females have become involved in most delinquencies and crimes. Further, analysis of the Illinois data by means of factor analysis—computed separately for males and females—yields very similar patterns of involvement in misbehavior for boys and girls. Young women and men, in other words, are becoming very similar in their patterns of crime and delinquency. Higher percentages of males are delinquent and criminal, but the gap between males and females is narrowing, and when they are delinquent, their behavior is very similar.

Harris and Hill's (1977) careful analysis of arrest data reaches similar conclusions. The most dramatic change in arrests for crimes reported to the FBI has been the increasing involvement of young females in crimes traditionally thought of as male. The ratio of male to female arrests for six major propety crimes (burglary, larceny, motor vehicle theft, forgery and counterfeiting, fraud and embezzlement, and possession of stolen property) decreased from 10.4:1 in 1953 to 3.8:1 in 1974 (compared to a decrease from 9.1:1 to 7.9:1 for six major crimes involving violence or its threat). Importantly, the drop in ratios was greatest for females under eighteen years of age, compared to their adult counterparts.

Consider also the fact that persons under the age of eighteen account for nearly half of all arrests for serious (Class I) common property crime and nearly a quarter of the most serious violent crimes.[3] Extend the age period to twenty-one and these figures become two-thirds and 40 percent, respectively; extend it to under twenty-five and they were 77.5 percent and 57.8 percent in 1976. Perhaps more dramatically, in 1977 more sixteen-year-olds than any other single age category were arrested for the serious property crimes, followed by fifteen-year-olds, then seventeen-year-olds, after which the numbers declined rapidly. In the same year more eighteen-year-olds were arrested for serious violent crimes than any other single age, followed closely by seventeen-year-olds, nine-

[3] Serious (Class I) property crimes in the UCR system include burglary, larceny-theft, and motor vehicle thefts. Class I violent crimes include murder, forcible rape, robbery, and aggravated assault.

teen-year-olds, twenty-year-olds, and sixteen-year-olds. All of these figures have been reasonably stable over the past several years.

Youth Crime in the Future

While I do not wish to add to the "gloss of psychopathology" associated with adolescence (Skolnick, this volume), it would be naive not to recognize that an important social context of the Child Rights Movement is the high rate of involvement of the young in serious delinquency and crime. The figure cited above will inevitably decline as current demographic trends work their way through the age pyramid.

Common crime already has leveled off in recent years, largely, one suspects, as a result of these demographic changes. Before becoming too sanguine concerning prospects for further reductions, however, it is well to remember that present levels remain very high compared to most other parts of the world and that prospects for reduction in serious crime are influenced by more specific demographic changes than those cited above. Projections of urban minority populations, those with the highest involvement in serious street crimes, suggest that urban crime rates are likely to remain at a high level in the foreseeable future. For example, Zimring (1975) projects a rise in minority youth population, ages 12 to 17, from 12 percent of the urban population in 1970 to 20 percent in 1990. Miller's (1975) comparison of 1970 white, nonwhite, and black male populations with projections for 1980 in six "gang-problem cities" yields similar results. Without allowing for differences in either mortality or migration, the white male population aged 10 to 19 (the most active gang-age grouping) is projected to decrease by 5.2 percent by 1980 for the six cities (New York, Chicago, Los Angeles, Philadelphia, Detroit, and San Francisco), but nonwhite males in this age range are expected to increase by 8.4 percent and black males by 9.4 percent during this period. There is considerable variation from city to city in these respects, but for all six cities the prospect is for the age and ethnic groups already most heavily overrepresented in police and prison statistics to increase in the immediate future. It is difficult to be sanguine about the future of these young men and those slightly older, who already crowd the unemployment roles, especially as the burdens of the post–World War II population bulge passes from schools and other youth-serving agencies to the labor market.

Institutional Contexts of Child Rights and Delinquency

A variety of institutions serve as social contexts, at both micro- and macrosociological levels, for the behavior we define as delinquent and for the promotion and the exercise of child rights. Microsociological contexts most salient to the behavior of children occur in families, in community institutions, and on the streets, where juveniles interact with one another and with adults. While these are important in triggering particular episodes of behavior and in shaping that behavior (its delinquent or nondelinquent nature, its episodic nature, and varying patterns of participation by children and others), because the primary focus of this chapter is on social change, our interest is mainly at the macro level. There is a certain timeless quality to the interaction of young people with one another—their grouping and their behavior—and with parents and others. Differences in these microsociological contexts are bounded and heavily influenced by changes in macrolevel phenomena of culture and social structure.

Changes in family life, particularly as they are affected by demographic trends, are discussed in Davis's chapter in this volume. The impact of lowered fertility rates, alternative family styles, and changing values related to childrearing have only recently been studied systematically (Berger and Hackett, 1974; Eiduson and Alexander, 1978) and their long-term effects are far from clear. In the past, single parenting has been associated with higher rates of dependency and delinquency. As single parenting becomes more institutionalized and acceptable, member of such families may become less dependent and less threatening to the larger society. In the short run, however, the concentration of single parenting among the poor, the young, and the black does not encourage optimism in this respect.

Child Rights and the School

Another institutional context of special relevance for child rights and behavior is the school. While the "blackboard jungle" problems of urban schools have been documented by National Education Association and National Institute of Education studies and by testimony before congressional committees, serious studies are rare (Wenk and Harlow, 1978). Schools have increasingly been the focus of attempts to deal with major social issues by government and by nongovernmental organizations and social movements. This is especially the case with respect to civil rights, stemming from the 1954 *Brown* decision of the U.S. Supreme Court. Court decisions and board of education policies, compounded by racial antagonisms at the local level, have made schools a battleground of contending interests.

There is, of course, much variation in the extent to which individual schools have experienced developments such as these and in their adaptations to them. A thoughtful and penetrating analysis of two national surveys (the Equality of Educational Opportunity survey of 1965 and the 1970 Survey of Disruption in Urban Secondary Schools), supplemented by extensive interviews with school administrators in the San Francisco Bay area, nevertheless suggests some important similarities in perceptions of these problems and adaptations to them by school personnel (Meyer et al., 1971).

While there is a widespread belief that ethnic and racial problems and student crime and disorder have increased, school administrators relate those problems primarily to problems of the larger society rather than of the schools per se. Meyer et al. refer to this conceptualization of problems as one of *externalization*. In this view drug use, vandalism, theft, and racial and ethnic conflicts stem neither from relationships between students and schools nor from relationships between schools and communities. Rather, they reflect problems in the larger society, especially as these problems involve relationships between young people and society. Concomitantly, young people are viewed as less dependent, requiring less protection by schools, and as more independent; in short, they are regarded as citizens. These developments have been encouraged by widespread public discussion and general agreement that youth problems are not the primary responsibility of schools but are nationwide in scope.

The results of these developments, Meyer and his colleagues report, are a retreat from traditionally *in loco parentis* roles of schools and adapation to these problems rather than efforts directed toward their solution. Vandalism is responded to by target hardening. Drug abuse is handled on a case-by-case basis. Racial and ethnic conflict and concern over national problems are recognized as legitimate, and "the main and most successful method of handling disruptions and activism has been the creation of regularized channels of communication between student groups and the administration and the initiation of new programs attempting to meet the demands of student groups" (Meyer et al.: 77). In summary:

We believe that a major social change is occurring in the position of young people in society. They are increasingly asserting, and tacitly being allowed and encouraged to assert, their independence from familial and school controls. The schools have by and large been forced to acknowledge much of this independence, and have developed more limited controls and demands on student behavior.

The surrender of paternalistic authority by the schools of which we find so many examples creates two potential problems. First, it means that social attempts to regulate the behavior of young people are less and less able to work through the schools as mechanisms. The political, ethnic, and cultural (including drugs) tastes of young people, if they are to be defined as a problem, are a *societal* problem: the schools are making fewer efforts to restrict and control them. This creates a strain on all sorts of social control mechanisms outside the school. The contemporary conflicts between young people and the police reflect this strain—issues which the police and others used to turn over to families and schools for management can no longer be treated in this way.

The second problem created by the social change we are describing is not primarily a crime, or social control, problem at all. It is an educational problem—the schools have acknowledged the legitimate independence of young people, and now have to find more and more ways to appeal to this newly-defined constituency . . . there have . . . been great increases in student absenteeism, and other forms of student non-participation in secondary schools. Most of the administrators with whom we talked, in fact, discussed *this* rather than the problem of disorder as their major concern. Young people are seen as having the right to make many more choices than in the past. Large numbers of them are choosing nonparticipation in schools—so many that the truancy control system in many areas has completely broken down. In any case, it is no longer completely legitimated by anyone, since young people are now seen as having more authority to decide their own behavior. . . .

Thus the schools have adapted to the present turbulence by limiting their authority over the total lives of their students, and by responding to these students as independent persons and groups. They have, in a period of increasing youth turbulence, managed to get out of the line of fire. This has created an educational problem of new dimensions—how to appeal to the educational interests of young people—and has left many aspects of the problem of controlling the relation of young people with the wider society to other agencies or mechanisms. (Pp. 8–10)

Meyer et al. acknowledge that documentation of these changes is incomplete. However, widespread experimentation with alternative schools, emphasis on negotiation of school conflict (DeCocco and Roberts, 1978), on democratization of school authority relationships (Scharf, 1978; Wenk, 1978), and calls for increasing attention to problems of internal school organization (Ianni, 1978) suggest that the trends identified are real and continuing. Recognition that "the traditional reliance on the school as the primary medium for resolving social problems is no longer tenable" (Ianni, 1978, p. 34) and calls for changes in school-community relationships (e.g., Pink and Kapel, 1978) suggest that specialization of institutional roles and the resulting fragmentation of social-control mechanisms remain major problems.

Child Rights and the Juvenile Court

This conclusion is reinforced by a nationwide study of the juvenile justice system. The National Assessment of Juvenile Corrections project surveyed "more than 2,000 judges, court administrators, probation officers, detention supervisors, and other court staff" (Sarri and Hasenfeld, 1976). Analyzing "the Juvenile Court and its environment," Hasenfeld (1976:93) notes "a persistent central finding": "In their transactions with key external organizations, the courts experience only limited influence from them and very little conflict with them." He says further that

these findings have some important implications with regard to the character of juvenile courts . . . they imply that juvenile courts do not make extensive use of resources in the environment, which prevents a dependence on any of these resources from developing. Concomitantly, the courts do not seem to make efforts to mobilize such resources or challenge existing agencies to serve youth in trouble. . . . Nor is there any evidence to suggest that such agencies are willing to serve such youth; rather, it seems that they prefer the court to assume responsibility for them. Children under court jurisdiction are likely to be thrust into a very narrow and limited pool of court services and be excluded from a wide variety of community youth services just at the time they need access to as many services as possible. (Hasenfeld, 1976:94–95)

Specific responses of juvenile court judges, court administrators, and probation officers in this survey indicate that the principal demands on the court made by schools are for isolation of juvenile offenders from the community and the development of more services within the court (Hasenfeld, 1976:87–89). Hasenfeld terms this finding "not surprising . . . since the schools always try to harness the court into removing troublemakers from the schools on their behalf" (p. 860).

Thus, two of the institutions most central to youth-community relations—the school and the juvenile court—appear to have adopted strategies of limiting their responsibilities for youth and specializing their functions. These strategies protect schools and courts from dependence and conflict with one another and from excessive demands from the community.

These strategies also are part of the continuing retreat from *in loco parentis* roles and philosophies that have characterized schools and juvenile courts throughout their histories in this country. This change is itself the product of complex forces, including changes in beliefs about the nature of childhood, controversies concerning institutional practices, and the law, and changing relationships among groups in the larger society (see, e.g., Empey, 1978; Finestone, 1976; Sennett, 1976; Moore, 1977; Silberman, 1978). Implications of these developments for the social fabric of society and for the ability of large-scale societies to act are profound. These developments reflect the breakdown of traditional patterns of authority and increasing reliance upon legal processes in regulating social relationships that were traditionally the province of other institutions. In addition to the family, the school, and the court, institutions of economy and polity are of special importance for child rights and delinquency.

Economy and Polity

While economic projection remains an inexact science, there is a general agreement that high rates of inflation and unemployment are likely to be with us for the foreseeable future. The economic drain of high military expenditures and foreign trade deficits, capital-intensive, rather than labor-intensive economic policies will be slow to change, if they change at all. This means that, despite recent gains (Farley, 1977), there will continue to be a very large pool of unemployed, and probably unemployable, young people, particularly of minority status. It is these who will continue to flood our court dockets and our prisons, placing additional strain on public willingness to support either child rights or the experimental policies needed to reform our justice systems.

There is yet another crime-related factor in the economic equation. Ianni (1974) has documented the movement into organized crime by minority groups who were previously excluded, except in the most menial capacities, from the most lucrative rackets—narcotics, gambling, and loansharking. The participation of increasing numbers of blacks and persons of Latin American extraction in this "queer ladder of social mobility" in American society (Bell, 1953) is not likely to encourage the extension of further rights to the young among these age groups. And, if not to them, can rights be extended only to the already privileged? Indeed, if we are unwilling as a nation to extend equal rights to women, who constitute approximately one-half our population, are we likely to be able to agree that equality in all matters should be extended to children?

The latter consideration is, of course, a reflection of political climate. There is already evident a new conservatism with respect to correctional policies and juvenile justice, despite the four D's (*due process* in courts, *diversion* from juvenile and criminal justice systems, *deinstitutionalization* and reintegration in local communities, and *decriminalization* of behavior not seriously injurious to others) that have characterized recent juvenile justice changes (Empey, 1978). LaMar Empey in his book *American Delinquency: Its Meaning and Construction* notes that the "hands-off" ideology of the movement to reintegrate children with their communities and the larger society, rather than isolating them by means of incarceration (i.e., deinstitutionalization), together with the other three D's reflects recent social changes with respect to child rights (Empey, 1978:563 ff.). He cites lowering the age of political suffrage to eighteen; court decisions protecting freedom of expression; the considerable rethinking that has occurred concerning child-labor restrictions, which often restrict more than they protect children; sexual freedoms not enjoyed by previous generations; and "freedom without responsibility," resulting from affluence and delayed entry into the labor force. Empey interprets these trends to mean "that we are in a transitional phase in our beliefs about childhood" (p. 568). But "transition" implies change from one state to another. It seems more appropriate to think of the present and future state of society as one of change, with no implication of static condition.

It is also the case that, while social movements and other attempts to create change by institutional means are important factors in social change, these and other trends have developed crescively more than by enactment. Changing legal and other institutional rules and practices react to and reflect changing conditions more than they create them. The call for "liberation" and "self-determination," if too vigorously and naively pursued, may work to the disadvantage of child rights, both to protection and nurturance *and* to self-determination. There is evidence, also, albeit of unknown representativeness, of adult resentment regarding "special privileges" already accorded youth, especially troublesome youth. A policeman is quoted by Carter (1976) as saying that "juvenile justice is slow. Jesus, the rights these kids have got. They have more rights that I have. . . . I'm not talking about the Mickey Mouse cases; I mean the hoodlums" (Carter, 1976:124).

My own research into the consequences of War on Poverty programs for gangs and programs oriented toward them makes a related but somewhat different point. A former detached worker with Chicago's Vice Lords noted that "many local adults are resentful over the public attention received by the gangs, and particularly so of funds granted in support of businesses. 'How is a guy going to feel who has run a business when he sees a bunch of young gang boys without experience getting money to run a competing business? Or if he has had to quit that business because he didn't get that sort of help?' " (Short, 1976:144–5). These quotes represent an unknown but, I suspect, significantly large counterreaction by adults to the movement for child rights. More generally, the new conservatism is fueled by the generally low level of confidence in those who "run" major social institutions in this country. A compilation of survey results from the General Social Survey (GSS) of the National Opinion Research Center and the Harris organization documents these declining levels of confidence among carefully drawn samples of U.S. adults (see Smith, 1977).

The GSS reports that only about 14 percent of the adults sampled expressed "a great deal of confidence" in either the Congress or the Executive Branch of the federal government in 1976, and the trend over past years was declining. In contrast, fully a quarter of respondents indicated "hardly any confidence" in these institutions in 1976, and this trend was rising. The U.S. Supreme Court fared better, with slightly more than a third expressing "a great deal of confidence," only 15 percent "hardly any," and with no clear trend. Organized labor fared even worse than the federal government in these surveys (12% "a great deal," 33% "hardly any" with similar trends), while "major companies" fared slightly better (equal percentages—22%—expressing "a great deal" and "hardly any" confidence, both trending unfavorably to the companies). Harris surveys, meanwhile, report similar trends but find even less confidence at both ends of the scale.

A few institutions are more favorably viewed by the general public. Medicine and the scientific community lead the list of "high confidence" institutions, with the GSS reporting 54 percent at this end of the scale for medicine in 1976 (compared to Harris's 42%) and only 9.2 percent expressing "hardly any" confidence (Harris, 11.7%). Both surveys report declining confidence in medicine over time, however. The scientific community is slightly less favored at the "great deal" end of the scale (43% GSS, 48% Harris, in 1976), but the trend in both surveys is positive; and somewhat fewer respondents express "hardly any" confidence in the scientific community than in medicine (about 7.5% in both surveys with only a slightly rising trend). The educational establishment also is more favored than the federal government (with the notable exception of the Supreme Court), 37.5 percent reporting "a great of confidence" in the 1976 GSS survey, and 15 percent "hardly any." The former has fluctuated but with no clear trend, while the latter has risen slightly. Banks and financial institutions are also favored with a relatively high degree of confidence (39.5% GSS; 33.5% Harris), with only 1 in 10 respondents in both surveys expressing "hardly any." The two surveys disagree as to trends at both ends of the scale.

TV and the press are viewed similarly to major companies in these surveys, with the press receiving slightly better marks than TV. Finally, the two surveys disagree the most in their reported assessment of the military, with the GSS reporting 39 percent high confidence, compared to only 22.5 percent by Harris, GSS finding no trend, Harris a declining trend. As the "low confidence" end of the scale, GSS reports less unfavorable assessment of the military (13% compared to 21% by Harris) and stability in trend compared to Harris's slightly rising trend of low confidence.

It would be unwise to read too much into these data so far as public support of any partiuclar social movement or other projected social change is concerned. Viewed together with a spreading tax revolt and other evidence of disillusionment with big government, as well as with big labor and big business, and a generally more conservative atmosphere than existed in the 1960s, they suggest that the public may be less willing to experiment, less tolerant of experimentation, than has been the case in the immediate past. People who do not trust their institutions are likely to be conservatively suspicious of innovation, and it is difficult to envision children's rights as the sort of bold new initiative that could reinstate confidence in these institutions. Recent setbacks experienced by the Gay Rights movement in municipal elections—a principal component of which has been concern over the influence on children of homosexuals—suggest that the public is in no mood to alter in fundamental ways traditional patterns of childrearing, including the granting of additional legal rights.

These developments again seem to suggest that, while political and economic changes affect us all, they have their greatest impact on the young, whose future jobs are most often altered, created, or eliminated. Ideological currents likewise have their most profound influence on the young. Older age groups are more set in their ways. They must, or feel that they must, make vocational and ideological commitments in a variety of institutional contexts, which render them less vulnerable to ideological appeal. These same commitments make radical change difficult for the older generation. By way of contrast, the young are more often free to participate in changing life-styles and social movements because of their prolonged period of dependence, which now extends well into young adulthood. Yet it is paradoxical that this same freedom militates against involvement of the young in their own behalf, for their interests are so diverse and their energies so diffused that potential support for the Child Rights Movement is dissipated.

The young, in fact, have been the foot soldiers of many fads, fashions, social movements, and revolutions. Their elders generally have provided intellectual and operational leadership for the latter two, and they have profited enormously from the former. And, of course, the young have been the primary victims of wars fought by nations throughout the centuries, just as they are of crime.

Considerations such as these highlight the vulnerability of the young and their special needs, in contrast with civil rights per se—a distinction recognized by child advocates of both the "self-determination" and "nurturance" orientations (Baumrind, 1978). It is apparent, also, that youth are much involved in many aspects of their own self-determination and fulfillment of their needs. Then involvement often takes the form of youth subcultures.

Youth Cultures, Child Rights, and Political Advocacy

After consideration of numerous technical reports and discussions, the panel on youth of the President's Science Advocacy Committee (Coleman et al., 1974) highlighted two themes: (1) increasing age separation in social and economic affairs, including separation of children of different ages, within and outside the family, and between young people and adults; (2) increasing options for youth with respect to recreation, education, and vocation.

The first theme is especially important insofar as creation

of an interest group out of an age category is at issue. Segregation of the young provides a basis for such an eventuality.
Glaser describes as "probably the most powerful explanatory
proposition in our discipline" the "law of socioculture relativ-
ity"; that is, that "social separation produces cultural differentiation" (Glaser, 1976:257). There can be little doubt that
separation of the young, from adults and among themselves,
conduces powerfully to the fromation of youth cultures in
great variety. But that is the point: youth cultures are hardly
of a piece. Indeed, variation in the extreme has been their
hallmark, so much so that it is difficult to identify common
cause among them. What they do share however, are certain
functional characteristics, all tending to meet certain fundamental needs among youth: learning and experiencing interpersonal relationships, social as well as more narrowly sexual
in nature; defining, achieving, and maintaining status. Beyond
this, some are highly specialized in the interests served, some
extremely broad in scope, some countercultural, and others
merely subcultural and highly conventional. Some involve values, artifacts, and practices that pit youth against youth. Others
are more cooperative, even altruistic, in goal orientations.
Some are aggressive, others withdrawn in their orientation
to the world at large and particular segments of it. Both the
variety of youth subcultures and the similarity of their functional characteristics have special implications for meeting the
needs of children and for child rights.

Political Advocacy

The increasingly politicized nature of social issues and social
problems has been noted many times. Historian Hugh Davis
Graham (1972), for example, notes that our capitalistic, federal
structure has historically pitted our racial, ethnic, and economic groups against one another rather than against the state.
Expansion of the power of the federal government during
the depression of the 1930s and following World War II has
altered this process, with the result that groups in increasing

numbers look to government for redress of grievance and promotion of special interest. But, as we have seen, the young appear not to be a viable political constituency. In addition to all other considerations, the young have the great handicap that they do not long remain young. This is precisely the point of population projections. The young grow older, and, as they do so, their social, economic, and political interests change.

Even the most enthusiastic supporters of children's liberation recognize that children are not likely to unite in support of the cause and that adult advocacy is necessary, though they hope for the day when "those adult efforts will give way . . . to the self determined efforts of children themselves" (Farson, 1974:8 ff). A recent survey of high school and college students, including adults enrolled in continuing education classes, finds that all groups give stronger support to nurturant than to self-determination rights in five content areas (health, education, economics, safety, and politics) but that high school students are generally less supportive of nurturant rights and more supportive of self-determination than are undergraduate education majors, other undergraduates, or adults. At the very least this suggests the importance of carefully studying a variety of youth and other segments of the population with respect to the questions at issue.

Farson also notes that "America has a long tradition of people helping oppressed groups to which they do not themselves belong, even when they themselves are regarded as oppressors. Whites were active in the emancipation of blacks. Men have been helpful in reducing the oppression of women. So it is that adults are working to help children." (See also chap. 13, pp. 213 ff.)

But the history of other liberation efforts and their real and potential conflicts with efforts to advance children's rights are not encouraging. Newman et al. (1978) find that advances toward black liberation, for example, have required powerful and persistent action on the part of blacks and that, without such efforts, advocacy by others has been relatively ineffective. Likewise, it is difficult to conceive of a successful feminist movement without heroic efforts on the part of women.

Hence, it is questionable whether more can be expected of adults to liberate the young.

The issue becomes even more problematic in view of (1) extensive youthful involvement in other social movements, such as minority civil rights (in each of which minority youth have played significant roles), women's rights, conservation and environmental protection, consumerism, liberation movements on the left and right, transcendental meditation, and a host of therapeutic and religious movements, some of which eschew activism of all types; and (2) existing and potential conflicts between child rights (both nurturance and self-determination) and other social movements. The fact that the young have been the foot soldiers—and often among the leaders—of social movements might lead the politically naive to suppose that these movements need only combine their energies to insure success. But of course it does not work that way. There is some overlapping participation in the many organizations and movements to which young and old devote their energies, but there is also a good deal of competition, and one group will often sit on its hands when matters of moment to another group are at issue.

The aging of the U.S. population and the rapidly developing political power of the aged are also important vis à vis children's rights. There may be less room at the top (and at other locations in economic institutions) as some older people choose to take advantage of raised mandatory retirement age standards. Much will depend on the generosity of retirement incentives, but continued inflation is sure to work against the young in this respect, as older people choose continued employment as a hedge against its ravages.

Of equal or greater importance, an aging U.S. population, especially when it is well organized, will place additional burdens on the economy, demanding resources that might otherwise go to meet needs of the young. The very real need to provide additional resources for health, education, and opportunities for the handicapped, minorities, and the very young, for example, is likely to conflict with pressing needs of the elderly. While in the long run zero population growth seems likely to enhance prospects for a better life for all (Time Magazine, Februrary 28, 1977 p. 71), short-run prospects—exacerbated by a faltering economy and growing political conflicts—suggest that competition for scarce resources will increase rather than decrease in intensity.

Divided Priorities among Rights Advocates

All of this would seem to place an especially heavy burden on adults who choose to promote the causes of children's rights. There is no shortage of specific candidates for child advocacy: parents, educators and members of other helping professions, medicine, the law, politicians. Yet it is also clear that each of these groups is profoundly divided with respect to support for nurturance versus self-determination for children, support for children versus support for the elderly or the poor, the handicapped, or minorities. The priorities of advocates are not clearcut. They are further divided, moreover, with respect to various types and degrees of protection and self-determination for children and over the most desirable means for achieving these objectives (cf., for example, Rosen, Rekers, and Bentler, 1978, and Morin and Schultz, 1978, with respect to children and sexual preference).

It seems likely, also, that the credibility of the helping professions is at issue in these matters. Recent historical research (e.g., Rothman, 1971; Platt, 1969), as well as contemporary commentary on a variety of helping professions and institutions (e.g., Illich, 1970; Silberman, 1970; Szasz, 1961), is highly critical of their motives and achievements. "Alternative" institutional forms are being experimented with in great variety, especially in education, family life, religion, group and individual therapies. There is, in addition, great need for careful assessment of both scientific evidence and ethical issues related to child rights. Diana Baumrind (1978) argues forcefully that

to grant that children should have all the rights now possessed by adults contradicts four propositions which have gained wide popular and scientific support: a) children undergo successive qualitative transformations requiring commensurate changes in social status as they pass from one stage of development to the next; b) children are inferior to adults in the competencies required to survive independently and therefore require special protection; c) self-determination in adulthood is a product of maturation and not a gift bestowed by permissive caretakers; and d) adult authority properly exercised in the early years is positively related to later independence.

Baumrind argues, in addition, that "the ethically insupportable feature of the children's liberation movement is its failure to acknowledge that dependent status precludes possession of the full rights of the emancipated person; the principle of reciprocity in parent-child relations is thereby rejected" (pp. 181–82).

State-managed Childhood

In the final analysis, the most powerful thrust for extension of children's rights may come from the impact on socialization beliefs and practices of the "dominance of the ideology of differentiated and state-managed childhood." This ideology, Boli-Bennett and Meyer (1978:810) continue, "reflects the rise of both individualism and the rationalized nation-state." On the one hand, the conception that individuals are free agents requiring socialization and that socialization is properly a function of the nation-state creates pressures both for the extension of civil rights and for the proper alignment of individuals with the state (through socialization and other control mechanisms). On the other hand, the societal (nation-state) stake in children is based not only on individual rights but on responsibility of individuals as citizens as well; hence, authority over children is not really abandoned, only transferred.

The extent to which the state has become both arbiter and authority over socialization of children in the United States continues to be much debated and contested in other ways. The most thoughtful current debates suggest that further extensions of rights to children will be accompanied by attention to concordant but limited responsibilities for them (see, e.g., Skolnick and Zimring in this volume). But while it is not within the province of this paper to resolve or even to engage these arguments, the scientific and ethical issues they raise are relevant to the larger social context within which they will ultimately be resolved. Baumrind's (1978:180) further observation seems apposite: "Unfortunately, it is just those adults who are insensitive to the indignities daily inflicted on children, and unaware of the unique capacities of children and adolescents, who will be further turned off to youth by the . . . radical rhetoric" of the child liberators. Whether in any case extension of rights would achieve the goals of child liberators remains problematic. For, as Boli-Bennett and Meyer (1978:811) note, "The extension of citizenship to the kindergarten or anywhere else, is at best an ambiguous step on the path to true equality or freedom."

A Final Note: A Comparative Perspective

Social Scientists and child rights advocates in the United States, of whatever persuasion, characteristically ignore the rest of the world, especially the non-Western world and those vast areas often referred to as "underdeveloped" or "developing." We tend, also to be preoccupied with the here and the now, though a few of the papers in this volume offer a welcome corrective. These tendencies are understandable in view of complex empirical and theoretical issues related to child rights and pressing problems of action in this country. But neglect of the past and of other societies and nations severely limits the empirical base of knowledge concerning these issues, the scope of theoretical interpretations, and the generalizability of action taken.

Recent scholarship has begun to correct our historical myopia, but many areas of potential import remain virtually untapped (see Takanishi, 1978), and the history of childhood tends to be viewed somewhat ethnocentrically in terms of the Western world. Historical concern with child rights is even more limited in scope. Takanishi's recent "Chronology of Events Related to Movements for Children's Rights," for example, is limited to the United States, beginning in 1873 when the American Medical Association formed a section on obstetrics and diseases of women and children. Her second event, occurring a year later, in 1874, notes the organization of the New York Society for the Prevention of Cruelty to Children, "10 years after the Society for the Prevention of Cruelty to Animals" (Takanishi, 1978:21).

Comparative Study of Child Rights

A full-scale comparative study of child rights is, of course, a major undertaking far beyond the ambitions of this paper. A few examples must suffice to illustrate the importance of comparative study to the social contexts of child rights and delinquency. The spring 1978 issue of the *Journal of Social Issues,* an official publication of the Society for the Psychological Study of Social Issues, is devoted to a variety of historical, scientific, legal, philosophical, and ethical issues related to child rights. The papers provide an excellent summary of the state of knowledge regarding important issues and make a substantial contribution to knowledge in their own right. From a comparative perspective, however, their scope is quite limited. Thus, editors of this issue, Norma Deitch Feshbach and Seymour Feshbach, refer in their introductory paper to the need for research concerning "the values and perceptions of the consumer—children and their families"—as a basis "for child advocacy and sound intervention" (Feshbach and Feshbach, 1978:2).

Yet a case can be made that, throughout much of the world, the principal consumer in matters concerning child rights is neither child nor parents but increasingly the modern nation-state, demands for loyalty to which supersede those to family, tribe, or other primordial group. There remain vast differences, despite increased "integration and, in some key respects, homogeneity of national societies in the globally unified value and stratification system" (Boli-Bennett and Meyer, 1978:810).[4] While in the United States and other Western democracies the issue of child rights is often posed as a conflict between parental autonomy and children's legal rights (Stier, 1978), the ideal in the People's Republic of China, for example, subordinates both to the pursuit of revolutionary goals. As Whyte (1973:155) notes:

No aspect of the life of an individual is regarded as completely irrelevant to his organizational performance. Informal contacts within the organization, outside recreation with friends, marital relationships, and many other factors are seen as affecting the performance of individuals. The leaders of a Maoist organization are to try to make sure that all these influences support, rather than undermine, organizational goals. Internal activities are highly organized, spare time recreation is arranged, evening political study sessions are run, and at times efforts are even made to organize families and outside friends for organizational purposes.

While this might recall the paternalism of some larger corporations in Western-style bureaucracies, the difference lies in (1) the pervasiveness of the Chinese model and the extent to which organizational efforts permeate the lives of *all* members;[5] and (2) the primacy of political (revolutionary) goals in China versus corporate goals in the West. Traditional family ties and values of autonomy and self-determination are undermined both in ideology and practice. As the American Delegation on Early Childhood Development in the People's

[4] This comment continues: "States pursue progress within the agreed-upon frame. Among these formally similar states such institutions of modernity as collectively managed childhood, evolved organizationally in world centers and moved rapidly as institutional recipes for progress to the most distant peripheries" (Boli-Bennett and Meyer, 1978:810).

[5] These efforts tend to make Chinese organizations more total in scope and more pervasive than their Western counterparts (i.e., their members engage in more joint activities and there are more activities inside and outside the organization for which the organization sets norms; (see Etzioni, 1961:160–63) (Whyte, 1973:155). These and other practices may change, with changed relationships between the People's Republic and other nations, especially the United States, perhaps narrowing the cultural differences here discussed.

Republic of China notes from their 1973 visit to that country, " 'Serving the people' seems to carry an emphasis on helping the peasants, workers, and soldiers rather than an emphasis on strengthening and protecting the initial family" (Kessen, 1975:38). And, noting the larger historical and cultural context, "Chinese children are defined by a long history of the culture's respect for order, restraint, deference to authority, and for service to the group above individual achievement" (p. 216).

While the emphasis on individual socialization is no less strong in the People's Republic than in Western democracies—indeed, it appears more so—concern over children's rights to self-determination, as distinct from child protection and nurturance, are absent. These are rooted in Western notions of individualism that many nations find they either cannot afford or wish to avoid on philosophical grounds. "Minimal security concerns" for food, shelter, and personal safety dominate both personal activities and governmental policies where they remain problematic (Heginbotham, 1977). Only when minimal security is assured are further concerns related to nurturance likely to be attended to, or particular groups such as the handicapped, abused, neglected, delinquent, or dependent made the objects of special concern. Kessen (1975:45) and his colleagues concluded that, in the People's Republic of China, "the child is indeed prepared for a somewhat spartan future built on cooperation with and respect for others." Self-determination is devalued in the interest of collectivist goals, while self-dedication to these goals is stressed. Pressures for fulfillment of subsistence needs are even greater in many parts of the world. And, as noted earlier, they differ considerably within the United States, though on a scale somewhat reduced from the immediately prior discussion.

Comparative Study of Delinquency

A comparative perspective is equally important with respect to crime and juvenile delinquency, as recent research suggests (see, e.g., Clinard, 1979; Short, 1979). While problems of youth have certain universal qualities, variations under different economic and political systems may inform the nature of these problems in our own as well as other societies. Even against the background of ideological convergence on differentiated and state-managed childhood, the implications for children of such vast differences in resources, cultures, social structures, histories, and contemporary problems are profound.

It is possible to conceive many scenarios for the future. Even the most radical of the child liberationists speak of eminently reasonable strategies, such as "continuing escalation to the concerns of larger groups" and commitment of competing and conflicting groups "to a superordinate goal that requires their cooperation for its solution" for "Redesigning the American Way of Life" (Farson, 1974:233,224). Granted that much needs to be redesigned—and on a worldwide scale—perhaps we can agree upon strategies for addressing problems of human needs and rights at every level, from minimal security to human dignity, regardless of social system or cultural commitments. To do so, we must reestablish a sense of common interest—is "Community" too much to expect in our highly fragmented society? As a start we might rely less upon the law to redress grievance and maintain social order. Legal remedy, though often necessary, is a poor basis for the discovery of common interest. There is hope for such discovery in other institutions, whose functions remain despite greatly altered circumstances. In their resiliency—as opposed to their intransigence—may be the basis for renewed common interest and community.

References

Baumrind, Diana
    1978   "Reciprocal rights and responsibilities in parent-child relations." Journal of Social Issues 34:2:179–96.

Bell, Daniel
    1953   "Crime as an American way of life." Antioch Review 13:131–54.

Berger, Bennett M., and B. M. Hackett
    1974   "On the decline of age grading in rural hippie communities." Journal of Social Issues 30:2:163–84.

Blumstein, Alfred, and Daniel S. Nagin
    1974   Analysis of Arrest Rates for Trends in Criminality. Pittsburgh: Carnegie Mellon University School of Urban and Public Affairs.

Boli-Bennett, John, and John W. Meyer
    1978   "The ideology of childhood and the state: rules distinguishing children in national constitutions, 1870–1970." American Sociological Review 43:6:797–812.

Carter, Robert M.
    1976   "The police view of the justice system." Pp. 121–32 in Malcolm W. Klein (ed.), The Juvenile Justice System. Beverly Hills, Calif.: Sage

Clinard, Marshall B.
    1978   Cities with Little Crime: The Case of Switzerland. Cambridge: Cambridge Univ. Press.

Coleman, James S., et al.
    1974   Youth: Transition to Adulthood. Report of the Panel on Youth of the President's Science Advisory Committee. Chicago: Univ. of Chicago Press.

Dawley, David
    1973   A Nation of Lords. Garden City, N.Y.: Anchor Books.

DeCocco, John, and John Roberts
  1978   "Negotiating school conflict to prevent student delin-
          quency." Pp. 168–76 *in* Ernst Wenk and Nora Harlow
          (eds.), School Crime and Disruption. Davis, Calif.: Re-
          sponsible Action.

Eiduson, Bernice T., and Jannette W. Alexander
  1978   "The role of children in alternative family styles." Jour-
          nal of Social Issues 34:2:149–67.

Empey, LaMar T.
  1978   American Delinquency: Its Meaning and Construction.
          Homewood, Ill.: Dorsey.

Etzioni, Amitai
  1961   A Comparative Analysis of Complex Organization. New
          York: Free Press.

Farley, Reynolds
  1977   "Trends in racial irregularities: have gains of the 1960's
          disappeared in the 1970's?" American Sociological Re-
          view 42:2:189–208.

Farson, Richard
  1974   Birthrights. New York: Macmillan.

Ferdinand, Theodore N.
  1970   "Demographic shifts and criminality: an inquiry." Brit-
          ish Journal of Criminology (April):169–75.

Feshbach, Norma Dietch, and Seymour Feshbach
  1978   "Toward an historical, social, and developmental per-
          spective on children's rights." Journal of Social Issues
          34:2:1–7.

Finestone, Harold
  1976   "The delinquent and society: the Shaw and McKay tra-
          dition." Pp. 23–49 *in* James F. Short, Jr. (ed.), Delin-
          quency, Crime, and Society. Chicago: Univ. of Chicago
          Press.

Fry, John
  1969   Fire and Blackstone. Philadelphia: Lippincott.

  1973   Locked-Out Americans. New York: Harper and Row.

Glaser, Daniel
1976   "Marginal workers." Pp. 254–66 *in* James F. Short, Jr. (ed.), Delinquency, Crime, and Society. Chicago: Univ. of Chicago Press.

Graham, Hugh Davis
1972   "The paradox of American violence: a historical appraisal." Pp. 201–9, *in* James F. Short, Jr., and Marvin E. Wolfgang (eds.), Collective Violence. Chicago: Aldine.

Harris, Anthony R.
1977   "Sex and theories of deviance: toward a functional theory of deviant type-scripts." American Sociological Review 42:1:3–16.

Harris, Anthony, and Gary Hill
1977   "Changes in the gender patterning of crime, 1953–1974: opportunity vs. socialization." Paper read at the Annual meetings of the American Sociological Association, September (mimeo).

Hasenfeld, Yeheskel
1976   "The juvenile court and its environment." Pp. 72–95 *in* Rosemary Sarri and Yeheskel Hasenfeld (eds.), Brought to Justice? Juveniles, the Courts, and the Law. Ann Arbor: National Assessment of Juvenile Corrections, University of Michigan.

Heginbotham, Stanley J.
1977   "The study of South Asian conceptual systems." Social Science Research Council Items 31:3:34–36(April).

Ianni, Francis A. J.
1974   Black Mafia: Ethnic Succession in Organized Crime. New York: Simon and Schuster.

1978   "The social organization of the high school: school-specific aspects of school crime." *In* Ernst Wenk and Nora Harlow (eds.), School Crime and Disruption. Davis, Calif.: Responsible Action.

Illich, Ivan
1970   De-Schooling Society. New York: Harper and Row.

Janowitz, Morris
   1978   The Last Half-Century: Societal Change and Politics in America. Chicago: Univ. of Chicago Press.

Kaplan, John
   1971   Marijuana: The New Prohibition. New York: Podies.

Kessen, William
   1975   Childhood in China. New Haven: Yale Univ. Press.

Lipset, Seymour
   1971   "Youth and politics." Pp. 743–91 *in* Robert K. Merton and Robert Nisbet (eds.), Contemporary Social Problems. New York: Harcourt Brace Jovanovich.

Meyer, John W., Chris Chase-Dunn, and James Inverarity
   1971   The Expansion of the Autonomy of Youth: Responses of the Secondary School to Problems of Order in the 1960's. Technical Report #41. Laboratory for Social Research, Department of Sociology, Stanford University (mimeo).

Miller, Patricia Y.
   1977   "Delinquency and gender." Unpublished manuscript, Institute for Juvenile Research, Department of Mental Health, State of Illinois (mimeo).

Miller, Walter B.
   1975   Violence by Youth Gangs and Youth Groups as a Crime Problem in Major American Cities. National Institute for Juvenile Justice and Delinquency Prevention. Washington, D.C.: U.S. Government Printing Office.

   1976   "Youth gangs in the urban crisis era." Pp. 91–128 *in* James F. Short, Jr. (ed.), Delinquency, Crime, and Society. Chicago: Univ. of Chicago Press.

Moore, Barrington, Jr.
   1977   Injustice: The Social Bases of Obedience and Revolt. White Plains, N.Y.: M. E. Sharpe.

Morin, Stephen F., and Stephen J. Schultz
   1978   "The gay movement and the rights of children." Journal of Social Issues 34:2:137–48.

Newman, Dorothy K., Nancy J. Amidei, Barbara L. Carter, Dawn Day, William J. Kruvant, and Jack S. Russell.
1978   Protest, Politics, and Prosperity. New York: Pantheon.

Pink, William T., and David E. Kapel
1978   Decentralization Reconsidered: School Crime Prevention through Community Involvement. *In* Ernst Wenk and Nora Harlow (eds.), School Crime and Disruption. Davis, Calif.: Responsible Action.

Platt, Anthony M.
1969   The Child Savers: The Invention of Delinquency. Chicago: Univ. of Chicago Press.

Poston, R. W.
1971   The Gang and the Establishment. New York: Harper and Row.

Powers, Edwin
1970   "Crime and punishment in early Massachusetts, 1620–1692." Reprinted in Paul Lerman (ed.), Delinquency and Social Policy. New York: Praeger.

Rosen, Alexander C., George A. Rekers, and Peter M. Bentler
1978   "Ethical issues in the treatment of children." Journal of Social Issues 34:2:122–36.

Rothman, David J.
1971   The Discovery of the Asylum. Boston: Little, Brown.

Sarri, Rosemary, and Yeheskel Hasenfeld
1976   Brought to Justice? Juvenile Courts and the Law. Ann Arbor: National Assessment of Juvenile Corrections, University of Michigan.

Scharf, Peter
1978   "Democratic education and the prevention of delinquency." Pp. 220–37 *in* Ernst Wenk and Nora Harlow (eds.), School Crime and Disruption. Davis, Calif.: Responsible Action.

Sennett, Richard
1976   The Fall of Public Man. New York: Knopf.

Sherman, Lawrence W.
1970   "Youth, workers, police, and the gangs: Chicago 1956–1970." Master's thesis, University of Chicago.

Short, James F., Jr.

1974 "Youth, gangs, and society: micro- and macrosociological processes." Sociological Quarterly 15 (Winter):3–19.

1976 "Gangs, politics, and the social order." Pp. 129–63 in James F. Short, Jr. (ed.), Delinquency, Crime, and Society. Chicago: Univ. of Chicago Press.

1979 "Political implications of juvenile delinquency: a comparative perspective." In David Shichor and Delos H. Kelly (eds.), Critical Issues in Juvenile Delinquency: Facing the Last Quarter of the Twentieth Century. New York: Praeger.

Silberman, Charles E.

1970 Crisis in the Classroom. New York: Random House.

1978 Criminal Violence, Criminal Justice. New York: Random House.

Skolnick, Jerome

1969 The Politics of Protest: Violence Aspects of Protest Confrontation. A Staff Report of the National Commission on the Causes and Prevention of Violence. Washington, D.C.: U.S. Government Printing Office.

Smith, Tom W.

1977 "Can we have any confidence in confidence? G. S. S. Technical Report No. 1. Chicago: NORC.

Stier, Serena

1978 "Children's rights and society's duties." Journal of Social Issues 34:2:46–58.

Szasz, Thomas

1961 The Myth of Mental Illness. New York: Harper and Row.

Takanishi, Ruby

1978 "Childhood as a social issue: historical roots of contemporary child advocacy movements." Journal of Social Issues 34:2:8–28.

Wenk, Ernst

1978 "Tomorrow's education: models of participation." In Ernst Wenk and Nora Harlow (eds.), School Crime and Disruption. Davis, Calif.: Responsible Action.

Wenk, Ernst, and Nora Harlow
  1978   School Crime and Disruption. Davis, Calif.: Responsible Action.

Whyte, Martin King
  1973   "Bureaucracy of modernization in China: the Maoist critique." American Sociological Review 38:2 (April): 149–63.

Zimring, Franklin
  1975   "Dealing with youth crime: national needs and priorities." Unpublished manuscript. National Institute for Juvenile Justice and Delinquency Prevention.

Current Reforms and the Legal Status of Children

Monrad G. Paulsen

THE law respecting children is a part of the general law. Hence, any attempt to understand their treatment by family, juvenile, or criminal courts or their status as it relates to constitutional rights requires some grasp of the fundamental beliefs and attitudes which inform the general law. A reformist treatise written about the creation of the juvenile court at the turn of the century, for example, illustrates a linkage between the origins of that court and some ideas about criminal justice then prevalent (Lou, 1927:10–14):

> The traditional administration of criminal justice is characterized by the theories of retribution, of deterrence, and of law as an inflexible body of rules. This attitude of hostility toward the law-breaker . . . provides no principles for the eradication of crime, for returning the delinquent to normal social relations, or for stating the transgressed rights and institutions in terms of their positive social functions. They are the causes of many absurdities and distortions in the criminal law. They accomplish neither legal justice nor social good. This is why the traditional administration of criminal justice— police organization, prosecuting machinery, courts, bar, and penal treatment—spectacularly fails in the suppression of crime.
>
> With the advent of the sociological school of jurisprudence of the present century, which advocates the unification of all social sciences, of which law is but one, law is no longer regarded as a self-centered, self-sufficient science, isolated from the other social sciences. We are realizing more and more that law should be conceived as a means toward social ends. This new conception of law compels us to take account of social causes and social effects in relation to social conditions and social progress. This is sometimes called social justice.

The juvenile court is conspicuously a response to the modern spirit of social justice. It is perhaps the first legal tribunal where law and science, especially the science of medicine and those sciences which deal with human behavior, such as biology, sociology, and psychology, work side by side. It recognizes the fact that the law unaided is incompetent to decide what is adequate treatment of delinquency and crime. It undertakes to define and readjust social situations without the sentiment of prejudice. Its approach to the problem which the child presents is scientific, objective, and dispassionate. The methods which it uses are those of social case work, in which every child is studied and treated as an individual.

These principles upon which the juvenile court acts are radically different from those of the criminal courts. In place of judicial tribunals, restrained by antiquated procedure, saturated in an atmosphere of hostility, trying cases for determining guilt and inflicting punishment according to inflexible rules of law, we have now juvenile courts, in which the relations of the child to his parents or other adults and to the state or society are defined, and are adjusted summarily according to the scientific findings about the child and his environments . . . We have now socially-minded judges, who hear and adjust cases according not to rigid rules of law but to what the interests of society and the interests of the child or good conscience demand. In place of juries, prosecutors, and lawyers, trained in the old conception of law and staging dramatically, but often amusingly, legal battles, as the necessary paraphernalia of a criminal court, we have now probation officers, physicians, psychologists, and psychiatrists, who search for the social, physiological, psychological, and mental backgrounds of the child in order to arrive at reasonable and just solutions of individual cases. In other words, in this new court we tear down primitive prejudice, hatred, and hostility toward the lawbreaker in that most hide-bound of all human institutions, the court of law, and we attempt, as far as possible, to administer justice in the name of truth, love, and understanding.

The criminal law, thus, was seen as harsh and futile. It failed to take into account the scientific knowledge and humanitarian spirit of the twentieth century. Hence, even if the general public was unwilling to abandon the existing criminal justice system, surely problem children could be treated differently. But rather than granting them total leniency, affirmative action should be taken to diagnose and to correct the causes of their misbehavior.

Many of the supporters of the original juvenile court believed that it should serve as a clinic in which the sciences of medicine, psychology, psychiatry, and child development, orchestrated by a probation officer, would change the character of a crime-causing child into that of a productive, law-abiding citizen. Others saw the juvenile court as an extension of the school system, providing moral education. But, in either case, the strategy was to reduce the incidence of crime by changing the moral habits or improving the health and circumstances of individual children.

These ideas were inherent in Julian W. Mack's (1905:104) prescriptions for adjudicating a case by a juvenile court judge:

The problem for determination by the judge is not Has this boy or girl committed a specific wrong?, but What is he?, How has he become what he is?, and What had best be done in his interest and in the interest of the state to save him from a downward career? . . . A thorough investigation, usually made by the probation officer, will give the court much information bearing on the heredity and environment of the child. . . . The physical and mental condition of the child must be known, for the relation between physical defects and criminality is very close . . . In hundreds of cases the discovery and remedy of defective eyesight or hearing or some slight surgical operation will effectuate a complete change in the character of the lad.

Most of the children who come to court, moreover, would be the children of the poor (Mack, 1905:106):

In many cases the parents are foreigners, frequently unable to speak English, and without an understanding of American methods and views. What they need, more than anything else, is kindly assistance; and the aim of the court, in appointing a probation officer for the child, is to have the child and the parents feel, not so much the power, as the friendly interest of the state; to show them that the object of the court is to help them to train the child rights.

The institutional facilities recommended by Judge Mack (p. 107) also reflected the commonly accepted middle-class values of the day:

What is needed is a large area, preferably in the country—because these children require the fresh air and contact with the soil even more than does the normal child—laid out on the cottage plan, giving opportunity for family life, and in each cottage some good man and woman who will live with and for the children. Locks and bars and other indicia of prisons must be avoided; human love, supplemented by human interest and vigilance, must replace them. In such schools there must be opportunity for agricultural and industrial training, so that when the boys and girls come out, they will be fitted to do a man's or woman's work in the world, and not be merely a helpless lot, drifting aimlessly about.

In short, the power exercised by the juvenile court would not be the state's power to repress crime by the power of parents over their children. When parents failed, the state would employ a residual power to act in substitution for the parent—the state's power of *parens patriae.* Thus, the virtue of the court would lie in its capacity to redeem wayward and neglected children and to minimize the harm done to those taken into the criminal process.

Given these prescriptions for court intervention, the usual protections for those accused of crime—jury trial, charge by indictment or information, the right to the privilege against self-incrimination, the right to counsel, the right to cross examinations and the like—were not applicable in juvenile proceedings. Instead, they were to be civil, not criminal, in character. The entire process was to be very informal, nonadversarial, and devoted to reaching the truth without the impediments of "loopholes" and "technicalities."

Contemporary Concerns and Procedural Rights

Ideas change. The rise of the Nazi and Communist tyrannies taught us something about the values which support the constitutional protections of those who are accused. Restrictions on the powers of the police seemed more important to most Americans when the tyrants of Europe engendered the terror experienced when a policeman's fist knocks on the door in the middle of the night. It is unlikely that before the European experience of the 1930s and 40s, many Justices would have written as Justice Frankfurter (*Malinski* vs. *New York*, 1945) did:

The history of American freedom is, in no small measure, the history of procedure. But in addition, the procedural rules which have been fashioned from the generality of due process are our best instruments for the distillation and evaluation of essential facts from the conflicting welter of data that life and our adversary methods present. It is these instruments of due process which enhance the possibility that truth will emerge from the confrontation of opposing versions and conflicting data. Procedure is to law what "scientific method" is to science.

In the 1960s three states of large populations (Illinois, California, and New York) reworked their juvenile court laws and, in the process, provided some of the traditional procedural safeguards of the criminal law by legislation. In New York, for example, each youngster was given the right to invoke the right to silence, the right to counsel when charged on a delinquency petition, and the right to have separate adjudications on issues of fact and issues of disposition so that the facts relevant to the investigation of general character would not prejudice the judge in fact-finding.

Some state supreme courts also broadened the application of constitutional protection in juvenile cases. In *In re Winburn* (1966), for example, the Supreme Court of Wisconsin said:

The burden of the state's argument then is that, since this is not a criminal action, the child is not entitled to the usual safeguards of the criminal law. The validity of this position has long been questioned. While the avowed purpose of the children's code is that "the best interests of the child shall always be of paramount consideration," there is doubt that the strictly civil approach to the problem accomplishes that purpose. . . . A recent commentary on our juvenile court system by Professor Joel F. Handler of the University of Wisconsin Law School reported criticism that our juvenile courts on a nationwide basis represented "unfettered official discretion." He pointed out that "* * *the system allows intervention by the government into the affairs of people without their consent and without standards and controls." [Handler, "The Juvenile Court and the Adversary System," 1965 Wisconsin Law Review, p. 7] . . . Despite all protestations to the contrary, the adjudication of delinquency carries with it a social stigma. This court can take judicial notice that in common parlance "juvenile delinquent" is a term of opprobrium and it is not society's accolade bestowed on the successfully rehabilitated. It is common knowledge also that juvenile records do not, in fact, have a confidential status. Peace officers' records may be communicated to school authorities and to other law enforcement agencies. The Federal Bureau of Investigation have no difficulty in ascertaining whether an individual has a juvenile record. A juvenile record may be a substantial handicap to one who seeks employment with the United States Government. The confidentiality of records, even if kept inviolate, is no real safeguard to the ex-delinquent for, if asked whether he was ever so adjudged, he will be morally obligated to admit it whether or not that status was adjudicated by due process and fair play.

All this preceded the U.S. Supreme Court case *In The Matter of Gault* (1967). *Gault* held that a child responding to a juvenile court petition was entitled to written, timely, and specific notice of the charges. The right to counsel, the right to confrontation by witnesses, the privilege against self-incrimination, the right to have facts found by witnesses under oath— all are guaranteed in cases where the respondent youngster is in danger of losing liberty.

By the time of *Gault* (1967), the constitutional protections of adults accused of crime had become very extensive and highly valued. Juvenile court proceedings, in large degree, were to be made congruent with this new appreciation of the value of the rights of those accused of crime. "Under our Constitution," Mr. Justice Fortas wrote, "the condition of being a boy does not justify a kangaroo court" (*In re Gault*, 1967:28).

Two additional points were made in *Gault*. Justice Fortas affirmed that all of the traditional values of the juvenile court with respect to rehabilitation and informality could be achieved within the framework that also employed constitutional protections for juveniles. Secondly, the lower court had committed young Gault to a training school for, as a maximum, the period of minority (six years) because of a minor offense. Yet an adult could have been given only a small fine and not more than sixty days' imprisonment for the same offense. Hence, the Supreme Court suggested that simple justice requires some proportionality between severity of punishment and an offender's misdeed.

Limits on Discretion

Within the past fifteen years, prevailing thought regarding the criminal law has also reflected a very skeptical attitude toward the great discretion exercised by police officers, prosecutors, judges, and correctional authorities. There has been a strong demand that handbooks guiding police discretion be formulated and made available to both the police and the public. The practice of plea bargaining by prosecutors has never been subject to more severe attack. Serious proposals are constantly being made today for relatively fixed sentences. The parole system is less often seen as an admirable means for individualizing punishment than as a means for dispensing the most arbitrary of decisions.

In its report, *Doing Justice* (Hirsch, 1976), the Committee for the Study of Incarceration provided further examples of the attack on discretion. Chaired by Charles E. Goodell, former U.S. senator from New York, and comprised of other distinguished members, this committee was charged with considering "the fundamental concepts" that ought to govern the sentencing of offenders after conviction. The committee decided, however, that it could not accomplish this task without inquiring into the rationale for punishment, since it is punishment that usually governs the choice among various alternatives, particularly incarceration.

In pursuing this task, the committee concluded that the

concept of general deterrence does not provide a sufficient justification for punishing offenders. In the first place, the general deterrent impact of a particular sanction is not easy to establish. Further, some actions that might deter deviant conduct would also be very unjust or even inhumane. Indeed, if deterring others justifies punishment, every criminal becomes a kind of savior who suffers vicariously for the rest of mankind.

In much the same way, the committee also concluded that rehabilitation does not provide a justification for imprisonment. Whether employed in an institution, as a form of intensive probation, or as a part of community programming, rehabilitative methods have not worked. In addition, some techniques, such as psychosurgery or chemotherapy, are too painful, debilitating, or destructive to be inflicted upon a human being.

In light of these conclusions, the committee decided that the most acceptable justification for punishment is a theory of "just deserts." It is an offender's past conduct that should determine whether he receives pleasant or unpleasant treatment. Furthermore, "just deserts" should not depend upon questionable predictions of future dangerousness or upon the idea that the offender's character will be reconstructed. Instead, it has a close affinity to the phrase "community reassurance": that is, when a harmful act is committed, the community has a right to demand that a fitting response be made and that the malefactor suffer an unpleasant experience.

The committee's acceptance of the idea that the seriousness and the harmfulness of the offender's past conduct is the most acceptable reason for punishment was not an isolated suggestion. Much of the public outcry against "crime in the streets" is rooted in the opinion that "no one does anything about criminal conduct." Furthermore, it is widely reflected in the scholarly literature, as well as in the popular media (Morris, 1974; van den Haag, 1975; Wilson, 1975). Consequently, in response to fears of crime and to the pessimistic belief that nothing can be done to change offenders, opinion leaders have rediscovered classical criminology, namely, the view that it is an offender's deviant act, not his character or extenuating circumstances, to which society should respond.

Standards for Juvenile Justice

The impact of the "just deserts" philosophy has not been confined to adults and to the criminal justice system. It has also had considerable impact on new legislative actions and proposals for the juvenile court. The deep commitment of that court to the rehabilitation of offenders is now being undercut and drastic changes are being introduced.

These new changes are dramatically illustrated in the new *Standards for Juvenile Justice*, formulated by a joint committee of the Institute of Judicial Administration of New York University and the American Bar Association (IJA-ABA, 1977). These standards are set forth in twenty-three volumes, each devoted to a different subject.

According to those who drafted the standards, the underlying concepts of these volumes "are not easily assimilated." Nonetheless, they were described as "genuinely shattering" since they symbolized a rejection of the medical, or rehabilitative, model of juvenile justice and the establishment of a new model. Hence, among the underlying principles governing the new standards were the following (IJA-ABA, 1977:22):

1. Proportionality in sanctions for juvenile offenders based on the seriousness of the offense committed, and not merely the court's view of the juvenile's needs, should replace vague and subjective criteria.

2. Sentences or dispositions should be determinate. The practice of indeterminate sentencing, allowing correctional authorities to act arbitrarily to release or confine juveniles as the convenience of their programs dictates, should be abolished. Such sentences permit wide disparity in the punishment received for the same misconduct and create a potential for abuse that the public is helpless to prevent.

3. The least restrictive alternative should be the choice of decision makers for intervention in the lives of juveniles and their families. If a decision maker, such as judge or an intake officer, imposes a

restrictive disposition, he or she must state in writing the reasons for finding less drastic remedies inappropriate or inadequate to further the purposes of the juvenile justice system.

4. Noncriminal misbehavior [status offenses, PINS] and private offenses [victimless crimes] should be removed from juvenile court jurisdiction. [Possession of narcotic drugs, however, has been retained as a basis for court jurisdiction.] Juvenile court intervention in these areas have [sic] proven ineffective, if not socially harmful, damaging a significant number of children and frequently turning unruly juveniles into criminals. Voluntary community services to deal with these problems, such as crisis intervention programs, mediation for parent-child disputes, and alternative residences or "crashpads" for runaways, are proposed as more suitable responses to noncriminal misconduct. School disciplinary proceedings, alternate programs, peer counseling, and other remedies within the educational system are suggested for truants. Neglect or abuse petitions would be filed where children are found living in dangerous conditions.

As to procedural protections, the standards went beyond the holding in the *Gault* case by adopting the view that

the best way to protect juveniles was to ensure fair proceedings through procedural safeguards, representation by counsel, fixed criteria to guide official action, written decisions subject to judicial review, and full participation by juveniles in consultations with counsel and their parents if the parents' interests are not adverse to the juveniles'. By thus holding court officers accountable for their actions, the standards did not eliminate discretion, but merely subjected it to responsible scrutiny. (IJA-ABA, 1977:24)

In summary, then, the new IJA-ABA standards (1) would eliminate status and victimless offenses from the jurisdiction of the juvenile court; (2) would classify juvenile offenses in much the same way that adult crimes are classified; (3) would grant juveniles virtually all of the procedural protections afforded adults, including protections against adverse actions by parents; and (4) would impose determinate sentences on criminal offenders. Not only would court practices with respect to young criminals be altered but with respect to status offenders and dependent and neglected children as well.

Criminal Conduct

The IJA-ABA standards, like *Doing Justice*, reflect an abandonment of the belief that, given time, research, and money, the causes of juvenile crime could be discovered and young offenders reclaimed. Paradoxically, those who drafted the standards still cling to the belief that poverty, discrimination, and family breakdown are the causes of criminal conduct, but they feel that these causes are simply beyond the power of the juvenile justice system to address. Consequently, as with adults, our legal institutions should concentrate on doing justice, not on reforming offenders.

The kinds of punishments that are recommended in the standards are generally less severe than those which are imposed upon adults for the same offenses. Provision is also made for the use of conditional or suspended sentences, but these cannot be used unless the accused agree to the conditions attached thereto. In certain circumstances, restitution or the payment of a fine might be allowed or a remedial program might be imposed upon an offender. But under no circumstance should the duration of any penalty exceed the maximum established term for the offense in question.

As might have been anticipated, some legislators have been quick to translate the IJA-ABA Standards into law. Those who drafted them, after all, were prestigious persons and groups. Even before the standards were ratified, in fact, the State of Washington used them to redraft its entire juvenile code. According to the Juvenile Justice Act of 1977, the new system in Washington should be "capable of having primary responsibility for, being accountable for, and responding to the needs of youthful offenders, as defined by this chapter. . . . It is the further intent of the legislature that young, in turn, be held accountable for their offenses" (Rev. Code of Washington, 1977: Sec. 55).

Reflecting the emphasis upon "just deserts," community protection, and offender accountability, the stated purposes of the juvenile justice system are to:

a) Protect the citizenry from criminal behavior;
b) Provide for determining whether accused juveniles have committed offenses as defined by this chapter;
c) Make the juvenile offender accountable for his or her criminal behavior;
d) Provide for punishment commensurate with the age, crime, and criminal history of the juvenile offender;
e) Provide due process for juveniles alleged to have committed an offense;
f) Provide necessary treatment, supervision, and custody for juvenile offenders;
g) Provide for the handling of juvenile offenders by communities whenever consistent with public safety;
h) Provide for restitution to victims of crime. (Rev. Code of Washington, 1977:80)

Not only do these stated legislative aims emphasize the imposition of "responsibility" on the juvenile offender, but other portions of the statute seek to minimize the use of official discretion (see Sec. 57).

In a unique provision, all complaints alleging the commission of an offense are referred directly to the prosecutor. The prosecutor, in turn, "shall" screen for "legal sufficiency," that is, whether the complaint brings the case within the jurisdiction of the courts, and whether, on the basis of available evidence, there is probable cause to believe that the youth did commit the offense charged.

Once this is done, the discretion of the prosecutor is limited. If the alleged offense is serious (e.g., a Class A felony or an attempt to commit a Class A felony, a Class B felony or an attempt to commit such a felony, and some other offenses as well), the prosecutor "shall" file on the case with the juvenile court. If, however, the offense is less serious, the prosecutor "may" file on the case but, apparently, it is not mandatory.

Once charged, the respondent must be advised on his rights: of a right to counsel at all critical stages of the proceeding, a right to a transcript of the proceedings, a right to the privilege against self-incrimination, a right to adequate notice, to discovery as provided in criminal cases, a right to be heard, to cross-examine and to be free from the introduction of illegally seized evidence. Further, an out-of-court statement or a confession made by the child "is insufficient to support a finding" that the child has committed the alleged act.

With regard to sentencing, the new Washington Code requires the secretary of the Department of Social and Health Services to propose to the legislature, no later than November 1 of each even-numbered year, "disposition standards" for juvenile crimes. These standards are to present a range of punishment for each category of wrongdoing: a maximum and a minimum term, the minimum defined as a certain percentage of the maximum. In that way, presumably, the determinate sentences for various crimes will keep pace with society's evolving definition of "just deserts."

In applying these standards, the juvenile court is constrained in two ways. First, it is supposed to utilize only age, prior offense history, and current offense in determining sentence. Secondly, it is required to make a disposition within the standard range set for the instant offense unless that disposition would result in an instance of "manifest injustice"—an instance in which an excessive penalty was placed upon the juvenile or in which a clear danger to the community was created. But if a "manifest injustice" is declared, the judge must justify in writing his or her departure from the predetermined range.

Another example of treating juveniles according to a principle of "just desserts" is found in the State of New York. In 1976 that state enacted a series of bills that provided for "restrictive placement" in the case of fourteen- and fifteen-year-olds who have been found to have committed one of several "designated felony acts" (New York Family Court Act, 1977-78:184). Such placement involves a greatly extended period of confinement with a mandatory period of secure confinement. Then, in 1978, Chapter 478 of the Session Laws of New York extended to thirteen-year-olds the special treatment of those who commit "designated felony acts." Later in the year, as a result, a thirteen-year-old charged with homicide was made a respondent under the new law (New York News, Sept. 24, 1978).

The justification for the new legislation in New York was

remarkably like that for the new code in the state of Washington:

A common theme of this program is accountability and responsibility—for the juvenile and for the agencies and individuals who make up the juvenile justice system.

All too many juveniles who get into trouble—even those who commit violent crimes—have not been helped, treated or punished (Barksy and Gottfried, 1977–78:186–87).

Now, if young criminals are not helped, at least they can be punished.

Noncriminal Conduct

Almost all juvenile codes provide for the exercise of state power over children who engage in noncriminal conduct that is thought to be harmful to themselves. The statutes of Alaska and New York contain typical formulations. The Alaska Statutes, 47110.010 (a) (2), (3) and (6) define "a person in need of supervision" as one who

by reason of being wayward or habitually disobedient is uncontrolled by his parent, guardian or custodian;

Is habitually truant from school or home, or habitually so conducts himself as to injure or endanger the morals or health of himself or others;

Associates with vagrant, vicious or immoral people, or engages in an occupation or is in a situation dangerous to life or limb or injurious to the health, morals, or welfare of himself or others.

The New York Family Court Act (Sec. 732) defines "a person in need of supervision" as "an habitual truant" or a child "incorrigible, ungovernable, or habitually disobedient and beyond the lawful control of his parent, guardian or lawful custodian."

Such statutes have been criticized on several grounds. First, they are said to be unconstitutional because of vagueness. Secondly, they permit juvenile court judges to confine too many children in training schools who are merely in conflict with their parents. Finally, it is said, young persons should be given the freedom to order their own lives without interference from parents.

The last argument, that children should be freed from parental constraints, has been bolstered by an opinion of Mr. Justice Douglas. He dissented in *Wisconsin v. Yoder* (1972), which upheld the right of Amish farmers to refuse to send their children to high school in defiance of the law in Wisconsin. His contention was that, "on this important and vital matter of education, I think that children should be heard." "Moreover," he wrote in a footnote to the same opinion, "there is substantial agreement among child psychologists and sociologists that the moral and intellectual maturity of the fourteen-year-old approaches that of the adult."

The Douglas footnote, which has disturbed a good many persons, calls to mind the fact that, in all the debate about children's rights, there is a concealed argument over age. The Justice may be right about fourteen-year-olds, but what about younger children? Is it to be assumed that six-, eight-, or ten-year-olds are capable of making wise decisions about life's fundamental choices? The question is a significant one because, without having paid apparent attention to the issue, those who drafted the IJA-ABA Standards Relating to Noncriminal Misbehavior would take away from juvenile court jurisdiction "juvenile acts of misbehavior, ungovernability or unruliness which do not violate the criminal law." Their justifications for doing so were as follows:

> State intervention has proven a poor buttress of parental authority and family harmony in handling the problems of rebellious children. As American society moves toward granting young persons greater rights at an earlier age, it is increasingly less adroit in giving the weight of legal authority to what is frequently rigid and arbitrary parentage. . . . Furthermore, there appears to be no evidence that "the viability of the family will be jeopardized by more freedom for the children," or that the present possibilities of judicial intervention as a parent surrogate, under the status offense jurisdiction, help to restore harmony to the dysfunctional family or benefit the child.

Judicial intervention in beyond-parental-control cases would appear to encourage parents to resign their parental roles to the court. The studies discussed in the Introduction suggest that parents of ungovernable children regard the juvenile court and detention facilities as there to provide the "control" they cannot; they also demonstrate that the court has been visibly unsuccessful as a surrogate parent in such cases.

Moreover, the family problems encountered in the exercise of the status offense jurisdiction range from seemingly trivial matters to complicated and many-faceted dilemmas that virtually defy solution. All present, to a greater or lesser degree, failures of communication within the family unit that are likely to be worsened by judicial intervention and that in most cases will be better served by non-coerced assistance. Many status offense cases are in reality cases of neglect, abuse, or delinquency and should be dealt with on that ground. The line is often exceedingly thin and decisions to invoke the status offense jurisdiction in a particular case may be based on such fragile considerations as having no evidence to proceed on another ground. . . .

School attendance is properly the business of the schools, not the courts. Judicial coercion can at best (and that very seldom, short of twenty-four hour confinement) dragoon the physical presence of the youth's body, with strong indications that the "heart and mind" will not only not follow, but will be strongly repelled. (IJA-ABA, 1977:35–38).

The draftsmen of the standards emphasize the point that the use of state force to shore up parental authority is likely to be futile. Love is a vagrant emotion. It will not obey the state's commands nor the pleas of persons involved.

As they did with respect to young criminals, legislators in the State of Washington agreed with the IJA-ABA standards with respect to status offenders (Rev. Code of Washington, 1977). First, they eliminated the jurisdiction of the juvenile court over this group. If, in the opinion of the Department of Health and Social Services, help of some kind is needed for runaways, truants, or incorrigibles, it will be provided by welfare workers, not legal authorities. Secondly, in a chapter (23) entitled "Juvenile Court Procedure for Families in Conflict," the new statute provides that any child, as well as its parents, may petition the juvenile court to permit alternative residential placement for the child. The court, in turn, may approve the request if it finds that the request is not capricious and that the family conflict cannot be resolved by counseling or crisis intervention. In short, the court may approve family separation but it may not use any coercion in an effort to keep the family together.

In a similar way, the IJA-ABA Standards provide no coercive sanctions for the child who will not attend school or who is defiant of school authority. But while there is logic in the contention that legal coercion is a poor way to insure that learning will take place, there is less logic in the argument that coercion cannot help to reduce truancy. While some children will resist attendance at any cost, compulsory education will bring others to school, whereupon they benefit. Were it not for some compulsion, in fact, many persons who are well-educated today would not have achieved that state. Indeed, in light of the handicaps imposed upon the untutored in modern society, some effort to prod young persons toward education would seem desirable, particularly for those families whose own resources are exhausted in trying to do so.

Since even more persuasive arguments might be made with regard to the use of alcohol or marijuana or with respect to such other "victimless" offenses as teenage prostitution, the position of the IJA-ABA toward status and victimless offenses has drawn considerable criticism. The Council on Children, Adolescents and their Families of the American Psychiatric Association, for example, has expressed its disagreement with the proposed standards, arguing that, without the presence of the court, many youngsters simply go unattended:

There are numerous examples in which the authority of a judge has brought about positive and effective changes when all efforts of social services have failed, notes the APA. The psychiatrists said that children are, by nature, involuntary patients and must, therefore, be coerced to treatment.

The APA disagrees with the proposed IJA/ABA standards concerning status offenders, explaining that in many communities, absent the court, youngsters would simply go unattended. (*Juvenile and Family Court Newsletter*, 1978:7)

The National Council of Juvenile Court Judges also opposed the proposal:

The committee strongly disagrees with the recommendations of the Non-Criminal Behavior volume in that the authors thereof fail to recognize the need to provide court services as a last resort for truants and runaways who refuse to avail themselves of voluntary services. The volume as written would not allow for the police to detain any runaways for more than six hours and would in essence eliminate court jurisdiction including power of placement, and if necessary, detention, then these youngsters will be able to run away from home at any age and compulsory education would cease. (*Juvenile and Family Court Newsletter*, 1978:8–10)

Thus despite the fact that the state of Washington had already legislated the proposed IJA-ABA Standards for noncriminal children, they were withdrawn from consideration by the ABA House of Delegates in its meeting in February 1979. Because their defeat seemed almost certain, Judge Irving I. Kaufman, the Chairman of the commission which drafted the standards, stated that they would be reintroduced at some future convention. The *New York Times* (Feb. 18, 1979), however, suggested otherwise. "For one thing," its article stated, "the Joint Commission of the Juvenile Justice Standards Project is out of money, having spent $2.5 million since 1971. For another, the delegates seemed greatly relieved to have finally cleared the subject from their agenda."

There seem to be two basic reasons why the jurisdiction of the juvenile court over noncriminal children was retained. First, many people apparently feel that the court should continue to provide backup support for the family and, indirectly, for the school. Typically, in the case of a very young person who fails to heed adult authority, the family seeks court assistance to carry out its responsibility. Without such support, it is contended, the traditional role and autonomy of the family would be weakened.

This point of view is not without opposition. A significant segment of the American populace would like to see a comprehensive program of child development and child-care centers developed across the country, supported by the federal government. In response to one such proposal, however, President Nixon voiced traditional sentiments by vetoing the child-development provisions of the Economic Opportunity Act of 1964. In support of his veto, he commented:

the child development envisioned in this legislation would be truly a long leap into the dark for the United States Government and the American people, I must share the view of those of its supporters who proclaim this to be the most radical piece of legislation to emerge from the Ninety-second Congress. . . .

. . . all other factors, being equal, good public policy requires that we enhance rather than diminish both parental authority and parental involvement with children—particularly in those decisive early years when social attitudes and a conscience are formed, and religious and moral principles are first inculcated.

. . . for the Federal Government to plunge headlong financially into supporting child development would commit the vast moral authority of the National Government to the side of communal approaches to child rearing over against the family-centered approach.

This President, this Government, is unwilling to take that step. (Nixon, 1971: 46057–59)

To this day traditional sentiments of this type seem to have remained the stronger, since federal legislation favoring comprehensive child-care centers has not been passed.

A second reason the authority of the juvenile court over status offenders was not eliminated is that there is a residuum of youngsters who will neither seek out nor follow the help which a voluntary agency might offer. Without some coercion they will continue to run away, to defy authority, or to remain out of school. Hence, as Judge Lindsay G. Arthur (1977: 631,632) has written, "courts . . . argue for continued judicial authority to handle the residuum of juveniles who cannot or will not accept diversion [from legal processing], those children who need help but will not get it voluntarily."

Abuse and Neglect

Recent thinking with respect to child abuse and neglect, while not eliminating the authority of the court, has tended to reduce some of its earlier power and to lend greater support to family autonomy. The IJA-ABA Standards, for example, provide that intervention by the state to assist a child should be authorized only when the child is clearly threatened with severe physical or emotional danger. No longer is the court able to impose its morality on the family, as it once was. Instead, the aim of current thinking is to protect children from serious, objectively verifiable harms. In short, while such an aim raises obvious questions as to how "severe," particularly "severe" emotional, harm can be objectively verified, current standards are weighted in favor of the notion that unusual life-styles, single parenthood, or sloppy housekeeping, by themselves, should not be grounds for removing children from their homes.

Support for this view comes not only from current beliefs that stress the rights of children as well as parents to live as they like but from deeply rooted cultural beliefs about the sanctity of the family. The comments of Justice Erwin, of the Supreme Court of Alaska, illustrate the depths of this feeling.

We note . . . that there is more to the parent-child relationship than simply custody. It is love and trust and a responsibility toward each other which cannot be defined legally. It is impossible to discuss severing this relationship without considering the heartache and anguish of the parents who must ultimately live with themselves and the decision after the child reaches adulthood. Further, the consideration of such an issue must accept the limitations of the State to be a parent; good itentions are not adequate substitutes for the day-to-day relationship which we have come to accept as necessary to the growth of children into responsible adults. (*L. A. M.* vs. *State,* 1976).

Conclusions

This paper has revealed some striking changes in the legal status of children. For three-quarters of a century the juvenile court reserved the right to act as a parent surrogate for children. And just as few procedural restrictions were placed on the powers of parents to control their offspring, so few were placed on the court's power to intervene in the lives of the young. In the name of redeeming wayward youth, the court enjoyed great latitude and power and few procedural restrictions.

In response to a growing distrust of legal authority and to mounting cynicism over the philosophy of rehabilitation, remarkable changes have been introduced into the legal rules governing childhood. Court decisions, standard-setting groups, and new laws have served to reduce the discretion and autonomy of legal authorities and to enhance the importance of procedural safeguards. No longer are children without recourse to protections from unbridled legal controls.

Despite the strong sentiments that have produced these changes, they are not without paradox. Under the traditional philosophy of the juvenile court, all children, criminal or otherwise, were to be treated as status offenders. The concern of the court, ideally at least, was to treat problems, not acts. Now, however, sharp distinctions have been drawn between criminal and noncriminal children. While the power of the court has been reduced over the latter, the former are to be subjected to procedures which differ only in degree from those to which adults are subjected. While due process for young criminals will be insured, "the just deserts" philosophy will tend to dictate the treatment they receive. Rather than rehabilitation, the primary purposes of the juvenile justice system will be to see that justice is done, that children are accountable for their crime, and that the community is protected.

References

The Alaska Statutes

Arthur, Lindsay G.
    1977   "Statute offenders need a court of last resort." Boston
            Law Review 57.

Barsky, Simon K., and Richard N. Gottfried
    1977–78   Supplementary Practice Commentaries to Sec. 711,
            712 (found in Cumulative Annual Pocket Part).

Haag, Ernest van den
    1975   Punishing Criminals. New York: Basic Books.

Hirsch, Andrew von
    1976   Doing Justice: The Choice of Punishments. Report of
            the Commission for the Study of Incarceration. New
            York: Hill and Wang.

In re Gault
    1967   387 U.S. 1, 18L, Ed. 2nd 527, 87 S.Ct. 1428.

In re Winburn
    1966   32 Wisc. 2d 152, 145 NW 2d 178.

Institute of Judicial Administration and the American Bar Association (IJA/ABA)
    1977   Standards for Juvenile Justice: A Summary and Analysis.
            Chicago: American Bar Association.

The Juvenile and Family Court Newsletter
    1978   "IJA/ABA standards." 8(Dec.)

L.A.M. v. *State*
    1976   547, p. 2d 827 (Alaska).

Lou, Herbert H.
    1927   Juvenile Courts in the United States. Chapel Hill: Univ.
            of North Carolina Press.

Mack, Julian W.
    1909   "The juvenile court." Harvard Law Review 23:104–22.

Malinski v. *New York*
    1945   324 U.S. 401, 412.

Morris, Norval
    1974   "The future of imprisonment: toward a punitive philosophy." Michigan Law Review 72:1161–80.

New York Family Court Act Sec. 732
    1977–78   Sec. 711, 712 (Cumulative Annual Pocket Part).

Nixon, Richard
    1971   Senate Document No. 92–48, 92nd Congress, First Session (Dec. 9, 1971), in the Congressional Record—Senate (Dec. 10).

Revised Criminal Code of Washington
    1977   Title 13. Juvenile Courts and Juvenile Delinquents: 66–90.

Wilson, James Q.
    1975   Thinking about Crime. New York: Basic Books.

Wisconsin v. *Yoder*
    1972   403 U.S. 205.

Disillusion with Rehabilitation: Theoretical and Empirical Questions

Daniel Glaser

A hundred years ago rehabilitation was usually not stressed as the major objective of government agencies that dealt with young lawbreakers. Then, as now, the vast majority of arrestees were children of the poor. Apparently little valued by society, their criminal conduct was usually ascribed to unalterable defects. Only during the twentieth century has it been customarily stated that their reformation is the primary goal of correctional agencies (Empey, 1978:chaps. 2–4, 17). Yet in the past decade this concern has been increasingly disavowed by both academicians and officials who once espoused it.

Efforts to change delinquents and criminals by means other than punishment reached a peak about twenty-five years ago. Psychiatry had become the most prestigeful and influential profession in juvenile courts and corrections. When psychiatrists were unavailable, which was most of the time in most places, clinical psychologists and psychiatric social workers served in their stead. When these were insufficient, guards, probation officers, and others were trained in group counseling. "Treatment" of offenders implied primarily getting them to talk with staff or with each other in front of staff. "Rehabilitation" denoted individual or group psychotherapy or counseling, plus academic and vocational training. Occasionally these terms were used even more broadly, as when playing ball was called "recreational therapy."

Although these usages continue, support for such methods of reforming wayward youths is much less widespread now than it was a quarter-century ago. The advocates of most rehabilitation efforts can *illustrate* their success by describing selected cases that make their claims of having a net positive impact seem plausible; few, however, can *demonstrate* such effectiveness by follow-up statistics that show less recidivism in treated than in similar untreated offenders. Advocates of psychotherapy, counseling, special education, or other programs for delinquents have usually been embarrassed by reports from the most rigorous evaluative research. Why has scientific assessment been so disillusioning? To answer this question it may be best to determine what ideas have guided treatment and then to assess their validity.

Theory and Treatment

Reactions to offenders express a variety of emotions as well as ideas. Many policies are based mainly on outrage at the defiance of conventional life-styles by some lawbreakers (even by those who do not victimize others). Also, widespread fear of victimization evokes much demand for containment of offenders. In addition, sympathy for victims of predations arouses a desire to avenge them by assuring that violent offenders get extreme penalties. Yet some interventions in the lives of lawbreakers are rationalized as efforts to reform them so as to reduce the prospects of their committing further crimes. Whenever this attitude exists, some theory on the causes of illegal conduct is implied.

Prevailing explanations for delinquency and youth crime and consequent justifications for methods of trying to change young offenders are all variations of a few ideas repeatedly voiced throughout recorded history. The behavior-causation theories underlying policies for the reformation of criminals can be grouped under four headings: control, insight, experience, opportunity.

Control Theories

An old idea about crime, often expressed in the Bible and in other ancient writings, ascribes wrongdoing to evil impulses and temptations. It implies that individuals achieve virtue by self-control or by controls on them (for example, through surveillance for misconduct, accompanied by threat of punishment). The demand for such government control assumes that potential offenders are rational enough to recognize their risks of being punished and that they are capable of self-control.

Biologically-oriented criminologists in the nineteenth century speculated that lawbreakers, because of hereditary defects, had stronger criminal instincts, less rational intelligence, or weaker capacities for controlling their emotions than noncriminals. Thus they advocated killing, incarcerating, or sterilizing offenders rather than trying to reform them. Psychoanalytic theory, still influential, portrays all persons as delinquent at birth because of unfettered ids and as achieving reformation if they develop sufficiently strong ego and superego controls over their persistent, although often unconscious, libidinal drives.

Hirschi asserts that we would all be offenders "if we dared" (1969:34) but that if our bonds to conventional society are sufficiently strong we do not dare to jeopardize them by delinquent acts. For this social-psychological control theory he offers statistical evidence, confirmed in other studies, that such indices of these bonds as favorable attitudes toward nondelinquent peers, parents, teachers, and school markedly differentiate nondelinquents from delinquents (see also Empey, 1978:chap. 9, and Glaser, 1978:chap. 8).

These variants of control theory yield somewhat different guidance for correctional policies. The traditional punitive version implies that offenders should be (1) confined, or (2) given alternative punishment, or (3) placed under surveillance with threat of penalties if they recidivate. The biological theories support confinement policies, but not other penalties or threats, as their ideas create doubts about the capacity of many offenders for self-control. Psychoanalytic theories inspire efforts to strengthen the egos and superegos of lawbreakers to enhance their self-control, as well as to identify unconscious psychological mechanisms, but the latter focus places them also in our insight category, discussed below. Hirchi's explanation for delinquency is compatible with the correctional policies of traditional control theory but also suggests that efforts be made to build social bonds between offenders and conventional persons to create in offenders a stake in conformity that they would not wish to jeopardize by new crimes.

Insight Theories

Many philosophers have shared the views of the ancient Greek Protagoras that humans are guided by a search for the good, so that evil behavior results only from lack of insight into what is good. Socrates, Aristotle, and others seemed to assume that a person who knows what is good will be good (Windelband, 1901:chaps. 2 and 3).

Freudian-inspired psychotherapy implies that when offenders understand how their unconscious minds repress and transform libidinal cravings, they will cease to express these mental processes as delinquent conduct.

Especially influential in correctional group therapy and counseling during the 1950s and 1960s was Carl Rogers's (1951) nondirective, or "client-centered," therapy. Rogers claims that people "actualize" their basically good selves when they can verbalize how they have failed to accept their better sentiments consciously or how they have distorted them in their defensive reactions to disturbing experiences.

By the late 1960s O. Hobart Mowrer's *New Group Therapy* (1964) and William Glasser's *Reality Therapy* (1965) had stimulated some abandonment of prevailing psychotherapies. These authors contend that delinquency and crime are not products of unconscious mental disturbances but of deliberate (and even therapist-encouraged) avoidance of moral responsibility for personal conduct. They insist that offenders can change only if they first admit wrongdoing. Glasser's many followers in correctional counseling urge clients to identify the causes of their current difficulties in achieving life-styles that are alternatives to crimes, such as getting and holding a job and budgeting their money, rather than analyzing the past and blaming others.

Recently, a more extreme emphasis on personal responsibil-

ity has attracted widespread attention. Yochelson and Samenow (1976) assert that criminals simply decide at an early age
to be criminals. These authors claim that offenders can reform
only if they are sufficiently disgusted with the consequences
of their criminal ways to accept about three hours of daily
instruction on their faults, for as long as it takes to reeducate
them. Insight advocates thus have been highly diverse in speci-
fying what the truth is that criminals should see and how
an awareness of this truth can be inculcated.

Experience Theories

The philosopher John Locke is usually credited with the conception of the human mind as blank at birth, then shaped
by experience (although this view had been asserted earlier,
notably by the Sophists in ancient Greece). Today, emphasis
on behavior as learned entirely by experience is particularly
identified with B. F. Skinner and behavioral psychology, but
it was also implied in earlier psychological theory, such as
Thorndike's "Law of Effect."

Adherents of this view assume that pro- or anti-criminal
conduct is not merely the result of learning abstract ideas,
and thus is rarely changed by words alone. They assert that
habits are shaped mostly by the experiences that are immediate consequences of conduct, particularly its gratifying results
(positive reinforcements), such as approval from peers and a
favorable self-image. Both delinquency and non-delinquency·
are thus ascribed mainly to the rewarding or aversive outcomes of social learning, although some influence is occasionally credited also to verbal communications and conduct
models, such as those provided by the mass media (Bandura,
1969).

Opportunity Theories

If learning good or bad conduct is primarily the product of
rewarding experiences, it follows that learning opportunities

determine character. Therefore, persons reared in homes and communities where they can readily acquire immediate gratification from good conduct should exhibit better behavior than those who were much less encouraged in conventionally approved activities. Conversely, persons reared with extensive exposure to delinquency and crime and with much favorable response to their participation in it are especially likely to develop patterns of lawbreaking.

Opportunity theories imply (1) that offenders can be reformed by helping them find alternatives to crime, especially jobs and acceptance in anticriminal social circles; (2) that they must, at the same time, be made to find little comparable attraction in crime. Such theories have been expressed since ancient times, but especially since Marxist claims that crime would be prevented by increasing social equality. The most influential proponents of opportunity expansion in the United States, however, are generally classified as liberals but not Marxists.

Labeling theory in its usual formulations in sociology can be considered a variant of opportunity theory. It asserts that being called delinquent or criminal stigmatizes a person who is then rejected in conventional circles but accepted among offenders. This is Schur's (1973) argument for a policy of "radical nonintervention" in delinquency; he claims that official reactions to offenses generally impede a juvenile's achievement of a conventional way of life.

An alternative interpretation of labeling that appears to have more empirical support is a type of differential-control theory. It observes that labeling persons as offenders when they break the law deters them from further lawbreaking if they already have a strong stake in a conventional reputation and have aspirations that they do not wish to jeopardize by such a label. It also recognizes, however, that the same labels further criminalize persons who lack conventional bonds, especially if they value a reputation among delinquents as being advanced in criminality. Among several factors complicating this differential control by stigmatizing labels is how readily the labels can be shed by appropriate conduct and whether the labels motivate extra effort by family and friends to help the offenders improve their reputations (Thorsell and Klemke, 1972; Glaser, 1978:118–21).

Testing the Theories

Because offenders differ in their bonds with criminal and anti-criminal persons, in their experiences in both legitimate and illegitimate pursuits, and in other relevant ways not yet discussed here (for example, their use of alcohol or other narcotics), reformation efforts could have contrasting effects on different persons. Therefore, disappointing evaluations of correctional programs could result largely from failure to note variations in their impacts on diverse participants. Thus, adequate assessment of the four types of theory distinguished here (control, insight, experience, and opportunity) requires that we identify the kinds of data on both treatment and subjects that would test each theory and inquire whether such data have been collected.

To evaluate a correctional-treatment program, researchers must first decide on appropriate criteria of effectiveness. The most salient criterion, it is generally agreed, is reduction of recidivism. This effect (the dependent variable) is measured by following up the research subjects to learn what offenses they commit after they are in the program and by assessing how these crimes—if any—compare in number or seriousness with those of similar offenders not in the program. There are various ways of measuring recidivism rates, for example, by arrests, convictions, or reconfinement for new offenses. Although each of these methods yields a very imperfect index of criminal activity, each is potentially useful when applied to comparing the recidivism rates of two or more large groups, if it can be presumed that the rates for all groups have about the same proportion of error (Glaser, 1973:chaps. 1–7; Lipton et al., 1975:chaps. 1 and 10; on pitfalls in this procedure, see Hawkins et al., 1977).

In most assessments of rehabilitation effects, the independent or causal variables are measured by grouping research subjects only according to whether or not they were in the program to be evaluated. Yet, to test a theory, one must know what the offenders got out of the program. Did it give them what the theory indicates would alter their recidivism rates? Thus, to evaluate education as a means of rehabilitation, inmates should be classified not merely by enrollment in an institution school but by improvement in test scores or earning a diploma. Similarly, they should not be differentiated by whether they were given vocational training but by the skills that they gained in it. Also, they should not be designated only as having received counseling or psychotherapy but by the quantity and quality of this verbal activity. For example, did it deal mainly with institutional adjustment or with such theoretically crime-relevant topics as family conflicts and job-retention difficulties? What was their participation in it? Failure to find that certain kinds of rehabilitation efforts reduce recidivism rates may often result more from deficiencies of the evaluation than from defects in the treatment.

In the correctional literature, the optimum evaluations described in the preceding paragraph are the exception rather than the rule, but enough studies approximate these standards to merit review here. A major resource for this purpose is the Lipton, Martinson, and Wilks (1975) landmark survey of 1945-67 correctional treatment evaluations (hereafter called Survey). On most topics it can be supplemented by data from more recent investigations. What does available evidence indicate is the utility of the four types of theories in guiding efforts to reduce recidivism?

Control Theories

Traditional control theories are concerned with what, since at least the early nineteenth-century writings of Jeremy Bentham, has been called *special* or *individual* deterrence—the idea that *punishment of known offenders reduces their recidivism*. It contrasts with general deterrence, the idea that national, state, or community crime rates are lowered by the threat of punishing any persons who break the law, a threat made viable by the publicized punishment of some who do (Zimring and Hawkins, 1973:72–74).

To test traditional control theories, one must determine if recidivism rates vary with differences in the speed, certainty, or severity of punishing released offenders for new crimes. Certainty, of course, depends upon the degree of surveillance. Therefore, if there is individual deterrence, the close supervision of probationers and parolees should diminish their recidivism.

The Survey seems to validate this traditional control theory: "A clear finding is that intensive probation supervision is associated with reduction in recidivism among males and females under 18 years of age. This conclusion is based on five studies in which youthful subjects were randomly assigned to various forms of intensive supervision and to standard supervision" (Lipton et al., 1975:27).

The implications for traditional control theory are less clear, however, from studies that compare probation and incarceration as alternative penalties. According to Wisconsin research reported in the Survey, *first offenders* given probation have significantly lower recidivism rates than similar lawbreakers imprisoned and then paroled, but there was little difference for those with prior felony convictions. The Survey also reports a study in Israel that found first offenders *under 20* less recidivistic with suspended sentences than with imprisonment, but no significant differences for older ones (Lipton et al., 1975:52–55).

Another set of contrasting results with alternative penalties was seen in the 1961–69 phase of the California Youth Authority's "Community Treatment Program" (Palmer, 1974). In this experiment Sacramento and Stockton youths in Authority custody for the first time were promptly screened to eliminate from the study about 25 percent of the boys and 5 percent of the girls whose crimes were mostly violent, hence for whom it was presumed that the public would demand rigid penalties. The remainder were then classified into nine categories based mainly on "interpersonal maturity" and were randomly divided into experimental and control groups. The experimental cases were paroled within a month to officers with small caseloads (8 to 12), trained to treat each category somewhat differently, and usually assigned only the types with whom they were most compatible. The control cases received the Authority's traditional incarceration, averaging eight months, then were paroled. Both groups were under Youth Authority jurisdiction for two to four years, and were followed up for four years thereafter.

In the final report on this experiment, the nine types were consolidated into fewer categories, thus increasing reliability (Palmer, 1974). About half, called "neurotics," did not seem highly committed to delinquency and were regarded as more psychologically mature than the others, especially in being less impulsive. They had lower recidivism rates during and after supervision if in the experimental group (paroled immediately) rather than in the control group. About a fifth, called "power oriented," were the most enculturated in delinquency and showed the most defiance or manipulation of authority figures. They had lower recidivism rates if in the control group (with regular correctional confinement and parole) rather than in the experimental community program. For the remaining 30 percent in residual categories, there was no clear advantage with either treatment. Unfortunately, the latest available official publications on this experiment's results (e.g., Palmer, 1974) do not provide statistics that are sufficiently detailed and clear to answer all questions raised by Lerman's (1975) more lucid report on this experiment, but Lerman does not analyze the typologically differentiated or the four-year post-discharge data which seem to contradict some of his conclusions. (Two books with later findings and analysis by Palmer and associates are forthcoming.)

Much publicized support for traditional control theory has come from Charles Murray and associates (1978), who found that "chronic juvenile offenders" in Chicago had significantly lower arrest rates immediately after, rather than just before, any major government intervention. This "suppression effect" on crime was about the same for youths whether in a correctional institution or UDIS, an intensive community-treatment program, but there was less "suppression" of new offenses with the allegedly more lenient regular probation. Empey and associates (1971, 1972) in earlier Utah and California studies, also found that offense rates declined after correctional interventions.

A report to be issued by four Chicago-area social scientists purports to invalidate Murray's claim of a "suppression effect" by maintaining that the observed decline in crime rates from the prearrest to the postrelease period was due to: (1) a "maturation effect" (the reduction in crime rates of most offenders as they grow older); (2) a "regression effect" (the return of released offenders to their average rates of crime after release, but their arrest most frequently when they are committing crimes at above their average rates); (3) a "mortality effect" (lost from Murray's postrelease sample were offenders still in UDIS or incarcerated when the follow-up crime tabulation was made, but those released last presumably were considered the most persistently criminal, so earlier releasees should have lower offense rates) (based on correspondence with Richard McCleary). Given the unresolved character of these contrasting interpretations, therefore, only time will tell whether claims for the existence of the "suppression effect" will be forthcoming.

Nonetheless, Murray's finding of there being about the same crime rates after release from either UDIS or incarceration cannot properly be compared to the California Community Treatment Program results because

1. The Chicago youths were not differentiated by type;

2. These youths averaged ten prior arrests and three prior detentions (hence most were not newly labeled "delinquent") and apparently they resembled California's "power-oriented," who had lower recidivism rates after institutional rather than community treatment;

3. Over half the days of service given by the UDIS staff were devoted to "youth advocacy," the provision of staff to speak to any authority figures (e.g., teachers, police, parents)

on behalf of the delinquents, a treatment that may often be the opposite of control. As a result, some interpretation of the differing outcomes for different types of offenders is needed.

Hirschi's (1969) social-psychological control theory implies that the main deterrent to crime is fear of losing bonds with conventional society. This view seems to be supported by the cited findings that release to the community with threat of confinement for new crimes, as compared with actual confinement, reduces recidivism most for young first offenders and for "neurotics." These two groups presumably have stronger conventional bonds than do the recidivist lawbreakers for whom immediate release with surveillance was less effective or scarcely different in crime-reduction from traditional incarceration and parole. For those with a stake in conformity, fines alone have been repeatedly shown to be an adequate deterrent for many offenses, and to be equitable if based on ability to pay (approximated by the Scandinavian practice of fining persons a certain number of days' income). Weekend public-service work is another alternative penalty.

The Survey's finding that intensive parole supervision did not clearly influence recidivism rates for any age group suggests that the prior *criminal* bonds of previously confined offenders affect recidivism rates more than the tested variations of supervision. On the other hand, Hirschi's theory may be deficient when applied to advanced offenders in not being "differential," for it does not consider the strength of criminal bonds. The recidivism-prevention advantages of probation, suspended sentence or prompt release of unadvanced offenders, when compared with incarceration, may be due more to institutional life strengthening the criminal bonds of many first-timers than to its weakening their ties with conventional persons.

The Survey found only one evaluation study of adult offenders (over-18-year-olds) which had randomly assigned offenders to different sized caseloads, a federal probation study for which it concludes that "intensive supervision had a lower rate of new offenses, and a higher rate of technical violation than the other types of supervision[11] (Lipton et al., 1975:46). Of course, tighter supervision probably made the probation officers aware of technical violations they would not have known about with less frequent surveillance. The differences with varied caseloads in this study were small, perhaps because, as other research shows, federal probation officers (and probably nonfederal as well) give higher priority to presentence investigation and report-writing on adults than to the supervision of probationers (Glaser, 1969:299–302).

One noteworthy exception to any conclusion that intense supervision has little impact on recidivism rates of advanced offenders in the community occurs for opiate addicts, if supervision includes nalline or urine tests. Research indicates that these types of relatively precise checks on new lawbreaking do reduce readdiction and crime, but do not have very lasting effects after the controls cease (Bailey, 1975; McGlothlin et al., 1977). Indeed, the Survey notes that these tests were effective as behavior controls only while the threat that further drug use would result in imprisonment was kept credible by actual arrests and confinements (Lipton et al., 1975:375).

Such findings on individual deterrence are consistent with the conclusions of a wide variety of behavioral studies on humans and animals. This research has repeatedly shown that conduct which is gratifying in a given type of situation will cease if punished with sufficient promptness, certainty, and severity, but that unless an alternative behavior then proves gratifying, the previous conduct tends to be resumed when the punishment ceases or is evaded or endured (Bandura, 1969: chaps. 5 and 8). Punishment presumably makes criminal acts less rewarding. But how can one increase the bonds of punished offenders to conventional society and thus make crime less gratifying to them?

Hirschi (1969:19–26) distinguishes four elements in conventional bonds: *attachment* to conventional persons; *commitment* to conventional pursuits; *involvement* in conventional activities; and *belief* in conventional values. Accordingly, such control may be furthered not only by increasing the ties of offenders with anticriminal persons but also by what the other three types of theories (still to be assessed here) suggest: inculcating conventional beliefs in former offenders and expanding their gratifying experiences and opportunities in law-abiding activities. But if Hirschi's theory is reconceptualized as one of differential control, it should also call for efforts to alienate offenders from delinquent or criminal persons, to alter their acceptance of rationalizations for crime, and to reduce their involvement in lawbreaking.

Intensive supervision, of course, may focus not just on closer surveillance but also on assistance. It is sometimes especially directed at developing good relationships between offenders and conventional persons, particularly the supervising officers. Yet how likely is it that such bonds can develop to the point where they rival ties among youths active in delinquency for many years, who usually "hang out" with one another during most of their waking hours? Not only does the potentially punitive authority of the officers make it difficult for offenders to be fond of them, but the officers and these youngsters usually contrast in age, ethnicity, social class, and education.

Most prisoners, even if young, have had years of conflict with the law. They retain few bonds with anticriminal persons, yet these bonds may have more chance of being preserved or expanded under some confinement conditions than under others. Hence, three propositions on the impact of incarceration are especially important:

1. The larger and more regimented the place of confinement, the more likely it is that inmates will develop very personal relationships there only with other inmates rather than with staff.

2. The less privacy there is for inmates (e.g., the more continuously they are in rooms with many other inmates whom they cannot choose and the more they are unsupervised by staff), the more they must adapt to the conduct norms established by the toughest and usually the most criminalistic and predatory inmates.

3. The less the personal contact that inmates can maintain or cultivate with conventional persons while confined, the more they are controlled by their bonds with criminal persons.

Only the last of these three assertions has been fairly well tested as an approach to recidivism reduction. Holt and Miller's (1972) California study found that maintenance of family ties during imprisonment was distinctly associated with success on parole. This seemed to justify the facilitation of family visits to inmates, including conjugal visits for married prisoners, and furloughs that permit some inmates to go home for a few days, usually when their parole date is not far off. In California, also, the services of M-2 Sponsors, an organization that arranges visits of conventional persons to prisoners who lack satisfactory visitors, were distinctly associated with recidivism reduction at both youth and adult correctional institutions (Lewis, 1976; M-2 Sponsors, 1978). None of these studies had the rigor of a controlled experiment that would eliminate the possibility that their findings result only from the better risks among the prisoners receiving visitors. Nevertheless, these researches had fairly good quasi-experimental designs, including controls for variables that might differentiate the groups compared. One M-2 assessment compared recidivism rates of inmates who requested visitors but did not get them because of a period of administrative difficulties in the program with rates for those who did get such visitors in other periods.

Massachusetts Department of Correction follow-ups of 1973 and 1974 releases showed that inmates who received one or more home furloughs had significantly lower recidivism rates than similar prisoners who got none (LeClair, 1978a). Incidentally, many institutions have had 98 or 99 percent of the furloughees return without serious tardiness or other infractions, even when such leaves were most liberally granted (Serrill, 1975).

In conclusion, although the evidence of postpenalty "suppression" of crime suggests that the traditional control theory of individual deterrence is valid, other data are more supportive of a differential social-psychological control theory. Such a theory, for example, explains the repeated finding that "radical intervention" by suspended sentence or supervision in the community reduces crime rates of young and unadvanced offenders more than does incarceration but does not have these effects for older or advanced young lawbreakers. Hirschi's nondifferential formulation of control theory suffices to explain the finding that recidivism is reduced by encouraging and facilitating contacts between prisoners and conventional persons in the community. Since Hirschi links the building of bonds also to beliefs and to commitment and involvement in legitimate activities, complete testing of his perspectives cannot readily be separated from evaluation of other types of theories considered here.

Insight Theories

Psychotherapy and counseling in corrections try to change behavior by giving offenders insight into the causes of their misconduct. They are perhaps the most frequently and enthusiastically prescribed treatment methods, but the least demonstrably successful in reducing recidivism rates, and they are probably the treatments most extensively assessed by controlled experiments. These programs are extremely diverse, yet all have one feature in common: they are deliberately devoted to talk.

In psychotherapy, the person in charge is generally a psychiatrist, psychologist, or psychiatric social worker, while in counseling this individual may be one of these or someone with other qualifications. Despite such differences in staffing, however, the content and style of the sessions called psychotherapy or counseling in corrections overlap, and the many dimensions on which they both vary include:

1. Whether they are provided on an individual basis to one client at a time or to a group;

2. Whether participation of offenders in them is voluntary or required, or allegedly voluntary but so rewarded as to create strong pressures to join;

3. The number of hours per day or week devoted to them,

often negligible but sometimes reaching almost continuous involvement of many participants, in which case they may be called "therapeutic community" or "milieu therapy";

4. How greatly the content and style of the talk is dictated by staff or by client(s), hence whether the communication is staff-directed, nondirected, or something in between, perhaps called "guided group interaction," with other procedural variations also possible (e.g., role playing, video feedback);

5. The theory that guides them, with the variations already indicated, such as psychoanalytic or reality therapy, and others;

6. Somewhat independently of the broad type of theory, the topics discussed, for example, relationships among participants, their early childhood traumas, criminal careers or immediate personal problems, and concerns about the future;

7. Linkage with other programs, for example, with academic or vocational training, social casework or methadone maintenance;

8. Whether they are conducted in institutions, in the community, or both (e.g., periodically bringing parolees back to the institutions for counseling sessions);

9. The types of participants (e.g., young or old, males or females or both, sex offenders, drug abusers).

Obviously, each of these variations and others, especially in the personalities of the staff, may affect the impact of such programs on the recidivism rates of their clients. Therefore, it is understandable that no uniform conclusion can be made about the consequences of all psychotherapy and counseling; yet the evidence suggests that talk sessions are not alone responsible for the reformation of most lawbreakers who go straight.

The Survey classified efforts to change the thinking of offenders into four categories that reflect several of the above dimensions (Lipton et al., 1975: 182–83, 107–68):

1. From seven studies of what it calls "casework and individual counseling," it concludes that some recidivism reduction occurred when the programs did not focus on psychodynamics but on helping their clients with immediate problems in the

community, such as obtaining financial assistance or a job (and these problems may have been alleviated by casework without much counseling).

2. In thirteen assessments of "individual psychotherapy," mainly in agencies for juvenile delinquents, recidivism reduction was reported only where the talk was oriented to practical problems rather than to achieving psychological insight and, especially, with sixteen-to twenty-year-old males. In the PICO Project such youths had lower recidivism rates following individual counseling in prison if they were initially deemed "amenable" (i.e., articulate and seeking counseling), whereas those classified in advance as nonamenable but placed in counseling groups anyhow had higher recidivism rates than the noncounseled nonamenables.

3. The eighteen evaluations of "group methods" yielded no evidence of major reduction in recidivism rates but indicated some benefits for first offenders, especially in groups with the same staff leader for more than a year (suggesting that personal bonds with this individual are influential). In general, there appears to have been little prevention of crime form the massive proliferation of group-counseling programs in California prisons during the early 1960s in which (a) prisoners were motivated by the prospect that their participation would result in a favorable recommendation for parole; (b) staff in almost every position were encouraged to train for largely nondirective counseling and to run at least one group session of inmates per week; (c) some of the most rigorous evaluation research in correctional history was undertaken to assess the counseling's impact (e.g., Kassebaum et al., 1971).

4. The twenty studies of "milieu therapy" show no clear evidence that these almost daily sessions of several hours of talk greatly affect recidivism rates, whether with juvenile delinquents in correctional residences or with youths on probation in the community.

Inculcating insight may often be attempted by purely didactic methods, in special classes, or in study and writing assignments designed to teach conventional values. Such "social education" has been offered in several juvenile and youth correctional institutions but with lettle objective evaluation. In one of the rare cases of a controlled experiment in sentencing, a Salt Lake City juvenile court in the 1960s randomly selected four groups of juvenile traffic violators for different penalties: fines, restraint from driving, attending traffic school, and writing a paper on traffic violation. A one-year follow-up revealed that those who wrote papers had distinctly the lowest rates of new violations, and those who were fined had the highest; traffic school was second highest; restraint from driving was second lowest (Mecham, 1968).

In 1974 in California's Fresno County the probation office of the juvenile court instituted a "Youth and Law Class" dealing with the juvenile-justice system. Attendance at this three-hour presentation in classes of up to twenty students was required for first offenders, with each to bring one parent. Other family members were invited to attend voluntarily, and some recidivists were also referred to it. Those in the first eighty four classes in 1976 had a 16 percent new offense rate, in a six-month follow-up, compared to a 29 percent rate for a random sample of first offenders in the previous year (Erdman, 1978).

To test insight theories more adequately (e.g., psychoanalytic, Rogerian, reality, or Yochelson and Samenow), therapists and counselors must (1) identify the theory they apply and (2) rate the insight achieved by their clients at the end of treatment. The correlation of these ratings with subsequent recidivism rates could then be determined, but perhaps the similarity of counseling by those who claim to be guided by the same theory should also be checked. In addition, any variables likely to affect the validity of these ratings of insight, such as ethnic similarity of rater and client, or the rater's total amount of contact with the client might well be investigated. Alternatively, to assess gains ascribable to the treatment, insight might be estimated from responses to a special questionnaire for each type of theory, administered at the beginning and end of a person's participation in therapy. Finally, in correlating measurements of insight to recidivism rates, statistical controls to differentiate offenders would be

desirable (e.g., by age, criminal record, education, work record).

To my knowledge, the types of assessments indicated above
have not been done in corrections, so that it is difficult to
test insight theories. When the correlations between counseling or psychotherapy and recidivism rates are made without
assessing the insight gained by the clients, it is uncertain
whether their subsequent crime reduction, if any, is due to
the talks, to the personal bonds that they develop with staff,
or to other simultaneous assistance, such as casework services,
schooling, or employment.

Counseling in the community seems to reduce recidivism
rates most when concerned with immediate problems of
achieving a conventional life-style, such as school, jobs, budgets, and family relationships. To alleviate problems in these
areas, however, the talk sessions are often combined with a
variety of social casework, financial aid, tutoring, vocational
training, and other assistance. Such services, as well as much
personal counseling, accompanied the close supervision that
was found to reduce recidivism rates of "neurotics" in California's Community Treatment Program (described under "Control Theories"); diverse casework also supplemented the
counseling credited with success for the "amenables" in the
PICO Project.

The most supported general conclusion on insight theories
from the many studies covered in the Survey and from others
(e.g., Carney, 1969; Shore and Massimo, 1973) seems to be
that unadvanced offenders probably are helped in avoiding
further crime by counseling alone if (1) it is available extensively, and with good rapport, when offenders wish to discuss
their problems in conventional pursuits (e.g., in school, work,
or being accepted in conventional social circles); and (2) they
already have other resources for resolution of these problems,
such as relevant skills, and persons willing to give them tangible assistance.

When offenders have been long involved in delinquent or
criminal groups or have taken alcohol or other drugs to excess,
they are usually wed to subcultures that rationalize or even

extol such conduct. When this type of learning has been regularly reinforced by intimate associates, it usually is too strong an influence for most counseling or therapy to overcome. Indeed, counseling in institutions often is little concerned with combatting criminal values and ideas, but is preoccupied instead with fostering adjustment to institutional life.

Correctional counseling of advanced offenders in the community may have to be supplemented by a variety of controls if it is to achieve extensive recidivism reduction. The Provo Experiment illustrates how such controls may include peer-group pressure for conformity to some conventional behavior standards, backed up by peer-sanctioned penalties, even temporary confinement, for gross misconduct (Empey and Erickson, 1972). Thus, wherever diminished crime rates are ascribed to counseling in the community, it is usually impossible to know how much of this achievement is due to the insight instilled through counseling, how much to the accompanying controls, and how much to the simultaneous fostering of successful experience in work or other alternatives to crime.

Experience Theories

The learning of criminal and anticriminal thought and behavior is usually a social process that begins at an early age. It appears to be especially influenced by experience during adolescence, that transitional period when the young person is neither child nor adult. Indeed, adolescence is a stage of great ambiguity where there is disagreement both in the family and in the community on how much independence and responsibility youngsters should assume or be given. The crucial significance of adolescence for crime is suggested by the fact that over half the arrestees for serious offenses in the United States are under eighteen. The ages with peak arrest rates (the modal years) for the FBI's Index Crimes are sixteen for theft and burglary, eighteen for robbery and aggravated assault, nineteen for rape, and twenty for murder (Glaser, 1978:75).

The home and the school are the institutions most concerned with preparing children and adolescents for adult roles. In the last few decades, however, the functions of the home in this regard have diminished, especially during adolescence, divorce rates and single parent homes have increased, more mothers are employed, and children are less likely to be needed for household chores or family businesses. Meanwhile, the span of life spent in school has increased about one year per census decade. Hence, the median amount of education of the U.S. population, aged twenty five and older, has risen from somewhat over eight years in 1940 to more than twelve in 1970. Accordingly, poor schoolwork or simply disliking school is supplanting home conflict as the main predictors of admitted or official delinquency (Empey, 1978:235–38, 286–88, 301–2; Glaser, 1978:162–65). Furthermore, once secondary-school students get into difficulty with the law, their prospects of further arrests diminish if they drop out of school, especially if they get married or go to work and thus assume adult roles (Elliott and Voss, 1974).

Sociologists studied the nature of slum life in our large cities from 1920 to 1940 in order to explain the high rates of delinquency and youth crime among the children of its poor families, most of whom were migrants from abroad or from our rural South. They concluded that, because slums overcrowd and concentrate families with problems that impede child care, juveniles there are on their own and in the streets more than in other neighborhoods. In addition, they noted that slum children are much more likely to encounter crime and vice and to become the members of youth gangs that both legitimate, and provide rationalizations for, the commission of criminal acts. Hence, they concluded that slum children are likely to be much more delinquent than others because of their more criminogenic experiences (Tannenbaum, 1938; Shaw and McKay, 1942).

These explanations were supplemented after World War II by writings that portrayed delinquent subcultures as collective responses to the strain that is induced by the lack of legitimate access to culturally valued goals (Cloward and Ohlin, 1960; Cohen, 1955). These publications reflected research which revealed that rates of self-reported delinquency did not differ nearly so much from one neighborhood to the next as did official rates of arrest or adjudication. In addition, these studies also showed that delinquent activities everywhere are especially supported and rationalized by the adolescents who are most alienated from teachers and parents and that these youths have life-styles suggesting that they are the main transmitters of delinquent subcultures. Although there is reason to suspect that the interpersonal bonds among these delinquents are not nearly so strong as previously thought (Hirschi, 1969), the gangs they perpetuate, particularly in slum areas, are still violent and still deadly (Miller, 1975).

It has also become clear that age-group segregation in our society now produces much more widespread contrasts between adolescents and adults in some types of illegal experience (such as marijuana use) than in others (such as burglary and assault). All persons, delinquent or nondelinquent, seem to be especially shaped by the experiences in which they are most successful socially, and those who get social and other rewards for legitimate behavior are the least involved in crime. Such experiences, of course, go hand-in-hand with the presence or absence of bonds to conventional persons. Whether one is delinquent or nondelinquent is a consequence of many contingencies that affect learning experiences, probably including not only home and community environments but also individual temperaments and abilities that are partly biological in origin (Glaser, 1978:chap. 7 and 8).

From this social-learning view of delinquency and crime causation, it follows that the best way to reduce recidivism is to help offenders experience more success at alternatives to lawbreaking. For many, such attainments would be easier if they improved their academic and vocational education. But efforts to provide schooling for offenders have been quite variable in their effects.

The Survey's review of fifteen studies that assess relationships between the development of skills and the reduction of recidivism suggests many pitfalls in these evaluation efforts.

Thus, the average inmate's length of time in a prison's academic or vocational-training program increases with time confined, but the fact that the most advanced offenders tend to have the longest terms may produce a positive correlation between time spent in prison schools and recidivism rates. Indeed, the least criminalistic offenders are often placed in minimum security settings (e.g., prison farms or forestry camps) where there is no school program or it is brief. Yet some recidivism reduction has been reported for inmates who raised their academic grade level appreciably in prison, instead of merely attending school there, and for youthful offenders who received vocational training, whether in institutions or in the community (Lipton, 1975:184–207).

In a methodologically unique study, McKee (1972, 1978) compared California prisoners who received vocational training with similar inmates who did not, and he procured not only their recidivism rates but also their postrelease earnings as shown by federal unemployment-insurance deductions. These data revealed that former inmates who received vocational training in prison had lower recidivism rates and earned more than the comparison group. The contrast occurred primarily for those who had over one thousand hours of vocational training in prison. Furthermore, the income advantages (hence the economic benefits to society in excess of training costs) were greatest from instruction and practice in machine shop, welding, sheet metal, auto repair, and electronics. Income changes were negative from training in shoe repair, dry cleaning, masonry, or landscaping. In addition, McKee found that the longer the lapse between completion of the vocational instruction and release from prison, the less was the gain in earnings associated with training.

At many correctional institutions in recent years, conflict among inmate gangs has greatly curtailed vocational training. The most realistic way of providing work instruction and experience for prisoners is demonstrated by Minnesota, and to a lesser extent by Illinois and Connecticut. They contract to have private industry operate factories within state prisons to produce goods for intrastate commerce. A minimum wage

scale, or higher, is given to inmate workers, who then pay
the state a part of their earnings for room and board. Prisoners
so welcome these programs that they are highly motivated
to maintain order (Business Week, July 18, 1977; Christian Science Monitor, July 13, 1978). Federal laws dating from the
depression bar interstate commerce in goods made in prison,
but possibly not those from juvenile correctional facilities.

Manpower expert Richard Tropp (1978) maintains that hard
physical labor which appeals to the masculinity concerns of
delinquents, and is remunerated (e.g., in conservation camps
and "Outward Bound" programs), is the type of vocational
training most consistently found to reduce recidivism. This
may well be because these work-group projects nurture a collective pride of accomplishment and prepare youths for the
physical demands of many of the jobs available to them after
release. Contrastingly, on the manpower training centers in
large cities, which have been widely criticized as maintaining
a casual and indolent atmosphere, he observes: "The volunmi-
nous evaluation literature indicates that participants do have
modestly higher earnings, a modestly greater probability of
non-subsidized employment, and marginally greater employment stability in the immediate post-training period of several
months to a year. The earnings and employment gains wash
out at a steep rate after a year, however." He also indicates
that the differences between trained and untrained youths
in stability of employment soon disappear too.

Perhaps the central problem in preparing most advanced
delinquents for the work world is that early humiliation in
school leads to their being much more comfortable in informal
groups than in the formal settings of today's jobs, which are
mainly in large organizations. Delinquents spend less time
than nondelinquents on homework but much more time on
"hanging out" with friends (Hirschi, 1969:chap. 10). Seldom
do they participate in formally organized extracurrilar programs, and their group life is characterized by a joshing, ineffi-
cient, informal, and often irrational style of communication
and decision-making (Loeb, 1973). These poor habits are en-

couraged by the "social promotion" policies of many schools that require only minimal effort and barely tolerable conduct for annual advancement to the next grade, an ambience perhaps duplicated in the manpower training centers discussed above. Furthermore, the unfitness for work thus generated in such schools is doubtless intensified by the forced time-killing and the slow pace of activities in correctional institutions and by the fact that the choices available to inmates are so limited that they cannot individually manage their daily lives as the outside world requires. These experiences may explain why released offenders not only have difficulty obtaining employment but have high quit and discharge rates when they do get work (Wiederanders and Luckey, 1977).

Several correctional institutions have introduced programmed instruction to replace traditional classroom procedures. These new teaching methods use specially designed books and even machines, some of them computer controlled, which break up lessons into small units that each student masters at his or her own pace. The students receive immediate individual aid (from the teacher, from the computer, or from both) when they have difficulties, and they are rewarded when they complete units and pass tests on them, at first after each brief unit. These procedures make studying a more continuously successful experience for most offenders than it ever was for them before, and many advance several grade levels per year. Unfortunately, there has been scant analysis of the impact of grade advancement on recidivism reduction, but ther is some strong evidence that programmed instruction is rehabilitative, especially as part of community rather than institutional programs (Cohen and Filipczak, 1971; Odell, 1974; Hackler and Hagan, 1975).

Programmed instruction is used mainly in elementary and secondary education, but several prisons permit qualified inmates to enroll in nearby colleges. Evaluations indicate that some of these college programs reduce recidivism rates but that most have no clear impact; and at least one program was actually associated with increased recidivism rates (Blumstein and Cohen, 1974; Seashore et al., 1976). Possibly more extensive research would reveal that variations in program administration, in student selection, or in evaluation methods account for these diverse findings.

Both theory and some evidence suggest that a change in experience reduces recidivism rates most in those for whom the change is greatest. Thus, large educational gains seem to make the greatest reduction in lawbreaking for youths who had least prior school, work, or criminal experience (Blumstein and Cohen, 1974; Beha, 1977). But skills learned do not provide much new experience unless they can be applied.

Opportunity Theories

Obviously, efforts to rehabilitate offenders can be promising only if the job market provides a chance to engage in what usually must be a key component of their reformation, earning an honest living. They are handicapped in seeking employment, not only by poor school and work histories, but by criminal records. Furthermore, since most offenders are either juveniles or are members of minority groups, or both, they are doubly handicapped. Taken separately, each has about twice the national unemployment rate, while young minority-group members have about four times the national rate.

Radical criminologists stress such unemployment figures in pointing out that youth adjudged delinquent or criminal have always come disproportionately from the marginally employed labor force in capitalist societies. The Schwendingers (1976) note that because these youths usually have marginally employed parents and because the children of the poor are handicapped in competing at school or work with offspring of the more affluent, our competitive educational system tends to perpetuate the existing class structure. Indeed, Quinney (1977) implies that capitalists deliberately keep many people in little-employed careers because the availability of "reserve" work force facilitates their exploitation of labor. These criminologists contend, therefore, that the only significant reduction in delinquency and crime will come when capitalism is replaced by socialism.

Nevertheless, most released offenders in our capitalist society sooner or later do procure legitimate employment and do refrain from serious crime. According to follow-up studies, the percentage of former prisoners who are reconfined has ranged from a little under a third to about two-thirds. Indeed, even those who recidivate generally do not immediately revert to felonies, and few depend on crime for a livelihood most of the time when they are out (Petersilia et al., 1977). Thus, the releasees most likely to fail are those who are younger, who have more prior criminality, and who live in areas with high crime rates, or who are followed up longer (see Glaser, 1969:chap. 1; Kitchener et al., 1977).

The democratic countries with advanced capitalism, notably in northwest Europe and North America, have usually had in the past century or two an accelerating trend of "inclusion," of providing more of the population with greater participation in, and benefit from, government (Parsons, 1977). Although this erratic but recurrent trend has not produced full equality, it has reduced racist and sexist discriminations and has furthered a variety of welfare state services. These developments expand more often than they contract. They gradually reduce the handicaps in career-seeking that children suffer because of the low education or status of their parents, handicaps that are also evident in socialist states. Governments of capitalist countries do not always guarantee employment for everyone as they are presumed to do under socialism, but their expansion of the assistance and opportunity available to their most deprived citizens is always a realistic political possibility. Our concern here will be with the criminological implications of economic developments that are conceivably feasible in the United States during the current era.

Opportunity theories on rehabilitation have been tested in the United States by efforts to increase tangibly the postrelease resources of prisoners. Two practices will be considered here which make it less probable that desperate financial need soon after leaving confinement will be a major factor in recidivism:

"Pay parolee" programs. These provide the "purest" way of making it easy for newly released prisoners to avoid being out of money; these programs give them cash when they are unemployed. During 1971–74, for example, an experimental group of newly released Maryland parolees was paid up to $60 per week when out of work, for a total of up to thirteen weeks (U.S. Department of Labor, 1977). In 1973–74 California's experiment issued up to $80 per week to unemployed parolees for a maximum of twelve weeks (Reinarman and Miller, 1975). In both states less crime and a better work record distinguished the assisted parolees from the control groups. The Maryland study found that this difference was only in rates of new property offenses. The California analysis did not differentiate recidivism by type of offense but found that success on parole occurred only with payments to persons previously convicted of property or drug crimes rather than of violent offenses. At any rate, considering that the government spends $10,000–$15,000 or more annually to incarcerate someone, as well as the suffering of victims from recidivism, the overall decline in new crime that resulted in these studies made the unemployment payments a profitable public investment.

The California legislature was so impressed by these experiments that it passed a bill, effective in 1978, whereby state prisoners receive credit for work and good conduct in prison toward eligibility for payments if they are unemployed in their first year after release. This was necessary because, regardless of their earlier work record in the community, released prisoners (as well as persons who recover from long-term physical or mental illness) usually are ineligible for unemployment compensation because they cannot meet the federal and state requirement of having had, in each of two different quarters of the preceding year, at least minimum earnings on which their employer(s) made payments for unemployment insurance.

In Maryland and California, those for whom recidivism declined most if they received unemployment payments were the least educated parolees, or the oldest, or both. In the Maryland study, only those younger offenders who had more than one year of prior work experience seemed to benefit from this experiment. The California study found that improvement in parole outcome was greatest when prior work history was "steady" (rather than "sporadic" or "none"), but it did not probe whether this finding varies with age.

The Maryland project excluded women, first offenders, alcoholics, and heroin users, presuming that its experiment was thus with parolees most likely to change their recidivism rates if paid when unemployed. The California study only excluded parolees with prior civil commitments for drug addiction, but so few women were in its cross-section of all other parolees that no control group was drawn for them and they are excluded in the evaluation. The experimental group, however, included many users of soft and hard drugs who were never civilly committed for addiction. The property offenders and drug users who received unemployment benefits had, when compared to controls, the lowest recidivism rates of all. Conversely, experimentals who were alcoholics before their prison terms were those who had higher recidivism rates than comparable controls. The finding on property offenders suggests that the greatest crime prevention achieved by paying parolees when unemployed occurs among those most likely to use the money for sustenance. Yet perhaps there was also crime reduction when parolees used the payments to maintain a manageable interest in drugs. It is clear that variations of substance abuse still not fully explored may diversely affect the impact of financial aid.

In 1976 the federal government funded pay-parolee experiments in Texas and Georgia, but preliminary reports indicate that the overall results are disappointing (Tropp, 1978), although details are not yet available. An ideal assessment would probe whether any aspects of program administration, as well as offender attributes, produce variations in outcome.

Halfway houses and work or school release or furlough. These were created to provide tangible assistance to persons just out of prison. The idea was that in halfway houses released offenders would receive room, meals, companionship, and, often, access to various recreational facilities and social-work services. The earliest houses of this type were established by private groups, frequently religious, to aid releasees who came voluntarily to them. Later, when opened by government agencies, halfway houses sometimes were the required first residence for parolees, and failure to obey the rules there could result in parole revocation. Many residents then resented these house restrictions, not traditional with parole.

In 1961 the U.S. Bureau of Prisons began its halfway-house program in urban areas, often using a section of a large YMCA or hotel to which some prisoners were transferred three or four months before parole. Although legally still prisoners, when these residents moved from a traditional prison to the halfway house, they traveled alone, by public transportation, and in civilian clothes. About 99 percent arrived there, and after a few days of orientation and possibly family visits, they went out to seek work or hold jobs. Then they were increasingly permitted to leave in their leisure time also, taking overnight or weekend passes when their parole dates were near. Many state-prison systems have now copied this federal model, as have some county jails. LeClair (1978b) shows that release through such state centers in Massachusetts distinctly reduces recidivism rates, but especially when it follows earlier home furloughs from prison.

In California and some other states, residents in the correctional system's halfway houses are among many prisoners legally designated as on work or school release or furlough. This terminology, however, may also mean departing daily from a traditional prison or jail to nearby paid employment or school enrollment. Such an arrangement may enhance the experience of inmates at legitimate roles in the free community, but it will not necessarily augment their resources when seeking a postrelease residence and job.

Only if halfway houses, prisons, or jails are in or near the postrelease communities of the prisoners are temporary releases and furloughs likely to expand their subsequent opportunities. By contrast, those benefiting most from piecemeal rather than complete return to freedom in the community are individuals who would not have enough funds at release to last until they could get a job, would have no prearranged housing, would have no noncriminal persons with whom they could talk readily, and would have no place to relax, to watch television, to read or to play except in bars or other commercial establishments. Although halfway houses can meet all these needs, the neediest inmates are often the least likely to receive such graduated release. Indeed, in many states (California, for one), only a minority of prisoners is released this way, and first priority is given the best risks, who generally have the most resources without this aid.

In halfway houses and work-release or furlough programs, releasees are usually charged for room and board, but at lower rates than are readily available elsewhere, and without obligation to pay when they have not yet received wages and lack other funds. Often, staff have much skill at maintaining a congenial atmosphere, as well as in sensing and solving problems that residents experience. Staff also enforce rules, however, such as banning drug use on the premises or unwarrented absences, and they can arrange return to regular imprisonment as well as recommend cancellation of a scheduled parole. Thus, these methods of graduated release are forms of increased control and containment as well as expansions of opportunity, when compared to the traditionally abrupt parole or discharge from an institution.

All the release arrangements discussed here are labeled by the Survey as "Partial Physical Custody" programs. It found no clear pattern in the results from five evaluations of halfway houses, but some interesting findings resulted from a two-year followup of the first 231 youthful offenders paroled from the first four federal community-correctional centers (in New York, Detroit, Chicago, and Los Angeles), and of 1,000 similar parolees from federal reformatories in the preceding years. The prisoners with records of repeated auto theft (most of them starting as juveniles) had markedly lower recidivism rates if released through these centers in their home communities rather than paroled from the distant reformatories.

Other categories of federal youthful offenders had much greater postrelease success rates than these recidivist auto thieves, but the outcomes of the other types were not so much affected by graduated release through the halfway houses.

It should be noted that these young recidivist federal auto thieves were charged with interstate transportation of stolen vehicles, usually taken as part of a juvenile pattern of joyriding and truancy from home rather than as professional theft. My observations of these centers indicated that these rather "flighty" youths often acquired and lost several successive jobs in their four months there, but by their parole date had the longest full-time and adult-type employment experience that they had ever had (Glaser, 1969:277–82).

The Survey also presents descriptive data on seven work-release programs but concludes: "claims for and assumptions underlying work release remain largely untested. . . . There is no convincing evidence that work release has any impact . . . in terms of recidivism" (Lipton et al., 1975:277, but see also pp. 269–80).

Finally, one summary of halfway-house evaluation literature through 1975 states that (1) there were only two controlled experimental studies, both of which found no differences in recidivism rates between residents and their control groups; (2) of the seventeen quasi-experimental studies, eleven found that residents had less recidivism, five found no difference, and one found higher recidivism in the halfway-house releasees (Seiter et al., 1977). By contrast, Massachusetts research concluded that halfway-house releasees were distinctly less recidivistic than similar prisoners paroled directly from institutions (Landolfi, 1976a and 1976b), but, surprisingly, this advantage of halfway-house aid was greatest for persons with prior drunkenness arrests, as well as for those with little prior employment (LeClair, 1975a). Possibly both of these categories consist of inmates least likely to have food and shelter at release unless in a halfway house, and the drunkenness cases may also be kept out of drinking places partly by the controls and the companionship at the houses.

Confounding the Massachusetts evaluations is the fact that they are based upon follow-ups only of persons completing their assigned period of residence in these houses. Those returned to prison for misconduct before completing this period had about the ame recidivism rates as other releasees from the prisons (LeClair, 1975b; Beha, 1976). These houses also augment control, for they permit officials to know about and act on deviant conduct by the releasees with more swiftness and certainty than is generally possible with ordinary parole, probation, or discharge.

As previously stated, daily leave at a prison located far from an inmate's postrelease residence contributes more to learning by new experience than to postrelease resources. A rigorously controlled experiment in such releases for Florida prisoners finds that it had no impact on recidivism rates (Waldo and Chiricos, 1977). When daily release occurs at a county jail, however, especially in a metropolitan area, the releasees are usually all residents of that locale. Therefore, county work-release or furlough programs may provide new jobs or preserve old ones for postrelease lives of the inmates.

Two other studies also find that these jail programs of opportunity expansion reduce recidivism rates (Rudoff and Esselstyn, 1973; Jeffery and Woolpert, 1974). The latter study noted that "work furlough is most beneficial to those having the highest risk of failure after release . . . the unskilled, unmarried men who had three or more convictions." Although these remained relatively poor risks, their recidivism rates diminished more by prerelease employment opportunities than did those of other types of jail inmates.

Even though the types of expansions of opportunities described here were rather small in scale and even though few programs received very adequate evaluations, there are sufficient data to justify some confidence that appreciable aid to the neediest releasees can reduce recidivism rates.

Summary and Conclusions

Theories justifying efforts to change the conduct of criminals can be grouped into four categories: control, insight, experience, and opportunity. Evaluation research that can be construed as testing these theories has been very deficient in quality and quantity. It indicates, nevertheless, that each type of theory provides some guidance for reducing recidivism rates but that each is relevant only to a limited segment of the lawbreaking population.

Individual deterrence of known offenders merely by threat of punishment (the traditional type of control theory) seems to be clearly effective only against persons with much stake in conformity and little in crime. Even for them the most effective punishments are those that do not impair their bonds with conventional society or increase their ties with other offenders; thus, probation, rather than incarceration, generally gives us most protection from further crimes by unadvanced offenders. The social-psychological control theory identified with Hirschi is also supported, notably by evidence that prisoners' retention of old bonds with law-abiders and the cultivation of new ones, if facilitated by visits and furloughs, reduces recidivism rates.

Unadvanced offenders were also shown to be the only ones for whom there may be prospects of recidivism reduction from efforts to inculcate insight by purely verbal methods. Yet to achieve such benefits even for them alone, only a small fraction of the vast array of correctional counseling, psychotherapy, and instruction methods have proved effective. Other types of theories and the findings of evaluation research indicate why this may be the case.

Most persons charged with felonies today are relatively young and have never very successfully made the transition from the dependence of childhood to economic self-sufficiency and acceptance in legitimate adult roles. Their lawbreaking is especially related to their difficulties in school, and their subsequent arrests to their inability to procure or hold jobs. Experience and opportunity theories, which indicate that these problems of offenders must be overcome if their recidivism rates are to be reduced, find support from the few instances of appreciable and well-evaluated aid.

This research indicates that the rate of return to crime tends to decline most when a correctional service makes the largest advance in the prospects of offenders at legitimate occupations and helps them to avoid desperate need. Thus, large improvements in academic attainment or in vocational training, as well as tangible aid to the neediest releasees, seem to be correctional investments that can best protect us from crimes.

The dictionary defines *rehabilitation* as "restoration to a former state," but most arrestees for felonies in the United States began their difficulties with the law as young teenagers, or even preteenagers, who never, or hardly ever, led a law-abiding or self-supporting life. Thus, the central problem in recidivism reduction is to habilitate them, to help them experience legitimate adult roles long and successfully for the first time. Habilitation efforts are sabotaged, however, if not utterly destroyed, if they are undertaken in institutional or community conditions that are *de*habilitating. For example, it is difficult to counter the criminogenic effects of regimenting offenders in large institutions where idleness is enforced, where there is extreme isolation from conventional society, and where the inmate ambience is determined by the most aggressive and exploitative prisoners.

Our disillusion with rehabilitation efforts only starts to vanish where we have correctional agencies that clearly build strong ties between offenders and law-abiding persons, where there is erosion rather than cultivation of bonds among serious criminals, and where great improvements occur in the qualifications and opportunities of former lawbreakers who seek a legitimate occupation. Programs which supply such opportunities, however, are far too scant and too scattered. Perhaps this is because it requires less thought, less effort, and les research merely to punish offenders than to provide effective rehabilitative services for them.

References

Bailey, Walter C.
    1975   "Addicts on parole: short-term and long-term progno-
             sis." International Journal of the Addictions 10
             (September):417–31.

Bandura, Albert
    1969   Principles of Behavior Modification. New York: Holt,
             Rinehart & Winston.

Beha, James A., II
    1976   "Testing the functions and effect of the parole halfway-
             house: one case study." Journal of Criminal Law and
             Criminology 67 (September):335–50.

    1977   "Innovation at a county house of correction and its
             effect upon patterns of recidivism." Journal of Research
             in Crime and Delinquency 14 (January):88–106.

Blumstein, Alfred, and Jacqueline Cohen
    1974   An Evaluation of a College-level Program in a Maxi-
             mum Security Prison. Pittsburgh: Carnegie-Mellon
             University Urban Systems Institute.

Carney, Francis J.
    1969   "Correctional research and correctional decision-
             making: some problems and prospects." Journal of Re-
             search in Crime and Delinquency 6 (July):110–22.

Cloward, Richard A., and Lloyd E. Ohlin
    1960   Delinquency and Opportunity: A Theory of Delinquent
             Gangs. New York: Free Press.

Cohen, Albert K.
    1955   Delinquent Boys: The Culture of the Gang. New York:
             Free Press.

Cohen, H. H., and J. Filipczak
    1971   A New Learning Environment. San Francisco: Jossey-
             Bass.

Elliott, Delbert S., and Harwin L. Voss
 1974   Delinquency and Dropout. Lexington, Mass.: Heath.

Empey, LaMar T.
 1978   American Delinquency: Its Meaning and Construction.
         Homewood, Ill.: Dorsey.

Empey, LaMar T., and Steven G. Lubeck
 1971   The Silverlake Experiment. Chicago: Aldine.

Empey, LaMar T., and Maynard L. Erickson
 1972   The Provo Experiment. Lexington, Mass.: Heath.

Erdman, Phillip M.
 1978   "Can education effectively reduce crime and delin-
         quency? Fresno's Youth and Law Class." Crime Pre-
         vention Review (Attorney General of California), 5
         (July):1–6.

Glaser, Daniel
 1969   The Effectiveness of a Prison and Parole System (rev.
         ed.). Indianapolis: Bobbs-Merrill.

 1973   Routinizing Evaluation: Getting Feedback on Effec-
         tiveness of Crime and Delinquency Programs.
         Rockville, Md.: National Institute of Mental Health,
         Crime and Delinquency Issues Monograph, Depart-
         ment of Health, Education, and Welfare, Publication
         No. (HSM)73–9123. Washington, D.C.: U.S. Govern-
         ment Printing Office.

 1978   Crime in Our Changing Society. New York: Holt, Rine-
         hart & Winston.

Glasser, William
 1965   Reality Therapy. New York: Harper & Row.

Hackler, James C., and John L. Hagan
 1975   "Work and teaching machines as delinquency preven-
         tion tools: a four-year follow-up." Social Service Review
         49 (March):92–106.

Hawkins, J. David, Christine H. Cassidy, Nancy B. Light, and Cathy
 A. Miller
 1977   "Interpreting official records as indicators of recidivism
         in evaluating delinquency programs." Criminology 15
         (November):397–424.

Hirschi, Travis
    1969   Causes of Delinquency. Berkeley: Univ. of California Press.

Holt, Norman, and Donald Miller
    1972   Exploration in Inmate-Family Relationships. Research Report No. 46. Sacramento: California Department of Corrections.

Jeffery, Robert, and Stephen Woolpert
    1974   "Work furlough as an alternative to incarceration: an assessment of its effects on recidivism and social costs." Journal of Criminal Law and Criminology 65 (September):405–15.

Kassebaum, Gene, David A. Ward, and Daniel M. Wilner
    1971   Prison Treatment and Parole Survival. New York: Wiley.

Kitchener, Howard, Annesley K. Schmidt, and Daniel Glaser
    1977   "How persistent is post-prison success?" Federal Probation 41 (March):9–15.

Landolfi, Joseph
    1976a   An Analysis of Recidivism among Residents Released from the Pre-Release Centers Administered by Massachusetts Halfway Houses, Inc. Boston: Massachusetts Department of Corrections.

    1976b   Charlotte House Pre-Release Center for Women: A Profile of Participants and a Recidivism Follow Up. Boston: Massachusetts Department of Corrections.

LeClair, Daniel P.
    1975a   An Analysis of Recidivism among Residents Released from Boston State and Shirley Pre-Release Centers during 1972–1973. Boston: Massachusetts Department of Corrections.

    1975b   A Profile of Characteristics Distinguishing between Program Completers and Program Non-Completers in Massachusetts' Pre-Release Centers. Boston: Massachusetts Department of Corrections.

    1978a   "Furloughs and recidivism rates." Criminal Justice and Behavior (September) (in press).

1978b   "Societal reintegration and recidivism rates." Paper to be presented at the Annual Meeting, American Society of Criminology, Dallas.

Lerman, Paul
1975   Community Treatment and Social Control. Chicago: Univ. of Chicago Press.

Lewis, Roy V.
1976   M-2 Project Evaluation: Final Parole Follow-Up of Wards in the M-2 Program. Sacramento: California Youth Authority.

Lipton, Douglas, Robert Martinson, and Judith Wilks
1975   The Effectiveness of Correctional Treatment: A Survey of Treatment Evaluation Studies. New York: Praeger.

Loeb, Rita
1973   "Adolescent groups." Sociology and Social Research 58 (October):13–22.

M-2 Sponsors, Inc. of California
1978   Successful Habilitation of Ex-Offenders. Hayward, Calif.: M-2 Sponsors, Inc.

McGlothlin, William H., Douglas Arglin, and Bruce D. Wilson
1977   An Evaluation of the California Civil Addict Program. Washington, D.C.: National Institute on Drug Abuse (Services Research Monograph Series: Department of Health, Education and Welfare, Publication No. (ADM) 78–558).

McKee, Gilbert J., Jr.
1972   A Cost-Benefit Analysis of Vocational Training in the California Prison System. Ph.D. dissertation in economics, Claremont Graduate School. (Ann Arbor, Mich.: Xerox, University Microfilms, No. 72–26,241).

1978   "Cost effectiveness and vocational training." In Norman Johnston and Leonard D. Savitz, Justice and Corrections. New York: Wiley.

Mecham, Garth D.
1968   "Proceed with caution: which penalties slow down the juvenile traffic violator?" Crime and Delinquency 14 (April):142–50.

Miller, Walter B.
  1975   Violence by Youth Gangs and Youth Groups as a Crime
          Problem in Major American Cities. Monograph. Na-
          tional Institute for Juvenile Justice and Delinquency
          Prevention, Law Enforcement Assistance Administra-
          tion (LEAA). Washington, D.C.: U.S. Government
          Printing Office.

Mowrer, O. Hobart
  1964   The New Group Therapy. Princeton, N.J.: Van No-
          strand.

Murray, Charles A., Doug Thomson, and Cindy B. Israel
  1978   UDIS: Deinstitutionalizing the Chronic Juvenile Of-
          fender. Washington, D.C.: American Institutes for Re-
          search.

Odell, Brian Neal
  1974   "Accelerating entry into the opportunity structure: a
          sociologically-based treatment for delinquent youth."
          Sociology and Social Research 58 (April):312–18.

Otto, Luther B.
  1976   "Social integration and the status-attainment process."
          American Journal of Sociology 81 (May):1360–83.

Palmer, Ted
  1974   "The Youth Authority's Community Treatment Pro-
          ject." Federal Probation 38 (March):3–20.

Parsons, Talcott
  1977   The Evaluation of Societies (Ed. Jackson Toby). Engle-
          wood Cliffs, N.J.: Prentice-Hall.

Petersilia, Joan, Peter W. Greenwood, and Marvin Lavin
  1977   The Criminal Career of the Repetitively Violent Of-
          fender. Santa Monica, Calif.: Rand Corporation.

Quinney, Richard
  1977   Class, State and Crime. New York: McKay

Reinarman, Craig, and Donald Miller
  1975   Direct Financial Assistance to Parolees. Research Re-
          port No. 55. Sacramento: California Department of
          Corrections.

Rogers, Carl R.
    1951   Client-centered Therapy. Boston: Houghton-Mifflin.

Rudoff, Alvin, and T. C. Esselstyn
    1973   "Evaluating work furlough: a followup." Federal Proba-
             tion 37 (June):48–53.

Schur, Edwin
    1973   Radical Nonintervention. Englewood Cliffs, N.J.: Pren-
             tice-Hall.

Schwendinger, Herman, and Julia R. Schwendinger
    1976   "Marginal youth and social policy." Social Problems
             24 (December):184–91.

Seashore, Marjorie J., Steven Haberfeld, John Irwin, and Keith Baker
    1976   Prisoner Education—Project Newgate and Other Col-
             lege Programs. New York: Praeger.

Seiter, Richard P., Eric W. Carlson, Helen H. Bowman, James J.
    Grandfield, and Nancy J. Beran
    1977   Halfway Houses. National Evaluation Program, Phase
             1 Summary Report. Washington: U.S. Department of
             Justice, Law Enforcement Assistance Administration
             (LEAA).

Serrill, Michael S.
    1975   "Prison furloughs in America." Corrections 1 (July/
             August):3–7. (Reprinted in Norman Johnston and Leon-
             ard D. Savitz, Justice and Corrections, New York: Wi-
             ley, 1978).

Shaw, Clifford R., and Henry D. McKay
    1942   Juvenile Delinquency and Urban Areas. Chicago: Univ.
             of Chicago Press.

Shore, Milton F., and Joseph L. Massimo
    1973   "After ten years: a follow-up study of comprehensive
             vocationally oriented psychotherapy." American Jour-
             nal of Orthopsychiatry 43 (January):128–31.

Spady, William G.
    1970   "Lament for the letterman: effects of peer status and
             extracurricular activities on goals and achievements."
             American Journal of Sociology 75 (January):680–702.

Tannenbaum, Frank H.
 1938   Crime and the Community. Boston: Ginn

Thorsell, Bernard A., and Lloyd W. Klemke
 1972   "The labeling process: reinforcement and deterrent?"
         Law and Society Review 6 (February):393–403.

Tropp, Richard A.
 1978   "Suggested policy initiatives for employment and
         crime problems." *In* Leon Leiberg (ed.), Crime and
         Employment Issues. Washington, D.C.: Office of Re-
         search and Development, Employment and Training
         Department, U.S. Department of Labor.

U.S. Department of Labor
 1977   Unlocking the Second Gate: The Role of Financial As-
         sistance in Reducing Recidivism among Ex-Prisoners.
         R & D Monographs 45, Washington, D.C.

Waldo, Gordon P., and Theodore G. Chiricos
 1977   "Work release and recidivism: an empirical evaluation
         of a social policy." Evaluation Quarterly 1 (Febru-
         ary):87–108.

Wiederanders, Mark, and Albert V. Luckey
 1977   Job Survival Skills Project Interim Report. Sacramento:
         California Youth Authority.

Windelband, Wilhelm
 1901   History of Philosophy. (2nd ed., trans, James H. Tufts).
         New York: Macmillan.

Yochelson, Samuel, and Stanton E. Samenow
 1976   The Criminal Personality. 2 Vols. New York: Jason
         Aronson.

Zimring, Franklin E., and Gordon J. Hawkins
 1973   Deterrence: The Legal Threat in Crime Control. Chi-
         cago: Univ. of Chicago Press.

Some Empirical Questions concerning the Current Revolution in Juvenile Justice

Maynard L. Erickson

CURRENT controversies over juvenile justice policy in America attest to the fact that it is torn between three competing ideologies: (1) the "helping hands" ideology, which stems from the traditional belief that juveniles should be rehabilitated rather than punished; (2) the "hands off" ideology, which is derived from labeling theory and suggests that kids should be left alone whenever possible; and (3) the "heavy hands" ideology, which represents a revival of classical theory and the belief that justice policies should stress deterrence, retribution, incapacitation, community protection, and normative validation.

It seems clear that the recent emergence of the "hands

NOTE: The data presented in this chapter come from several sources. Some of the data were collected as part of a larger research project: "Measures of Delinquency and Community Tolerance," supported by Public Health Service Research Grant, MH22350, NIMH (Center for the Study of Crime and Delinquency). Other data were made available by Maricopa County Juvenile Court Research and Planning Division, Phoenix, Arizona, and by Pima County Juvenile Court, Tucson, Arizona. Appreciation is expressed to both courts. A special debt of gratitude is owed to William McCarthy and Carol Burgess of Maricopa County Juvenile Court, not only for the data they provided, but for their analysis as well. Other data were also collected under the auspices of a research evaluation grant from the U.S. Department of Justice, Law Enforcement Assistance Administration (Grant 78-JN-AX-0020). I wish to express my gratitude to my research assistants and colleagues, James Galliher and Mark Warr, for their assistance in completing the analyses presented in this chapter. And finally I wish to express my thanks to LaMar T. Empey and Malcolm W. Klein for comments on an early version of this Chapter.

off" approach and the resurrection of the "heavy hands" approach are due in part to the failure, real or imagined, of the rehabilitative approach.[1] Many people are disillusioned with the concept of rehabilitation, or at least with all of the activities currently associated with that concept. Many people apparently believe such criminologists as Robert Martinson (1974), who contends that "nothing works"; and many assume that the rehabilitative approach is unacceptably ineffective

---

[1] Whether the rehabilitative approach to the delinquency problem has been a real failure remains problematic. The issue remains controversial because of the incredible diversity in (1) the quality of the activities which claim to be rehabilitative and (2) the evaluative research organized to assess rehabilitative programs. This diversity in quality makes it highly questionable to generalize about all such activity and the research on it. Until standards can be developed for classifying both programs and studies into reasonably homogeneous groups, it would be wise not to draw any final conclusions about the efficacy of the rehabilitative approach. It must also be noted that attempts to judge program effectiveness by some general, overall outcome measure are probably counterproductive. Surely we know enough about human behavior not to expect all kinds of people to be affected in the same way by any social or psychological experience. The implication is of course that it is reasonable to expect any treatment program to have different effects on different kinds of people (some people ought to be affected positively and others negatively by the same experience).

The implication of this observation is simply that evaluation research must make provisions to reveal both negative and positive outcomes for different kinds of people (e.g., different types of offenders, ages, races, etc.). It is not only possible but probable that the conclusion that "nothing works" is due to the fact that most past research has failed to specify results in such a way that those individuals who were positively affected by the treatment experience could be located—and, conversely, so that those affected negatively could be located. If there were approximately equal numbers affected in both directions and another group that was not affected at all, it is very likely that when one final conclusion is drawn (based on aggregate outcome measures), the conclusion would be that there is no effect.

Obviously, the debate over the efficacy of rehabilitation is not over. In fact, there are good reasons to believe that the decisive arguments both for and against the rehabilitative approach are yet to be made. Of one thing we can be reasonably sure: many people will continue to hold steadfast to the rehabilitative approach. They will continue to cling to those beliefs regardless of the empirical evidence that has been and will be generated by social scientists.

and costly. Yet their willingness to believe these things cannot be explained solely by the persuasiveness of the "nothing works" argument or by the amount and quality of empirical evidence on the effectiveness of rehabilitation. Rather, many are willing to believe existing criticisms of rehabilitation because of their desire to find *any* reasonable explanation for the ever rising crime rates. Thus when the "hands off" and the "heavy hands" ideologies also provide theoretical rationales for discrediting rehabilitation, they gain adherents. Although they are based on incompatible assumptions, each ideology provides a plausible explanation for the failure of rehabilitation.

This state of affairs requires an examination of the basic premises of both approaches. Meanwhile it would be well to remember that, while ideological battles rage over the relative merits of all three approaches, the "helping hands" approach remains pretty much in place; rehabilitation continues to direct the practices of juvenile justice professionals. This point is made simply to emphasize the fact that major social policies—and perhaps criminal justice policies in particular—do not disappear simply because a large number of social reformers, citizens, policymakers, or politicians become disillusioned with them.

The Current "Hands Off" Approach to Juvenile Justice

Empey (1978:525–58) refers to this approach as the most recent "revolution" in juvenile justice and characterizes the revolution in terms of four policy concerns or trends (i.e., due process, decriminalization, diversion, and deinstitutionalization). This approach to dealing with youth problems is of fairly recent origin. Its emergence as a major policy in juvenile justice occurred partially by default, owing to the fact that traditional institutions (e.g., the juvenile court) and the rehabilitation approach to juvenile justice have lost favor in recent years. The popularity of the "hands off" approach is also due in part to a major shift in the emphasis of delinquency theories from

strain, opportunity, and cultural transmission theories to labeling theory (Becker, 1963; Erikson, 1962; Kitsuse, 1962; Schur,
1969). The "hands off" approach is directly deducible from
labeling theory and is the single most important policy implication to be derived from that theory.

It is, of course, very difficult to explain the changing popularity of theories in the social sciences. Most of us would like
to believe that some of these changes reflect scientific development—that is, they reflect the cumulative results of scientific
research. However, the phenomenon of theoretical popularity
is much more complicated than that.

The rising crime rate and reported high recidivism rates,
linked with the apparent failure of many of the war-on-crime
programs, had a significant effect both on the demise of subcultural and opportunity theory, the falling out of favor of the
rehabilitative approach to corrections, and thus the rise in
popularity of labeling theory and the "hands off" approach
to juvenile justice. However, the absence of convincing alternative explanations for the rising crime rates and high recidivism rates left labeling theory in a position to inherit center
stage. Obviously, this interpretation of the events leading to
the emergence of labeling theory is debatable. But whatever the true historical reasons behind its emergence, it is
presently the most widely accepted theory on which juvenile
justice policy is predicated.

Labeling theory argues that official reactions serve to increase, rather than to decrease, the frequency of delinquent
behavior. Tannenbaum (1938:19–20) suggested long ago that
"the harder they (officials) work to reform the evil, the greater
the evil grows in their hands." Lemert (1951:76) asserts th it
the most important and "effective" causes of serious delinquent behavior are not such primary causes as poverty or
bad homes but the labeling and stigmatizing processes initiated by officials. When a child is repeatedly processed, he
begins to play the delinquent role assigned to him by others.
To the extent he does this, his deviation is "secondary deviance." Similarly, Tannenbaum (1938:19) suggested that "the
person becomes the thing he is described as being."

The policy implications of these theoretical arguments are as follows. (1) Refuse to dramatize evil in the first place. "The less said about it, the better" (Tannenbaum, 1938:20). (2) "If there is a defensible philosophy for the juvenile court, it is one of judicious nonintervention. It is properly an agency of last resort for children (Lemert, 1967:96). And (3) "Leave kids alone whenever possible. Our policy should be one of nonintervention" (Schur, 1973:155). In short, labeling theory and the theory of secondary deviance suggest that it is an overzealous juvenile court that is responsible for the rising crime rates. Rehabilitation has not only failed to cure the problems of essentially innocent children, it has made them worse. Hence, the goal of the "hands off" policy should be to avoid escalating childish behavior into acts of criminal behavior.

As noted above, the "hands off" approach has been translated into a variety of policies and programs notably, decriminalization, diversion, deinstitutionalization, and due process. One of the most recent and significant of these policies focuses attention on status offenses and offenders. Nearly every state in the United States is now involved in attempting either to decriminalize, deinstitutionalize, or divert status offenders.

On the surface this movement seems logically sound. It makes sense not to hold juveniles legally responsible for behavior that is not illegal for adults. Furthermore, status offenses are the least serious of all of the offenses for which juveniles may be legally prosecuted. Finally, removing status offenders from juvenile court jurisdiction by one method or another might relieve the present burden of the juvenile court and thus make it possible for it to deal more effectively with hardcore juvenile delinquents—perhaps at an even lower cost to the public.

However logical the "hands off" policy may appear, certain questions must be asked before it can be accepted, questions to which all too little attention has been paid:

1. The "hands off" philosophy suggests that the juvenile court should no longer have jurisdiction over status offenses and offenders since they involve acts and persons that are not really criminal. Does this mean, then, that the number

of *juveniles* appearing in court would be significantly reduced if status offenses were no longer grounds for legal action or if the people who commit such offenses were diverted to other agencies?

2. The notion that status offenses should not be subject to legal action implies that there *are* such things as "pure" status offenders. Is this assumption correct? Are status offenders really different from delinquent offenders?

3. Proponents of the "hands off" philosophy argue that status offenders are the least serious of all offenders. Yet the concentration on status versus delinquent offenses overlooks the possibility that status offenders may be frequent violators of the criminal law. To what degree, therefore, is it accurate to assume that the frequency of law violation is lower among status offenders than among delinquent offenders?

4. The "hands off" philosophy implies that, if the legal stigmatization of status offenders occurs, serious patterns of delinquency will result. Their behavior will be characterized by movement from the most trivial offenses to the most serious. Is this assumption correct? Does legal processing actually escalate, rather than reduce, the likelihood of a criminal career?

In bringing empirical evidence to bear on these questions, I shall utilize both self-reported and official delinquency data. The first two data sets are self-reports of offenses and arrests obtained through questionnaires administered to two different samples of Arizona teenagers. The first sample includes 3,209 students attending six Arizona high schools. The second sample is comprised of 515 adolescents selected randomly as an evaluation sample for status-offender projects in Pima County, Arizona, all of whom were referred to one or more of numerous newly developed projects specifically designed to deal with status offenders.

Tests of Assumptions about Offenses and Offenders

The first set of data to be utilized in testing assumptions about status offenses and offenders it based on the survey of high school students. In 1975 self-reports of involvement in eighteen different offenses were obtained from each of 3,209 respondents: these included five status offenses (running away from home, truancy, defiance of parents, drinking alcohol, and smoking tobacco), five misdemeanor offenses (shoplifting, petty theft, fighting, vandalism, and being drunk), and eight felonies (burglary, grand theft, assault, auto theft, armed robbery, unarmed robbery, use of marijuana, and drug use). Respondents were asked to report their violations of each offense and any arrests (referrals to juvenile court) for each of the offenses over the past twelve months. For the present analysis, reports of violation were truncated at 365; that is, any response that exceeded 365 was recoded to 365. For most offenses, this procedure was of no consequence. However, for smoking tobacco and defiance of parents this procedure was needed to make aggregate frequency figures more interpretable. Technically speaking, however, every cigarette an adolescent smokes constitutes a violation of the juvenile code—likewise for defiance of parents, having an alcoholic drink, etc. For classifying individuals into types of offenses, these tabulating issues are of little consequence. In analysis to be presented later, however, these issues are important.

Types of Offenses among High School Students

Among the sample of 3,209 high school students, the number of violations reported is very great indeed. Collectively, the sample reports 672,901 violations. With smoking included, 423,918 (63%) are classified as status offenses while 248,983 (37%) are delinquent offenses (misdemeanors and felonies combined). When smoking is excluded from the frequency tabulation, there is almost an equal number of status and delinquent offenses: 250,887 (50.19%) status offenses and 248,983 (49.81%) delinquent offenses.

Clearly, many status offenses were committed by these students. Yet, as will be seen later in Table 1, the number of "pure" status offenders is miniscule when compared with the

Table 1. Types of offenders based on self-reports among high school adolescents

Types of offenders	Number of cases	Percent of sample	Percent of offenders (N = 2,647)	Percent of offenders arrested
Pure conformists (no violations)	562	17.51	—	—
Pure status offenders (only So)	369	11.50	13.94	2.17
Pure misdemeanor offenders (only Mo)	71	2.21	2.68	4.22
Pure felony offenders (only Fo)	25	0.78	0.94	8.00
Mixed (So and Mo)	557	17.36	21.04	4.00
Mixed (So and Fo)	87	2.71	3.29	6.00
Mixed (Mo and Fo)	27	0.84	1.02	10.00
Mixed (So, Mo, and Fo)	1,151	47.09	57.08	21.00
Totals	3,209	100.00	100.00	—

So = Status offenses
Mo = Misdemeanor offenses
Fo = Felony offenses

number of status offenses committed. Indeed, Table 1 shows that only 13.9 percent of the total were "pure" status offenders and only 3.62 percent "pure" delinquent offenders. All the remainder were mixed.

Interesting facts are also revealed when one considers the frequency of self-reported arrests for this sample of high school students. The total sample accounted for 2,390 arrests (referrals to court) during the one-year period covered by the survey (including arrests for smoking). Of these, 43 percent were for status offenses and 57 percent for delinquent offenses.

If arrests for smoking are excluded, the total number of arrests is 2,258, of which 39.7 percent are for status offenses and 60.3 percent are for delinquent offenses. Taken together, these data show that a large number of status offenses were committed in the community, many of which never came to the attention of the juvenile courts. Nonetheless, the number of status offenses handled by the court was still quite large. Hence, from a policy standpoint, it is clear that the decriminalization of status offenses *might* significantly reduce the number of cases (petitions, court hearings, etc.) that the juvenile court would have to deal with. However, an important question survives these facts, namely, What proportion of the offending population would escape the juvenile court if status offenses were decriminalized or otherwise removed from juvenile court jurisdiction? Stated otherwise, are status offenses concentrated among a particular portion of offenders, or are they part of the offense patterns of most offenders?

Types of Offenders Based on Self-Reported Violations and Arrests

In order to answer questions about "pure status" and "pure delinquent" offenders, an analysis of the violation patterns of adolescents is required. Table 1 presents the results of such an analysis.

Some rather interesting, perhaps even surprising, facts are revealed in Table 1. Note first that pure status offenders (respondents who reported committing only status offenses) constitute only 11.5 percent of the total sample and only 13.9 percent of the offending population. Said another way, if *all offenses* resulted in official reactions (as unlikely as that is), only 13.9 percent of the offenders would escape juvenile court *if status offenses were decriminalized.* This is in dramatic contrast to what one might conclude by examining only the volume of status offenses or arrests for status offenses.

While it is still true that the volume of work in the typical juvenile court would be reduced by nearly half if status offenses were decriminalized, the population of offenders receiving attention would not be significantly reduced. This is true because the overwhelming majority of offenders are involved in several kinds of offenses. As the figures in Table 1 show, 82.4 percent of offenders are mixed, and 57 percent are involved in all three types of offenses (status, misdemeanor, and felony). As a matter of fact, pure offenders are not common for any of the types—only 13.9 percent are pure status offenders, 2.68 percent pure misdemeanants, and only 0.94 percent pure felons.

Even more dramatic facts can be brought to light by examining the arrest (referrals to court) patterns among the types of offenders displayed in Table 1. Perhaps most astounding is the finding that among the 369 pure status offenders in this sample, only 2.17 percent were brought to court at all. In other words, only 2 percent would be brought to court for status *offenses* and be truly "pure status offenders." All other adolescents brought to court for status offenses would be "mixed offenders."

Further examination of the arrest patterns among types of self-reported offenders (see Table 1, Column 5) reveals a number of other noteworthy findings. For example:

1. There is a positive relationship between offense seriousness and proportion of offenders arrested (viz., 2.17 percent of the pure status offenders were arrested, 4.22 percent of the pure misdemeanor offenders, and 8 percent of the pure felons).

2. Among the mixed-offender groups, the same pattern per-

sists (viz., for mixed status and misdemeanor offenders, 4 percent arrests; status and felony offenders, 6 percent arrests; misdemeanor and felony offenders, 10 percent arrests; and status, misdemeanor and felony offenders, 21 percent arrests).

3. Official arrest records provide a very poor basis for predicting the offending patterns of offenders. Treatment strategies directed solely toward the type of offense for which juveniles are referred to court will be incorrect far more than correct.

The decriminalization of status offenses, therefore, would not reduce the number of adolescents who appear in court by very much! To illustrate this point further, of the 3,209 students in the sample described above, only 268 (8 percent) were brought to juvenile court at all. Predicting offending patterns from offenses for which juveniles were brought to court proved to be accurate in less than 6 percent of the cases. The general tendency is for adolescents to be arrested for an offense more serious than the offenses they commit most frequently. This is due in large measure to the fact that the more serious an offense, the higher the probability of arrest (e.g., 2 percent of status offenses result in an arrest as compared to 8 percent for felonies).

Types of Offenders among Clients Diverted into Status-Offender Programs

Further evidence can be brought to bear on the distribution of "pure status" and "pure delinquent" offenders by examining self-reports among official offender groups. As in the previous analysis, self-reports were collected from a sample of teenagers. However, this sample included only cases officially referred to programs designed for status offenders. The sample included 515 adolescents. The questionnaire was similar to the one used in the survey of high school students, except that the list of acts varied somewhat and respondents were asked to report their violations and arrests (referrals to court) over a six-month period rather than for a whole year.

The questionnaire included eight status offenses—truancy (part-day), curfew, defiance of parents, drinking, defiance of teachers, runaway from home, truancy (all-day), sex relations; seven misdemeanor offenses—sniffing glue, carrying a concealed weapon, vandalism, stolen property, getting drunk, shoplifting, larceny (less than $50); and twelve felony offenses—auto theft, burglary, breaking and entering, assault, group assault, vandalism (more than $50), marijuana use, pills, (speed, downers), drugs (cocaine, heroin), selling drugs, larceny (more than $50), and robbery.

Using the self-reports of violations of the 515 teenagers, classes of offenders were created, following the same procedures used to classify offenders for Table 1. These results are presented in Table 2.

Although the percentages differ somewhat from Table 1, the distribution of types of offenders is remarkably similar. Note that even among those receiving treatment as status offenders, only 8 percent are "pure" status offenders (8.2 per-

Table 2. Types of offenders based on self-reports among adolescents diverted into status-offender projects in Pima County, Arizona

Type of offenders	Number of cases	Percent of sample	Percent of offenders (N = 500)
Pure conformists (no violations)	15	2.91	—
Pure status offenders (only So)	42	8.16	8.40
Pure misdemeanor offenders (only Mo)	3	0.58	0.60
Pure felony offenders (only Fo)	1	0.19	0.20
Mixed (So and Mo)	44	8.54	8.80
Mixed (So and Fo)	23	4.47	4.60
Mixed (Mo and Fo)	2	0.39	0.40
Mixed (So, Mo and Fo)	385	74.76	77.00
Totals	515	100.00	100.00

So = Status offenses
Mo = Misdemeanor offenses
Fo = Felony offenses

cent of the total sample and 8.4 percent of the offenders in the sample). Seventy-seven percent of the offenders were involved in offenses of all three types (status offenses, misdemeanor, and felony offenses).

It is also interesting to note that 2.9 percent of the sample of adolescents formally processed as status offenders claimed not to have committed *any* offenses; that is, they claimed to be "pure conformists." There are two interpretations of this finding. First, it may simply reflect on the reliability of self-reported delinquency data. However, it is known that several of the so-called status-offender programs in Pima County (from which the sample was drawn) were more realistically involved in prevention than treatment.

In other words, it is not unreasonable to assume that approximately 3 percent of the adolescents involved in the diversion programs had not yet committed a status or delinquent act. It is known that in the early months of the DSO (Deinstitutionalization of Status Offenders) project in Pima County, several programs recruited to get started and to justify their programs. Several programs also sent intake data to the evaluation team without recording a referral offense. Some even admitted that some of their kids had no official offense, but were "pre-status offenders" who needed help. It is obvious, in short, that in this instance, the net of the juvenile court was expanded by a "hands off" policy, not contracted.

Summary and Conclusions regarding Offenders Classified According to Self-reported Violations

Data presented in Tables 1 and 2 dramatically show that there are not many pure status offenders—either in the general adolescent population (13.9 percent) or in a sample of adolescents dealt with by various programs as status offenders (8.4 percent). In other words, the contention that there are distinct populations of delinquent and status offenders receives little support. In fact, the single most accurate prediction of offending patterns based on arrest (court referral) data is that *all* offenders have mixed patterns, arrests records to the contrary. Put another way, if one predicted that all offenders brought to official attention were mixed offenders, the predictions would be about 98 percent accurate for those arrested in the general population of high school adolescents and 91 percent accurate for offenders included in so-called status-offender treatment programs in Pima County, Arizona. It should be obvious that, to the extent that such findings can be used as a basis for generalization, present assumptions and policies regarding status offenders are highly questionable and may be without empirical foundation.

The data presented in Tables 1 and 2 and the additional analysis used to supplement those tables are, of course, subject to all manner of criticism. First of all, there are those who would not give a nickel for self-reports of offenses or arrests. And it is true, of course, that the reliability and validity of self-reports can be questioned. However, short of outright rejection of the data, the best criticisms of the present data sets are: (1) they cover only a short period of time (six months in one case and twelve in the other) and (2) agencies that deal with offenders (e.g., the juvenile court, police, and varieties of diversion and treatment programs) can only deal with official offenses—those known to authorities.

For although there may be few pure status offenders per se, officials must act on the basis of the offense for which a juvenile is apprehended. They cannot penalize him for other acts for which he has not been caught or perhaps for which he was punished heretofore. Therefore, these findings reveal a lack of support for the assumption that, if a juvenile is arrested for a status offense, he is only a status offender. Indeed, these findings could be used as fuel for the arguments of either the "helping hands" proponents or those who favor the "heavy hands" approach. The traditionalist, who favors rehabilitation, could argue that we should still be treating offenders, not offenses. Meanwhile, the neoclassicist might maintain that these data document clearly the need for a "justice" model. Since juveniles are usually involved in all kinds of delinquent acts, our efforts should be directed toward deterrence and incapacitation.

Frequency of Offending among Types of Arrested Offenders

Thus far little has been said about the relative frequency of offending among different types (classifications) of offenders. The relationship between arrests and frequency of offending is important for assessing the adequacy of the "hands off" approach because it assumes not only that the major behavior problems of status offenders involve status offenses but that status offenders are neophytes as well. The issue can be stated in the form of a question: Given information regarding the number of arrests and/or the type of offense for which arrests occur, what inferences can be made about the previous frequency of offending?

Table 3 presents the results of an analysis of self-reported violation rates according to self-reported arrests. This analysis utilized questonnaire data from the sample of 3,209 Arizona high school students previously used in constructing Table 1. Pure conformists (respondents who reported no violations) were not included in this analysis. This reduced the sample from 3,209 to 2,647, of which 268 (10 percent) reported one or more arrests.

Mean violation rates for each of three types of offenses— status offenses (excluding smoking), misdemeanor, and felony offenses—were calculated for each respondent. Respondents were then grouped into arrest-status categories and aggregate mean violation rates were then calculated. Thus, the means presented in Table 3 involve two levels of aggregation: (1) the aggregation of offenses into three categories for each individual, and (2) the aggregation of the offense means of individuals according to arrest status.

The findings presented in Table 3 demonstrate a rather strong relationship between frequency of offending and frequency of arrest. For status offenses there is a perfect stepwise

Table 3. Mean offense violation rates by arrest status of 2,647 Arizona high school students

Arrest status (N)	Mean status offense violation rate	Mean misdemeanor offense violation rate	Mean felony offense violation rate	Total mean offense violation rate
Offenders: No arrests (2,379)	19.29	6.31	4.51	8.44
Offenders: one arrest Status offense (53)	34.96	13.28	15.05	19.16
Offenders: one arrest Misdemeanor offense (68)	29.51—33.80	10.98—13.73	10.59—14.15	14.94—18.62
Offenders: one arrest Felony offense (50)	38.41	17.97	18.02	23.04
Offenders: Two arrests (6)	47.21	31.67	19.76	29.89
Offenders: Three arrests (26)	49.94	23.02	12.93	23.85
Offenders: Four arrests (16)	53.33	33.00	16.10	29.50
Offenders: Five or more arrests (49)	72.64	40.11	28.58	41.77

pattern. The mean status-offense violation rates for the respondents with no arrests is 19.29; for offenders with one arrest (ignoring the offense for which the arrest occurred) is 33.80. The means for offenders with two, three, four, and five or more arrests during the past year are 47.2, 49.94, 53.33 and 72.64, respectively.

The patterns for the other types of offenses (misdemeanors and felonies) as well as the total violation rate are similar, but there is not a perfect stepwise relationship. The exceptions involve those arrested twice. For some reason not presently apparent, those arrested twice have mean violation rates equal to or higher than those arrested three or four times. Overall, however, it must be concluded that *frequency* of arrest is closely related to frequency of offending.

Interesting evidence is brought to light by examining frequency of offending among offenders arrested once when they are separated according to the type of offense leading to the arrest. Note that for offenders arrested once for a status offense, the mean status-offense violation rate is 34.96, the mean for misdemeanors is 13.28, and, somewhat surprisingly, the mean felony violation rate is 15.05. Interestingly, the three rates for those arrested once for a misdemeanor offense are 29.51, 10.98, and 10.59 for status offenses, misdemeanors, and felonies, respectively. Note that all three rates are lower for this group than for those arrested for a status offense. In contrast to this, the rates for offenders arrested for a felony offense are higher than either of the other two groups: 38.41, 17.97, and 18.02 for status offenses, misdemeanors, and felonies, respectively.

The ranking of the three groups is further illustrated by examining the total mean violation rates. Notice (in column 4) that those arrested once for a felony offense have a total mean violation rate of 23.04, whereas the rate for those arrested once for a status offense is 19.16 and finally the rate for those arrested once for a misdemeanor offense is 14.94.

From a policy standpoint, it would appear that if diversion or deinstitutionalization is intended to remove from the system that group of offenders least involved in illegal behavior, it would *not* be aimed at status offenders but rather at misdemeanor offenders. It is that group (arrested once for a misdemeanor offense) that has the lowest violation rates for all three kinds of offenses, including misdemeanors.

Types of Offenders Classified According to Juvenile Court Records

In order to perform the best possible analysis of official records, two additional sets of data were obtained. Both sets reflect the entire official delinquency careers of the cases included. In one sense they constitute birth cohorts; that is, all individuals included in each data set were born during the same year and thus became adults (turned 18) during the same year. The data sets included only individuals who during the childhood-adolescent years (birth to 18) were referred to court at least once. In other words, the data sets include no information about official nondelinquents. For some kinds of research this limitation would be fatal. However, for present purposes the absence of data on official nondelinquents is without serious consequence.

The analyses of these data are aimed primarily at illustrating the career patterns of official offenders—especially the distribution of status offenders. The analysis is relevant to many of the assumptions explored earlier using self-reports. In addition, however, these data reflect on other assumptions of the "hands off" approach, specifically, those that imply long-term effects of official labeling.

The first of the two data sets was obtained from the Research and Planning Division of Maricopa County (Phoenix), Arizona. The data pertain to 9,559 individuals born in 1956 (and turned 18 in 1974). The information covers a total of 24,616 court referrals (an average of 2.58 per case). Of these referrals, 17 percent were for status offenses, 48 percent for delinquent offenses, and 35 percent involved mixed charges (most of these apparently were treated in court as status offenses).

The second data set was obtained from Pima County Juvenile Court (Tucson, Arizona). It includes 2,843 cases, covering 6,616 court referrals (2.33 referrals per case). These individuals were born in 1957 and turned 18 in 1975. Of the 6,616 court referrals, 34 percent involved status offenses, 35 percent misdemeanors, 22 percent felonies, and the remaining referrals (8 percent) involved multiple mixed charges.

In Table 4 the career offense patterns of both birth cohorts are presented.

Note first that for both cohorts a sizable proportion of the cases was referred to the juvenile court but once (58 percent of the Pima cohort and 56 percent of the Maricopa County cohort). Of the first-time offenders, about one-third were status offenders (35 percent for the Pima cohort and 30 percent for the Maricopa cohort).

The most dramatic finding revealed by Table 4 is the fact that there are so few pure offenders—either status or delinquent. There is a steady and even dramatic decline in the percentage of pure offenders as career length increases. Note, for example, that less than 6 percent of pure status offenders have careers longer than five offenses in both cohorts. Furthermore, if one-time offenders are excluded, only 13 percent of the Pima County cohort are pure status offenders. The comparable figure for the Maricopa cohort is 10 percent. The majority of the career patterns are mixed; that is, they include court appearances for both status and delinquent offenses sometime during the childhood-adolescent years. In addition, the longer the career length, the more likely that the career will be mixed. Note that all careers longer than 11 offenses are 100 percent mixed for the Pima cohort and all careers longer than four offenses are at least 90 percent mixed. The figures are lower for the Maricopa cohort but, nonetheless, the majority of careers are mixed and there are very few pure status offenders.

The conclusion, therefore, is that policy based on the assumption that there are separate populations of status and delinquent offenders is based on scant empirical evidence.

Table 4. Types of official offenders according to length of official delinquent careers for two Arizona birth cohorts

Career length or number of offenses during adolescent years	Pima County, Arizona birth cohort of offenders				Maricopa County, Arizona birth cohort of offenders			
	Number of cases	Percent pure status offenders	Percent pure delinquent offenders	Percent mixed offenders	Number of cases	Percent pure status offenders	Percent pure delinquent offenders	Percent mixed offenders
1	1,649	35	65	—	5,376	30	70	—
2	458	19	20	61	1,567	17	53	30
3	251	15	9	76	804	11	39	50
4	133	8	2	90	491	8	34	58
5	94	7	2	91	311	6	26	68
6	65	5	2	93	226	5	24	71
7	42	2	2	96	151	1	16	83
8	44	2	0	98	126	2	20	77
9	23	4	0	96	100	0	16	84
10	17	6	6	88	83	0	23	77
11	23	0	0	100	61	0	26	74
12	8	0	0	100	41	2	17	81
13	15	0	0	100	39	0	10	90
14	7	0	0	100	34	3	12	85
15 or more	14	0	0	100	149	0	11	89

Whether based on official or self-reported data, the preponderance of offenders is involved in both status and delinquent offenses. However, even when taken collectively, these findings do not necessarily refute another assumption of the "hands off" approach, namely, that reactions to petty offenses will only produce more serious delinquent conduct.

Official Reactions and Secondary Deviance: The Escalation Hypothesis

The "hands off" philosophy seems to imply a particular career-development pattern characterized by movement from the most trivial offenses (i.e., status offenses) through misdemeanor offenses and ending up with felonious acts. This assertion will be referred to hereafter as the "escalation hypothesis." Of course the theoretical basis for the escalation hypothesis is labeling theory, or, more specifically, the theory of secondary deviance. As indicated earlier, the idea here is simply that the official labeling process makes offenders worse. The theory asserts that due to official stigma—produced by referral to court and detention—individuals continue to violate the law and become involved in more serious offenses.

Some may argue that the theory of secondary deviance does not necessarily imply an escalation in the seriousness of offenses but merely in the frequency of offending. Regardless of which interpretation is attributed to labeling theory, those in a position to set juvenile justice policy reflecting the "hands off" approach often make both arguments in their justification for the approach. Here tests are aimed only at the former interpretation.

Figure 1 provides a percentage breakdown of the entire Pima County birth cohort according to length of career patterns (N=2,843). Fifty-eight percent of the cohort had only one offense (Box I), while 42 percent involved multiple (two or more) offenses (Box II).

The multiple-offense careers are divided into three subgroups: (1) static careers involving two or more offenses (15

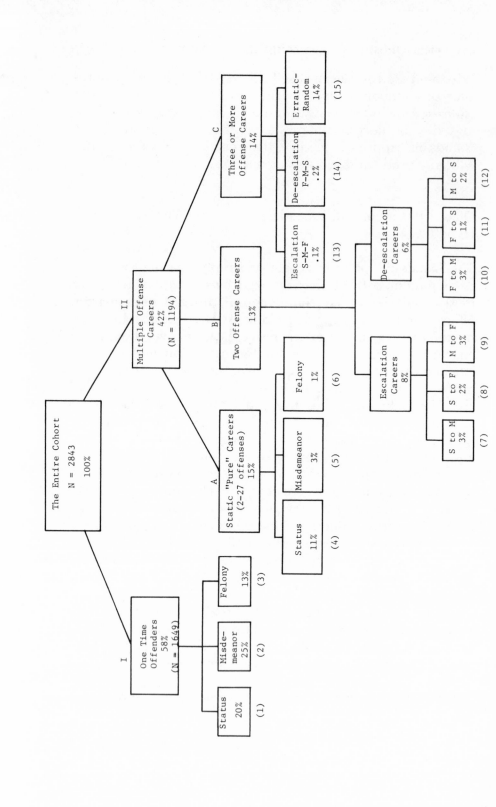

percent of the cohort, Box A). These careers are characterized by exclusive involvement in only one of the three types of offenses (status offenses, misdemeanors, or felonies). (2) Mixed two-offense careers (13 percent of the cohort, Box B). And (3) mixed careers involving three or more offenses (14 percent of the cohort, Box C).

The distribution of one-offense careers and static careers has been discussed previously (see Table 4). Therefore, the discussion here will focus on those parts of Figure 1 that are most relevant to the escalation hypothesis. The crucial figures are in Boxes 7-12 and 13-15.

Examine first the figures presented under Box B, mixed two-offense careers (Boxes 7-12). Note that only 8 percent of the cohort had career patterns that would support the escalation hypothesis. Interestingly, 6 percent showed the opposite tendency, namely, de-escalation (Boxes 10-12). It should also be noted that only 5 percent (adding the figures in Boxes 7 and 8) of the cohort disclosed movement from status offenses to delinquent offenses. In short, there is very little support for the escalation hypothesis when examining two-offense careers.

Even less evidence is found for the hypothesis when careers longer than two offenses are examined (see Boxes 13–15). Less than 1 percent (actually 0.1 percent) of the cohort fit an escalation pattern (Box 13). Only 0.2 percent fit a de-escalating pattern (Box 14). All but a small fraction of the cases with careers between 3 and 27 official offenses show no stepwise pattern. To the contrary, nearly all cases (397 of 406) have erratic— almost random—patterns involving the three types of offenses (status, misdemeanor, and felony). In short, these patterns are not only mixed, they do not follow any discernable pattern.

In drawing conclusions about the findings presented in Table 4 and Figure 1, one must remember that these cases received traditional treatment. These cases were all processed before diversion and deinstitutionalization came to Pima County. (The entire cohort turned 18 in 1975.) With this in mind, other findings in Figure 1 are relevant in assessing the escalation hypothesis. For example, 58 percent of the cohort who were labeled and stigmatized by being brought to court never came back (see Box I, Figure 1). Of those who did come back, 15 percent returned *only* for the same kind of offense they were brought to court for originally (see Box A). When these facts are linked to the evidence on escalation patterns among multiple-offense careers, it is clear that the escalation hypothesis must be rejected.

A slightly different way of examining the figures presented in Table 4 and Figure 1 is most revealing. Careful examination of the figures reveals that exactly 50 percent of the cohort appeared in court for the first time for a status offense. Remembering that they were all labeled, that many spent time in detention, and that most were placed on probation, let us examine what happened to this half of the cohort.

Forty percent never came back to court a second time. In addition, 22 percent came back only for additional status offenses—no escalation occurred. Ten percent did have escalating patterns—6 percent came back to court for a misdemeanor offense only, the other 4 percent were for felonies. The remaining 28 percent of the cohort did return to court for additional status offenses—mixed liberally with misdemeanors and felonies. In summary, 38 percent did come back to court involving some kind of delinquent charges. When examined this way, the findings are not quite as negative as they might have appeared earlier; nonetheless, there is little empirical justification for a universal "hands off" approach.

Of course, the analysis of one data set can only be taken as suggestive. A great deal of additional research is needed. Six other offender birth cohorts have been examined using the same type of analysis. However, the findings from these other data sets are remarkably similar to what has been reported here.

In addition, panel data for a diverted sample will soon be made available for analysis. The analysis of self-reports and official records of cases not officially processed in traditional ways will provide an important contrast to the data presented in this chapter.

Prognosis for the Success of the "Hands Off" Approach

If the "hands off" approach continues at its present pace, it will only be a matter of years until status offenses will no longer be handled by juvenile courts in this country. To some, that will mark at least the partial success of the "revolution," The removal of status offenses from the juvenile court might have a profound effect on the work load of the court—it might reduce it by half or more.

However, if the findings presented in this chapter are not unique, the removal of status offenses from juvenile court jurisdiction will not change the clientele of the court very much.[2] The juvenile court will still see most of the same people because the overwhelming majority of offenders are involved in *both* status and delinquent offenses.

The removal of status offenses from the juvenile court jurisdiction is only one of the goals of the "hands off" approach. There is also a desire to soften the reactions to many kinds of offenders, nonserious offenders in particular. And apparently some believe that more humane and more effective treatment can be provided by private and voluntary organizations rather than the juvenile court or any other "establish-

[2] When one examines the characteristics of pure status offenders—using official juvenile court data—it is discovered that the removal of those offenders from the juvenile court's jurisdiction will for the most part remove females and Anglos. In the long run this may leave in the juvenile court an inordinately disproportionate distribution of males and particularly black males (and other minority groups as well). If our criminal justice system (and particularly the juvenile justice system) can presently be accused of discrimination toward minorities, that argument will be even more valid once status offenses have been decriminalized and/or diverted. For even now one can make the argument that the "hands off" approach is really a method for giving preferential treatment to the privileged classes of our society, specifically, middle-class white children, especially girls.

ment" system. Whether such organizations will be more humane, effective, and less stigmatizing remains open to debate. Only time and additional experience and research will resolve these questions.

One thing already seems clear. The national legal "hands off" policy concerning status offenders has been and will probably continue to be a boon for private enterprise in the business of treating juveniles. In a number of local sites where deinstitutionalization projects were conducted, there was tremendous growth in the development of programs and approaches to deal with status offenders (some were new, most were based on old concepts). There was, and will continue to be, a great deal of money to be made in developing *some* kind of program for dealing with status offenders and perhaps other types of offenders as well. But turning such problems, if indeed they are problems, over to private and voluntary organizations is not the same as delivering better service or treatment. For one thing, the success of nonlegal systems will depend almost completely on whether people are willing to submit to treatment in these programs.

The extent to which therapy can be successfully applied in a voluntary program is debatable. Evidence already available from deinstitutionalization sites suggests that the voluntary nature of participation in programs enormously reduces the potential impact of those programs and therefore increases the cost of each case actually treated. In short, juveniles simply do not show up for treatment when it is on a voluntary basis. For example, in the Pima County, Arizona, DSO Project, only 30 percent of the cases recommended for treatment actually showed up at all. When these data were examined more carefully, it was discovered that a large percent of those who did show up appeared only once and came from one of the referral agencies that transported children directly to the recommended treatment facilities the first time. When this was discontinued, meaning that the client had to find his or her own way to the treatment facility, those who actually showed up constituted only 17 percent of those recommended for help. It is unlikely that this is a transportation problem. Instead, it reflects the absence of a legal threat and perceived need for therapy. Therefore, all things considered, it is difficult to be optimistic about the success of the "hands off" approach in solving the problems it has set out to solve.

The Current "Heavy Hands" Approach to Juvenile Justice

There is a significant movement today in America to return to a classical penal policy stressing punishment and deterrence (Bentham, 1962; Beccaria, 1963). Empey (1978:584–86) interprets this to be a counterrevolution in response to the high rates of juvenile crime and the policies of the reintegrative revolution. Although he may be correct, it is also possible that the so-called counterrevolution is more a response to the presumed failure of the rehabilitative approach than to the "hands off" approach. In either case, the movement to return to a "heavy hands" approach to juvenile justice represents a dramatic departure from the policies of the last several decades.

Juvenile justice policies of the last several decades indisputably were intended to minimize punishment. In fact, since the creation of the juvenile court in 1899, punishment has consistently been de-emphasized in dealing with juvenile offenders. However, now we see major statutory changes occurring all over the country. For example, California has a new law that makes selected juvenile misdemeanants and felons sixteen years and older subject to adult court and, therefore, adult penal sanctions (California Welfare and Institutions Code, Assembly Bill No. 3121, 1976: Chapter 1071:1–24). In Washington State a new system of mandatory sentences has been adopted for juvenile offenders (Revised Criminal Code of Washington, 1977, Title 13:66–90).

In Arizona a completely new criminal and juvenile code was implemented in October of 1978. This code explicitly denies rehabilitation as one of its goals. Similarly, the new juvenile justice code of Washington lists "treatment" sixth in a list of ten purposes of the new code. It lists "protection of the community" first and "making the juvenile accountable for his acts" third. The fourth purpose of the code is "to provide punishment commensurate with the age, crime, and criminal history of the juvenile offender" (Revised Code of Washington, 1977:80). These are only examples; similar changes can be found in many states.

In general, the movement to return to a "heavy hands" approach can be characterized in terms of three major reforms: (1) lowering the age of accountability for crime (e.g., from 18 to 16), thus making adult penal sanctions applicable to more juvenile offenders; (2) abolition of the juvenile court; and (3) punishing and incapacitating offenders (Empey, 1978:584–85).

Since the counterrevolution is so new, it is not possible to assess its success. However, it is possible to examine some of the basic assumptions of these proposed reforms. All three reforms share in common: (1) a lack of confidence in the juvenile court, (2) an apparent belief that adult courts are more efficient and effective than juvenile courts, and (3) a belief that the juvenile crime rate—and thus the overall crime rate—can be significantly reduced by subjecting juveniles to punishment and/or incapacitating them.

Given the fact that the juvenile crime rate has been steadily increasing for years and that many people believe the court—especially the juvenile court—has been excessively lenient, it is not surprising that many have lost confidence in the court. But it is somewhat surprising that these same people apparently believe that the adult courts will be more effective. In fact, it is possible, perhaps even probable, that when juvenile offenders are dumped on the adult courts they will be even less efficient in dealing with juvenile offenders than the juvenile courts have been.

Perhaps more important, if the leniency of the juvenile court is the major reason for abolishing it, it is debatable whether the adult courts are any more severe. The point is that statutory provision for severe punishment does not guarantee imposition of severe punishments. Given the range of problems facing the adult courts, from plea bargaining to the increasing volume of cases, it is highly unlikely that shifting juveniles to adult courts will solve any of the problems it is intended to solve.

Beneath all the "heavy hand" reforms is a belief in deterrence and incapacitation as a means of reducing juvenile crime. Such beliefs presently lack strong empirical support.

The Deterrence Doctrine

A great deal of research has been conducted on the deterrence doctrine in the last ten years. However, the findings thus far are inconclusive (Zimring and Hawkins, 1973; Gibbs, 1975; Tittle and Logan, 1973). There is little in the published research that would justify broadening the use of punishment as a means for reducing the crime rate of adults. Therefore, there is no empirical justification for assuming that punishment would be effective if applied to juveniles.

Deterrence research over the last ten years has been aimed primarily at assessing the validity of "general" deterrence, rather than "specific" deterrence. General deterrence refers to the possible effects of fear of punishment on the general public (potential offenders in particular) because they have experienced, directly or indirectly, the punishment of others. "Specific" deterrence refers to the effects of fear of punishment on the future behavior of individuals actually punished. The basic proposition tested by most of the deterrence research over the last decade can be stated as follows: The higher the certainty and severity of punishments, the lower the crime rate.

The cumulative results of deterrence studies show that certainty is more important than severity. It remains problematic, however, whether these findings constitute evidence for a deterrent effect or some other social-psychological process. Gibbs (1978:34–50) lists nine possible additional processes that could be involved in producing a negative relationship between the crime rates and properties of punishment.

The fact that certainty of punishment has been found to

be more important than the severity of punishment has profound implications for contemplating the expanded use of punishment on juvenile offenders. We know that the certainty of reaction is incredibly low for juvenile offenders. Empey (1978:589) estimates that something less than 2.5 percent of all delinquent acts actually result in court action and conviction. Data reported earlier in this chapter indicate the percentage to be even lower. Depending on which offense is included in the calculations, the proportion of self-reported offenses resulting in court action varies between 0.01 to 10 percent. For all types of offenses combined the percentage is slightly larger than 1 percent.

Given certainty levels this low, it is questionable whether changes in the severity of statutory punishments will be sufficient to deter potential offenders. Obviously, the statutory changes being made throughout the country only affect the severity of punishment. They do not and probably cannot affect certainty.

The problem can be illustrated by an example. If the certainty of receiving a ticket for parking in a given location is absolute (1.0), the penalty (the fine) may not have to be very much to deter most people. Perhaps $5 to $10 would do the job. However, if the certainty of getting a ticket is near zero (between 1 and 5 percent), how much of a fine would be needed to obtain the same level of deterrence? For some the fine may not have to be very high, but for others not even $500 would get the job done.

Herein lies the prognosis for deterrence with juvenile offenders. Changing the severity of punishments may not be sufficient to reduce the juvenile crime rate because the likelihood of such punishments actually being imposed on an individual is very low—and is perceived to be so. Deterrence would work, I suppose, if (1) juveniles were universally informed of the changes in statutory severity, a problem of no small magnitude itself, and (2) their perceptions of certainty were high—even though actual certainty is low.

However, previous research has shown neither condition to be the case. We do a poor job in this country of informing the public of the specific details of the law. In addition, studies of perceived certainty of arrest and incarceration among juveniles (Teevan, 1975; Erickson, et al., 1977; Jensen, et al., 1978) show that while many juveniles tend to overestimate the certainty of official reactions, their estimates are still very low. In fact, if they were better informed of the actual certainty of official reaction, the juvenile crime rate would probably be even higher.

In conclusion, based on what we now know, it is unlikely that the statutory changes presently being made throughout the country will reduce the crime rate very much through deterrence.

Incapacitation

It is possible that the imposition of substantially more severe punishments on a few selected juveniles might bring down the crime rate through some other process other than deterrence. The process most likely to produce such an effect is referred to as "incapacitation" (Gibbs, 1978:43–50). Through incapacitation, opportunities for committing additional illegal acts are reduced or eliminated (Wilson, 1975). For example, incapacitation makes it all but impossible for auto thieves to contribute much to the auto theft rate. Thus, house arrests and detention of all forms might reduce the crime rate through incapacitation.

The potential for reducing the juvenile crime rate through incapacitation, however, is contingent on several factors. For example, the effectiveness of incapacitation hinges on incapacitating a specific proportion of the offending population namely, those who disproportionately contribute to the crime rate. In other words, if it were possible to remove from the streets the 25 percent of the offending population with the highest violation rates, the crime rate could indeed be expected to go down.

A reexamination of the figures in Table 3 will illustrate the potential of incapacitation. Consider how many violations might have been prevented had that proportion of the population arrested two or more times during a single year been deprived of opportunities for further violation after their first arrest. It would appear to be a tremendous reduction. Yet it is debatable whether such a reduction would actually occur! It is debatable because the preponderance of delinquent acts involves several offenders. Therefore, there is no necessary relationship between frequency of acts and the number of offenders. Instead, for example, for every burglary (known to the police), there may be several individuals who are candidates for incapacitation. Unless all are incapacitated, the future crimes of the clique or group will not necessarily be prevented. In addition, the removal of an individual from a delinquent clique, group, or gang may merely provide an opening (a position) for another potential offender rather than immobilizing the group.

In short, the potential effectiveness of incapacitation depends on a one-to-one relationship between offenses and offenders. Since we know from a vast amount of research on delinquency that this is not the case, the prognosis for incapacitation to reduce the juvenile crime rate must be pessimistic.

One Final Observation

In exploring empirical evidence relevant to the basic assumptions of current juvenile justice policies, I have not proceeded under the illusion that public policy—juvenile correction policy in particular—is decided and guided on the basis of empirical evidence. There is ample evidence to the contrary. Nonetheless, it is important, in my opinion, to examine the efficacy of any policy from the perspective of the best empirical evidence of the time.

We , as social scientists, often feel compulsive in our effort to judge social policy in light of empirical evidence—that is simply a natural product of our training. Unfortunately, in much of our activity—perhaps especially as it concerns work in juvenile justice and corrections—some of us may occasionally feel that we are mentally masturbating, that we are the only ones that are "really" involved, and somehow that diminishes the enjoyment. It is unfortunate, but our training does not usually prepare us to face the fact that most people— the public, policymakers, and practitioners—do not share our compulsion for empirical evidence.

References

Beccaria, Cesare
  1963   On Crimes and Punishments. Indianapolis: Bobbs-Merrill.

Becker, Howard S.
  1963   Outsiders. New York: Free Press.

Bentham, Jeremy
  1962   The Works of Jeremy Bentham, Vol. 1. (Ed. Bowring). New York: Russell and Russell.

California Welfare and Institutions Code
  1976   Assembly Bill No. 3121. Chapter 1071:1–24.

Empey, LaMar T.
  1978   American Delinquency: Its Meaning and Construction. Homewood, Ill.: Dorsey.

Erickson, Marynard L., Jack P. Gibbs, and Gary F. Jensen
  1977   "The deterrence doctrine and the perceived certainty of legal punishments." American Sociological Review 42 (April):305–17.

Erikson, Kai T.
  1962   "Notes on the sociology of deviance." Social Problems 9:307–14.

Gibbs, Jack P.
  1975   Crime, Punishment and Deterrence. New York: Elsevier.

  1978   "Preventive effects of capital punishment other than deterrence." Criminal Law Bulletin 14 (January–February):34–50.

Jensen, Gary F., Maynard L. Erickson, and Jack P. Gibbs
  1978   "Perceived risk of punishment and self-reported delinquency." Social Forces 57 (September):57–78.

Kitsuse, John I.
  1962   "Societal reactions to deviant behavior: problems of theory and method." Social Problems 9:247–256.

Lemert, Edwin M.
   1951   Social Pathology. New York: McGraw-Hill.

   1967   "The juvenile court—quest and realities." Pp. 91–106
           in the President's Commission on Law Enforcement
           and Administration of Justice, Task Force Report: Juve-
           nile Delinquency and Youth Crime. Washington, D.C.:
           U.S. Government Printing Office.

Lipton, Douglas, Robert Martinson, and Judith Wilks
   1975   The Effectiveness of Correctional Treatment: A Survey
           of Treatment Evaluation Studies. New York: Praeger.

Martinson, Robert
   1974   "What works? questions and answers about prison re-
           form." The Public Interest (Spring 1974).

Schur, Edwin M.
   1969   "Reactions to deviance: a critical assessment." Ameri-
           can Journal of Sociology 75:309–22.

   1973   Radical Nonintervention: Rethinking the Delinquency
           Problem. Englewood Cliffs, N.J.: Prentice-Hall.

Tannenbaum, Frank
   1938   Crime and the Community. New York: Columbia Univ.
           Press.

Teevan, James J., Jr.
   1975   "Perceptions of punishment: current research." Pp.
           146–54 *in* R. L. Henshel and R. A. Silverman (eds.),
           Perceptions in Criminology. New York: Columbia Univ.
           Press.

Tittle, Charles R., and Charles H. Logan
   1973   "Sanctions and deviance: evidence and remaining
           questions." Law and Society Review 7 (Spring):371–92.

Washington State. Revised Criminal Code of Washington.
   1977   Title 13 Juvenile Courts and Juvenile Delinquents: 66–
           90.

Wilson, James Q.
   1975   Thinking about Crime. New York: Basic Books.

Zimring, Franklin E., and Gordon Hawkins
   1973   Deterrence: The Legal Threat of Crime Control. Chi-
           cago: Univ. of Chicago Press.

Privilege, Maturity, and Responsibility: Notes on the Evolving Jurisprudence of Adolescence

Franklin E. Zimring

> *Any interest the parent may have in the termination of the minor daughter's pregnancy is no more weighty than the right of privacy of the competent minor mature enough to have become pregnant.*
>
> JUSTICE BLACKMUN, *Planned Parenthood of Central Missouri* v. *Danforth*, 428 U.S. 52, at 75

A student of American culture might well be puzzled by the crosscurrents of contemporary trends in legal policy toward the young. At a time when law-and-order rhetoric dominates public and political debate on criminal justice, some current reform proposals concerning juvenile justice favor lessening punishment for youthful offenders (Schur, 1973; Task Force, 1976). At the same time, critics of the juvenile court favor extending privilege to the young by abolishing the power of the state to enforce age-related prohibitions against drinking, smoking, and disobedience.[1] Further, despite long-term move-

NOTE: Fred Ackerson, a second-year student at the University of Chicago Law School, provided valuable research assistance on this project. Robert Burt, Norval Morris, and Margaret Rosenheim supplied helpful comments on an earlier draft on this paper.

[1] The National Advisory Committee on Juvenile Justice and Delinquency Prevention favor immediate elimination of jurisdiction over noncriminal misbehavior. The Advisory Committee on Standards, however, would retain

ment toward lengthening periods of financial dependence and social marginality for the young, there is a discernible trend toward extending privileges and choices usually reserved for adults to young persons at earlier ages.

It might appear that these various social trends rest on different and inconsistent images of the middle and late adolescent in American law and social policy. If one views the conferring of rights and privileges as an aspect of adulthood, why the trend toward privilege without full responsibility? If immaturity is used to justify leniency toward young criminal offenders, why should not that same perception of adolescent judgment restrict the privileges of the young and justify state intervention to protect the adolescent from noncriminal conduct that threatens the young person's future and well-being?

This essay is an attempt to address these questions by struggling toward a theory of adolescence that explains these apparently contradictory trends in legal and social policy. The first section is devoted to an outline of the coherent, consistent, and currently quite unfashionable view of adolescence which produced the state interventionist tradition of juvenile justice and which has dominated legal policy for most of this century. It is only after some discussion of the original premises of juvenile justice that one can begin to make sense out of the movement to reform and to reformulate the balance between child, parent, and state that is currently underway.

The second section summarizes four major themes in the antipaternalistic reform movement in juvenile justice and outlines some of the different grounds on which a principled argument against state intervention might be based.

The third section examines the argument for a symmetrical view of privilege and punishment, rejecting the view that the images of adolescence that have extended privilege earlier into the process of social development require parallel downward shifts in such matters as criminal punishment and coerced economic self-sufficiency.

---

jurisdiction over noncriminal misbehavior, while providing that juveniles not guilty of criminal misbehavior could not be held in secure custody (see National Institute of Juvenile Justice, 1976:11–16).

Finally, the last section outlines a theory that attempts to explain the reforms now being proposed. At the same time the paper stops short of judging the ultimate validity of the image of adolescence implicit in current reform thinking. Whether a particular set of social policies toward adolescence is good or bad depends on empirical and value judgments rather than logical coherence. An examination of basic principles, however, is of particular value in the ideologically charged and fast-changing domain that now constitutes the legal universe of the young.

Paternalism and Parity: The Juvenile Court Tradition

Recent reform movements in juvenile justice are, in large measure, reactions against the philosophy and practice of the "progressive era" of the juvenile court movement. The original juvenile court was constructed on the theory that the state has both the power and the responsibility to foster the proper development of the young. The juvenile court was to pursue child welfare by using the agencies of state government to assure that "the care, custody, and discipline of a child shall approximate . . . that which should be given by its parents" (Illinois Juvenile Court Act, 1899). Indeed, many of today's critics hold a similar view of the ends of juvenile justice, namely, that the welfare of the child, in almost every case, is the paramount value of the juvenile court.

Given these premises, it is not a misuse of language to suggest that the original theory of juvenile justice was centrally concerned with children's rights. The state assumed power over the lives of neglected, dependent, and delinquent youth to protect these children from threats to their healthy maturation. In Professor Burt's phrase (1976:225), the court was pursuing rights *for* children: intervening whether or not the particular minor consented to pursue his best interest.

At the same time, this way of defining children's rights meant that the juvenile court was to be relatively unconcerned with the rights *of* children to exercise decisional power over their immediate environments. Indeed, the crucial distinction between rights *for* children and rights *of* children is the locus of decisional power. The paternalistic tradition of the juvenile court was to do what was best for the child, with or without his consent. By contrast, to honor the rights *of* the child would be to allow his or her will to prevail over the opinions of others as to where the minor's best interests might lie.

In choosing between the child's welfare and the child's will, the philosophy of the juvenile court was unambiguous and consistent. The minor who was the subject of the juvenile court's concern was immature and thus in need of coercive guidance for his or her best interest. (Mack, 1909:107). Immaturity was the reason why the child's needs should replace the criminal law in determining appropriate response to young persons who violated the law. Since the fundamental purpose of exercising delinquency jurisdiction was to save the child rather than to punish him, there was no need to confine the court's delinquency jurisdiction to persons who violated the law (President's Commission, 1967:84). Instead, almost any young person whose behavior indicated a need for help could qualify for the court's assistance under the broad and vague definition of delinquency. Similarly, since the aim of the court was to pursue the welfare of the child, informal proceedings were considered appropriate. Under this formulation, a child did not need a lawyer in juvenile court; he or she already had one—the sitting judge—with the additional protective participations of probation and social work professionals.

This same image of immaturity justified age-specific prohibitions and duties. Minors could not drink, smoke, willfully absent themselves from school, or stay out late because they were too young to exercise appropriate judgments. The young could not disobey their parents, educators, or the court because such disobedience would put the child's welfare at risk. In the mindset of the original reformers, the "right" to custody was the primary vehicle for achievement of the child's welfare, and a minor's wants were consistently to be subordinated to a minor's needs.[2]

While the image of childhood and early adolescence that emerged from juvenile court philosophy was internally consistent, many of its assumptions about child welfare were naive. The belief that a judge should or could be guided only by the best interests of the child who happens to commit a number of armed robberies is difficult to sustain after even the most cursory review of juvenile court history or current practices (Zimring, 1978:46–57). The informality of the court's processes were compared unfavorably to the Star Chamber by Dean Pound (1937:xxvii) of the Harvard Law School forty years ago. More recently a decline in social confidence in paternalistic intervention and in coerced rehabilitation has created grave doubts that so one-sided an allocation of power was either a proper or an effective mechanism for safeguarding the interests of children. The classic liberal critique of juvenile justice in the mid-1960s was that it provided the worst of both worlds: "neither the protection afforded to adults nor the solicitous care and regenerative treatment postulated for children" (*Kent* v. *United States*, 1966).

This core of dissatisfaction is the origin of the most recent generation of juvenile justice reforms. Indeed, it is symbolic of a broader distrust of coercion that has become the benchmark for what has loosely been called the Child Rights Movement.

Deregulating Adolescence: Antipaternalistic Reforms and Their Origins

In an era of rapid social change, the legal meaning of adolescence has shifted from the paternalism of the juvenile court

---

[2] "The early reformers . . . believed that society's role was not to ascertain whether the child was 'guilty' or 'innocent' but 'what is he, how has he become what he is, and what had best be done in his interest and in the interest of the state to save him from a downward career' " (*In re Gault*, 1967).

tradition in a variety of important ways. The voting age, a symbol of citizenship, has shifted from age twenty-one to age eighteen, and the minimum age for valid marriage, after drifting upward for an extended period, has now been reduced for males in those states that previously had higher minimum ages of marital eligibility for males than for females.[3] Where age-related prohibitions are still enforced, as in alcoholic beverage control, the age of permissible purchase has drifted downward in many states from twenty-one to nineteen or eighteen over the last decade. During the same period courts have held that "mature minors" may obtain abortions without parental consent and may be given access to contraceptive devices without parental notice *(Population Service International* v. *Wilson,* 1975; *Carey* v. *Population Services International,* 1977; Colorado Revised Statutes, 1973).[4]

Within the juvenile court there is a powerful movement to deprive the court of jurisdiction to intervene coercively in the lives of disobedient and truant minors, and a growing consensus that enforcement of age-related prohibitions on smoking, drinking, and other victimless behaviors should be de-emphasized. Modern reform proposals for the juvenile court often include giving children the right, having run away

[3] The national average statutory minimum age for marriage without parental consent rose, between 1919 and 1959, from 20.5 to 20.6 years for males, and from 18.3 to 18.9 years for females. But the average dropped to 18.4 and 18.1 years for males and females in 1976 as states reduced minimum age for males to match that of females, usually at 18 (see, e.g., Cal. Civ. §4101 (West) as amended by 1971 Cal. Stats. c. 1748 p. 3747 §26; Ind. Code §31-1-1-4 as amended by 1973 Ind. Acts P. L. 295; Mass. Gen. Laws Ann. ch. 207 §7 as amended by 1971 Mass. Acts 255 §1). Meanwhile, the national percentage of first marriages at less than eighteen years has decreased from 6.6 percent of marriages by males in 1900–1919 to 3.8 percent in 1965–70, and from 23.4 to 14.3 percent of marriages by females over the same period (Hall and Brooke, 1919:32–33, 51–132; U.S. Bureau of the Census, 1973:77–79; Sussman, 1977:229–230).

[4] "There can be no doubt but that a female's constitutional right to an abortion in the first trimester does not depend upon her calendar age. . . . In the present area the rights of the minor outweigh the rights of the parents, and must be protected" *(Baird* v. *Bellotti,* 1975, 1976).

from home, to stay away from home in defiance of parental wishes.[5] Meanwhile, the courts have given recognition to the rights of minors to free expression in school settings *(Tinker v. Des Moines,* 1969), and accused delinquents in juvenile court proceedings have been accorded the right to an attorney to pursue the child's interests as the child perceives them *(In re Gault,* 1967).

Is all of this a tendency toward an earlier recognition of full maturity? I think not. In the advocacy for adolescent rights, an apparently similar pattern of shifting decision-making power from state and parental authority to the young is, in my view, a complicated set of social adjustments that have been pursued for at least four different conceptions of the best interests of the young: (1) the "autonomy," or maturity, rationale; (2) the principle of "least harm"; (3) delegating decision making as an instrument for insuring child welfare; and (4) "learning by doing"—the transition toward maturity.

Autonomy

The "autonomy" rationale for lowering the age of privilege seems the easiest of the four concepts to describe. Yet it has probably played a smaller role in motivating the extension of privilege than is often supposed. When autonomy is the only rationale, the age at which a particular privilege may be exercised is reduced because the reform advocates believe that younger persons are capable of exercising fully mature judgments. Thus, some have argued that a constitutional shift of minimum age for exercising the franchise from twenty-one to eighteen is a recognition of earlier maturation and adulthood (Kuh, 1978:21–24). Some commentators have also suggested that the same reasoning explains the emerging rights of young persons to free speech, to participation in

---

[5] "If the juvenile refuses to return home . . . the staff of the facility should arrange transportation for the juvenile . . . to a temporary nonsecure residential facility licensed by the state" (Institute of Judicial Administration/American Bar Association, 1977:3. 2B).

the labor force, to freedom of decision making in relation to sexual conduct, and to determining the outcome of pregnancy (Empey, 1978:565–68).

What might appear to be a simple case of lowering the age of privilege under an autonomy rationale is the extension of the franchise. However, a brief review of the history surrounding this extension suggests that the matter is somewhat more complicated. The two most frequent arguments for the lower minimum voting age were: (1) the greater sophistication and earlier political literacy of young persons (early maturity), and (2) the burdensome roles that were imposed on eighteen-year-olds ("If you are old enough to fight, you are old enough to vote").[6]

Lying behind the formal rhetoric of the debate was the political activism of the 1960s and the felt need to focus the political energies of the young into legitimate channels.[7] The degree to which the extension of the franchise rested on accommodating the youth movement or other grounds of expediency is difficult to reconstruct. But the Vietnam War and campus upheavals of the late 1960s played important roles.

Yet even if the eighteen-year-old vote is a relatively pure case of an autonomy rationale at work, it is also a striking illustration of two different kinds of autonomy theory—general and specific—with importantly different implications.

A general theory of autonomy views an individual as a child

[6] Senator Birch Bayh (Congressional Record, 1971) has argued that "first, younger citizens today are mentally and emotionally capable of full participation in our democratic form of government. Second, 18-year-old citizens have earned the right to vote because they bear all or most of an adult citizen's responsibilities." He then went on to cite statistics showing that, of 11 million 18–21-year-olds, about half were married, 1.4 million served in the armed forces, 3 million were full-time employees and taxpayers, and 49 states treated 18 year-olds as adults in their criminal courts.

[7] Senator Pearson argued in 1968 that "many (young people) join demonstrations simply because they feel it is the only way they can be heard. The fact remains that many of the participants are involved because of their inability to find meaningful political outlets elsewhere to express their concern. For them, certainly, the right to vote is an opportunity for rewarding involvement in public affairs" (Subcommittee on Constitutional Amendments, 1968).

or an adult without regard to the specific context in which a privilege or responsibility is being discussed. Thus, some support for the eighteen-year-old franchise was built on the notion that eighteen should be an age of majority governing all transactions.

It is equally rational, however, to proceed from a less monolithic theory of maturity and to make judgments about appropriate autonomy in the specific context of the issue under discussion. Thus, one could survey the literature on moral development, literacy, and political awareness and come to the conclusion that many eighteen-year-olds are old enough to vote without making any implicit judgments about the appropriate age border for the exercise of other adult privileges and responsibilities. For example, a law which may reflect on the most finely articulated of these functional distincitons is found in the Gun Control Act of 1968. Rather than granting all persons the right to own guns, this act creates separate legislative age boundaries for the ownership of handguns (twenty-one) and long guns (eighteen) (Gun Control Act of 1968, 1978). A similar gradation appears in laws that allow late adolescents to purchase beer and wine a few years before they can purchase hard liquor (Ill. Ann. Stat., 1978).

It is quite clear that these two approaches to autonomy have sharply different implications. If an extension of privilege to adolescents is based on a strict theory of general autonomy, parity between privilege and responsibility would be an integral part of the reasoning behind the reform, since the implicit syllogism of the theory begins with the major premise that those of a particular age are adults. Accepting that premise should lead to one uniform boundary between childhood and adulthood, whether the issue involved the language of rights or the language of responsibility.

Arguments for the extension of privilege that rest on theories of specific autonomy, by contrast, involve a more complex, case-by-case inquiry before one can make a judgment about whether the age at which a particular privilege is extended carries any implications for determining the age at which particular responsibilities should be imposed. One must inquire whether the particular inventory of skills and judgments that inform an argument for privilege are relevant to consideration of appropriate age for a specific responsibility, and vice versa. In this sense, equating the age of draft eligibility with the minimum age for exercising the franchise—whatever its appeal as an argument for quid pro quo—is not a strong basis for using the same age boundary for both types of maturity, unless the repertoire of skills and social development required for the two roles are similar.

There may have been a time when life was sufficiently uncomplicated that a single benchmark birthday was an appropriate border between immaturity and full citizenship. But in most contemporary debates, arguments based on specific indices of maturity would seem to be a more prudent, if more complicated, path toward determining when, on grounds of maturity, an individual should be held responsible for or entitled to full citizenship.

Least Harm

Most of the contemporary disenchantment with the paternalism of the juvenile court tradition is based more on skepticism about coercive state and parental power than on any notion that adolescents are optimal decision makers. In this view, a distrust of state intervention can lead to a reallocation of power to adolescents as the lesser of two acknowledged evils. This is the principle of "least harm."

In my view it is this principle, and not the belief that adolescents are mature, which is the most important motivation for contemporary reform proposals that purport to deregulate adolescence and thus to redistribute power from adults and the state to minors. The fourteen-year-old who runs away from home may be granted the right to resist his parents' efforts to have him returned home, because giving parents, and ultimately the state, total authority runs the risk of doing more harm than giving all immature minors some veto power over the placement decision that their parents might make (Institute of Judicial Administration, 1977). Likewise, the sexually active minor is given access to birth control information, not because adults suddenly recognize that his or her judgment is mature, but because withholding that information risks senseless, unwanted pregnancy and disease. Indeed, it could be argued that the *less* equipped a particular individual is for the burdens of parenthood, the stronger the argument is for providing access to birth control information for him or her. Conversely, attempts to use coercive state power to restrict the sexual adventures of adolescents—even if it is a legitimate end—may produce a classic pattern of costly, intrusive, and futile intervention. Similarly, those who argue for reducing the power of the state to intervene in the lives of disobedient and truant youth do not usually invest such minors with the moral and social judgment of the mature. Instead, they typically rest their case on the abuses that coercive state power has produced in the regulation of noncriminal behavior.

Despite the current effort to minimize harmful intervention, the use of the principle of least harm to distribute power among the state, parents, and children can never lead to a distribution of decision making which is as satisfactory as that which occurs between state and adult because children and adolescents lack the capacity for fully mature judgment. As a result, there is a search for the least harmful trade-off between the cost of attempting to regulate adolescence and the cost of leaving the immature to the mercy of their own judgment. To be sure, it results in a sticky kind of social policy, one that often calls for pragmatic judgments rather than broad policies derived from sweeping first principles. But it is a process that is common.

Privilege as the Means to Other Ends

In the imprecise language of children's rights, the extension of due-process procedural guarantees to delinquency proceedings is sometimes cited as an important benchmark in the Child Rights Movement (Empey, 1978:533, 547).

If these procedural guarantees and rights to counsel are seen as a recognition of early maturity, the basis upon which these rights have been granted has been misconstrued. An adolescent accused of delinquency is not extended constitutional protections as a safeguard against the arbitrary use of state power, not because he is viewed as fully mature. For example, the argument advanced in the majority opinion of *In re Gault* (1967) is that these procedural rights do not inhibit the child-welfare mission of the juvenile court and may indeed facilitate it. In his majority opinion Mr. Justice Fortas said:

The appearance as well as the actuality of fairness, impartiality and orderliness—in short, the essentials of due process—may be a more impressive and more therapeutic attitude so far as the juvenile is concerned. When procedural laxness . . . is followed by stern disciplining, the contrast may have an adverse effect upon the child, who feels that he has been deceived or enticed. While due process requirements will, in some instances, introduce a degree of order and regularity to Juvenile Court proceedings to determine delinquency, . . . nothing will require that the conception of the kindly juvenile judge by replaced by its opposite. *(In re Gault,* 1967:26–27; Empey, 1978:583)

The rationale of cases like *In Re Gault* is a third basis upon which decisional rights may be allocated to those who are not fully mature, what I will call the "instrumental" rationale. Here it is argued that giving accused delinquents the right to an attorney who will serve their wishes also best serves the overall notion of child welfare because it guards against mistakes in the system that would otherwise disserve the larger goals of the juvenile court. As a result, this concept need not depend on the assumption that the child knows his own best interest or that the child's attorney is representing a course of action that is invariably in the child's best interests. The extension of due-process rights can best be understood as an expression of the general belief in procedural protection, as both a contribution to the legal process and as a means of effecting just results. In this view, procedural rights are a vehicle to achieve a greater number of just results rather than a greater number of results that reflect the desires of the child. Given this rationale, it is possible to argue that due-process guarantees and legal representation should be extended to children, without having to take the position that they should be granted the rights of adults. Instead, a welfare orientation is retained that defines rights in terms of a child's needs. Hence, the due-process revolution is not tied to any theory of maturity or autonomy.

Learning by Doing

The fourth, and final, justification for granting privileges to children is based on the notion that chronological age is a notoriously unreliable indicator of capacity for many social roles. It would be absurd, for example, to pick any birthday as the only qualification for becoming an engineer, a doctor, or a lawyer, because more than maturity is required to competently practice any of these specialized social roles. The law may, and usually does, prescribe certain minimum ages of eligibility based on a judgment that those younger than the minimum are too immature for the duties inherent in competent performance, but age alone is not enough.

Although the point is obvious with respect to specialized professions, it also applies to other nonchronological skills that most adults, as well as children, have to master. For instance, there is no acceptable answer to the question, How old is old enough to drive? Any starting point—sixteen or sixty—involves a learning process that must start short of competence. Hence, the sixteen-year-old, like the sixty-year-old, must learn by doing. Each is more of a risk than those who have already learned, but each is less of a risk than he would be in later years without earlier practice. For similar reasons, a young attorney should not begin his practice with a capital case; rather, the mistakes he will inevitably make should be confined to less momentous cases.

In this view of adolescence, privilege is extended to the young, not because they are already competent, but because they can never be ready without a learning period. Hence, the question is not whether a young person is old enough to drive but whether he or she is old enough to *learn* to drive. Indeed, although the extension of privilege is a gamble that must be made sometimes, it is often concentrated in the adolescent years. In many other pursuits, as well as driving, the notion is that, if the sixteen-year-old driver survives until twenty-one, he may be a better driver as a result of the five-year experience. The "learning permit" theory of adolescence, in short, is yet another motive that has been used to justify the granting of privilege to the young.

Confusion in the Reform Movement

Given the different motives have been responsible for justifying the reduction of coercive state power over the life of contemporary adolescents, one would expect some confusion of purpose in the reform literature. Yet it is still surprising that so few attempts have been made to state explicitly what rationale is being used to justify some particular change in the legal meaning of childhood and adolescence. At times the contemporary movement for reform appears to be one army marching under four separate flags, with the combatants paying very little attention to the specific justifications and basic images that underlie the call for a particular change in the legal status of children or their relationship to adults. On both sides of almost every question, the nebulous concept of "youth welfare" seems to be employed as a substitute for a detailed exploration of those aspects of childhood that makes the extension or withholding of a privilege consistent with the welfare of children. The next section addresses one issue that illustrates some of the confusion generated by the multiple overlapping rationales for antipaternalism.

In Rights Begin Responsibilities?

In his recent review of American delinquency, LaMar Empey (1978:583) poses two questions that often represent responses to the Child Rights Movement by its conservative opponents.

They evoke what I shall call the "new parity" argument: (1) Child advocates suggest that children have the right to live with the same guarantees of freedom that adults enjoy. If that is the case, why should they not be subjected to the same responsibilities, including punishment for their crimes? (2) If status offenders are different from young criminals and are simply misbehaving youngsters who should be diverted or ignored, why not get tough with the real culprits—the young criminals?

In suggesting that autonomy may be a double-edged sword, this commentary reverses the sequence of the late sixties slogan: "If you're old enough to vote, you're old enough to fight." Usually, the reasoning behind this slogan is implicit rather than explicit in contemporary calls for a law-and-order approach to adolescent criminality. For example, in objecting to a series of "lenient" policy recommendations for sentencing young offenders, Richard Kuh (1978:21), the former district attorney of Manhattan, comments, "In its consideration of 'youth crime' the task force construes the word 'youth' very broadly. Were the term applied solely to those who I have heretofore regarded as juveniles—youngsters who have not reached puberty or those who have obtained it within three or four years—I would have no problems with such a lenient approach. But the task force has applied the term to individuals as old as twenty." Kuh (p. 21) then went on to suggest that, because "eighteen-year-olds today can vote and those between eighteen and twenty-one both typically are working or able to work or completing college, are sexually and physically mature (and mentally as close to being mature as they ever will be), and are in many cases married or the equivalent," they should be held responsible for their criminal acts.

Of interest here is the logic rather than the policy conclusion implicit in Kuh's analysis. Both the right to vote and the observation that many adolescents are married or living together are employed as grounds for inferring the kind of maturity that should translate into full criminal responsibility, whatever that nebulous phrase may mean.

I propose to address the validity of that argument and the value of the approach it entails: first, using the four rationales for granting privileges to adolescents, I shall make general statements about when an age of privilege can be validly used as a benchmark for an age of full penal liability; second, I will attempt to apply this analysis to a number of specific privileges presently available to middle and late adolescents.

The Logic of Different Rationales

The four rationales for adolescent privilege imply contrasting outcomes:

1. If the extension of privilege is based on a theory of *general autonomy,* the age at which the privilege is extended to adolescents also becomes the proper benchmark for assessing their full social and legal responsibility.

2. If the rationale for the extension of a particular privilege is *special autonomy,* the relationship between that age border and the adolescents' social responsibility should be determined by how closely the concerns that animated the finding of special-purpose maturity are relevant to the specific form of responsibility under discussion.

3. If a right or privilege is extended to adolescents under a principle of *least harm* or as a means of achieving child welfare, there is no logical reason to make the age of responsibility coterminous with the age of privilege.

4. If a minimum age for exercising a right or privilege is based on *learning by doing,* full accountability for wrongdoing seems inappropriate to the transitional status of the learner. It may be argued, however, that no learning role is complete without learning, in some measure, responsibility. In this view, therefore, part of the initiation into adult roles is the socialization into adult responsibilities. Just as a learning theory of adolescence posits a transition toward adulthood, so it may also imply a progression toward adult levels of responsibility. Thus, while the adolescent is protected from the full force

of adult responsibility, he is pushed along by degrees toward the moral and legal accountability that characterizes the legal image of adulthood.

Some Specific Examples

With respect to punishment for violating penal laws, the list of roles and privileges outlined by District Attorney Kuh serves as an instructive set of examples for detailed study. Of what relevance is the voting age to the age of appropriate penal liability equivalent to adults? If, on the one hand, it represents a social judgment that the eighteenth birthday is the beginning of adulthood, it argues tautologically for full criminal responsibility under the same umbrella theory of adulthood. If, on the other hand, it represents a special-purpose judgment of maturity, the strength of the argument depends on how persuasively the indicia of maturity that lead to the downward movement in voting age can be tied to the benchmarks of maturity that should properly demark the age of total criminal responsibility. In short, different rationales for granting privilege to adolescents imply different outcomes.

What of the sexual freedom evoked by Kuh's quotation? Physical sexual maturity would seem to have no discernable relationship to the cognitive, emotional, and social correlates of criminological adulthood. The privilege of living together, to the extent that it exists in American law, seems more closely related to a "least harm" or a "learning" rationale for adolescents than to any notion of complete autonomy for them.

The eligibility of eighteen-year-olds to enter binding legal marriages is a somewhat more complicated case. Historically, the minimum age of marital eligibility has been on the rise until quite recently (see note 3). At the same time, consistent with social mores, the minimum age for marriage has been higher for males than for females, an impediment that is now probably a violation of the constitutional right to equal protection under the law. While there is some nostalgia about early maturity in the discussion of where the new equal-age boundary should be located, the fact that the prohibition could be considered an encumbrance made it legally more likely that the uniform age chosen would be eighteen. Moreover, the traditional earlier age of marriage for females would have made a single standard of twenty-one a socially much more revolutionary move than a shift to age eighteen. Hence, it is difficult to derive from the peculiar history of the age of marriage eligibility in the recent past any evidence directly relevant to penal liability.

A similar conclusion seems warranted when addressing Professor Empey's question concerning status offenders. If the movement toward diversion of status offenders is based on a principle of least harm, it is not strong support for considering those young offenders who violate the criminal law as equivalent to adults because their noncriminal deeds are no longer the subject of coercive state control. The same can be said for the reallocation of power as between parent and child in the state control of runaway youth, when done for prudential purposes. The teenage girl who is allowed access to contraceptives without parental permission because we cannot control her sex life without doing more harm than good (and we do not want her pregnant) is no more mature and no closer to an appropriate border of responsibility because we have made that decision. In this view, current efforts to reduce the social control of status offenders may help us to focus on young criminal offenders as special policy problems, but it cannot help much in deciding when it is appropriate to disregard an offender's age in making punishment decisions.

Adolescence as a Learner's Permit

In the traditional milieu of Jewish society, thirteen-year-old boys are told, "Today you are a man." The phrase remains with the ceremony, but neither the rabbi nor the subject takes it literally. In the last quarter of the twentieth century, thirteen-year-olds are not old enough to fight or to vote. It is true that, in most cases, teenagers have the economic, social, and physical power to obtain harmful substances or means of transportation that the larger society would rather deny them. Likewise, early sexual maturity and activity are becoming a rule rather than an exception. But adulthood is more distant than ever in developed Western society. Physical maturity comes at an earlier age, but the roles of adulthood are further down the road; thus, adolescents with the physical equipment of last century's adults are thrust into a holding pattern of unprecedented length.

In these circumstances, any attempt to control the lives of adolescents is an expensive and often futile task. Hence, much of the movement toward the deregulation of adolescence can best be viewed as a strategic withdrawal from ineffective and intrusive efforts that were not worth their considerable costs. Yet, these costs notwithstanding, there is also reason to believe that the adventures of the teen years, if survived, add to the quality of the mature social adjustment in later life. An optimistic view of the teen years would suggest that adolescence is a period of planned transitional risk—a period when privilege is extended, not because the subject is ready for adulthood, but because there is hope that learning by doing will produce a survivable transition toward adulthood. Sex, driving, drugs, and political commitment are avenues of exploration we cannot, in any event, deny our older children. Faced with this fait accompli, those who have not planned American adolescence can nonetheless reconstruct, perhaps after the fact, a rationale for its existence. To some extent, deregulation of adolescence was inevitable. But the image of adolescence as a learner's permit can also be viewed as a planned period of experiment and enrichment, a transition that allows the young to develop toward adult roles and the ability to make intelligent life choices.

In this view, some consequences must attach to the serious misdeeds of youth, lest the learning of these transitional years be misunderstood. But the young are protected from the full consequences of misbehavior for the same reason—an investment in future personal development that permits the extension of privilege. How long this transitional period should or can last and how much the full extent of adult responsibility can be muted are the subject of lively debate. But a "learning permit" theory of adolescence is, in my view, one important cultural and legal image underlying proposals for children's rights and juvenile justice reform.

This image of adolescent life would suggest that policies should be avoided that permanently impair the life chances of an adolescent: when the young violate the law, permanent labels, exile from the community, and exclusion from school and other paths of opportunity should be viewed with disfavor. In the economic sphere, work experiences would be encouraged, but not at the cost of pushing the young away from even greater skill development or the ability to change directions. Likewise, necessary experiments with sex and affection should be shielded, insofar as is practical, from lifetime commitment.

At the same time, the "learning permit" concept of adolescent life is best viewed as an ideal; hence, its aspirations must be balanced against the legitimate needs of the rest of society and of physical reality. We cannot produce riskless driving, sex without pregnancy, or unlimited economic opportunities for all. There is also no reason to totally abandon concern for public safety because offenders are passing through a developmental phase. Nonetheless, the ideal suggests that policy choices should usually be less polar and that the value of protecting growth can often be served at an affordable cost.

This glowing portrait of the teen years as a learning adventure leads to a provocative question: why not adolescence for everyone? Since human social development ends on no particular birthday, why should the social policies (and resources) that facilitate growth be reserved for the young? To some extent, there is a movement toward greater developmental flexibility for adults in career and family matters. But there also may be costs associated with the impermanence of a lifelong adolescence that differ from those of transitional learning periods. Thus, the arguments for providing less fatefulness in the choices of the adolescent may stand apart from a more general movement away from the social order of permanent commitment.

A Concluding Note

In considering the legal images of childhood and adolescence, one is surprised by the gross categories of human development represented in the language of the law. Terms such as *child, juvenile,* and *minor* encompass a substantial period of human growth and a variety of different stages of physical, cognitive, and emotional development. Concepts such as "majority" and "adulthood" convey an absolute quality which is both arbitrary in the abstract and which does not accurately convey the complexity and variety of legal policies toward age-related rights and responsibilities.

Perhaps one by-product of the gross categories of legal classification is the misleading labels that often accompany the reform proposals of the Child Rights Movement. For example, in considering whether a runaway child should be routinely returned to its parents, it would strike me as important to know whether the child is six or sixteen-years-old. It would be the most extraordinary of coincidences if the appropriate legal response to six- and sixteen-year-old bids for independence were identical. Thus, it seems to me that much of what has been associated with the Child Rights Movement is really a bid to deregulate adolescence rather than to deregulate the larger and more diverse universe of childhood. American adolescence is a period in life that is complicated and particularized enough to deserve a jurisprudence of its own, complete with important distinctions between differing stages within its lengthening boundaries, without attempting to include earlier phases of childhood as well. To give special attention to the legal meanings of this particular stage of human development will not solve any major problems, but it can help us to define them with much more clarity and specificity than is presently the case.

References

Baird v. *Bellotti*
    1975   393 F. Supp. 847, 855–857 (D. Mass).

Bellotti v. *Baird*
    1976   428 U.S. 132.

Burt, Robert A.
    1976   "Developing constitutional rights of, in and for children." Pp. 225–45 *in* Margaret K. Rosenheim (ed.), Pursuing Justice for the Child. Chicago: Univ. of Chicago Press.

Carey v. *Population Services International*
    1977   431 U.S. 678.

Colorado Revised Statutes
    1973   §13–22–105.

Congressional Record
    1971   117:5488–89.

Empey, LaMar T.
    1978   American Delinquency: Its Meaning and Construction. Homewood, Ill.: Dorsey.

Gun Control Act of 1968
    1978   §102, 18 U.S.C. §922 (b) (1) (Supplement).

Hall, Fred and Elisabeth Brooke
    1919   American Marriage Laws. New York: Russell Sage Foundation.

Illinois Annual Statutes
    1978   ch. 43 §131 (Supplement).

Illinois Juvenile Court Act
    1899   §21, Illinois Laws. 137.

In re Gault
    1967   387 U.S. 1.

Institute of Judicial Administration/American Bar Association
    1977   Juvenile Justice Standards Project: Standards relating
             to Noncriminal Misbehavior. Cambridge: Ballinger.

Kent v. *United States*
    1966   383 U.S. 541.

Kuh, Richard H.
    1978   "Dissent." *In* Confronting Youth Crime: Report of the
             Twentieth Century Fund Task Force on Sentencing
             Policy toward Young Offenders. New York: Holmes and
             Meier.

Mack, Julian
    1909   "The juvenile court." Harvard Law Review, Vol.
             XXIIIl.

Population Service International v. *Wilson*
    1975   398 F. Supp. 321 (S.D.N.Y.).

Pound, Roscoe
    1937   "Foreword." Pauline V. Young, Social Treatment in
             Probation and Delinquency. New York: McGraw-Hill.

President's Commission on Law Enforcement and Administration
    of Justice
    1967   The Challenge of Crime in a Free Society. Washington,
             D.C.: U.S. Government Printing Office.

Schur, Edwin M.
    1973   Radical Nonintervention: Rethinking the Delinquency
             Problem. Englewood Cliffs, N.J.: Prentice-Hall.

Subcommittee on Constitutional Amendments of the Senate Com-
    mission on the Judiciary
    1968   Lowering the Voting Age to 18: Hearings on S.J. Res.
             8 90th Congress, 2d Session.

Sussman, Alan N.
    1977   The Rights of Young People. New York: Avon.

Task Force to Develop Standards and Goals for Juvenile Justice
    and Delinquency
    1976   Standard 14115. Washington, D.C.: U.S. Government
             Printing Office.

Tinker v. *Des Moines Independent Community School District*
   1969   393 U.S. 503.

U.S. Bureau of the Census
   1973   Subject Reports: Age at First Marriage. Washington, D.C.: U.S. Government Printing Office

National Institute of Juvenile Justice and Delinquency Prevention
   1976   Report of the Advisory Committee to the Administrator on Sandards for the Administration of Juvenile Justice. Washington, D.C.: U.S. Government Printing Office.

Zimring, Franklin E.
   1978   "Background Paper." *In* Confronting Youth Crime: Report of the Twentieth Century Fund Task Force on Sentencing Policy toward Young Offenders. New York: Holmes and Meier.

Capitalism, Socialism, and Delinquency

Alexander Liazos

THE amount of crime in any society reflects social, political, and economic conditions. Crime, like any human action, does not arise spontaneously. It results from unmet needs, from conditions of oppression and exploitation, from the deterioration of social relations. To understand crime is to understand the quality of life in any society.

The Problem Today

Today there is a great concern with crime and delinquency. It is not a new concern. As I have shown elsewhere (Liazos, 1974), we can trace concern and alarm with delinquency to at least the 1820s. The headlines of newspaper and magazine articles alone give us an indication of the current perception of the problem of delinquency: "The Youth Crime Plague" (Time, 1977); "The Rising Tide of School Crime" (Katz, 1976); "Gangs on the Corners, Strife in the Streets" (Kenney and Taylor, 1976); and in a very recent four-part series in the *Boston Globe*, Larkin and Taylor (1978: part 1) open with alarming words. They write of "a generation of street-corner teenagers who have seized control of the sidewalks and parks after dark, converting them to their own use. It has become a nuisance of startling proportions. Boston police call it their no. 1 problem. Suburban officials spend inordinate time searching for solutions." In 1975 the Boston police received 68,000 complaints about such groups of teenagers. The series by Larkin and Taylor reports that citizens are terrorized, especially old people, in some Boston neighborhoods.

But vandalism, theft, and terror are not limited to the cities. School vandalism in the suburbs constitutes a large part of the over $500 million annual cost (Liazos, 1978;365–66). Larkin and Taylor (part 1) write of teenagers shooting out $3,000 worth of windows in Belmont, a Boston suburb. Generally, there is general property destruction of cars, playgrounds, mailboxes, and so on. (In Lexington, where I live, I have seen no playground without extensive destruction.) Wynne (1977:19 ff.) reports increasing suicides, drugs, and destruction among teenagers in U.S. suburbs. (Few commit suicide, of course, and not all use drugs—but they are the visible portion of the pressures experienced by all youth.) He goes on to cite studies showing increasing withdrawal, privacy, and alienation among suburban college freshmen.

One very common reaction to these claims is to argue that they are overreactions; indeed the media do sensationalize. But, as Platt cautions (1978), we must not dismiss a very serious problem. He cites the various victimization surveys, carried out by LEAA, which show there is much more crime than is reported to the police. Since there were 11.5 million crimes reported to the police in 1976 and since victimization surveys show that 4 to 5 times more crimes are committed than reported, we are talking of about forty million crimes (murder, rape, assault, armed robbery, theft, auto theft, and burglary).

It is true, of course, that corporations and the government commit even more serious crimes against people. But that reality does not diminish the threat of street crimes. It is especially important to note that the victims of crimes committed by the poor and minorities are often other poor and minorities (Platt, 1978:29–30). Thus, the fear and fact of crime are realities in the lives of millions of Americans and we must try to understand their causes and search for solutions.

So far I have spoken of both crime and delinquency. It is unclear how many of these crimes are committed by juveniles. FBI statistics show that about 25 percent of crimes are committed by people under eighteen. Williams and Gold (1972) show that most (87%) juveniles commit chargeable offenses, with about 25 percent committing serious offenses. They also show that the rate of delinquent behavior is about the same for all classes. In conclusion, even though we may not know how many of the crimes are committed by juveniles, certainly a great proportion are.

In what follows I will argue that delinquency results from social and economic conditions under capitalism (which include the powerlessness of youth) and that only under socialism can we even begin to search for solutions. Certainly, the record of delinquency prevention and reform since the 1820s, one of continual failure, permits no other conclusion.

Causes of Delinquency

Any delinquency textbook describes the great variety of theories which have attempted to explain delinquency. Many human conditions have been cited as causes. Biological theories have abounded, as have psychological ones. Too much love or too little, too much discipline or little discipline, and so on have been cited as causes. Sociologists have focused on urbanization, poverty, culture conflict, the family, and other conditions. Some recent attempts at explanation have focused on learning disabilities, nutrition, and aesthetics (people vandalize to destroy unaesthetic objects and environments) (Allen and Greenberger, 1978).

Before outlining a brief socialist theory of delinquency, I want to make some observations on the family as the cause of delinquency. Directly or indirectly, it is the focus of much theorizing and research and many solutions. Even in Cuba, the U.S.S.R., and other socialist societies, they point to the importance of the family in preventing or causing delinquency.

Data on the percent of delinquents from broken homes are unclear (Haskell and Yablonsky, 1974). Initially, the definition of a broken home is unclear. Secondly, some studies show that a majority of delinquents come from broken homes, others only about 25 percent or so. Thirdly, as many people have pointed out (see Williams and Gold, 1972), delinquent behavior differs from juvenile delinquency. We think broken homes lead to delinquency; thus, to control that delinquency, juveniles from broken homes who commit delinquency offenses are labeled and treated more than are juveniles from other homes.

Lastly, to the degree that home life contributes to delinquency, we must be clear that disordered family life is itself the result of other conditions. After all, people who leave their families, get divorces, have arguments at home, and so on, arise from social and economic conditions. Since Marx, we have become aware how capitalism destroys community and family. The immigrants, blacks, and poor whites who crowd slums, where family life is precarious, are the source of cheap labor for capitalist enterprises and are recruited to be exploited. In a very real sense, both family life and the rate of crime are shaped by political, social, and economic conditions. Family life cannot be improved while those conditions persist.

Delinquency and Capitalism

The conditions of and opportunities for children are related to social, economic, and political conditions. The needs of the ruling class (whether it be small upper class or the whole working class in socialist societies) shape what happens to children (and everyone else). The behavior of children and the responses to that behavior are related to the economic system and the quality of life it creates (see Chambliss, 1973; Liazos, 1974).

As socialists, we focus on material conditions, the political economy, and the changing economy (Quinney, 1977:31–32). But we do not see crime as merely a mechanical response to economic conditions. The political economy of capitalism not only creates material inequalities and physical suffering, it also destroys communities and human relations. People do not relate to each other as people but, rather, as competitors and strangers. Where there is no community, people can justify stealing from each other, and they also feel alienated and thus do not help each other. Pervasive alienation, boredom, powerlessness, worthlessness, and distrustful social relations can only diminish the quality of life and drive people to crimes. Thus, we can understand the crimes people commit against their own, the extensive vandalism by juveniles of all classes, and the terrorizing of old people. These cannot be acts by people who live in real communities. They arise from lack of community and destroy further any remnants of community.

As many writers have noted, about 90 percent of reported street crimes involve theft or destruction of property. The other 10 percent, involving personal violence, are a small minority, but, as Platt (1978) has noted, they are important in destroying human relations. Moreover, many of the other 90 percent also act to destroy trust and community, and thus they contribute to the deterioration of the quality of life, to fear and to distrust.

In examining crime, organized crime, and white-collar crime, Gordon (1973) urges that they are a *rational response* to life under capitalism. Since 90 percent of all crimes are property related, we see that in each case people resort to crimes to optimize their economic conditions. Poor people steal, pimp, and so on because they make more money this way than they could by most legitimate jobs available (or not available) to them; organized crime finds a market for goods and services which guarantees high profits; and business people resort to white-collar theft, price-fixing, and so on in order to maximize profits (maximization of profits is the first priority of a capitalist economy).

These are true statements, but limited. As I have said, and I want to stress this issue, crime is hardly a mechanical response to economic conditions. For the amount stolen is usually small, under $100 (Platt, 1978:33), and vandalism and similar acts result in no economic gain. Crime is a response to the total way of life created by capitalism and indicates the poverty of human relations and social conditions.

One of those conditions is alienating and demeaning work.

Many books have shown the social, personal, and emotional destructiveness of work, foremost among them Braverman's *Labor and Monopoly Capital* (1974), Terkel's *Working* (1974), and Garson's *All the Livelong Day* (1975) (for a summary of this work see Liazos, 1978). Many young people refuse to look forward to such lives, and their aimless rebellion results in vandalism, theft, and drugs.

Blum and Smith (1972:98) summarize well the feelings of poor youth:

Reform schools often try to rehabilitate by training kids for socially accepted and useful jobs. But these kids already view the jobs in question—and we would agree—as dead-end occupations. For the most part these are working-class kids who are being trained to stay in working-class jobs. Their parents, neighbors, and schools are working-class, and these kids have found the life surrounding them oppressive and intolerable. They want out, and society tells them there is no way out.

The death of Larry Largey (in Cambridge, Mass., in Oct. 1972), a working-class youth, exposed the uselessness and despair of youth in working-class neighborhoods. Indeed, what showed best the emptiness of their lives was the satisfaction they felt from even temporary jobs, such as picking up garbage (Kirchheimer, Hartnett, and Sales, 1973).

For, in fact, even before we talk of the alienation of most jobs, we must note that for many teenagers (especially black ones) there are no jobs at all. Official unemployment among black teenagers is 40 to 50 percent, but in fact in many areas it reaches 90 percent, as in Charlotte, North Carolina (Rich, 1976:592). The result is predictable (Rich, 1976:594):

As an example of the city's unemployed and under-employed black teenagers, Cleo is far from unique. That becomes clear after three weeks of hanging out with other Cleos on street corners, in chilly, dark housing-project parking lots, and on rocky, red clay clearings that pass for basketball courts and baseball diamonds. There the acrid, depressing stench of cheap marijuana blends with the gloom of corroding lives.

Black teenagers in housing projects like Dalton Village, Earle Village and Boulevard Homes, sitting in groups on cars or concrete apartment steps, are mistrustful of strangers, fearful of police harassment, angry, idle, frustrated, not really sure if they are criminals, as adults say they are, or the victims.

It is for alienating work that schools prepare youth. The vandalism and other crimes which abound in school and which are worrying authorities result from youth's reaction to this socialization for demeaning and exploiting work. Schools, work, and the general quality of life conspire to produce juvenile delinquency (see Liazos, 1978) for an elaboration of this issue).

Boredom and aimlessness are predictable. An eighteen-year-old woman told Larkin and Taylor (1978: part 1) that she and her friends hang around in street corners because they have nothing to do. "If there was something to do, we wouldn't be here." They think little of the future and they are very bored, "just looking for something to do," and "they complain of being excruciatingly bored" (1978: part 2).

In a recent study of increasing violence in San Francisco's Chinatown, Takagi and Platt (1978) provide us with another exploration of the political economy of juvenile delinquency. They show that the increased violence is not caused by gangs in Chinatown, nor by "culture conflicts" between Chinese and American culture: "delinquency is on the increase in Chinatown, and peer group formations among Chinese youth are quite common. But there is no evidence to support the argument that *the violence* is related to youth gangs. Organized violence appears to be related to the business of protection rackets and political intimidation of progressive organizations rather than to an 'irrational' youth 'subculture' " (Takagi and Platt, 1978;22). Chinese youths resort to crime in reaction against the exploitation of their community and the degrading conditions in which they live.

Chinatown was created and is sustained by capital to accumulate profit. Its cheap labor force creates superprofits for the garment industry and contributes to San Francisco's reputation as a profitable convention center. . . . With the exception of a very small bourgeoisie and petty bourgeoisie, Chinatown is a community of superexploited labor: women in the sweatshops, men in the restaurants and able-bodied youths out of work and on the streets. With long hours of work for little pay, both parents working to make ends meet, crowded and inadequate housing, few recreational facilities and regular police sweeps to keep the streets clear for tourists, it is not surprising that there is an increase in family fights and tensions, and in petty theft and vandalism among adolescents. Under these conditions, individualism replaces reciprocity as the basis of social relations. (Takagi and Platt, 1978:22, 22–23)

The crimes committed by the youth of Chinatown, like crimes by people anywhere else and of any age, are rarely political. They are individual responses, not conscious political statements. But they do reflect political conditions. It is thus that we must understand street crime. As Platt (1978) argues, we must neither romanticize it as political rebellion nor dismiss it as meaningless and politically irrelevant.

What I have said so far would seem to explain crimes committed by poor, minority, and working-class youths. What explains the equally pervasive crime in suburbs among middle-class youths? The answer has three parts.

1. Youth of all classes are powerless (I develop this point below).

2. The deterioration in the quality of life and the loss of community are not limited to the poor cities. They are found everywhere. Wynne (1977), among others, shows how the special isolation of suburban life creates alienation and delinquency. In fact, there is less of a community in most suburbs than in many ethnic and working-class neighborhoods.

3. But, above all, I think we are wrong in the distinctions we make between the middle class on the one hand and the poor, minorities, and working-class on the other. First of all, most jobs, not only typical working-class ones, are alienating (see Terkel, 1974). To be sure, factory and similar work may be more destructive to mind and body than being a doctor or lawyer, but most people are not doctors, lawyers, or top managers. As Terkel shows, the typical white-collar job is very alienating. Young people see the pressures under which their parents work, and these pressures effect major changes in

family and community life. Furthermore, most families do not make enough to live the life-style defined as "comfortable" by the U.S. Bureau of Labor Statistics. In 1976, 85 percent of all families made under $25,000, which is where the supposed comforts of middle-class life begin (Statistical Abstract of the U.S., 1977:450).

In short, all youth are exposed to life under capitalism. Some are affected by some conditions, others by different conditions. Very poor youths are shaped by the sheer poverty and exploitation of their community; suburban youths experience meaningless life, alienation, competition, and insecurity; all youths are exposed to diminished status; and youths, like adults, live without community.

Adolescence and Powerlessness

The very existence of a special category of criminals and crimes reveals the special social status of adolescents. A standard sociological and anthropological issue is a discussion of the development of adolescence as a special age. Here, I will make only a few comments.

Certainly, in no society have infants and little children been accorded equal status with adults. But some societies have treated infants and children very differently from modern societies. Childhood, for one, has not always covered a long period; people reach adult status early. Secondly, as some anthropologists have argued, children often assume responsibilities early in life, herding livestock and carrying out other duties. Thirdly, the individuality and autonomy of all children are respected. Good Tracks (1973) shows that even today most native American tribes raise their children on the principle of "noninterference." Adults respect the autonomy and person of the child (and of each other). In turn, children reciprocate, from early life, with the same noninterference of adults' autonomy.

In short, children have often been autonomous, have enjoyed real responsibilities, and have become adults soon. People today lack all these; they remain children for a very long time. For suburban youth, the situation may be even worse, for they are isolated from many experiences and conditions of their society (Wynne, 1977:12). Margolin (1978:449) cites a survey of seven- to eleven-year-olds which shows most are happy with their home and school; two-thirds said they felt their parents treated them more as grown-ups than babies. That may be what the survey showed and what the children said. But any comparison of the daily life and experiences of children today with children of native American tribes (Good Tracks, 1973) shows vast differences in autonomy.

This extended childhood makes thirteen- to seventeen-year-olds (and older ones) powerless. And powerlessness leads to resistance. Resistance may bcome rebellion or revolution, or it may involve individual attempts to deny the degraded status. Thus, status offenses, peculiar only to juveniles, and vandalism strike at the heart of the juveniles' position. Other offenses may reflect both the powerlessness of adolescence and the conditions I described above. Marwell (1966) wrote a theory of delinquency focusing on powerlessness as the essence of delinquent behavior. Delinquent acts are attempts to deny and to overcome powerlessness. They inconvenience and anger the adult world, they give status to juveniles in their peers' eyes, and they also provide them with money and objects denied them as "children."

Christie (1975:226–27) has summarized well much literature on the crime-producing effects of adolescence:

Left to each other during the years when their physical strength (and sex-drive) is at its zenith, they are forced into basic inactivity with regard to meaningful work. It is difficult to imagine a situation better designed for giving a group a greater risk of clashing with the formal agents of control in a society. . . . Since young persons are not participants in the ordinary work force, they are outside the most easily applicable systems of rewards and punishments. They are not given money for their efforts, nor can they be punished for deviance through withholding of monetary rewards. . . . Members of segregated units could become difficult to control because they create a sub-system of equals. This means that as negative sanctions from the adults are given less consideration, such sanctions could even be converted into possible rewards.

Since they are deprived of work, money, and status and kept as children for a long time, we should expect adolescents to resort to more defiance. Christie (1975:229) cites figures from Norway for the years 1860 and 1970. They show that the average age of those committing crimes has lowered drastically. This lowering of the age of crime arose with the raising of the age of childhood and the invention of adolescence. There are no similar statistics readily available on the United States but Marwell (1966) does argue that delinquency has been lower when the status of youth, because of increased responsibility and work, has been higher. He cites the examples of the Great Depression, when young people worked to contribute to the family survival; rural times, when youth were an integral part of a farm family's work; and others. (I note below that the status of youth is becoming higher in some socialist societies.)

Crimes against Youth

Finally, no discussion of the status of youth can avoid the crimes committed against youth (a point made clear to me by James Brady). Schools that degrade, as many writers pointed out in the 1960s; harrassment by adults; joblessness and low-paying jobs (whole industries, like hamburger chains, operate by paying the minimum wage to teenagers); the denial of educational opportunities for the poor and the minorities, the degradation of city schools; the grinding poverty and degradation of lower-class parents; and, for all teenagers, the conditions I described above, especially the use of school as socialization for alienating lives and work. We have here a group more threatened than threatening (see Liazos, 1978, for a summary of the work which shows the oppression of youth by schools).

A Brief Summary

Adolescents, unlike blacks or women, soon outgrow their condition. The powerlessness of adolescence ends, but most people find inequalities, powerlessness, and exploitation in their adult life. Moreover, one generation of adolescents is immediately replaced by another. So the individuals change quickly, but the group persists.

Not all adolescents resort to serious crime, but 25 percent do, and 87 percent do commit some chargeable offense (Williams and Gold, 1972). Nor should we think that crime is the only reaction to powerlessness. Emotional problems of various sorts, destructive drugs, physical or emotional running away from home, and other reactions also reveal the problems of young people. Indeed, far too many adolescents internalize the alienating conditions and powerlessness and resort to drinking, drugs, glue-sniffing, and similar outlets.

In short, capitalism and its effects on human relations; the destruction of community; poverty and exploitation for some, insecurity for most of the rest (Levison, 1974); and the powerlessness of youth—all combine to produce delinquency. Adolescence arose under industrial capitalism, which has no useful work for young people and keeps them in school for too many years. Schools serve to keep young people out of the labor market and to socialize them for the alienating work they must eventually do.

Reforms

Since the founding of houses of refuge in the 1820s, there has been an unending search for programs and institutions to prevent delinquency and reform delinquents. The search continues because delinquency has continued; indeed, in the eyes of many people, it is becoming more of a problem. It continues because no proposed solution has worked, at least not on any large scale (Liazos, 1974).

The civil rights movement, the Vietnam War, and the general unrest of the 1960s and 1970s have had lasting effects. An increase in crime and delinquency and an intensified search for solutions (Quinney, 1974) have been among those effects. The Law Enforcement Assistance Administration (LEAA) has been the instrument of the war on crime. It has funded new prevention and reform programs, funded research on solutions, and disseminated programs and solutions by distributing free literature. The "exemplary projects" have sought to publicize "successful" delinquency-prevention and control efforts (I examine two below). In short, except for the obviously discredited reform schools, nothing seems to have been excluded as a possible solution to stem the tide of crime and delinquency.

The Characteristic of Reforms

"Diversion" and "community alternatives" seem to characterize all reform programs. They keep juveniles away from juvenile courts and institutions and work to rehabilitate them in the community. There they provide counseling, education, work training, and other services. Frequently, juveniles are assigned volunteers to work with them, whether they are known as "volunteer probation officers" or by other names. In many cases, especially in the last three to four years, rehabilitative methods consist of some form of restitution or community service, such as the cleaning of a pond by a group of sentenced delinquents (Beha, Carlson, and Rosenblum, 1977; Longscope, 1977; Calhoun, 1978:30-31; Kenney, 1978).

Most of these programs deal with adolescents after they have committed offenses, usually serious offenses. Little is still done about prevention. Also, most programs are small, dealing with under 100 people. Finally, LEAA funding (partial or total) is very common.

Work is central to most of these programs. It involves actual paid work, work training, and development of proper attitudes about work. I will return to this issue, but here I want to note that the primary concern of many work programs is the prevention of trouble by idle teenagers. The headlines of three *Boston Globe* stories are very revealing: "Job Plan Urged to Curb Violence" (Cohen, 1976); "Jobs for Youth Needed to Avert Violence" (Jordan, 1977); and "Summer in the City: Few Jobs for the Young, Time for Trouble" (Barnicle, 1978).

The Massachusetts Department of Youth Services

One of the better-known reforms has been taking place in Massachusetts. First, it involved the closing down of institutions in 1972, followed by the use of many other approaches to delinquency control. Nonetheless, controversy still rages over this reform since Massachusetts is the only state to have taken this step. Yet places of confinement remain for about one hundred youths deemed too dangerous to be left totally free, although the terms used to describe them are euphemisms designed to hide their real meaning (see Calhoun, 1978:16).

After he was hired in 1969 as director of the Department of Youth Services, Jerome Miller soon decided that reform of the old training schools was hopeless. So, even though alternative programs and places were not yet available for many youths, he closed down the reform schools, obviously on the theory that anything was better.

The resulting fiscal and administrative chaos was severe, programs were in disarray, and juvenile court judges, politicians, and others were very angry at Miller. Indeed, the latest annual report of the Department of Youth Services (Calhoun, 1978) is devoted mostly to meeting the criticisms of disorganization. Nonetheless, the institutions were and remain closed. Miller left Massachusetts in January, 1973, and his successors have been both carrying on his mission and trying to organize the department to meet criticism.

On any given day, about two thousand youth are under DYS care. The latest DYS annual report lists the programs and the number of youth in each (Calhoun, 1978:13–14).

1. Six hundred youth are at home receiving casework services. For the most part these children have been through other DYS programs, are somewhat stabilized, and approach termination from DYS.

2. Five hundred fifty children are receiving nonresidential services, some in their own homes and some while in alternative placements. Nonresidential services include, but are not limited to, tracking, Neighborhood Youth Corps, on-the-job training programs, alternative schools, and work/restitution programs.

3. Five hundred-fifty youth receive residential care, of which foster care comprises the largest part. Indeed, since foster care represents the most normal of alternative placements used by DYS, the foster care model is one with which DYS has experimented extensively. DYS has "normal" foster care (one or two kids with a family), intensive foster care (foster care plus intensive day service), and intensive foster care for girls. Other variations on the foster care model are being contemplated.

Also under the aegis of residential care are halfway houses, which are now called group homes. Placements in psychiatric settings represent the most expensive and extreme form of residential placement. They are used very infrequently.

4. Forty-nine children are in long term (6-12 months) secure care. An additional twenty are in Department of Mental Health locked settings.

5. Thirty-five children are attending the 28-day "Homeward Bound" Forestry Program on Cape Cod.

6. Three hundred youth are in detention, ninety-two in locked settings, and the rest in foster care or shelter care (e.g., YMCA's).

The same basic principle holds for detainees as it does for committed youth, namely, youth are placed in the least-restrictive settings. Detainees remain with DYS for fourteen days on the average. Almost 7,000 youth pass through DYS's detention system annually, of which 10–15% eventually become DYS commitments.

The Massachusetts Experiment has received close attention. LEAA awarded $500,000 to Lloyd Ohlin and the Harvard Law School to study the effects of the closing down of institutions and community treatment. A preliminary report (Ohlin, Miller, and Coates, 1977) has been released. Comparing 1968 and 1974 recidivism rates, the authors conclude that there has been neither a "substantial increase" nor a "substantial decrease" in violation rates (p. 60). Some regions of the state do show a substantial decrease, while others show an increase. Ohlin et al. also indicate that "youth from secure care recidivate at a faster rate than youth in less secure programs" (p. 76). In short, as the *Boston Globe* said in an editorial, the recidivism rate did not increase after the closing down of the reform schools.

Exemplary Projects and Others

Project New Pride (Blew, McGillis, and Bryant, 1977) and The Adolescent Diversion Project (Ku and Blew, 1977) have been designated "exemplary projects" by LEAA. Both claim success.

New Pride provides four types of services to improve "the youth's typically very low esteem for themselves and others" (Blew et al., 1977:2). The four services are: (a) education, which includes an "alternative school" providing personal, one-to-one, supportive teaching and a "learning disabilities center"; (b) counseling, involving counselors who work closely with youth and their families; (c) employment, which includes the teaching of skills, attitudes, and "realistic appraisals of career ambitions and requisite skills"; (d) cultural education, which includes sports events, restaurant dinners, and "many other educational and recreational events" (pp. 8, 51–63).

The project served 200 youth from 1973 to 1976. The recidivism rate was 27 percent, and a control group had a rate of 32 percent (pp. 8, 51–63).

The Adolescent Diversion Project was run by the University of Illinois. It was conceived and administered by faculty and graduate students, but the work was carried out by undergraduates, each of whom was assigned to a juvenile.

The youngster and assigned volunteer typically spent several weeks getting to know each other. Once the two had established a relationship, the volunteer assessed the needs and problems of the client and, with the help of peers and supervisor, developed a program using one or a combination of techniques known as *behavioral contracting and child advocacy.* Volunteers using behavioral contracting would monitor and mediate written contractual agreements between the youth and the parents concerning real-life issues such as privileges to be available to the child in return for complying with curfews, house chores, and personal appearance. Contracts with teachers were also frequently drawn up. The principle of a behavioral contract is that clearly detailed responsibilities must be fulfilled by the youngster as well as by the other participants in the contract.

The volunteers using child advocacy would personally act to secure the rights of their clients when the clients faced crises, such as suspension from school. Moreover, the advocate would introduce the child to available educational, welfare, health, mental health, and vocational resources that could be used on the child's behalf. In each of the intervention strategies, the students attempted to ensure that their clients could serve as their own monitors and advocates after the students' involvement in the project had ended. (Ku and Blew, 1977:3–4)

One-year and two-year follow-ups showed much lower recidivism for this group than for a control group. For example, the 1973–74 group a year later had an 0.76 average number of police contacts per child versus 1.75 contacts for the 12 in the control group (p. 7)

It must be stressed that the samples were small, the time lapsed (even 2 years) was too short, and the authors did not know the reasons for the positive effects. They are unsure whether the effects came from any "counseling technique" or from "just having a sympathetic and helping figure" (p. 72).

Gold (1978) has proposed "alternative schools" as a reform for many delinquents. He begins by arguing that schools "have the capacity to prevent and reduce delinquency, independently from other institutions in their community" (p. 290); they "can mount an ameliorative effort whose effectiveness would not be contingent upon other influences" (p. 291). Delinquent behavior is a defense of one's derogated image and identity (p. 292). To support this conclusion, Gold cites studies which tend to show that better students "tend to have a higher self-esteem" (p. 294), that there is a correlation between delinquent behavior and scholastic achievement (p. 296) and that low self-esteem leads to delinquent behavior (p. 299).

Following this background, Gold goes on to argue that alternative schools are one answer to delinquency. Such schools should create more successful educational experiences and "a warm, accepting relationship with one or more adults" (p. 303). Gold cites some schools which follow these principles and which show some scholastic improvement and lower recidivism rates but which, generally, do not collect data on their effectiveness (p. 305).

Many other programs can be cited: youths tried by their peers; forestry camps which end in a three-day survival experience on one's own (which show substantial reductions in recidivism); and old ideas in new guise. It may be appropriate to end with a suggestion which shows the poverty of capitalist solutions. Walter Miller "quietly harbors an . . . innovative approach, one he calls his 'pie in the sky' idea. 'It's a recreational program that would involve risk for kids. Maybe a demolition derby out in an isolated place where it wouldn't bother anyone. We could wean them away from the corners with it' " (Larkin and Taylor, 1978: part 4).

A Socialist Critique

Perhaps the LEAA programs will reduce delinquency. In time we will know the answer. But we already have an answer for all past reforms.

The Record of Failure. Very simply, the ongoing search for new programs is an admission of failure of old ones. No prevention or control program has proved successful. Most successes turn out to be exaggerations or badly done studies (Krisberg and Takagi, in Krisberg and Austin, 1978:460) or are limited and of short duration.

Dixon (1975) examined reports or studies of nine types of programs: volunteers, counseling, street workers, and so on. The programs examined had to have included some data and study of their effectiveness. Dixon concluded that all of these programs had little or no effect in reducing delinquency among those they worked with. Larkin and Taylor (1978: part 3) also claim that traditional solutions are not working.

Indeed, Joan McCord (Bruzelius, 1978), who followed the boys of the famous Cambridge-Somerville project thirty years after counseling ended, argues there may have been a negative effect on those in the experimental group. Those who "received the most intensive treatment were 'slightly more' likely than those in the untreated control group to have committed at least one serious crime, were more likely to show signs of mental illness" (Bruzelius, 1978:1). Even though some may dispute these findings, no one can claim that the Cambridge-Somerville study prevented delinquency and crime.

Reasons for Failure. As I argue elsewhere (Liazos, 1974), programs have not confronted the causes outlined above. The juvenile justice system is part of a larger system of control, aiming to perpetuate a class society and its inequalities. Welfare, prisons, courts, schools, mental health, and so on, all work to oppress, not to liberate (Krisberg and Austin, 1978:571).

The skills and attitudes taught to those in the juvenile justice system are preparation for low-prestige, low-paying jobs and limited lives (see Liazos, 1974:7 ff.). Wellman (1968) shows in detail how one antipoverty program functioned as "cooling-off" socialization for low-paying jobs or no employment at all. And Project New Pride, with its claim of success, was no exception. "Most positions [of New Pride graduates] are janitorial positions or are in the service industries" (Blew et al., 1977;46)

No work or job is, in itself, demeaning. But under capitalism, the jobs for which delinquents are trained have low prestige and are low paying. Occupational prestige studies, in which people rate the prestige of each of 100 jobs, show clearly that the jobs for which youth in the juvenile justice system have been and are prepared are low in prestige, and thus demeaning (Landis, 1977:145). They are the jobs which are most alienating and least paying (Liazos, 1974; Terkel, 1974; Braverman, 1974; Garson, 1975).

Motives of reformers. Some reformers, to be sure, are truly interested in the welfare of youth. Others want to protect capitalism and perpetuate inequalities. And at least some reforms are instituted to save money.

Scull (1977), in a very detailed study, shows that the movement to close down (or reduce) institutions for the mentally ill, criminals, and delinquents arose from the fiscal crisis of the state. These institutions were created to deal with the human and institutional failures of capitalism, but the costs now are so high that "decarceration" is seen as the only alternative.

The evidence is long and detailed. Scull shows that the destructive effects of institutions were described, often movingly, a hundred years ago. Although the argument did not prevail in the nineteenth century, it has prevailed now (in part) because it coincides with the fiscal crisis of the state. In addition to all the evidence cited by Scull, there is the evidence from every LEAA publication I have received. Each new program cites its reduced costs as one of its main attractions. New Pride claims that it cost $12,000 annually to keep a youth in an institution, but its program costs only $4,000 (Blew et al., 1977:9).

And, ironically, the private sector (especially nursing homes and group homes) are among the primary beneficiaries of decarceration. Unionized state workers could ask for a semidecent wage, but those who work with the "deviants" in the private sector can be exploited by low wages (Scull, 1977:150).

Claims of reduced recidivism. Not only are the reports of program success often based on poorly designed and biased studies (Scull, 1977:101) but they also do not cover more than two or three years after the end of treatment. Yet despite the weaknesses of these studies, the most fundamental critique of reform programs does not focus on discrediting the claims of lower recidivism. Indeed, even if the claims were accepted, the fundamental issue is the quality of life of those who are supposedly reformed. What happens to them, to those who never commit any offenses? Schools and the juvenile justice system consider them successful people. But our vision is limited and distorted if all we expect of people is law-abiding behavior. Our essential concern should be the quality of life most people lead.

Terkel's (1974) *Working* is populated by men and women who, at least outwardly, have accepted their fates and have settled down to the jobs our economy provides. But what kinds of lives do they lead? What does their work do to them? When Terkel listened to people talk about their buried feelings and aspirations, the wounds, hurts, and discontent poured out. Those who "succeed" by accepting degrading work are as oppressed as those who "fail." The discontent, safely buried most of the time, does arise on some occasions. One man asked Terkel to replay their taped talk. In amazement he said, "I never realized I felt that way."

Everyone is happy that most working-class youths eventually get a job and settle down. They would like all youths to do the same. But what do these jobs do to the workers?

Socialist Justice

The causes and solutions of crime reveal fundamental social realities. Just as we see that capitalism leads to crime and makes solutions impossible, so we must understand that the fundamental realities and values of socialism cause certain crimes to disappear, some to persist, and new ones to arise. Solutions too are influenced by the development of a socialist society.

Socialist Principles

Since crime reflects social conditions, we must look briefly at socialist principles and how they work in socialist societies. It should be clear that socialists do not agree on the definition of socialism. All seem to agree on the eventual goal of a stateless communist society, but there are different ideas and practices on the road to that end. These differences form the causes and solutions of crime under socialism.

I think that socialist principles can be divided into two related areas. The first one deals with economic and material conditions. Here we see the need to abolish profit and private ownership of the means of production, to guarantee life's essentials (food, shelter, health, work, education) to every person, to produce goods for *use* by all people, not profit for the few, and to produce other changes of this type.

I believe that most, if not all, socialists agree on these goals although they may differ on the means to achieve them. Because of these differences, therefore, the quality of human relations under socialism will differ. For example, it is obvious that there are two approaches to socialism: (1) the Soviet model and its variants in Eastern Europe, and (2) the Chinese model under Mao and the Cuban experiment under the principles of Che Guevara. While the Soviet model relies on central organization, bureaucracy, and conformity to the party line, the Chinese model (which I would call popular participation) calls for true control by the workers of all institutions: work, health, education, criminal justice and law, and so on. The Great Proletarian Cultural Revolution in China, despite its excesses, shortcomings, and ultimate failure (at least for now), was its finest hour (Hinton, 1972; Pfeffer, 1973; Chen, 1975; Bettelheim, 1974, 1978).

Those who follow the Soviet model do not disavow popular participation and the withering away of the state. They believe, however, that the road there must be slower and that it must be preceded by the creation of an advanced socialist economy. By contrast, Mao, Guevera, and others feared that, unless popular participation and control begin to be instituted immediately, a bureaucracy and a new ruling class would arise and socialist goals would be forgotten. The reason is that socialism is not only a change of economic system and a guarantee of material necessities, it is also, and equally, a transformation in human relations, the creation of true communities. It means cooperation rather than competition, concern with the common good rather than only one's own benefit. Indeed, without such a transformation, even the goals of a classless society will not be achieved (Sweezy, 1977; Gandy, 1976). As Mao and others have taught us, and as we may learn from experience, the struggle to abolish classes is a long and ever changing one. New classes do arise under socialism and must be struggled against.

Some Principles of Socialist Justice

For those who may still be uncertain of my bias, I believe in the popular participation model of socialism. I am aware that in reality socialist societies go through many changes and that at any given moment a socialist society may easily embody parts of both models. Indeed, China and Cuba today seem to be such examples, with the Soviet model gaining at the expense of popular control (Bettelheim, 1978). To that degree, the solutions of crime seem to be changing.

The principles I outline here assume popular control in a socialist society. I do not think a long-term solution to crime and delinquency is possible without such true democracy. China and Cuba seem to have embodied some of the principles of socialist justice, but they are far from exemplifying it. (I must also note that my knowledge of justice in socialist societies is limited. There has been very little direct, long-term observation of justice under socialism. In part, I have not read and assimilated all the available literature.)

Although no socialist society is crime free, most writers on the issue seem to agree that crime is less of a problem than in the United States and other capitalist societies (Connor, 1972). At least some of this reduction in crime is due to the reduction in inequalities, elimination of exploitation and oppression, and the guarantee to everyone of life's essentials. Some of the material conditions for crime have been eliminated. To put it differently, crimes against the people have been eliminated: a capitalist ruling class has been abolished and oppression and exploitation are virtually gone.

But alienation and other problems persist. Alienation may persist at work, where the workers still toil under the same environment as before. To be sure, the product of their labor may not be expropriated for the benefit of a capitalist ruling class, but workers still only execute the demands of managers and they have no part in the *conception* and *control* of their work (Braverman, 1974). Hence, some of the alcoholism, crime, and delinquency in the Soviet Union (Connor, 1972) may be attributed to the alienation of work.

The creation of community and neighborhood is equally important, for most crime, delinquency, and deviance must be prevented and controlled locally or it will not be prevented at all. Let us look at child abuse as an example. It is simply impossible to train and hire specialists to detect and deal with every case. We are becoming aware of this condition in the United States. From what I have read about China, it seems that neighbors and neighborhood committees deal with all such cases of abuse and the condition of children. Without real community and neighbors who care, we cannot solve any of our human problems: crime, loneliness, health, and so on (Sawyers, 1977). Communities have been destroyed in capitalist societies; socialism must create them, or it cannot succeed in improving the quality of life (Burchett and Alley, 1976).

In addition, of course, justice institutions, like all institutions, must be transformed. In the wake of the success of socialist revolutions, postrevolutionary societies use the previous legal systems. Many seem to preserve some of the capitalist legal forms. But they must proceed on new principles to form new institutions.

Why Does Crime Continue?

Some crime does persist in socialist societies. According to Salas (1978a, 1978b), for example, Cuba has a serious crime problem, often discussed by Castro and other leaders. We do not know how much, since statistics are either not kept or are not released. Wald (1978:289) cites the figure of 100,000 crimes in Cuba in 1968, compared to 200,000 in 1958. Murders were reduced to 475 from 2,650. With limited documentation, many writers have proclaimed China virtually crime free (Chen, 1975; Burchett and Alley, 1976). Whatever the truth may be, we can safely conclude that crime has been reduced from capitalist days, but some (or much) still exists under socialism.

Why? Without explanation or documentation, I will list some of the causes. Some alienation persists. Although inequalities have been reduced, some still exist. Indeed, Bettelheim (1978) shows how they are spreading throughout China again. At times, some material deprivations also continue. Thus, the measures created to deal with them (e.g., rationing in Cuba) lead to new forms of crime (cheating on rations). And as important as any of these is the perpetuation of old habits, customs, institutions, practices, and morality. Liberal critics seem to ridicule the socialist explanation of capitalist remnants as a cause of crime, but let them think about the difficulties of changing basic values and institutions in any society. Socialist societies must not only combat captialist remnants within their own societies, but also existing examples in other societies today. At any rate, it is obvious that the old order does not die easily, as we have seen everywhere, and the new order adds its own problems (Hinton, 1972; Bettelheim, 1978).

Criminal Justice under Socialism

To combat the commission of crimes, both those that are traditional and those that are against the socialist order, new institutions must be created. Old criminal justice institutions served the capitalist ruling class; to serve the new ruling class, the workers, there is a need for new institutions.

What I describe below is mostly ideal. It has existed in part at times, and parts persist (in China and Cuba). It is not a blueprint for actual practice, for practice creates its own principles and theory. The fundamental guiding principles involve *community* and *control by the people.* (For the case of China in the late 1960s and early 1970s, see Brady, 1977.)

As before, I list some basic principles with little elaboration. Those interested should see some of the longer studies (Berman, 1969; Brady, 1977; Salas, 1978a, 1978b).

Most crimes are not handled in formal legal institutions. Neighborhood groups and committees, whose functions include more than crime, detect cases of minor crime, or people who are heading for crime, and try to reeducate them without coercion (Li, 1973). The same nonpunitive justice operates in workplaces, schools, and so on. The prevention and control of crime are the concern of all citizens, not of experts (as in tribal societies; see Turnbull, 1961:chap. 6).

When there is a need for more formal institutions of social control, the same principles of popular control arise. These institutions, such as the popular tribunals of Cuba and lower courts in China, are least concerned with punishment. Education of the accused *and* the audience are essential. It is education of the new socialist morality. It involves an emphasis on the need for a continuing class struggle, to prevent the appearance of old values and new classes.

They are to be run by workers, not experts (judges and lawyers). Their laws are written in plain language, and their concern is for the truth and for education, not legal technicalities. Everyone speaks about what they know, and everyone expresses their opinions. Justice institutions are true community institutions.

Youth under Socialism

So far, I have written about crime in general. Obviously, young people are affected by the same conditions as older people. But there are specific conditions and institutions for youths (delinquent and nondelinquent), and I will describe them immediately below. Here I want to make a few general comments.

It is only logical that socialist societies, seeking to create a new order, should focus mostly on those people least encumbered by the old order: young people. Cuba, as one example, has placed tremendous emphasis and many resources on the education of young people (Wald, 1978). Education, nutrition, and health have received enormous emphasis, beginning before birth.

And in societies where much work needs to be done to alleviate deprivation and suffering, young people have a sense of mission, urgency, and a feeling of being needed. Whatever I read on youth in new socialist societies (Burchett and Alley, 1976:chap. 18; Wald, 1978) communicates this sense of mission and responsibility.

But I do not know enough to say whether youth have achieved equality. It is obvious that they have a central position and importance and that they also seem to have some voice in law-making (Wald, 1978:289–91), but equality does not seem there yet. Nor, of course, is there autonomy, when autonomy has not been achieved for adults either. (I should note that in tribal societies autonomy coexisted with cooperation and community. Autonomy did not mean unbridled individualism and concern only for one's own self.) Ehrenreich (1974) describes Chinese schools in 1973 where students were challenging the teachers' powers, the grading system, and so on, and where open discussions between students and teachers were common. But this challenge to authority seems not to have lasted (Bettelheim, 1978).

The Soviet Union

The following discussion is based entirely on Connor (1972). It is unclear whether he talked with Soviet youth or visisted institutions for delinquents. He did talk with Soviet academicians in Moscow and elsewhere. Moreover, Connor does not appear to be a socialist, and that bias (like any bias) must color some of his findings.

The Soviet press considers delinquency a "problem of significant proportions" (p. 82). Although there are no statistics on its prevalence, some data do exist on characteristics of juvenile offenders. In Estonia for 1964–67, 83.4 percent of all fourteen- to seventeen-year-olds were in school, versus only 24.4 percent of the first offenders. Meanwhile, only 6.4 percent of all juveniles worked, versus 47.1 percent of the first offenders; and the percentages of those who did neither were 2.0 percent and 17.6 percent, respectively (p. 92). Thus, the percentages of detected delinquents show a clear class bias in Soviet society. Not only were delinquents less likely to have the benefit of schooling, but were forced to work instead. Furthermore, they were more likely to be living with only one parent (p. 89).

Despite the evidence of class bias, Soviet criminologists focus on two courses. First, they argue that institutions like the family, school, and work fail to socialize youth. Secondly, others argue that the growing pains of the adolescent male contribute to delinquency (pp. 94–95). For example, families cause delinquency by being too lenient and giving children too many things, or by being too strict, or by paying no attention to their children (p. 97). Plant managers are also said to focus mostly on production and to ignore the training and socialization of young workers (p. 104).

By contrast, the following quote from Connor (p. 112) reads as if it could apply to the United States. Many youths, being in the bottom of a class society, with limited jobs and boredom ahead, are driven to delinquency. The elimination of starvation, the guarantee of some type of job, the free medical care, are not enough for them.

The adolescent from a working-class family will frequently find that, for a variety of reasons, he may not do so well in school as his peers from more culturally advantaged backgrounds. Dropping out after six or seven years of school with an indifferent or poor record, he finds only menial jobs available with little perceived opportunities for advancement, and even these jobs are scarce. Entering a trade school, he may find the instructors unqualified, uninterested, and incapable of dealing with a population of students similar in many ways to himself. Neither he nor his peers will find museums, theaters, or hobby circles—approved forms of leisure—very attractive. He has little to offer by way of marketable knowledge or skills to Soviet society, and it offers him correspondingly little. Is it going too far to speculate that his frustrations and boredom may find some outlet in delinquent behavior, whether aimed at the aquisition of goods he does not possess or violent, aggressive behavior with no particular aim in view? This, at least, must be a partial explanation.

Solutions follow logically from the perceived causes. Help families make better work training available, provide more constuctive leisure activities, and so on. Connor (p. 116) describes preventive efforts of various sorts, aimed at helping and reeducating youths. There are some citizen groups working with youths and delinquents, and citizens are exhorted to join such groups (p. 118). There is also a program very similar to the Big Brother program found in the United States (p. 119).

Youth taken to juvenile courts face four options: commitment to an institution, suspended sentence, probation and counseling, and others such as "social censure" (pp. 126–27). Connor describes institutions for delinquents, but his information does not seem to come from direct observation. The institutions appear strict and formal (pp. 131–33), but not as brutal as many are in the U.S., and they claim to try hard for rehabilitation. I do not know how much we can believe.

In conclusion, the Soviet Union is still largely a class society and exhibits serious problems of delinquency, though less serious than the United States. The proposed solutions do not seem to confront the basic causes of conditions in a class society. There seems to be a minimum of socialist justice.

Cuba

Delinquency in Cuba seems to present a more complicated picture. Wald (1978), who visited Cuba (even had her baby there) in 1973–74 and studied education, prevention, and control of delinquency, shows that some delinquency exists but that virtually all delinquents are reeducated. It is a very positive description with delinquency under control. Salas (1978a), basing his research on many Cuban publications, notes that Cuban leaders are worried about the seriousness of the problem, since 40 to 50 percent of all crimes are committed by juveniles. The causes, as seen by Cubans and interpreted by Salas, focus on failures of the revolution: on inadequate educational resources, too few teachers, disorganization caused by changes brought about by the revolution, some continuing material deprivations, and old values and habits. It reads much like Connor on the Soviet Union.

I do not know enough to judge whether Wald or Salas presents us with a better version of the truth. I tend to think both allow their visions to shape their presentations. One might argue that in comparison to prerevolutionary days, Cuba has made enormous progress in eliminating crime and delinquency, despite continuing problems. But Salas, looking at the same conditions, takes a dimmer view, comparing the situation to conditions in capitalist countries. It is clear that socialist justice is only partial and that popular control of justice institutions (as of other institutions) has been undone in the last three to four years.

Delinquency does exist in Cuba. Rafael stole a tractor and crashed it (Wald, 1978:300). Others steal from people on the streets, especially luxury goods. There is also much loitering and aimless hanging about. Few of these youths are conciously against the revolution. They do seem to react to material, economic, family, and other conditions. Not least among them are still vivid capitalist values, institutions, and morality.

Without citing any statistics, Wald (p. 287) says that there are very few repeat offenders, and "almost none" of the delinquents become adult criminals (if so, in time crime should be virtually nonexistent).

Unless youths commit very serious offenses, all efforts are made to help them outside justice institutions. Social Prevention, a commission made up from members of various groups, or the school authorities, or someone else, "visit and talk with family members, friends, teachers, and classmates in the case of a pattern of minor antisocial acts, trying to resolve the problem in this way" (p. 293). If all efforts fail and delinquency continues, a juvenile court (structured much like U.S. juvenile courts, only claiming to work closer to the ideal) becomes involved. Here psychologists and others study the child and his or her environment carefully. In some cases, children are committed to institutions (called "reeducation centers"). Here, as in all forms of reeducation, youths are not excluded; they are made to feel part of the revolution. Although reeducation may seem to resemble reform of delinquents in the United States, the content and the context are vastly different (p. 283).

Reeducation centers have from 60 to 250 youths, with an average of 100. Most are arranged like open campuses (p. 293). The goal is rehabilitation, not punishment, which is possible and real when jobs with adequate income and prestige are guaranteed to all (p. 291). Wald spoke to many youngsters, all of whom said their teachers were "loving" and they had "close rapport" with them (p. 294). Suspicious that the students told her what they were expected to, instead of what they believed, Wald probed time and again. The story did not change. Rafael told her that he was never hit or treated badly and insisted he really meant what he said (pp. 300–301). It does not seem that Wald lived in one of these institutions, so we do not know the truth of what she was told.

The daily routine of school, work, study, and play formally resembles that of U.S. institutions (p. 315). However, there are differences. Boys and girls mix regularly in social events (p. 296). And the work they do teaches them skills which are valued and needed by the revolution, with a guaranteed job at the end. All centers have farms and grow their own food. Students work on the farm, and they may make infant shoes, perfume, and other things, or fix radios and TV's (pp. 296–309).

Wald asked a center official about youths who want to go to the university. She was told that, given their very low education skills, few do. Those who can, and work hard, do go on to higher education (p. 298). We may see this as an admission that reeducation centers, like U.S. reform schools (Liazos, 1974), function to perpetuate the class structure. Or we may argue that the work for which they are trained, even though mostly manual labor, is not degrading to them, for such labor has prestige. The context of what the society values and rewards does make a difference. It also makes a difference whether one's labor is exploited for the benefit of a capitalist ruling class or benefits the society as a whole (oneself included).

Indeed, it appears that the entire Cuban educational system increasingly focuses on combining work and study. Manual labor is to have dignity, respect, and prestige. To the degree that this movement succeeds, one of the fundamental causes of alienation may begin to disappear. For example, many native Americans have suggested that "learning to work was like play." At five or six children began to do real work, and work and play were not separated. A child who cares for two or three family sheep is not oppressed, rather he or she combines play and work.

In their own way the Cubans are striving for the same goal. All junior high schools combine three hours of work with five hours of study. This means that children either work on a farm or a factory near the school (Wald, 1978:346–47). Some fourth graders are doing two hours of work daily. When kindergarten and first to third graders saw this, they also wanted to do some work, and they were given two to six hours a week (p. 348). Whenever possible, work is related to school studies, such as biology to farm work (p. 352). In addition, schools have no janitors; instead, students clean their own schools (Wald, 1978:364; Ward, 1978:101).

Ward (1978:101) has some doubts about the results of children's farm work: "any but the most casual observer will note incredible inefficiency as students spend hours playing and talking in fields." But this is said from a profit-making, capitalist perspective, where slave-driving discipline is demanded. Here, work is to be fun, educational, and productive. And with the play, the children take their work seriously. Each day after work they discuss what they did, how much they accomplished, how to improve it and so on (Wald, 1978:350). Certainly, this is not anything like the child labor in early capitalist industries, with long hours, abominable working conditions, low wages, and so on.

Children are exposed to work and workers early. An old worker spoke warmly of the respect children have for workers (p. 356), while a child told Wald (p. 360) that "when children see that they're being mistreated, they don't like to work. But if they could have a revolution the same as ours, they'd be just as happy to work as we are. We start working here when we're five years old, but no one forces us to. We do it for the Revolution. And when we finish with our work, we sit down at the table and eat what we produced ourselves!" Thus, Wald is justified in concluding that the children's work does more than help improve living conditions (p. 371):

Combining work and study has many effects in terms of the development of the children. In the United States, children think food comes from the supermarket. In Cuba they know it comes from the ground, and that somebody planted it, weeded it, harvested it and transported it. They know this because they have taken part—even if in only a small way—in this entire process. . . . This process also helps in building a sense of discipline among the students and a respect for the material things they have. The Cuban people have learned that they are the owners of their products and resources, and that it is now in their interest to protect and develop them. Children today are much less likely than before to drop out of school, miss classes, or misuse and destroy books and equipment. "Teach children to plant trees and nobody will have to punish them for destroying trees," Fidel suggested. "We can teach respect for goods by teaching people to create goods."

Finally, there is the serious problem of creating an elite. The best students do get to attend top schools. How can they avoid becoming an elite, thus leading to a new class society, and the delinquency and other problems which follow? Wald was told that top students know they got to the best schools through collective effort, so they do not feel special. They also do the same work everyone else does. They too clean toilets (p. 365). I am not sure this is a convincing answer. The prevention of a new elite is a yet unsolved problem in socialist practice.

China

In China, too, work and education are combined. Students usually do a month a year of practical work, either on a farm or factory, and workers come to lecture them (Burchett and Alley, 1976:305–6). As a result, work now brings prestige, the shame attached to manual labor is gone (pp. 303, 305). Young people are given positions of power and responsibility. They work closely with older workers. There is no alienation or generation gap (p. 311). Young people are very involved in such pioneering work as the reclaiming of desert lands (pp. 308–9). In short, they seem to have no serious problems: they feel secure, they are assured work and all work has prestige if done well (pp. 304–5, 311). Whether these achievements will continue now that the cultural revolution has ended is another matter; they may be lost.

I have read little about delinquency in China. It appears that delinquents are treated with the institutions and practices of socialist justice I described above. A student who visited China in June 1976 related an example she was told. A student had been defacing desks in school. Even though people knew his identity, he was told nothing. Instead, the whole class visited the factory where the desks were made. This seems to have stopped the destruction.

The claims of Wald and of Burchett and Alley may be only partly justified. We will not know how socialism effects crime and delinquency for some time. It is true, however, that only a truly changed society can lead to the virutal elimination of crime and delinquency. Although it is useless to discuss a total elimination of all crime, we can make vast improvements to what exists today, both in capitalist and socialist countries.

Socialist Solutions under Capitalism

I want to stress that socialism provides no automatic solutions to delinquency. It does, however, make it possible and realistic to struggle for a solution.

What can we do until socialism provides us with that opportunity? I have no clear answer. We could say, "Wait 'till socialism arrives." But socialism will not come without a struggle. Thus, the answer involves the search for solutions to delinquency as part of a struggle to abolish capitalism. Such a fight for socialism can raise our consciousness and make the end of capitalism more possible.

Struggles for the community control of delinquency prevention, for the political transformation of young people, especially delinquents, and for a change in the status of youth constitute some general principles of a socialist strategy to delinquency prevention. But they must take place within a general movement toward a socialist society so that the quality of life will be improved for everyone.

According to Krisberg and Austin (1978:573–74), there have been only three efforts at community control of delinquency prevention. Two were attacked as "communist-inspired" and in time destroyed (the authors do not mention the fate and effectiveness of the third). All sought to improve the quality of life for all the people in the area.

The community-controlled approach to delinquency emphasizes placing power and resources at the disposal of those people closest to the needs and problems of youth. Community programs generally seek to assist children in their growing-up process through support and encouragement. Since such programs recognize the contributions of poverty, racism, and sex-discrimination to delinquency, they challenge the existing structure of privilege on behalf of youth. Misbehavior by children is treated firmly, but with the compassion nurtured by a communality of persons who view the child as an individual. (Krisberg and Austin, 1978:573)

It does not seem that any of these programs were based on any socialist ideology or strategy. Thus, their inevitable failure must have been very frustrating, for the people involved did not realize that no solutions are possible under capitalism, only steps to eventual solutions.

The political transformation of individuals and gangs has led some people to abandon crime and delinquency. George Jackson and Malcolm X are primary examples. Groups like the Black Panthers, the Young Lords (Browning, 1970), and the Black Crusaders (Helmreich, 1973) were very effective in reducing delinquency, at least of their members. Involved in a struggle to improve their lives and the lives of others, their lives gained meaning and they saw the futility and destructiveness of crime. Efforts to feed hungry children, to rid the community of drugs, and to provide protection from crime became the best solutions to delinquency. In time, of course, all groups failed (in part through sabotage and infiltration), as they could be expected to fail under capitalism. They did teach us, however, the way to delinquency prevention: young and old, delinquents and others, all must fight for a better life, and the fight gives meaning. Delinquency is not ended, nor is justice achieved. But if the struggle is, and is seen as, part of a total socialist strategy, we have made progress.

Finally, there is the need to gain equality for children. I have little to say, for little has been written from a socialist perspective. A recent collection by Gross and Gross, *The Children's Rights Movement* (1977), contains reports of the latest struggles for children's liberation. But they are not waged from a socialist perspective, and they are waged mostly by adults. If liberation must be gained by those oppressed, there is a profound contradiction here. And talk of changing the *system* oppressing children (Gross and Gross, 1977:9), without a realization of the material and political conditions necessitating the oppression of children, does not contain the promise of a successful struggle.

As part of a total socialist strategy, we can see the end of the exploitation of poor and minority children. We may even envision some system, like Cuba's, which combines work and study. But I do not know how we can even begin to think of the true autonomy of children. It seems to me that socialist theory and practice have paid little attention to the liberation of children. The hope is that a society which liberates adults (a difficult enough task) will also liberate children. We should be weary of such assumptions and automatic solutions.

Conclusion

As socialist societies move closer to direct control by the people and as they allow for true equality for youth, crime and delinquency diminish drastically. But as they follow the Soviet model, they will tend to repeat the experience of the Soviet Union: a serious problem of crime and delinquency will exist. For a short time it may be possible for youth to find meaning in their lives through involvement in the pioneering work of reclaiming the land, abolishing abject poverty, and so on (Burchett and Alley, 1976:308–9). But once these goals are achieved, it is very likely that delinquency will become a problem unless there is autonomy and equality for all people and all people run the institutions of their society.

Can a socialist society keep youth subordinate? If so, will there be delinquency without adult crime? Can youth remain subordinate where adults have gained equality with each other? Is it ever possible for adults to be free and autonomous but not their children? I think not.

Marwell (1966) assumes that the only possible solution to delinquency is for youth to gain social and personal power, just like adults. But it seems to me that is no solution. Rather, we need a society where responsibility, autonomy, and life's essentials are guaranteed to people of all ages. Thus, since in the United States, we are a long way from achieving a truly socialist society, we need to wage a long struggle to take the state away from the control of the capitalist ruling class. Meanwhile, the liberal reforms I discussed may work for a few people, at least for a while. But since they do not begin to deal with the basic problems of alienation, exploitation, destructive work or none, and the absence of community, they cannot make much difference to the problem of delinquency.

There is no separate problem of delinquency—there is the existence of an oppressing, exploiting ruling class in a capitalist society. As we move toward a just society, to socialism, and as youth are liberated and find a useful place, delinquency will begin to disappear. Not otherwise. History speaks too clearly on this issue. That became very clear to me in researching and writing "Class Oppression: The Functions of Juvenile Justice" (1974); more years of research on crime and delinquency in the United States and in socialist countries have strengthened that conclusion.

References

Allen, Vernon L., and David B. Greenberger
    1978   "An aesthetic theory of vandalism." Crime and Delinquency 24:309–22.

Barnicle, Mike
    1978   "Summer in the city: few jobs for young; time for trouble." Boston Globe (July 13):17.

Beha, James, Kenneth Carlson, and Robert H. Rosenblum
    1977   Sentencing to Community Service. Washington, D.C.: U.S. Government Printing Office.

Berman, Jesse
    1969   "The Cuban popular tribunals." Columbia Law Review 69:1317–54.

Bettelheim, Charles
    1974   Cultural Revolution and Industrial Organization in China. New York: Monthly Review.

    1978   "The great leap backward." Monthly Review 30 (July-August):37–130.

Blew, Carol Holliday, Daniel McGillis, and Gerald Bryant
    1977   Project New Pride. Washington, D.C.: U.S. Government Printing Office.

Blum, Jeffrey D., and Judith E. Smith
    1972   Nothing Left to Lose. Boston: Beacon.

Brady, James
    1977   "Political contradictions and justice policy in People's China." Contemporary Crises 1:127–62.

Braverman, Harry
    1974   Labor and Monopoly Capital: The Degradation of Work in the Twentieth Century. New York: Monthly Review.

Browning, Frank
    1970   "From rumble to revolution: the Young Lords." Ramparts (October):19–25.

Bruzelius, Nils J.
    1978   "Did counseling 40 years ago harm boys?" Boston Globe (January 10):1, 7.

Burchett, Wilfred, and Rewi Alley
    1976   China: The Quality of Life. Baltimore: Penguin.

Calhoun, John A.
    1978   Commonwealth of Massachusetts Department of Youth Services. Annual Report, 1977. Boston.

Chambliss, William J.
    1973   "The Saints and the Roughnecks." Society 11:1 (Nov.-Dec.):24–31.

Chen, Jack
    1975   Inside the Cultural Revolution. New York: Macmillan.

Christie, Nils
    1975   "Youth as a crime-generating phenomenon." Pp. 221–30 in Krisberg and Austin (eds.), The Children of Ishmael: Critical Perspectives on Juvenile Delinquency. Palo Alto, Calif.: Mayfield.

Cohen, Muriel
    1976   "Job plan urged to curb violence." Boston Globe (Oct. 21).

Connor, Walter D.
    1972   Deviance in Soviet Society. New York: Columbia Univ. Press.

Dixon, Michael
    1975   Juvenile Delinquency Prevention Program. Nashville: Peabody College for Teachers.

Ehrenreich, Barbara
    1974   "Democracy in China." Monthly Review 26:4 (Sept.): 17–32.

Gandy, Ross
    1976   "More on the nature of Soviet society." Monthly Review 27:10 (March):11–14.

Garson, Barbara
    1975   All the Livelong Day. Garden City, N.Y.: Doubleday.

Gold, Martin
    1978   "Scholastic experience, self-esteem, and delinquent be-
             havior: a theory for alternative schools." Crime and
             Delinquency 24:290–308.

Good Tracks, Jimm G.
    1973   "Native American non-interference." Social Work 18:6
             (Nov.):30–35.

Gordon, David
    1973   "Capitalism, class, and crime in America." Crime and
             Delinquency 19:163–86.

Gross, Beatrice, and Ronald Gross (eds.)
    1977   The Children's Rights Movement. Garden City, N.Y.:
             Anchor/Doubleday.

Haskell, Martin, and Lewis Yablonsky
    1974   Juvenile Delinquency. Chicago: Rand McNally.

Helmreich, William B.
    1973   "Black Crusaders: the rise and fall of political gangs."
             Society 11:1 (Nov.-Dec.):44–50.

Hinton, William
    1972   Turning Point in China: An Essay on the Cultural Revo-
             lution. New York: Monthly Review.

Jordan, Robert A.
    1977   "Jobs for youth needed to avert violence." Boston
             Globe (April 27).

Katz, Tonnie
    1976   "The rising tide of school crime." Boston Globe (May
             23).

Kenney, Michael
    1978   "Youths earn money to pay back victims." Boston
             Globe (May 7).

Kenney, Michael, and Jerry Taylor
    1976   "Gangs on the corners, strife in the streets." Boston
             Globe (Sept. 5).

Kirchheimer, Anne, Ken Hartnett, and Bob Sales
    1973   "The legacy of Larry Largey." Boston Globe (Feb. 5).

Krisberg, Barry, and James Austin (eds.)
1978   The Children of Ishmael: Critical Perspectives on Juvenile Delinquency. Palo Alto, Calif.: Mayfield.

Krisberg, Barry, and Paul Takagi
1978   "Ethical issues in evaluating criminal justice demonstration projects." Pp. 454–63 in Krisberg and Austin (eds.), The Children of Ishmael: Critical Perspectives on Juvenile Delinquency. Palo Alto, Calif.: Mayfield.

Ku, Richard, and Carol Blew
1977   The Adolescent Diversion Project. Washington, D.C.: U.S. Government Printing Office.

Landis, Judson R.
1977   Sociology: Concepts and Characteristics (3rd ed.) Belmont, Calif.: Wadsworth.

Larkin, Al, and Jerry Taylor
1978   "The streetcorner generation." Boston Globe (July 9–12): parts 1–4.

Levison, Andrew
1974   The Working-class Majority. Baltimore: Penguin 1975.

Li, Victor
1973   "Law and penology: systems of reform and correction." Academy of Political Science 31:144–56.

Liazos, Alexander
1974   "Class oppression: the functions of juvenile justice." Insurgent Sociologist 5:1 (Fall): 2–24.

1978   "School, alienation, and delinquency." Crime and Delinquency 24:355–70.

Longscope, Kay
1977   "Young offenders working things out." Boston Globe (Nov. 12):3.

Margolin, C. R.
1978   "Salvation versus liberation: the movement for children's rights in a historical context." Social Problems 25:441–52.

Marwell, Gerald
    1966   "Adolescent powerlessness and delinquent behavior."
            Social Problems 14:35–47.

Ohlin, Lloyd E., Alden D. Miller, and Robert B. Coates
    1977   Juvenile Correctional Reform in Massachusetts. Wash-
            ington, D.C.: U.S. Government Printing Office.

Pfeffer, Richard
    1973   "Leaders and masses." Academy of Political Science
            31:157–74.

Platt, Tony
    1978   " 'Street' crime: a view from the left." Crime and Social
            Justice 9 (Spring-Summer):26–34.

Quinney, Richard
    1974   Critique of Legal Order. Boston: Little, Brown.

    1977   Class, State, and Crime. New York: McKay.

Rich, Cynthia Jo
    1976   "Young, black and no place to go." The Nation. (May
            15):592–95.

Salas, Luis
    1978a   "Juvenile delinquency in the revolution: Cuba's re-
            sponse." Unpublished paper.

    1978b   "Popular courts in Cuba." Unpublished paper.

Sawyers, Larry
    1977   "Urban planning in the Soviet Union and China."
            Monthly Review 28:10 (March):34–47.

Scull, Andrew
    1977   Decarceration. Englewood Cliffs, N.J.: Prentice-Hall.

Statistical Abstract of the United States, 1977
    1977   Washington, D.C.: U.S. Government Printing Office.

Sweezy, Paul
    1977   "Theory and practice in the Mao period." Monthly Re-
            view 28:9 (Feb.):1–12.

Takagi, Paul, and Tony Platt
    1978   "Behind the gilded ghetto: an analysis of race, class,
            and crime in Chinatown." Crime and Social Justice 9
            (spring-summer):2–24.

Terkel, Studs
    1974   Working. New York: Avon, 1975.

Time
    1977   "The youth crime plague." (July 11):18–28.

Turnbull, Colin M.
    1961   The Forest People. New York: Simon and Schuster.

Wald, Karen
    1978   Children of Che: childcare and education in Cuba. Palo Alto, Calif.: Ramparts.

Ward, Fred
    1978   Inside Cuba Today. New York: Crown.

Wellman, David
    1968   "The wrong way to find jobs for Negroes." Transaction 5 (April):9–18.

Williams, Jay R., and Martin Gold
    1972   "From delinquent behavior to juvenile delinquency." Social Problems 20:209–29.

Wooden, Kenneth
    1976   Weeping in the Playtime of Others. New York: McGraw-Hill.

Wynne, Edward
    1977   Growing Up Suburban. Austin: Univ. of Texas Press.

Children's Liberation:
Dilemmas in the Search
for Utopia

LeMar T. Empey

REFLECTIONS on the bewildering status of today's children
are not confined to the esoteric world of academia. In a recent
essay in *Time Magazine* (1979:42,47), Lance Morrow wonders
in behalf of Middle America "if children are necessary."

In the *Leave It to Beaver* suburban world of the American '50s,
the family and the child were enveloped in a cherishing mythology.
Americans, it was said, had grown obsessively kiddified; they were
child-worshipers who sentimentalized their offspring in a compla-
cent land of Little League and Disney. . . .
Today some Americans worry that in the last decade or so the
U.S. has veered to the opposite extreme, that it has developed a
distaste for children that sometimes seems almost to approach fear
and loathing. . . .
Those who detect a pervasive, low-grade child-aversion in the
U.S. find it swarming in the air like pollen. They see a nation recoiling
from its young like W. C. Fields beset by Baby Leroy.

After weighing the issues, essayist Morrow happily concludes that Baby Leroy is not likely to dominate America's
future vision of the child. Despite the fact that 7 out of 10
parents told Ann Landers that they would not have children,
if given a second choice, that child pornography is flourishing,
and that enlightened elitists consider childbearing nothing
more than an ego trip, there are counterbalancing signs which
leave room for optimism.

In the first place Morrow suggests that this is not the only
generation of Americans which has been appallingly cruel

and stupid toward children. Early Calvinists considered the child to be a "lump of pure depravity." Later a forerunner of Dr. Spock, Dr. J. B. Watson, advised parents, in 1928, "never to hug and kiss" children; instead they should be treated with cold scientific detachment.

Secondly, some militant feminists and such founders of the National Organization for Nonparents as Ellen Peck or T.V. performer Hugh Downs have shown signs of repentance as they have grown older. Betty Rollin of NBC News, for example, says that, by not having children, she "feels like she has missed something." Hence, out of the confusion and wreckage of the '60s and early '70s, when a "lot of menacing nonsense got flashed around," a new, more sensible, consciousness has arisen: "Today, many new parents start with the lowest expectations about having children—everyone told them how sick the family is—and then awake in astonished delight to find that the experience is (or can be) wonderful. It is possible that the U.S., with its long history of elaborate delusions about children, is beginning to grow up on the subject?" (Morrow, 1979:47).

Mr. Morrow may be correct; perhaps we are "beginning to grow up." But, if that is the case, the essays in this volume suggest that we will still have to grapple with a number of issues which even Betty Rollin, Hugh Downs, and Ann Landers did not consider.

Child Liberation

One such issue is the Child Rights Movement. In his essay on the subject, Richard Farson agrees that, "when people deal with children, they respond almost entirely to childness, not to personhood." Thus, he would agree with Morrow that the *Leave It to Beaver* world of the 1950s was not good for children. It order to quarantine them from evil, they were stripped of all power, denied a sense of personhood, and confined in an age-segregated prison. But one wonders whether Morrow (or Betty Rollin) would agree with Farson that, in order to liberate children, they should be empowered against their adult oppressors, that the only way to really protect them is to grant them all the constitutional protections afforded adults, and that anything that is legally permissible for grownups should be permissible for children.

After having taken this stand, Farson himself confesses to uncertainty on the issue. One reason is that other liberation movements have not turned out the way he anticipated. He notes, for example, that when civil rights concepts appropriate to black liberation are applied indiscriminately to other groups, such as to women and children, some serious errors result. While distinctions between blacks and whites are often inappropriately drawn, there are qualitative differences between men and women, or between adults and children, that should be taken into account. But people often fail to do this. Thus, rather than improving the quality of family life or the relations between the sexes, the Women's Movement has sometimes contributed to "sexual hostility and male impotence, and reduced interest in procreation and family building."

Farson suggests, as a result, that we should continue to advocate liberation for children, but with moderation. Full equality for them should be approached with caution, humility, and a full appreciation of the dilemmas that will inevitably be encountered. Indeed, while he believes "in using our powers of reason to end the senseless victimization that comes from superstitions, dogmas, and outdated taboos, [he] also believes that, when we discard many deeply held myths, we do so at our peril."

How, then, shall we interpret the Child Rights Movement? Is it possible for children to enjoy constitutional rights in moderation, something like being moderately pregnant? On the one hand, the movement has probably had more success in the past few years than Farson actually acknowledges in his essay. Children have been granted the right to due process and counsel in legal proceedings (even when in opposition to their parents), the right of free speech in the schools, the right to abortion without parental consent, and the right (in some states, at least) to leave school at an earlier age. The once vaunted image of the juvenile court as society's all-wise superparent has also been badly tarnished, and society's abiding faith in its capacity to rehabilitate youthful wrong-doers has been discredited. As a result, higher court decisions and recent legislation are tending to reduce legal controls over children for such offenses as truancy, incorrigibility, sexual promiscuity, or running away from home. Radical changes have occurred that prior generations of reformers would have found unthinkable.

On the other hand, the Child Rights Movement has created a dilemma for virtually every reform it has envisioned or produced: whether children are capable of unfettered self-determination, whether the nuclear family can or should survive under the onslaught of the Child Rights and other social movements, whether the institutional and demographic structures of society may do more to hinder than to facilitate greater freedoms for the young, whether current reforms in juvenile justice really correct the presumed excesses of the juvenile court, or whether juvenile justice per se should be scrapped and the young held fully accountable for their crimes. Indeed, these dilemmas are but a sampling of those requiring attention if the full implications of the Child Rights Movement are to be assessed.

Child Development

As an advocate for child liberation, Farson argues that social scientists, no less than parents and professionals, have been oppressors of children. Scientists are incapable of recognizing the inherent capacities of the young because they are the captives of developmental theories predicated upon the assumption that children are only *potential* adults. Thus, until they go through an invariant bio-psycho-social process of growth, they are incapable of responsible, informed behavior.

In her discussion of this issue, Arlene Skolnick tends to agree with Farson. Developmental psychologists "have tended to describe all young people in terms of their inadequacies rather than their competencies." But she does not seem to agree that this tradition has been entirely dysfunctional for children.

In the first place, psychologists, along with other reformers, were instrumental in securing what traditionally have been defined as nurturance rights *for* children—adequate housing and nutrition, a loving family, an education, and protection from abuse and neglect by parents and other authority figures. Hence, the efforts that are being made to extend civil rights *to* the young need not entirely discredit earlier efforts to secure nurturance rights *for* them.

Secondly, in the far more difficult arena of trying to determine the moral and cognitive capacities of children, recent research does tend to challenge the traditional assumption that children are incompetent. Asked to deal with problems that are relevant to the world in which they live, "children are capable of remarkably sophisticated reasoning." But, adds Skolnick, this does not mean that there are no differences among the preschooler, the schoolchild, and the adolescent. While young children are much less globally inept than previously thought, they "still do not do well at tasks involving sophisticated forms of abstract reasoning, and their use of their capacities is erratic and fragile."

A major problem in assessing the meaning of such findings, however, is the fact that the cognitive capacities of all people—adults as well as children—vary considerably, depending upon the cultural familiarity of the task they are asked to perform. If a task is related in some way to a person's background, he or she can do much better on it. But, since most studies of these issues have been confined to laboratory or otherwise artificially constructed situations, existing research makes generalization difficult. Nonetheless, Skolnick concludes that, with all their limitations, scientific findings do provide some guidelines for policy formation.

Relative to this discussion, the most noteworthy is the idea that civil rights should be extended further down the ladder of age. Indeed, the American Psychological Association joined other child advocates in supporting a class action suit which contended that children ages twelve and over should be accorded the same due-process protections as adults. Yet Skolnick also warns that, while the evidence suggests that children are often surprisingly sophisticated, "it does not say that children or adolescents are the same as adults." Indeed, if one compares the qualified support that research provides for child liberation with some traditional beliefs that have long been reflected in the law, some surprising findings emerge.

Both the English Common Law and the Catholic Canon Law have specified for centuries that children under the age of seven cannot be held accountable for knowing right from wrong, and that between the ages of seven and fourteen they might be presumed incapable of that knowledge unless proved otherwise. Significantly, modern research shows much the same thing: (1) that a major increase occurs in the child's moral and cognitive capacities at about age seven and (2) that children become even more capable at about age twelve. Hence, a cynic might be tempted to ask, "So, what else is new?" The congruity between the findings of modern science and the folk wisdom of centuries is striking.

Beyond these limited guides for action, Skolnick maintains that the sides people take on the issue of child liberation are based more upon the values they espouse than upon any compelling evidence they can cite. Depending upon whether they see the glass of age as half full or half empty, they conclude that children should, or should not, have the same rights as adults. Hence, a more objective stance would be to suggest that the developmental literature cannot provide a definitive answer for children of all ages.

Family Life and Child Liberation

There is a certain irony in the current effort to empower children against their parents. A series of recent historical works tends to suggest that our current concept of childhood is a product largely of the past few centuries (Aries, 1962; Mause, 1974; Stone, 1974). Before that time children were treated with indifference, at best, and with outright cruelty, at worst. Unwanted children, particularly girls, were put to death at birth, were deliberately abandoned, were sold into prostitution, or were left to be raised by others. Consequently, as Skolnick points out, such eighteenth-century reformers as Rousseau pleaded with parents to exercise greater concern and control over their children. In contrast to contemporary reformers, he argued that children require patience, special care, and guidance, not autonomy. Rousseau, in short, was one of the first philosophers to advocate nurturance rights for children.

By contrast, because new, late twentieth-century beliefs are so different, they create unfamiliar problems. In a time when it has become fashionable to argue that everyone, not just children, requires liberation, Rousseau's preoccupation with childhood and family life seems anachronistic. Indeed, even Skolnick may sound reactionary when she says that "the roles of children and adults . . . have been out of balance." By contrast, a more popular view among militant feminists is that "you won't find those sacrificial mothers any more" (Time Magazine, 1977). Women, as well as men, want to forge their own destinies, and children can be distinct hindrances in doing so.

Given the other pressures under which the modern family operates, this added tension may make its continued existence even more tenuous. For example, many of the essayists in this volume underscore the well-known fact that modern parents enjoy few of the traditional rewards associated with parenthood—children who are economic assets, offspring who will provide monetary and emotional supports in old age and who will remain obedient subordinates throughout life. As a result of the Child Rights Movement, indeed, the few remaining psychological and symbolic rewards associated with parenthood may well be threatened. In 1972, for example, a fifteen-year-old girl in Minnesota brought a court action against her parents because they wanted to take her on a trip around the world for two years and she did not want to go. Consequently, the increasing tendency for children, as well as for adults, to resort to complex legal procedures to solve family squabbles has led Harvard law professor Frank Sanders to conclude that "we're going to make being a parent tougher and tougher. We're going to have to explain our actions to the courts. The ultimate absurdity would be if my son, who gets mad at going to bed at 10:30, goes to court and asks for a later bedtime. This is a trend one need to worry about" (see Goodman, 1976). Perhaps liberated moderns will not be "missing something" after all by not having children.

But if the rewards for parents are declining, what about the impact on children of the changing character of family life? In his demographic analysis of this subject, Kingsley Davis highlights the dramatic finding that, because of high divorce rates and the current trend toward single parenthood, "the likelihood that an American child will remain with both parents throughout childhood has been reduced to about the same level it was in the preindustrial era." More and more children are being raised by a single parent or by a state-run surrogate. Not only has the divorce rate tripled since 1933, but the ratio of illegitimate births has gone up 314 per cent since 1947. Furthermore, as Bureau of Census projections suggest, there is no sign that the trend is leveling out. By the time of the next census in 1980, there may be half again as many unmarried couples as existed in 1978 (Timmick, 1979).

Opinions relative to these trends are divided. An unmarried mother believes they are healthy. "A man," she says, "is pressure, all that relating emotionally. I don't want to be told how to raise my child. . . . After seven years of going it alone, I can't imagine delegating 50% of it to someone else" (Los Angeles Times, January 17, 1979).

As might be expected, many child psychiatrists disagree with this liberated mother. "The single parent phenomenon is going to bring many problems," says Dr. Saul Brown, director of psychiatry at Cedars Sinai Community Mental Health Center in Los Angeles. Dr. Sidney Berman, past president of the Academy of Child Psychiatry, agrees. "A single parent family," he says, "becomes a matriarchal family in which various types of unsatisfactory substitutes for the father are sought—a series of men, a big brother, uncle, grandfather—

and all of them transitory and of a quality not conducive to meaningful psychological support" (see Timmick, 1979). Berman believes that the young not only need consistency of guidance but the presence of both parents so that the child can develop a sense of what it means to be male or female.

If history is any guide, these fears may be excessive. Peter Laslett (1977) indicates that there have been marked fluctuations in the illegitimacy ratio in England from the sixteenth century to the present. This ratio reached a peak in 1600, declined to a low about 1650, reached a new high about 1840, declined again about 1900 and, then, reached a new peak in recent years. Thus, if patterns in England are any guide, the recent upsurge of single parenthood in this country may be followed by a decline in the years to come.

The results of contemporary studies on the subject, however, are equivocal. On the one hand, those who conducted a survey of attitudes toward marriage in California concluded that wedlock is in a healthy condition in that state (Dye, 1979). Not only did the overwhelming majority of the respondents express satisfaction with marriage as an institution and with the sexual fidelity it implies, but those single persons who were living together outside of marriage expressed monogamous sentiments. Furthermore, 3 out of 4 respondents felt that children now enjoy too much freedom.

On the other hand, a national survey conducted by investigators at the University of Michigan found that between 1957 and 1976 the tendency for people to evaluate marriage positively had dropped dramatically, particularly among women (Douvan, 1979). Although 70 percent of the men versus 56 percent of the women felt that marriage had more advantages than single life, 80 percent of the total sample approved of divorce. Furthermore, the persistent tendency for women to reject traditional family values more strongly than men indicates quite clearly that feminist attitudes have had a marked impact in the past twenty years. "Today, marriage and parenthood rarely are viewed as necessary, and people who do not choose those roles are no longer considered social deviants" (Douvan, 1979;4).

Such surveys, as well as other popularized discussions of single parenthood, are limited, however, because they usually express the world view of the middle and upper classes. Whereas single parenthood and children's liberation are trendy, provocative issues for white, employed, young and middle-aged adults, fatherless households have long been an established fact among underprivileged Americans, particularly blacks. With blacks unmarried cohabitation and single parenthood have not only been a matter of economic convenience but also are a legacy of slavery, which was antifamily by nature. These pragmatic practices, moreover, have increased in recent years, not decreased.

In 1950, 18 percent of all black families were famale-headed; in 1969 the proportion had risen to 27 percent; and by 1977 it had reached 41 percent (Bronfenbrenner, 1974; Monahan, 1957; and Davis in this volume). Indeed, as Kingsley Davis points out in his essay, the ratio of female-headed households per 100 two-parent black families could reach as high as 117.9 by 1985 if present trends continue versus 19.1 percent for whites.

The implications of such trends are nothing short of profound. In the first place, the facts are that the majority of unmarried mothers are not successful liberated women, as so much of the popular literature would lead one to believe, but uneducated, unemployed teenagers, many as young as thirteen or fourteen. Secondly, it is among these mothers and their offspring that the rates of infant mortality, of school failure, of poverty, of mental and physical disease, of criminal victimization, and of child abuse are the highest. Thirdly, high rates of illegitimacy, particularly in our urban ghettos, are not a symbol of disgrace, but a means of survival. Unacquainted with other means, the daughters of the poor regard pregnancy as a way to welfare, and welfare as a way to independence. For them, the American Dream has been reduced to these proportions.

This life-style, while often unfamiliar to whites, is not lost on black leaders. As the founder of PUSH (People United to Save Humanity), the Rev. Jesse Jackson toured the country in 1979, speaking to children and seeking to acquaint them with other alternatives (Krier, 1979). Jackson dramatized the issues by pointing out that he, too, is the offspring of unmarried children: his mother was seventeen while her mother, in turn, was fourteen. Furthermore, neither his parents nor his mother's parents ever married. But, says Jackson, it need not be this way. Life is not a one-thrill experience, dominated by unwed parenthood. Instead, there can be many thrills: graduating from school, marrying, finding employment, and seeing one's own children follow the same pattern. Like so many other people from backgrounds of poverty and discrimination, Jackson is a conservative when it comes to the virtues of the monogamous family. He sees it as an important, if not indispensable, source of stability and guidance for children. As a result, there is no little irony in his message.

By taking a point of view opposite that of Jackson, one could satirize some of the more extreme features of the Child Rights Movement by arguing that the children of the poor have long enjoyed most of the freedoms oppressed middle-class children are denied: freedom from two-parent controls, freedom from compulsory education, freedom from sexual taboos, and freedom from stultifying routines of work and practice. Whereas middle-class children have been constrained in all these activities, lower-class children have been licensed to experience life in its fullest.

What this parody overlooks, of course, is the fact that license and freedom are not the same thing. As indicated above, it would be difficult to argue that the "freedoms" of poor children have provided unadulterated benefits. Indeed, Jesse Jackson seems to be saying that, until lower-class children receive the nurturance rights so long taken for granted by middle-class children, they cannot realize their full potential. There is virtue in institutionalized patterns that constrain childish license until that license can be tempered by self-control, education, opportunity, and experience. Rather than espousing a new set of values, therefore, Jackson seems bent on reasserting the importance of traditional virtues for children: self-discipline, hard work, respect for authority, and deferred gratification of sexual impulses—virtues first enunciated by the child savers of the eighteenth and nineteenth centuries, not those that are advocated by today's reformers. As a consequence, it seems quite clear that, when the Child Rights Movement is viewed from below, it takes on a quite different cast than when viewed from above.

Given the conflicting prescriptions for family life and child-rearing, it should come as no surprise to find that Americans, especially young people, feel a growing sense of disorientation and anxiety. According to the University of Michigan survey mentioned earlier, young people in particular "are having greater difficulty integrating into society today compared to a generation ago" (Veroff, 1979:4–5):

Compared to the 1957 sample, the 1976 sample found their social integration to be a problem and their social roles and their interpersonal relationships to be more of a source of distress. The advantage of traditional social roles which were more prevalent in the fifties was that they facilitated automatic coping with life problems. In our less rigidly defined society, people are forced to cope with their own very personal integrations of experience. The price is increased worry and anxiety.

Demographic and Social Contexts

Worry and anxiety among young people are increased not merely by changes in the American family. Change is also endemic to the changing social and demographic contexts of American life. Throughout the history of civilization, societies have been predominantly young. In the late seventeenth century the average life expectancy at birth was 32 years in England and about 27.5 years in Germany (Gillis, 1974:10). This meant that the ratio of young to old people was extremely high. "In Sweden in 1750 the ratio of those persons aged 15–29 years to every 100 persons aged 30 years and over was 63 percent. In France in 1776 the ratio was 65 percent; and as late as 1840 it was approximately 77 percent in England" (Gillis, 1974:11).

In the United States in 1900 the ratio of young people ages 14–24, to the population aged 25–64 was still about 52 percent. But by 1970 it had declined to 45 percent (Coleman et al., 1974:47). More to the point, Davis points out that, while 15- to 19-year-old adolescents constituted 10.5 percent of the population in 1890, they make up only 9.8 percent today and will constitute only about 7.8 percent in the year 2000.

The reasons for these decreases are twofold: (1) a decline in the birthrate and (2) an increase in life expectancy. Since 1957 the fertility rate has dropped from a peak of 3.76 children per woman to a record low of 1.75 in 1976. The United States may well be on its way to the goal of zero population growth. Meanwhile, average life expectancy at birth has increased to about 68 years for men and 72 years for women. "In 1890, only 4.0 percent of the American population was over 65. Today the figure is 10.9 percent. In the most probable projection of the Census Bureau, the proportion rises in the year 2000 to 12.2 percent" (Davis, this volume). What, then, are the implications of these trends?

One possibility is that, in a society that is growing progressively older, we will witness added support for the idea that our protective stance toward the young should be decreased. In terms of state rather than family responsibility, Western countries for three centuries have placed increasing emphasis upon the school as a vital institution for socializing the young, second only to the family in importance. Education has been described as the means by which our cultural life might be shaped into a new, more moral, pattern. But, as James Short points out in his essay, the belief is steadily gaining strength that schools should no longer play an *in loco parentis* role. Not only is it argued that children should be allowed to assert their independence from familial controls, but from school constraints as well. As a consequence, we should not be surprised that many of our schools have become unstable sources of training for the young, marked by defiance and violence as well as by a decrease in educational effectiveness.

Citing a series of recent studies, Short points out that educational authorities have responded to this state of affairs by absolving themselves of responsibility for high levels of turbulence in the schools. Current difficulties, they argue, are rooted in society as a whole. Given the emphasis upon child liberation and the autonomy of the individual, "the traditional reliance on the school as the primary medium for resolving social problems is no longer tenable" (Ianni, 1978:34).

Added to the declining influence of the family and the fact that many children may not be capable of mature cognitive and moral tasks, the loss of social control by the school might be enough to traumatize the traditionalist. Yet it could be argued that a decline in the functions of traditional institutions need not be traumatizing if new institutional arrangements are forthcoming for socializing the young. Innovative forms of social control and creativity might be sustained by new arrangements that decrease age grading and bring children closer to adults in productive and mutually rewarding pursuits. Relative to this issue, however, Kingsley Davis is not optimistic. Instead, he points out that, as a result of the changing population pyramid, the young have increasingly become competitors with the elderly for the largesse of society. Instead of only one dependent group in society, we now have two. But since older people now outnumber youth, and are more effectively organized, it appears that the battle will be won by them.

The growth in population from 1950 to 1970 was lowest for people under 45, 30.5 percent. By contrast, the population of people over 65 increased by 63 percent. Even more striking was the growth in the number of people over 75, 97 percent— from 3.9 million in 1950 to 7.6 million in 1970 (U.S. Department of Commerce, 1971). Indeed, "by the year 2020 there will be almost twice as many people over 65 (43 million) as there are today, exerting immense new pressures on the Social Security, pension, and Medicare systems" (Time, February 28, 1977a:71).

Interpretations of this new phenomenon are divided. Amitai Etizioni feels that it "means a less innovative society in which fewer people will have to attend, care, feed, house, and pay for a larger number" (Time, February 28, 1977a:71). Young people may enjoy more civil rights, but they may also be saddled with a great many more responsibilities. Charles Westoff, by contrast, disagrees. He believes that a better life is in store for everyone, even if our population is growing older. "Zero population growth," he says, "will reduce pressures on the environment and resources. It will probably increase per capita income. It will reduce pressure on governmental services. And it will give society an opportunity to invest more in the quality rather than the quantity of life" (Time, February 28, 1977a:71). If Westoff is correct, it could be that in a generation or two there will be fewer—but highly treasured—children and that opportunities for them will be unprecedented. But what about the more immediate future? Is there evidence that new roles are opening up for them?

Again, the evidence is not promising. Davis points out that between 1951 and 1976 the proportion of males over 65 who were employed declined from 44.9 percent to 19.4 percent. But, paradoxically, this decrease was not accompanied by a compensatory increase in the employment of the young. Instead, virtually all of the increase has been among women, particularly among married women (Carter and Glick, 1976:424). The Child Rights Movement, in short, is in direct competition with the Feminist Movement as well as with the elderly. As a result, almost half of the nation's unemployed in 1976 were between the ages of 16 and 24—3.5 million of them (National League of Cities, 1977).

Economists are concerned that large numbers of America's high school and college graduates cannot find jobs. But if employment is a problem for this group, consider the problems of unwed, adolescent mothers, and of their male counterparts, many of whom are school dropouts. Estimated unemployment rates for adolescents, in general, run anywhere from 20 to 40 percent, but for black and brown teenagers in urban areas they may be as high as 50 or 60 percent. "A generation of young people is moving into its 20s—the family forming years—without knowing how to work, since many have never held jobs" (Time, August 29, 1977b). Indeed, as pointed out earlier, welfare has become the road to independence for many of the young people in this group.

What all of this means is that the movement to grant greater freedoms to children is not yet matched by a set of institutional arrangements by which rights can become a reality, particularly for those whose economic and social status is the lowest. The notion that children's rights should be equal with those of adults is relatively empty unless it is matched with means by which they can become self-sufficient. Relative to this issue, for example, Alex Liazos argues in his essay that capitalist countries should emulate socialist societies by promoting age integration and combining work with study for young people. Children should be exposed to adult labor and laborers early in their lives. In this way the young would not only experience the dignity that is associated with contributions to the collective welfare but would be provided with a stake in conformist rather than predatory behavior. "As yet, however, youth's right to work is much farther from realization than the child's right to protection against certain kinds of work at too early an age" (Coleman et al., 1974:40).

This state of affairs raised a question relative to the rhetoric of the Child Rights Movement: Does it have substance beyond efforts to free children from traditional restraints? A kind of irreducible ambivalence is revealed that has characterized child savers throughout history.

In 1621 two Puritan reformers, Robert Cleaver and John Dod, warned that "the young child which lieth in the cradle is both wayward and full of affections; and though his body be but small, yet he hath a reat [wrongdoing] heart, and is altogether inclined to evil" (Cf. Illick, 1974:316–17). Thus, while parents should love and care for their babies, they should be "wary and circumspect" as well. Otherwise, the evil inherent in those same offspring would "rage and burn down the whole house."

Three centuries later, when America was in the depths of the Great Depression, the National Child Labor Committee declared that the continued employment of children had become an economic menace. "Children should be in school and adults should have whatever worthwhile jobs there are" (Coleman, et al., 1974:35). Once again, children were perceived as a threat to the welfare of adults.

Today's child savers notwithstanding, the same ambivalence seems to persist. On the one hand, many Americans not only advocate greater autonomy for the young but have taken steps which have had the effect of loosening familial, educational, and legal controls over them. The same logic that gave birth to the Civil Rights, the Feminist, the Elderly, and the Gay Rights movements has been applied to children. Yet, on the other hand, the concern of these other social movements with maintaining their competitive positions has had the effect of leaving children in a social vacuum. Rhetoric has not been matched with significant alterations in the traditional dependent status of the young. Hence, without new, more responsible positions to occupy, autonomy for children has meant little more than license. The scene, the characters, and even the plot have changed, but the historical theme remains the same.

Juvenile Justice

The paradox produced by ambivalence is no less evident when changes in juvenile justice are considered. First, as Jerome Miller, Monrad Paulsen, and Franklin Zimring indicate, the invention of the juvenile court was predicated on the following assumptions: (1) that children are qualitatively different from adults; (2) that legal intervention in their lives is justified because of their dependent and protected status; and (3) that the goal of intervention is rehabilitation, not punishment. As a result, children's rights were defined in terms of protecting them from parental neglect, physical abuse, immorality, excessive and dangerous work and insuring that they attended school in order to prepare themselves for adulthood.

But, as the foregoing review has indicated, our assumptions about children have changed markedly: (1) that children are not qualitatively different from adults, at least not so much as we thought; (2) that their right to self-determination should prevent legal interference into their lives for behavior which, if exhibited by adults, would not be considered illegal; and (3) that children should be granted all the constitutional protections afforded adults, including the protection of their rights against parents, the school, or the legal system itself. Hence, rather than worrying so much about nurturance rights *for* children, we should concern ourselves more with the civil rights *of* children. As Zimring puts it, "To honor the rights *of* the child would be to allow his or her will to prevail over the opinions of others as to where the minor's best interests might lie."

As we have seen, these new assumptions are not without opposition. Nevertheless, they have contributed to a series of reforms—decriminalization, diversion, due process, and deinstitutionalization—which, besides producing change, have also created dilemmas.

Decriminalization

Decriminalization is a reflection of the growing belief that children are less different from adults than previously thought and that the legal system should be prohibited from censoring their moral conduct. This point of view was clearly expressed by Edwin Lemert (1967:97) in his famous essay for the President's Crime Commission in 1967. "Individual morality," said Lemert, "has become functional rather than sacred or ethical in the older sense. [Hence], it has become equally or more important to protect children from the unanticipated and unwanted consequences of organized movements in their behalf than from the unorganized, adventitous 'evils' which gave birth to the juvenile court." Accepting Lemert's point of view, the Crime Commission concluded that "serious consideration should be given to complete elimination of the court's power over children for noncriminal conduct" (1967:85).

This point of view, however, has not yet been applied universally. Nonetheless, it appears to be only a matter of time until it is. Monrad Paulsen points out in his essay that statutes regulating the moral conduct of children have been criticized as unconstitutional because of vagueness, that higher court opinions have bolstered the argument that children should be freed from parental constraints, that the new IJA–ABA Standards Relating to Noncriminal Misbehavior would eliminate the jurisdiction of the juvenile court over acts of ungovernability, unruliness or immorality, and that the State of Washington has already written the new IJA–ABA Standards into its juvenile code.

These actions were bolstered by the presumed failures of the juvenile court as well as by the ideology of the Child Rights Movement. One of the most telling criticisms of the court has been the fact that the one type of offender most often referred to it has been the status offender and that this offender has been as likely as the criminal property offender to be sentenced to a correctional institution (see Empey, 1978:chap. 16). Such outcomes might not have offended the sensibilities of reformers had court referral and the confinement of status offenders proved to be of clear benefit to them, but such has not always been the case. Instead, the evidence suggests that confinement, in particular, has not successfully changed young people and has not returned them to society as healthy and productive citizens. Thus, in the interests of justice, if not rehabilitation, decriminalization has been hailed as a constructive reform.

Like other outcomes of the Child Rights Movement, however, decriminalization has done more to highlight undesirable practices than to promote desirable alternatives. We have already seen that, as the socializing influences of family and school have declined, that decline has not been matched by compensatory changes in other social institutions. Thus, it is significant that decriminalization represents more of the same. While few would disagree with the assertion that children should be protected from official abuse, it is quite another thing to suggest that they require no controls. What will happen if the juvenile court, along with other child-oriented institutions, loses its capacity to place limits on any behaviors except those that are clearly criminal?

Critics from both ends of the ideological spectrum have voiced cries of alarm. Herman and Julia Schwendinger (1979), who are radical theorists, argue that, while decriminalization may reduce the harassment of working-class children by the police, it might also do them lasting harm. Indeed, like the Rev. Jesse Jackson, they point out that working-class families already have a difficult time controlling their children in the face of meager family resources, poor public schools, and the attraction of unfettered gang and street life. Hence, if decriminalization is combined with all the other freedoms advocated by the Child Rights Movement, it would simply result in another instance of benign neglect, justified by high-flown but class-biased principles. While well-to-do parents may have sufficient resources to make recourse to legal controls unnecessary, the parents of the inner city need the juvenile court as a backup institution. Otherwise, their children will continue to suffer from ignorance, poverty, and high rates of illegitimacy and crime.

Writing as a traditional advocate of the juvenile court, former Family Court Justice Justine Wise Polier (1979) says much the same thing. In so doing, she cites a problem with which every police officer, judge, and correctional worker is familiar, namely, that such terms as "incorrigibility," "lewd conduct," or "truancy" usually cover a multitude of problems, as well as "sins." Desperate parents often come to officials asking for help, not only because their children are truant, stay out late, and get drunk but because they are drug users, gang members, prostitutes, or thieves. But because these children have been referred to officials by their parents, they have usually been defined legally as status offenders, since the officials have had no firsthand knowledge of any crimes having been committed. If, however, all status offenders are decriminalized, officials could not take action, parental wishes notwithstanding. Lacking proof of criminal behavior, they would have to ignore any pleas for help.

By way of example, a judge of the Family Court in Manhattan recently dismissed charges against a fourteen-year-old girl for prostitution on the grounds that "sex for a fee" is a "recreational," not a criminal, act. Reflecting contemporary libertarian views, the judge said that "however offensive it may be, recreational commercial sex threatens no harm to the public health, safety, or welfare, and therefore may not be proscribed" (Goodman, 1978:7).

For some people, however, this action pushed the outrage button. "It's absolutely bizarre," opined one columnist, "to have to prove that a young girl committed a crime, in order to help her. . . . The one thing on which everyone agrees is that a 14-year-old girl selling sex in Times Square needs and deserves help" (Goodman, 1978:7). Nonetheless, to the degree that status offenses are decriminalized, and are not otherwise addressed, help may not be forthcoming.

The same sorts of dilemmas are associated with the runaway problem. In 1976 there were from 519,000 to 613,000 runaway children (*ORC* Newsletter, 1976). Because they have no place to live, such children are often exploited and turn to crime and prostitution in order to survive. Consequently, concerned parents often implore officials for assistance in locating and controlling these children. But, to the degree that runaway behavior is decriminalized, officials lose their power to sustain parental requests, at least by coercive means. In states like California, for example, it is illegal to detain runaways in secure facilities unless they have committed a crime. Lacking coercive power, therefore, the police and other officials are less and less inclined to intervene when runaway or other status offenders are encountered.

Finally, there are the assumptions upon which the decriminalization effort is based. The first is that there are qualitative differences between status and criminal offenders. Whereas the juvenile court was originally intended to decriminalize all children, not just status offenders, current reforms imply that they should be divided into two groups: (a) "good" kids whose only sin might be that of violating outmoded moral standards, and (b) "bad" kids who have violated the criminal law. Secondly, it is assumed that, when status offenders are officially labeled and stigmatized, their so-called evil is dramatized and they are made worse. Innocent acts and identities are escalated into criminal careers by the misguided zeal of legal authorities.

In his provocative essay, however, Maynard Erickson provides empirical findings that seriously question both assumptions. Whether based on official or self-report offense data, he finds that, for the most part, the presumed difference between status and criminal offenders is a myth. The overwhelming majority of all juveniles have committed both types of offenses, and in no particular order. As a result, only a small fraction of all offenders would escape prosecution if status offenses were decriminalized.

Erickson also finds little support for the belief that criminal careers begin, first, when children are apprehended for minor offenses and then are gradually made more criminal as a result of official action. The commission of delinquent acts does not follow an escalating pattern from minor to major. Consequently, if one were to justify decriminalization as a social policy, one would be advised to rely less on the assumptions described above and more on the classical concept of justice, namely, that authorities should respond to acts, not to people. In so doing, of course, one would have to pay the price of discarding entirely the original philosophy of the juvenile court, which suggested that it is the social and psychological backgrounds of juveniles that require the greatest attention, not the particular offenses they have committed. Indeed, the libertarian concepts of freedom and justice imply that, if children are to be treated more like adults, they should be free to do all the harm to themselves they want, so long as they do not injure others. But, if they do injure others, they should be held fully accountable for their acts, and should gain no particular benefit from their immaturity.

Diversion

Perhaps because of the dilemmas created by decriminalization, the practice of diversion—turning offenders away from entry into the juvenile justice—has become the most popular of current reforms. As such, it represents an uneasy compromise between the older controls of the juvenile court and total freedom for children from moral constraints. Hence, by creating community alternatives to court referral for status offenders and petty criminals, diversion is supposed to provide remedies without stigmatizing children or infringing upon their civil rights. But, like decriminalization, diversion creates some dilemmas of its own.

The most salient has to do with the enthusiastic acceptance and widespread application of diversion. Although its ostensible purpose is to reduce the number of juveniles being inserted into the juvenile justice system, it has apparently not done that. Rather, study after study indicates that it has produced a new semilegal, semiwelfare bureaucracy that has widened, rather than reduced, the net of social control. Children who in the past would have been warned and released are now placed in treatment; meanwhile, about the same numbers and types of offenders are being inserted into the juvenile justice system as before (see Klein, 1979, for a comprehensive review). Thus, the use of diversion has not only run contrary to the injunction of labeling theorists and civil libertarians "to leave children alone wherever possible" (Schur, 1973), but it may be criticized as perpetuating many of the problems it was supposed to correct:

1. Children who are diverted to the new correctional bureaucracy do not have the same recourse to legal counsel, review, and appeal that they would have if they were referred to juvenile court. Whereas that court may have exercised excessive discretion in the past and denied children the rights of due process, such is less true today. Hence, we may eventually be confronted with a paradox in which those children who are most likely to enjoy the protection of their rights are those who are referred to court, not those who are diverted from it.

2. History has come full circle. Like decriminalization, diversion has also contributed to a situation in which young people are divided into two groups: the "good" and the "bad" kids, or as Jerome Miller describes them, the "deserving" and "undeserving." The implication is that, while good, deserving kids merit our concern and resources, those who are bad and

undeserving are best locked up in detention centers and training schools. In short, in seeking to decriminalize one group, we have recriminalized another (Polier, 1979).

3. Diversion programs reflect this division because they prefer to work with "good" rather than "bad" kids. Two national surveys reveal that only a fraction of the juveniles being diverted to, or accepted by, community diversion agencies would have been referred to court anyway (Klein 1979; Nejelski, 1976).

4. A careful review of the services rendered by diversion agencies reveals that they are both narrow in concept and highly traditional in character (Klein, 1979). Rather than removing marginal youth from the age-segregated vacuum in which they find themselves and creating new age-integrated programs of study and work, they are subjected to such traditional modes of treatment as psychological counseling and crisis intervention. Thus, rather than terminating or adding to the services of existing agencies, we may only be perpetuating them in new guise.

Radical theorists such as Alex Liazos argue that these outcomes are but further examples of discrimination by a class-conscious society. Diversion programs have expanded, not because they are designed to improve the rights of working-class children but because they are adaptable to middle-class needs. Rather, the kinds of diversion programs working class children should have are those that would provide a minimum family income, improve slum schools, and create job opportunities. Otherwise these children will continue to be defined as "undeserving" and to populate our courts and correctional institutions. Indeed, programs that fail to help marginal youth are, themselves, losers: the battle in behalf of youth will not be won; age, class, and racial barriers will persist; and the rights of other groups will take precedence.

Due Process

There is no belief in Anglo-American jurisprudence that has greater support than the belief that the rights of all litigants should be protected by the principle of due process. Indeed, as Monrad Paulsen points out, Americans have grown even more skeptical over official discretion in the past fifteen years and have sought even more refuge in formal procedure. Thus, when these trends are combined with the Child Rights Movement, it should not be surprising that procedural principles have been extended to children. Yet even they have their limitations.

On the one hand, various appeals courts have ruled that children as well as parents must have their day in court. On the other hand, the formalities of due process—raised benches, judicial robes, codified procedures, and the presence of law-yers—do not always guarantee better solutions for youth problems. Indeed, if the juvenile court follows the lead of our adult criminal courts, greater justice is by no means insured. There is every chance, instead, that one form of injustice will be replaced by another.

About 90 percent of all prosecutions in our criminal courts are now resolved by guilty pleas, many of them the result of plea bargaining, not adversary procedures and a careful analysis of the evidence (Lefcourt, 1971). For the most part, these guilty pleas are the result of poverty or ignorance, or both. Why, then, should we not expect such problems to char-acterize our juvenile courts unless a massive infusion of funds, facilities, and personnel is forthcoming?

Constitutional safeguards for children depend heavily upon the capacities of their parents to find and employ competent legal counsel. Poor or single parents, however, must usually depend upon overworked and less skilled public defenders to handle their cases. In some jurisdictions, in fact, public defenders are not available at all, while in others they may not even review a case until moments before they are ex-pected to try it in court. As a result, the parents and children who can afford it the least but who need it the most are the ones who do not have the means to guarantee that their cases will be capably presented and fairly judged.

Were this not enough, the Supreme Court has left a curi-ously ambiguous mandate for the juvenile court to follow.

On the one hand it has decreed that the informal discretionary practices of the past can no longer be tolerated. Yet on the other hand it has also decreed that the impersonal formality of the criminal court is not acceptable either. As Justice Fortas put it, "The observance of due process standards, intelligently and not ruthlessly administered, will not compel the States to abandon or displace any of the substantive benefits of the juvenile process: . . . nothing will require that the conception of the kindly judge be replaced by its opposite" (*In re Gault*, 1967:21).

In response to this seemingly contradictory mandate, the National Council of Juvenile Court Judges expressed confusion and anger (Rubin, 1976:136). How, the council seemed to ask, can judges remain impartial with respect to proving the acts that juveniles commit and yet appear to be partial and fatherly in the process? How can prosecutors and defense attorneys be persuaded to give up the traditional practice of concentrating more on winning a case than in seeing that justice is done? Even worse, will not adversary procedures destroy the informality of the juvenile court, create cynics out of children, and contribute to the belief that the best way to avoid responsibility for their criminal acts is to get a clever lawyer? Since such questions are incapable of full resolution, it seems likely that the emphasis upon due process will take precedence over the "kindly" judge image and move us much closer to a classical system of justice for children than to an individualized or rehabilitative one.

Deinstitutionalization

Deinstitutionalization has been rationalized on four grounds: (1) the destructive impact of places of captivity on children; (2) the belief that offenders require reintegration into the mainstream of American life, not isolation from it; (3) increased attention to the civil rights of juveniles; and (4) the excessive bureaucratization of correctional programs to which Jerome Miller alludes. Miller argues that the treatment afforded juveniles has never approached the goals envisaged for it. Correctional bureaucracies have become self-perpetuating organizations which use professionals and professionalism to bless and ratify their existence.

Under the guise of scientific diagnosis and treatment, these bureaucracies have been little more than isolated repositories for society's "undeserving" children. Since the nineteenth century, diagnostic labels and treatment procedures have changed markedly; yet the process of extrusion, exclusion, and isolation remains the same. Hence, Miller's sentiments are like those of Senator Birch Bayh (1973), who sums up the argument in favor of deinstitutionalized correctional programs for all but the most serious of criminal offenders: "Today, too many young people are thrown into custodial institutions who should be handled in the community. We want to find ways to establish meaningful alternatives to incarceration. . . . Punishment, isolation, neglect, and abuse seem to be the hallmarks of institutional life. This includes harassment, affront to human dignity, and the gross denial of human rights."

Perhaps the most debatable aspect of this reform is the tendency for its proponents to take an all-or-none position. By defining all institutions as bad, they condemn without distinction such diverse places as adult jails, archaic training schools, huge, prisonlike edifices and small public or private programs. Obviously, there are great differences among these "institutions." What is needed, therefore, is two things: (1) a clearer definition of the term *deinstitutionalization* and (2) an evaluation of any program to make sure that it serves the basic needs of children, whether it is residential or not. The goal of deinstitutionalization is to rid juvenile programs of social isolation, personal degradation, stultifying routines, and cruelty, not to rid them of helpful services.

As programs are deinstitutionalized, one goal would be to avoid what Polier (1979) calls the "turnstyle" child—the child for whom a return to the community is ordered without that child having a suitable place to live. Some children are mentally ill, mentally retarded, or severely lacking in interpersonal, academic, and work skills. All too often they are persons who are difficult to place and difficult to help. Hence, if adequate provision is not made for them, they may be dumped from one foster or group home to another, not placed back on the track that leads successfully from childhood to adulthood.

These and other problems do not justify keeping juveniles in institutions, but, as we have already seen, they do imply a need for caution. Indeed, our review of diversion programs indicated that few community agencies as yet have been successful in addressing the need for institutional and societal change, a sine qua non for successful deinstitutionalization. Rather, they come closer to ratifying Jerome Miller's belief that they do more to perpetuate the treatment bureaucracies of the past than to provide marginal youth with a realistic stake in conformity. Furthermore, there is precious little scientific evidence that community programs are more successful in reducing recidivism than correctional institutions (Klein, 1979).

What is revealed, then, is a theme that has pervaded our whole analysis of the Child Rights Movement as well as our review of justice reforms, namely, the striking contrast between rhetoric and reality. Neither has done much to increase the capacity and willingness of the schools or the employment sector of the economy to solve the problems of the disadvantaged, to reduce age segregation, or to provide youth with greater access to responsible adult roles. Hence, it would do little good to deinstitutionalize programs if children were left worse off than before.

The Counterrevolution

The final issue that merits attention is the historical tendency for any social revolution to generate its own counterrevolution. The same may be no less true of the current revolution in child rights and juvenile justice. That revolution, as we have seen, has been based upon the assumptions that the juvenile justice system has overcriminalized children, has labeled and stigmatized them unnecessarily, has denied them their civil rights, and has been excessively punitive.

Heightened by fears of crime, a striking counterideology has emerged in recent years, namely, the belief that, rather than being too harsh, the juvenile justice system has been excessively lenient, has denied the rights of victims, has eroded discipline and respect for authority, and now threatens to destroy social order (Miller, 1973:454–55). Although the proponents of this ideology would likely support current reforms favoring *decriminalization* and *due process*, their reasons for doing so are peculiar to a retributive, not a liberal, doctrine. They would agree that status offenses should be decriminalized because they believe the police should be in the business of fighting crime, not of enforcing morals; such enforcement should be left to others. Likewise, they would favor due process for juveniles because they see it as a means of insuring that strict rather than discretionary procedures are followed by heretofore lenient judges. Beyond these areas of agreement, however, the other reforms they advocate are of a far different nature.

Abolish the juvenile court. Now that the Supreme Court has ruled that the juvenile court must become more formal, some legalists have advocated an even more extreme step—doing away with the juvenile court altogether (McCarthy, 1977). It is a diseased organ that no longer performs any useful function. In its place should be only one court to handle all criminals.

Lower the age of accountability. Consistent with the view that children should be treated more like adults, various states have lowered the age of accountability for crime. In 1978 the state of New York lowered to thirteen the age at which it is mandatory that juveniles be confined for an extended period of time for committing one of several "designated felony acts" (Paulsen, this volume). Other states have lowered the age of accountability by making trial in adult court automatic if serious felonies are committed (Cf. California Welfare and Institutions Code, 1976).

Punish and incapacitate offenders. Finally, a growing number of philosophers, social scientists, and legal scholars have suggested that justice demands an elimination of the individualized rehabilitative approach to offenders and a return to punitive practices in which retribution and restraint are the governing principles (Morris, 1974; Wilks and Martinson, 1976; Wilson, 1975; van den Haag, 1975).

In their zeal these advocates may not have considered the implications of this reform for the nation's youth. Since teenagers commit at least half of all traditional serious crimes, it would have far greater impact upon them than upon any other group. But whether considered or not, the following are the steps that would be taken:

1. Since the rehabilitative philosophy is a proved failure, it is futile for the justice system to try to control crime by focusing on its causes. Rather, its principal purpose should be that of insuring that punishment is swift, certain, and uniform.

2. The preponderant majority of all crimes are committed by a small number of habitual offenders. Consequently, they must be incarcerated and isolated in the interest of community protection.

3. Such former tools of the rehabilitative philosophy as the indeterminate sentence and parole should be abolished. All sentences should be of determinate length and should be based upon seriousness of offense and the offender's prior criminal history. Significantly, this reform is similar to the one advocated by the new IJA–ABA Standards and is already reflected in Washington State's new juvenile code, which ranks the treatment of juveniles below such other objectives as community protection, accountability, determinate sentencing, appropriate punishment, and due process.

4. Each time an offender is reconvicted, the length of the sentence should be increased—doubled, perhaps, for a second

offense or tripled for a third (van den Haag, 1975; Wilks and Martinson, 1976).

5. Since most criminals are adolescents or young adults, the goal of increasingly stringent sentences would be to immobilize repeat offenders until at least age thirty-five. After that, the need for controls diminishes because the impulse to criminality drops sharply (van den Haag, 1975).

In short, since the concept of rehabilitation is bankrupt, efforts to reform offenders should be secondary to the goals of protecting the community, deterring further crime, and insuring that justice is uniform for all.

Implications

It is obvious, of course, that the "just deserts" philosophy is nothing new. It is simply classical criminology in twentieth-century guise. Nonetheless, its resurgence at this particular time is reflective of a new set of circumstances to which the changing concepts of childhood and juvenile justice have made a contribution.

Parity for children. First, as Franklin Zimring points out, the Child Rights Movement, when viewed through conservative eyes, can be seen as justifying a "new parity" argument. If children have the right to live with the same guarantees of freedom that adults enjoy, why should they not be subject to the same responsibilities, including punishments for their crimes? Why should children have their cake and eat it too?

Zimring argues, however, that it need not follow that, because young people are granted increased privileges, they should be held fully accountable for their acts. Instead, adolescence should be a period in which the young are granted a "learner's permit" to make mistakes—"a period when privilege is extended, not because the subject is ready for adulthood, but because there is hope that learning by doing will produce a survivable transition toward adulthood." To be sure, some consequences must attach to serious misdeeds, but the young should be protected from full responsibility for their acts as an investment in the future. Society has a stake in seeing that their inevitable mistakes do not permanently impair their life chances.

Zimring's argument is noteworthy, not because of its substance—the idea has been taken for granted for centuries that children should have a learner's permit to make mistakes—but because it had to be made at all. Perhaps more than we realize, fears of youth crime, along with the ideology of the Child Rights Movement, have moved us to a stage where the new "parity" argument makes sense. Otherwise, why the need to rejustify the traditional belief that an extended childhood should constitute a moratorium in the life cycle during which young people are granted greater latitude for making mistakes than are adults?

Brutal pessimism. If this reexamination of an old belief were the result of some newfound faith in the inevitability of human progress, as was the case during the nineteenth century, today's retributive doctrine might be dismissed as a passing fancy, but that is not the case. Instead, current demands for reform, whether liberal or conservative, are based upon the premise that benevolence, official discretion, and faith in human progress are not to be trusted and that we must take refuge in formal rules and procedure. Indeed, no better symptom of today's disillusionment can be cited than the attitudes that prevail toward the concept of rehabilitation. It is not merely that we lack evidence that rehabilitation can reduce crime but that we are losing faith in the belief that benevolently motivated intervention will work even with children.

By way of example, contrast the black forebodings of today's retributive doctrine with the overriding optimism expressed by Enoch Wines in his preamble to the Principles of Rehabilitation first enunciated in the Cincinnati Prison Congress of 1870:

A prison governed by force and fear is a prison mismanaged, in which hope and love, the two great spiritual, uplifting, regenerating forces to which mankind must ever look for redemption, are asleep or dead.

Why not try the effect of rewards upon the prisoner? Rewards, as truly as punishments, appeal to the inextinguishable principle of self-interest in his breast. (Wines, 1910:12)

Given the destruction of this kind of faith and optimism, it is entirely possible that we will see a decline in support, not only for rehabilitation, but for such newer reforms as diversion and deinstitutionalization. In their place an increasingly disillusioned populace may well turn to retribution, incapacitation, and deterrence as the appropriate responses.

Objections to this possibility have been raised on several grounds. The well-known jurist David L. Bazelon (1977:2) sees current developments as evidence of a "brutal pessimism:" "Rehabilitation . . . should never have been sold on the promise that it would reduce crime. Recidivism rates cannot be the only measure of what is valuable in corrections. Whether in prison or out, every person is entitled to physical necessities, medical and mental health services, and a measure of privacy. Prisoners need programs to provide relief from boredom and idleness . . . libraries, classes, physical and mental activities."

Yet, as Daniel Glaser points out, efforts to improve and to enlarge the vision of corrections is undermined repeatedly, not merely by retributionists but by academics and legalists as well. Thus, new efforts, no matter how humane, are defined as "rehabilitative" and treated with scorn. Nothing works! (Martinson, 1974:25).

Despite the prevailing cynicism, however, Glaser also argues that the evidence is by no means clear that "nothing works." Instead, the presumed limitations of rehabilitation are due as much to primitive theorizing, to a poverty of knowledge, to the poor implementation of correctional programs, and to poor evaluation research as to the inherent limitations of the concept itself. Yet even with all these limitations there are repeated signs that various kinds of programs have had beneficial effects on some offenders under some conditions. It cannot be said that all efforts have been fruitless.

Glaser also stresses a theme that has been noted repeatedly in our review of the Child Rights Movement, namely, that it is not *rehabilitation*—restoration to some prior state—that most marginal youngsters need but *habilitation*—the opportunity to be prepared for, and to experience, legitimate adult roles for the first time. In other words, the rehabilitation task has too often been approached negatively. Rather than conceiving of correctional programs as devices by which conformity and creative citizenship can be facilitated, we have concentrated on ways by which to control, and to undo, the criminogenic influences that are presumed to inhabit the individual. It is no wonder, then, that success has been so limited.

Conversely, in reviewing the literature on deterrence, Maynard Erickson finds little evidence to support the view that punishment and incapacitation—the "heavy hands" approach—would be effective if applied to juveniles. The reason is that *certainty* of punishment is far more important in deterring crime than is *severity*. Yet, because the likelihood of apprehension for any single offense is so low and because most delinquent acts are committed in groups, the chances that an offender will escape punishment are astronomical. Hence, unless Americans are willing to tolerate a totalitarian police state, in which civil rights are greatly reduced, little faith can be placed in the assumption that retribution will work.

Nonetheless, Erickson closes on a cautionary note that not only aptly summarizes his discussion of justice reforms but our entire review of the Child Rights Movement, namely, that we should not harbor the illusion that public policy will be guided by evidence. Indeed, if there is anything we should have learned, it is that public policy is based on vaguely perceived cultural and demographic changes, conflicts among vested interests, and the vagaries of chance. Consequently, it is probable that the future of childhood and juvenile justice will depend upon some uneasy compromise among all of these factors, not upon a rational awareness of the many issues that have been highlighted in this volume.

References

Ariès, Philippe
    1962   Centuries of Childhood (Trans. Robert Baldick). New York: Knopf.

Bayh, Birch
    1971   Statement to U.S. Senate Committee on the Judiciary, Subcommittee to Investigate Juvenile Delinquency, 92nd Congress, First Session, May 3–18.

Bazelon, David L.
    1977   "Crime and what we can do about it." LEAA Newsletter 6:2.

Bronfenbrenner, Urie
    1974   "The origins of alienation." Scientific American 231:48–59.

California Welfare and Institutions Code
    1976   Assembly Bill No. 3121. Chapter 1071:1–24.

Carter, Hugh, and Paul C. Glick
    1976   Marriage and Divorce: A Social and Economic Study (rev. ed.). Cambridge: Harvard Univ. Press.

Coleman, James S., et al.
    1974   Youth: Transition to Adulthood. Chicago: Univ. of Chicago Press.

Douvan, Elizabeth
    1979   "Twenty-year comparison: family roles." ISR Newsletter. Winter:4–5.

Dye, Lee
    1979   "Marriage—a healthy state in California." Los Angeles Times, January 14, Part I:1 ff.

Empey, LaMar T.
    1978   American Delinquency: Its Meaning and Construction. Homewood, Ill.: Dorsey.

Gillis, John R.
1974   Youth and History. New York: Academic Press.

Goodman, Ellen
1976   "Children's rights." Los Angeles Times, Nov. 10, 1976.

Ianni, Francis A. J.
1978   "The social organization of the high school: school-spe-
        cific aspects of school crime." *In* Ernst Wenk and Nora
        Harlow (eds.), School Crime and Disruption. Davis,
        Calif.: Responsible Action.

Illick, Joseph E.
1974   "Child rearing in seventeenth century England and
        America." Pp. 303–50 *in* Lloyd de Mause (ed.), The
        History of Childhood. New York: Psychohistory Press.

In re Gault
1967   387 U.S. 1, 18L, Ed. 2nd 527, 87 S.Ct. 1428.

Klein, Malcolm W.
1979   "Deinstitutionalization and diversion of juvenile of-
        fenders: a litany of impediments." *In* Norval Morris
        and Michael Tonry (eds.), Crime and Justice, 1978. Chi-
        cago: Univ. of Chicago Press.

Krier, Beth Ann
1979   "Carrying charisma to teen-agers." Los Angeles Times.
        March 16, Part IV:1 ff.

Laslett, Peter
1977   Family Life and Illicit Love in Earlier Generations.
        Cambridge: Cambridge Univ. Press.

Lefcourt, Robert (ed.)
1971   Law against the People. New York: Vintage Books.

Lemert, Edwin M.
1967   "The juvenile court—quest and realities." Pp. 91–106
        in the President's Commission on Law Enforcement
        and Administration of Justice. Task Force Report: Juve-
        nile Delinquency and Youth Crime. Washington, D.C.:
        U.S. Government Printing Office.

McCarthy, Francis B.
1977   "Should juvenile delinquency be abolished?" Crime
        and Delinquency 23:196–203.

Martinson, Robert
    1974   "What works: questions and answers about prison re-
            form." The Public Interest 35:22–54.

Mause, Lloyd de
    1974   The History of Childhood. New York: Psychohistory
            Press.

Miller, Walter B.
    1973   "Ideology and criminal justice policy: some current is-
            sues." Pp. 453–473 *in* Sheldon L. Messinger et al. (eds.),
            The Aldine Crime and Justice Annual, 1973. Chicago:
            Aldine.

Monahan, Thomas P.
    1957   "Family status and the delinquent child: a reappraisal
            and some new findings." Social Forces 35:250–58.

Morris, Norval
    1974   "The future of imprisonment: toward a punitive philos-
            ophy." Michigan Law Review 72:1161–80.

Morrow, Lance
    1979   "Wondering if children are necessary." Time Magazine
            113(Mar. 5):46–47.

National League of Cities
    1977   CETA and Youth: Programs for Cities. Washington,
            D.C.: National League of Cities and U.S. Conference
            of Mayors.

Nejelski, Paul
    1976   "Diversion: the promise and the danger." Crime and
            Delinquency 22:393–410.

Polier, Justine Wise
    1979   "Prescriptions for reform—doing what we set out to
            do?" *In* LaMar T. Empey (ed.), Juvenile Justice: The
            Progressive Legacy and Current Reforms. Charlottes-
            ville: Univ. Press of Virginia.

Rubin, H. Ted
    1976   "The eye of the juvenile court judge: a one-step-up
            view of the juvenile justice system" Pp. 133–59 *in* Mal-
            colm W. Klein (ed.), The Juvenile Justice System. Bev-
            erly Hills, Calif.: Sage.

Schur, Edwin M.
    1973   Radical Nonintervention: Rethinking the Delinquency
            Problem. Englewood Cliffs, N.J.: Prentice-Hall.

Schwendinger, Herman, and Julia Schwendinger
    1979   "Delinquency and social reform: a radical perspective."
            In LaMar T. Empey (ed.), Juvenile Justice: The Pro-
            gressive Legacy and Current Reforms. Charlottesville:
            Univ. Press of Virginia.

Stone, Lawrence
    1974   "The massacre of the innocents." New York Review
            14:25–31.

Time Magazine
    1977a   "Looking to the ZP generation." February 28, 110:71.
    1977b   "The American underclass." August 29, 110:14–27.

Timmick, Lois
    1979   "Single women opt for motherhood in growing num-
            bers." Los Angeles Times, January 17, Part I:29.

United States Department of Commerce
    1971   Bureau of Census Reports, 1950–1970. Washington, D.C.:
            U.S. Government Printing Office.

van den Haag, Ernest
    1975   Punishing Criminals. New York: Basic Books.

Veroff, Joseph
    1979   "Twenty-year comparison: feelings of well-being." IRS
            Newsletter. Winter: 4–5.

Wilks, Judith, and Robert Martinson
    1976   "Is the treatment of criminal offenders really neces-
            sary?" Federal Probation 3–8.

Wilson, James Q.
    1975   Thinking about Crime. New York: Basic Books.

Wines, Frederick H.
    1910   "Historical introduction." Pp. 3–38 *in* Charles R. Hen-
            derson (ed.), Prison Reform and Criminal Law. New
            York: Charities Publication Committee.

Contributors

KINGSLEY DAVIS is Distinguished Professor of Sociology, Department of Sociology and Population Research Laboratory at the University of Southern California. A Phi Beta Kappa Visiting Scholar in 1977, he is a member of the National Academy of Sciences and the World Academy of Art and Science. Davis is also a past Chairman of the United States National Committee for the International Union for the Scientific Study of Population.

LAMAR T. EMPEY is editor of this volume and Professor of Sociology at the University of Southern California and was Director of the Youth Studies Center there. He is the author of *American Delinquency: Its Meaning and Construction; The Silverlake Experiment* (with Steven Lubeck); *The Provo Experiment* (with Maynard Erickson); *Explaining Delinquency* (with Steven Lubeck); and *Alternatives to Incarceration*. Empey is the editor of *Juvenile Justice: The Progressive Legacy and Current Reforms*, the first KPAF volume on juvenile justice.

MAYNARD L. ERICKSON is Professor of Sociology at the University of Arizona. His areas of specialization include juvenile delinquency, criminology, social control, evaluation research, methodology, and statistics. He is the author of *The Provo Experiment* (with LaMar T. Empey).

RICHARD FARSON is a psychologist, author, and member of the faculty of the Humanistic Psychology Institute of San Francisco. He was Director of the Western Behavior Sciences Institute, La Jolla, Calif., which he helped found, and now serves as Chairman of the Board of Trustees. He has also been President of the Esalen Institute, Dean of the School of Environmental Design of the California Institute of the Arts, a psychotherapist and organization consultant in private practice and is the current President of the International Design Conference in Aspen. He is the author of *Science and Human Affairs, The Future of the Family,* and *Birthrights: A Bill of Rights for Children.*

DANIEL GLASER is Professor of Sociology at the University of Southern California. He has taught at the University of Illinois, was sociologist-actuary for the Illinois Parole and Pardon Board in Pontiac and Joliet prisons, and supervised German jails and prisons with the military government. His major evaluative study of the federal prison and parole system is reported in his book *The Effectiveness of a Prison and Parole System;* other publications include *Routinizing Evaluation, Handbook of Criminology, Correctional Institutions,* and *Crime in our Changing Society.* He is past Chairman of the Criminology Section of the American Sociological Association, current Chairman of the Crime and Juvenile Delinquency Division of the Society for the Study of Social Problems, and 1976 recipient of the Sutherland Award of the American Society of Criminology.

ALEXANDER LIAZOS is Associate Professor at Regis College in Weston, Mass. He was born in Albania, raised in Greece, and emigrated to the United States in 1955. A Marxist sociologist, his primary substantive interests are delinquency, criminology, and deviance. He has written "The Poverty of the Sociology of Deviance," "Class Oppression: The Functions of Juvenile Justice," and "School, Alienation, and Delinquency." His long-term interest is the nature of criminal and juvenile justice systems in socialist societies.

JEROME G. MILLER is Director of the National Center for Action on Institutions and Alternatives and is currently engaged in a study of the politics of de-institutionalization in Ohio, Pennsylvania, Florida, and Massachusetts under the auspices of the LEAA Institute for Research. He has been Commissioner of Children and Youth in the Pennsylvania Department of Public Welfare, and worked with youth services in Maryland, Massachusetts, and Illinois. Miller has taught at The Ohio State University and is the author of "Locking Them Out—The New Corrections," "Research and Theory in Middle Class Delinquency," "The Dilemma of the Post-Gault Juvenile Court," and other articles. He received the 1975 Award of the American Society for Public Administration "in recognition of significant national contribution to the advancement and professional development of criminal justice administration."

MONRAD G. PAULSEN is Vice President for Legal Education and Dean of the Benjamin N. Cardozo School of Law, Yeshiva University. He has been a Fulbright Professor at the University of Freiburg, where he received an honorary J.D. He has taught at the Salzburg (Austria) Seminar, Institute of Advanced Legal Studies at the University of London, and the University of Göttingen. He has served as consultant and chairman of the Advisory Committee to the Legal Services Program of Mobilization for Youth. Paulsen published a major study on the Abused Child Reporting legislation and is co-editor (with Sanford Kadish) of *Criminal Law and Its Processes*.

JAMES F. SHORT, JR. is Director of the Social Research Center and Professor of Sociology at Washington State University. He has served as co-director of Research for the National Commission on the Causes of Prevention of Violence. He was editor of the *American Sociological Review* and has served on the editorial boards of numerous professional publications. Short was a fellow at the Center for Advanced Study in the Behavioral Sciences, a Guggenheim Fellow at the Institute of Criminology and Kings College of the University of Cambridge. He is the author and co-author of numerous books and articles, including *Crime, Delinquency, and Society* and *Gang Delinquency and Delinquent Subcultures*.

ARLENE SKOLNICK is Research Psychologist in the Institute of Human Development at the University of California, Berkeley. Her major areas of interest are human development and the family and she has been a consultant to the Childhood and Government Project at the University of California Law School. She is the author of *The Intimate Environment* and the co-editor of *Family in Transition*.

FRANKLIN E. ZIMRING is Professor of Law and Director of the Center for Studies in Criminal Justice at the University of Chicago Law School. He is the author (with Gordon Hawkins) of *Deterrence: The Legal Threat of Crime Control.*

Participants

ROBERT A. BAUER is Director of the Kenyon College Public Affairs Forum at Kenyon College and Director of the American University Public Policy Symposium.

CHARLES M. BLAIR is Senior Program Officer of the Lilly Endowment Inc., in charge of youth programs, juvenile justice programs, minority leadership development programs, and youth employment programs.

KINGSLEY DAVIS (*see* Contributors)

LAMAR T. EMPEY (*see* Contributors)

MAYNARD L. ERICKSON (*see* Contributors)

RICHARD FARSON (*see* Contributors)

NANCY S. KUJAWSKI is Juvenile Justice Specialist in the Office of Juvenile Justice and Delinquency Prevention, Law Enforcement Assistance Administration, U.S. Department of Justice.

ALEXANDER LIAZOS (*see* Contributors)

CHARLES R. MAHER is a legal affairs writer with the *Los Angeles Times.*

JEROME G. MILLER (*see* Contributors)

RICHARD A. MYREN is Professor and Dean, School of Justice, College of Public Affairs of The American University.

MONRAD G. PAULSEN (*see* Contributors)

HOWARD L. SACKS is Assistant Professor of Sociology and Chair of the Department of Anthropology/Sociology at Kenyon College.

JAMES F. SHORT, JR. (*see* Contributors)

ARLENE SKOLNICK (*see* Contributors)

FRANKLIN E. ZIMRING (*see* Contributors)